Practical
Curriculum Study

Routledge Education Books

Advisory editor: John Eggleston
Professor of Education
University of Keele

Practical
Curriculum Study

Douglas Barnes

School of Education
University of Leeds

Routledge & Kegan Paul

London, Boston and Henley

First published in 1982
Reprinted in 1985
by Routledge & Kegan Paul plc
14 Leicester Square, London WC2H 7PH,
9 Park Street, Boston, Mass. 02108, USA, and
Broadway House, Newtown Road,
Henley-on-Thames, Oxon RG9 1EN
Set in IBM Press Roman and Universe 10/12pt
and printed in Great Britain by
St Edmundsbury Press, Bury St Edmunds, Suffolk
© Douglas Barnes 1982

Library of Congress Cataloging in Publication Data

Barnes, Douglas R.

Practical curriculum study.
(Routledge education books)
Bibliography: p.
1. Education. – Curricula.   2. Curriculum planning.
3. Curriculum evaluation.   I. Title.   II. Series.
LB1570.B327   1982   375   82-15136

ISBN 0-7100-0979-8 (pbk.)

Contents

Contents

Tasks

Tasks

Acknowledgments

The author and publishers are grateful to the following for permission to quote from the works cited:

Philip H. Taylor for *How Teachers Plan Their Courses*, NFER, Windsor, Berkshire, 1970.

Addison-Wesley Publishing Company, Inc., Reading, Mass., for *A Teacher's Handbook to Elementary Social Studies*, 2nd edn, 1971, by Hilda Taba, Mary C. Durkin, Jack R. Fraenkel and Anthony H. McNaughton.

Schools Council and Macdonald Educational, Ltd, London, for *With Objectives in Mind*, Schools Council Science 5-13 Project, 1972.

Doubleday Inc., New York and Faber and Faber, Ltd, London for 'The Meadow Mouse' from *The Collected Poems of Theodore Roethke*.

Schools Council and Thomas Nelson and Sons Ltd, London, for *Cities and People*, Schools Council Geography for the Young School Leaver Project, 1974.

Anne Yeadon for *Toward Independence: The Use of Instructional Objectives in Teaching Daily Living Skills to the Blind*, American Foundation for the Blind, New York, 1974.

Heinemann Educational Books Ltd, London, for *Scottish Integrated Science: Teachers' Guide 1-8*, Scottish Central Committee on Science, 1977.

Schools Council and Collins Educational, London, for *Curriculum Planning in History, Geography and Social Science*, Schools Council History, Geography and Social Science 8-13 Project, 1976.

Lawrence Stenhouse for 'The Humanities Curriculum Project', *Journal of Curriculum Studies*, vol. 1, no. 1, 1968, and 'Open-minded teaching', *New Society*, 1969, p. 356.

Denis Lawton for *Class, Culture and the Curriculum*, Routledge &

Kegan Paul, London, 1975.

D.K. Wheeler and Hodder & Stoughton Educational, London, for *Curriculum Process*, University of London Press, 1967.

Schools Council and Macmillan Education, London, for *The Aims of Primary Education*, Ashton *et al.*, Schools Council Research Studies, 1975.

Frank Musgrove for 'The contribution of sociology to the study of the curriculum' from *Changing the Curriculum*, J.F. Kerr (ed.), London, University of London Press, 1968.

Dennis Warwick and Michael Flude for a table from 'Some aspects of the sociology of the curriculum' in *Educability, Schools and Ideology*, M. Flude and J. Ahier (eds), Croom Helm, London, 1974.

Schools Council Publications for *Exploration Man*, Schools Council Integrated Studies Project, 1972.

Schools Council and Longman Group Limited for *Patterns I*, Schools Council Integrated Science Project, 1973.

Basil Bernstein for 'On the classification and framing of educational knowledge' from *Knowledge and Control*, M.F.D. Young (ed.), London, Collier-Macmillan, 1971.

Interstate Printers and Publishers, Inc., Danville, Illinois, for *A Curriculum Guide for Teachers of the Educable Mentally Handicapped* (The Illinois Plan for Special Education of Exceptional Children), H. Goldstein and D.M. Seigle (rev. edn, 1971, available from the publishers).

Peter Tomlinson for 'Moral judgment and moral psychology: Piaget, Kohlberg and beyond' in S. Modgil and C. Modgil (eds) *Towards a Theory of Psychological Development*, NFER, Windsor, Berkshire, 1980.

Ian Lister for 'The whole curriculum and the hidden curriculum' in *Deschooling: A Reader*, Cambridge University Press, Cambridge, 1974.

UNESCO for Yoloye, E.A. 'Observational techniques' in A. Lewy (ed.), *Handbook of Curriculum Evaluation*, © UNESCO, 1977.

Rob Walker and Clem Adelman for *A Guide to Classroom Observation*, Methuen, London, 1975.

Schools Council and HMSO, London, for a diagram from *Enquiry 1*, 1968.

J.M. Dent & Sons Ltd, London, for 'Reading and the school handicap score' by S. Froome in *The Fight for Education: Black Paper 1975*.

Maurice Kogan for *The Politics of Educational Change*, Manchester

University Press, Manchester, 1978.

National Union of Teachers for *Education in Schools: the NUT's response to the recommendations in the 1977 Green Paper*, NUT, 1977.

Department of Education and Science Assessment of Performance Unit and the Controller of Her Majesty's Stationery Office for *Science Progress Report 1977-8* (Appendix: 'List of science concepts and knowledge'); for *Language Performance* (1978); and for *Mathematical Development: Primary Survey Report No. 1* (1980).

Carl Parsons for 'Geography for the Young School Leaver' in *Curriculum Research and Development in Action*, L. Stenhouse (ed.), Heinemann Educational books, London, 1980.

Schools Council for *Second Interim Report of the Schools Council Impact and Take Up Project*, University of Sussex, 1980; and for 'Local curriculum development preliminary information sheet' (unpublished).

Jack Whitehead for *Improving Learning for 11 to 14 year olds in Mixed Ability Science Groups* (A Schools Council Local Curriculum Project located at Wiltshire Curriculum Development Centre, Swindon).

Malcolm Skilbeck for 'School-based curriculum development' (cyclostyled), 1972.

John Elliott for 'The case for school self-evaluation' in *Forum*, vol. 22, no. 1.

Accountability in the Middle Years of Schooling Project, University of Sussex, for their report to the Social Science Research Council.

Schools Council and Holmes McDougall Ltd, Edinburgh, for *The Mystery of Mark Pullen*, from *What is History?* Schools Council History 13-16 Project, 1976.

John Darke for worksheets from *Explore and Discover: Science for the Middle Years*, by J. Darke and G. Hughes, McGraw-Hill, New York, 1974.

Lancashire Education Committee for 'Primary School Evaluation: A schedule for self appraisal', 1980.

Schools Council, Patricia Ashton, Pat Kneen and Frances Davies, and Hodder and Stoughton Educational, London for *Aims into Practice in the Primary School*, 1975.

Schools Council and Longman Group Ltd, London, for 'In other people's shoes' from *Lifeline*, Schools Council Moral Education Project.

Acknowledgments

Thanks are also due to the following for permission to use unpublished materials:

Dewsbury and Batley Technical and Art College for a set of objectives for Communication Studies in TEC courses.

Sandford Middle School and Osmondthorpe Middle School, Leeds.

Teachers at South Hunsley School, North Humberside (Keith Bryant, Barbara Cussons, Linda Fendley, John Sharpe, Michael Smale and Keith Smith) for documents relating to an experimental course.

Geoffrey Holroyde, formerly Principal of Sidney Stringer Community College, Coventry, for 'Community Education'.

Rita Mansoukhani and Joyce Casserley, formerly students in the School of Education, University of Leeds, for examples of learning hierarchies.

Patrick Fathers, formerly geography teacher at Cross Green School, Leeds, and Michael Morgan, Department of Geography, University of Bristol, for a version of the game 'Micropolis'.

Elizabeth Hardman for the worksheet 'The Mob', originally prepared for the Nuffield Resources for Learning Project.

John Darke for transcriptions of extracts from lessons.

Paul Williams and Harold Rosen for a collection of school documents originally assembled for a conference of the National Association for the Teaching of English.

I should like to thank Margaret Rainbow for preparing the typescript of this book.

D.B.

Introduction

Practical Curriculum Study presents a view of how the curriculum should be studied. It is intended for use in colleges of education, teachers' centres and university departments of education, both in initial training and in courses and workshops for experienced teachers. The core and purpose of the book is to be found in the wide range of practical tasks which constitute a large part of the text. Some of these tasks require readers to reflect upon and analyse their preconceptions about teaching; others suggest ways of planning work for their pupils and trying it out; some require them to analyse and evaluate textbooks and worksheets, to study other teachers in action, to consider alternative ways of organising the curriculum, and so on. It is these tasks — which can be carried out by teachers working alone or in groups — that implicitly define a way of studying the curriculum.

The purpose of the text which accompanies the tasks is solely to provide a context for them: it seeks to present the issues briefly and without dogmatism. Explanatory text is often very resistant to interrogation by the reader; indeed textbooks by their simplification and compression of issues tend to discourage critical reading. In this case the tasks encourage reflective and critical thought by giving, as it were, institutional status to comparison, analysis, criticism, discussion and debate. They provide heuristic methods through which students, with or without a tutor, can explore the curriculum as it is, look critically at their own values and purposes, and plan and choose more reflectively than is often possible in the rush of classroom teaching. The reader, whether an experienced teacher or a student in training, is thus characterised as a responsible professional who does not wish to be given ready-made opinions, since teaching should be based upon considered principles. It would be absurd to treat curriculum theory as an esoteric body of knowledge, and thus ignore the reader's existing understanding of schools and schooling, particularly if he or she is a practising teacher who has daily commerce with aspects of the curriculum. Thus the practical tasks are so ordered as to encourage teachers to form systematic strategies for thinking about the curriculum, and to lead to the discussion of matters of principle as a basis for practical choices. It is in this sense that the book offers a model for the teaching of curriculum theory.

It is probably true that more study of the curriculum goes on in courses labelled 'primary education' or 'the teaching of geography' (or some other subject) or 'remedial and special education' and so on than in courses explicitly concerned with the theory and practice of the curriculum. Thus, although the overall structure of *Practical Curriculum Study* makes it suitable for courses concerned with the school curriculum as a whole, certain parts of it also take into account the needs of more specialised courses. For example, there is an extensive section concerned with life skills and socio-moral education; other sections suggest ways of studying a particular subject-area in detail, while the interests of both primary and secondary-school teachers are kept in mind throughout.

At a time when schools are being urged to take more explicit responsibility for curricula, the discussion of 'Course planning', 'The content of the curriculum', and 'Analysing and evaluating the curriculum' — the topics of the first three chapters of this book — is as useful to experienced teachers as to teachers in training. The final chapter, 'The control of the curriculum' takes some recent trends in the administrative and political control of education as an opportunity for raising permanent issues about the responsibilities of schools, the rights of parents and community, and the powers of administrators.

It is highly unlikely that one style of teaching or one view of curriculum priorities will ever gain universal approval, but this does not mean that any teaching is as good as any other. Although the research evidence is contradictory and imprecise, there are some general characteristics of good teachers that we can take the risk of naming. Good teachers reflect carefully on what they are doing, choosing on a principled basis the materials they use and the activities they give to their pupils: their work is deliberate rather than habitual or directed by fashion. They vary their teaching and organisational style according to the nature of the activity in hand, and according to their view of its relevance to their pupils' learning. In spite of their clarity of purpose and careful preparation, they are quick to understand their pupils' contributions, understandings and viewpoints. Such teachers enlist the collaboration of pupils and the respect of colleagues. The tasks in this volume are intended to provide a repertoire of critical and analytical strategies that can form a basis for principled teaching, whatever particular educational values a teacher may espouse.

Many of the tasks, originally devised for teachers who worked with me during the last ten years, have since been revised. They are often framed in highly specific terms; actual examples are quoted, particular subject-matter is referred to, or imaginary situations are outlined in some detail. It was impossible, however, to supply so many examples and tasks that every subject specialism and every stage of schooling is catered for on all occasions, so that when the book is used by a lecturer with students, he or she may in some cases wish to select other similar materials more specifically related to the students' interests. Many of the tasks have been planned so that they can best be carried out by a group working together. This approach assumes the importance of colleagues taking joint professional responsibility for the curricula they are making available to their pupils. For this purpose teachers need the experience of working together in developing strategies for planning and analysing, and also in becoming more adept at communicating with one another about these matters. Teachers who do not — who perhaps cannot — talk explicitly to one another about their work are unlikely to persuade the public that they know what they are doing.

Chapter 1

Course-planning

Teachers' responsibility for planning the curriculum varies from one country to another. In many countries, possibly in most throughout the world, there is an official set of goals for the school system, and curriculum guidelines are published by the government, which are intended to control, tightly or loosely, the content of the curriculum and, often, the teaching methods to be used. At this point all we need to notice is that in all countries teachers have some responsibility for planning their courses, and that in some countries they have – or at least seem to have – a great deal of autonomy.

In England and Wales the legal responsibility for curriculum lies with local education authorities under the loose supervision of the central government Department of Education and Science. In practice much of this control has been delegated, on the one hand, to the schools themselves and, on the other, to examination boards. In the USA, responsibility for curriculum is vested in local School Boards. These School Boards also control the financing of schools, and this has enabled them to play at times a very influential role in curriculum matters, for example in determining what biological topics can be dealt with and what works of literature read. Teachers in the USA and in England and Wales, and in a number of other European countries such as Denmark, are expected to take an active role in course-planning as part of their day-to-day professional work.

To take full responsibility for one's own teaching is not merely to plan and teach a series of lessons, but to be able to justify what one has taught and how one has taught it. This implies considerable reflection upon why one is teaching this rather than that, upon the methods one is using and why they are suitable, and upon what one hopes one's

1

pupils are gaining from the lessons. The purpose of this section is to provide practice in deliberate planning, and in looking critically at the results of one's own and other people's planning.

Explicit planning of this kind has two purposes: to improve the quality of one's own thinking about one's teaching, and to enable communication with other people. Practised teachers find that they do not need to write down exactly what they are doing and why: they find they can rely upon habit and well-formed intuitions. Yet this is precisely the stage at which they should be reflecting more deliberately upon their teaching; having mastered the elementary classroom skills they are in a position to choose to teach this way rather than that. In a study of an infants' school (Sharp and Green, 1975), one unfortunate teacher called Mrs Carpenter found when asked that she could not explain how she decided when a child was 'ready' to begin reading.

> 'You see it's all readiness really, when you're with little children, because you can't really (pause) they all do it at different stages and different times. The only thing you can do is just sort of provide as many different sorts of things so they've got every opportunity to go as far as they can — now I can't really, sort of (pause) I don't quite know how to put it (pause) again it's concentration, and if they're not really, sort of, ready, or going to understand something they're doing, then their concentration will go straight away, that's one of the first things.'

Of course, Mrs Carpenter *may* have been making admirable intuitive judgments, but since she was unable to say what criteria she was using, neither she nor anyone else was in a position to judge. It is valuable for every Mrs Carpenter to be clear about what she is trying to do and about the basis of her judgments, since otherwise she is not in a position to consider her teaching critically in order to improve it. Habit and unexamined intuition are the enemy of deliberate responsible choice. Explicitness is thus a tool of professional self-improvement. Moreover, the individual teacher is not the only person concerned: other teachers, parents, the pupils themselves, have a need or a right to know what the teacher's plans are, and why they have been selected. Collaboration and discussion is of great value to all teachers, both the more and less experienced.

In recent years, teachers have often been urged to base their planning upon explicit objectives. Other writers argue that planning by objectives is not suited to some kinds of learning in schools. Alternative methods, not open to the same criticisms, will be put forward so that the reader can select appropriate methods for different kinds of planning.

General aims

A distinction is usually made between 'aims' and 'objectives'. Aims are more general: a school might include amongst its aims the fostering of self-reliance in pupils. Although this might be useful in providing a reminder to teachers about an overall goal, it does not commit anybody to doing anything in particular. It still remains to be decided what activities, experiences or relationships foster self-reliance, and which areas of the curriculum — indeed which lessons — should include them.

Similarly there may be more general objectives within a subject-area. A science course might have the general objective of encouraging in pupils a critical habit of mind. Again, this is a useful reminder which does not commit anybody. How and when pupils should criticise has to be decided. Some middle path has to be chosen between entirely dogmatic teaching and the encouraging of pupils to criticise everything whether or not they have good grounds for doing so. Thus the more general kinds of aims and objectives are potentially useful, but can prove to be pious statements that are never put into effect. For this reason, many writers advocate the writing of specific objectives, including the extremely specific ones called 'behavioural objectives'. The first tasks in this book are, however concerned with more general aims.

Task 1.1 Writing and analysing general aims

1.1.1 Write ten *general aims* that you think would be the most important ones for a primary-school class, or for a remedial group in a secondary school. Choose whichever age-group you are most familiar with. Arrange the aims in order of importance, and justify your choice.

1.1.2 Write eight general aims for teaching a particular subject or curriculum area to an age-group of your choice. Put these aims in order of importance and justify your selection of

3

1.1.2 them. (You may, for example, decide to write aims for art and
contd   craft work with a junior class, or for environmental studies with
a class from the middle years, or for mathematics or physical
education with a secondary-school class.)

1.1.3 Aims are intended to express teachers' purposes. They do so by
specifying either (i) what teachers will do, or (ii) what they
hope their pupils will learn to do. Read each of the following
aims and decide which of the two kinds it is. (These aims were
decided upon by groups of secondary-school teachers, and are
quoted from Taylor, 1970.)

English

1 Written English is not to be isolated from other school
subjects.

2 The English department should work closely with other
departments so as to encourage the development of *creative*
pupils.

3 Command of English so that a person can express himself
orally or in writing with clarity and coherence.

4 To read fluently, with understanding and to get a response
to literature, thereby enriching a child's experiences.

Science

1 Knowledge of scientific principles and their application to
everyday life, i.e. household electricity, heat conductors,
air pressure, etc.

2 To give a training in scientific method, progressing from
known information through observation to a conclusion.
To emphasise the need for accurate observation, recording
and interpretation of data.

3 Providing an understanding of nature and man's use of it.

4 The basic science course acts as a basis on which a more
detailed approach to individual subjects can be built.

Do you see advantages or disadvantages in formulating aims in
one way or the other?

1.1.4 Look back at the list of aims which you wrote in answer to Task
1.1.1 or 1.1.2. Decide in respect of each aim whether it indicates (i) what the teacher is to do, or (ii) what the pupils are to
learn. Some writers argue that all aims should be formulated in
terms of what pupils are to do, since this helps teachers to

1.1.4 focus upon their pupils' learning rather than upon their own
contd intentions, but this is open to debate.

Informal planning of courses

General aims in their nature leave the teacher with the practical decisions still to be made, that is, the decisions about what to teach and
how to teach it. There has been much debate about how best to do this,
and some of the issues will be discussed in the next section of this
chapter. Here we will begin with the practical options.

Different kinds of subject-matter and of teaching methods require
different techniques for planning. The categories used here are no more
than rough guidelines, but they will help you to see how to modify
your planning for different purposes. The five categories are set out in
Table 1.1.

TABLE 1.1 *Planning techniques used for different subjects and teaching methods*

	Basis	*Description*	*Subject-matter*
(a)	Content	Based on an area of experience, a body of knowledge, or a group of phenomena, e.g. 'My brother's keeper', 'the Norman Conquest', 'floating and sinking'.	Most subjects, especially in their elementary stages. Can be interdisciplinary. Suited to subjects such as science, history, geography, environmental studies, religious education, literature.
(b)	Concept	Based on a concept or interrelated set of concepts; e.g. 'probability', 'energy', 'role', 'population'.	Any subject, especially in its advanced stages.
(c)	Skills	Based on a set of skills.	Some subject-areas such as mathematics or literacy or craft can more readily be

5

TABLE 1.1 *contd*

Basis	Description	Subject-matter
		defined in terms of skills than in any other way. In others, such as history and art, skills play a more subordinate role.
(d) Problem	Planning based on problems that pupils are to solve, as a means of enabling them to apply skills in a more complex and realistic situation or as a means of indirect access to concepts.	Can be used anywhere, but especially in skills-based subjects, such as mathematics, design and physical educa-tion and in some approaches to science.
(e) Interest	Since the onus is on the learner to select issues important to him, the teacher's role is to offer a starting-point and a range of possible options and methods.	Not predetermined by the teacher. Likely to be interdisciplinary and diffuse.

The next five sets of tasks are arranged in terms of these five categories. If you are a specialist teacher, you may find that some kinds of plan-ning will be more important to you than others. Teachers of general subjects in primary schools, or in remedial departments, are likely to find all of them appropriate for one purpose or another.

Content-based planning

This kind of planning is perhaps the commonest of all, since its starting-point is an area of experience, a body of knowledge or a group of phenomena. The teacher's task is to decide what possibilities the content offers, what conceptual learning might arise from it, what skills might be exercised, what activities the pupils should engage in. The tasks suggest some starting-points, but there is no reason why you should not choose other suitable ones.

Task 1.2 Content-based planning

1.2.1 Plan a course-unit* concerned with materials that float or sink in water. What concepts and principles would you wish your pupils to grasp? What activities would you plan to help them do so?

1.2.2 Plan a course-unit concerned with the Norman Conquest. What materials would you present to your pupils? What issues would you want them to be aware of? What range of historical and other skills would you want them to use? What sequence of activities would you plan to enable this?

1.2.3 Plan a course-unit based upon an anthology of poems. Devise a series of activities that will encourage your pupils to read poems individually and to one another, choose ones they like, represent and perform them in different ways, and perhaps talk about them.

1.2.4 Plan a course-unit for young children concerned with houses. Decide what different kinds of learning can arise from this topic; and plan appropriate activities to make this possible. What materials would you need for this?

1.2.5 Plan a course-unit called 'My brother's keeper', concerned with moral responsibility for others. What kinds of insight into moral responsibility are your pupils likely to be capable of? What everyday situations are likely to provide opportunities for them to deepen their insights and reflect upon them? Choose a sequence of situations and devise activities for the children that will encourage this.

* 'Course-unit' is a vague concept that refers to a group of lessons that have been planned together. It can vary in length from a morning's work to a course lasting a whole term. For these tasks you should choose whatever seems appropriate to the scale and importance of the subject-matter.

In carrying out these tasks, you will find it necessary to plan as if for a class of children whom you have taught, or at least to imagine one. This is essential because what you choose for them to do, and what you hope they will understand, needs to be matched to the level of understanding, and to the likely interests and knowledge of a group of pupils.

There now follows a suggested method for content-based planning, which breaks the planning down into a series of steps. Since these are intended to be used with a variety of subject-matters, they may need to be modified in your case. It may be necessary to omit some of the stages, if they do not seem to apply. (For example, it is unlikely in Task 1.2.3 that you will wish pupils to learn particular concepts from reading the poems.)

The following is a method for content-based planning.

Content. Select a suitable area of content.

Activities. Jot down briefly all the ideas you can think of for activities arising from the content, which seem appropriate for the children you have in mind. At this stage there is no need to sort out the activities.

Concepts. If it seems appropriate to the subject-matter, list all the concepts and principles which the children might at best be expected to learn from working with it. This is important even with younger children, since they may be brought to understand simpler ideas on which later concepts will be based. (For example, in Task 1.2.1 what preliminary concepts might be learnt from floating and sinking objects, which would later form the basis for an understanding of relative density?)

Information. Next decide whether there are parts of the content that you want to emphasise particularly and if so make a list of them. You might want your pupils simply to memorise some information, but nowadays it is more likely that you would wish to ensure they have understood central issues, to have grasped their importance, and seen their relationship to other matters. (In some subjects, such as history, this may prove a more appropriate way of organising the subject-matter than through concepts. In science, too, there may be knowledge to be mastered, as the 'content map' in the next paragraph illustrates.)

Making a content map. Now put together in a diagram the concepts, information and activities. Some 'content maps' are concerned only

8

with subject-matter. Table 1.2 is a simple content map for social studies in primary schools made by Hilda Taba and her team (Taba, Durkim, Fraenkel and McNaughton, 1967).

TABLE 1.2 *Content map 1: Structure of content*

Area or topic	Main idea	Sample of cultures	Dimensions studied or study questions
Middle and South America	Culture change in varying degrees when they come in contact with another culture.	Aztec Spanish Yoruba	What are the land and the climate like where the Aztec, Spaniard and Yoruba lived?
			How did these people secure their food, clothing and shelter? (Farming, trading, etc.?)
			What tools did they have?
			What evidence of trade is seen? (Market places, laws, money?)
			How were the people governed?
			What language did they speak?
			How did these people educate their children?
			If there were schools, who attended?
			What kinds of things did these people invent?

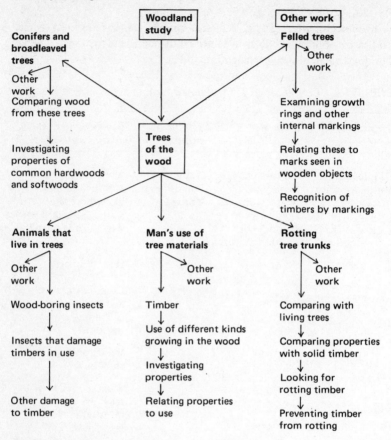

Figure 1.1 *Content map 2*

You may find it more useful, however, to include activities and concepts in the content map, as in the one made by the Schools Council Science 5-13 Project for pupils of top junior age (Ennever and Harlen, 1972) (see Figure 1.1).

You will notice that this is a mixture of concepts (Conifers and broadleaved trees), information (Insects that damage timbers in use) and activities for the pupils to do (Examining growth rings and other internal markings). If you follow the arrows you will see the sequence of ideas and activities that the teacher has planned. When you make your own map you will find out where there are gaps that need to be filled with activities, and whether there are any activities that seem to lead nowhere and would be better omitted. Most important of all, it will help you to work out a suitable sequence of activities. You may find it useful to number each of the arrows that come from the main box in whatever sequence seems to make best sense.

Activities and concepts.   At this stage you may need to consider whether the activities you have planned really do contribute to an understanding of the concepts you want to be learnt. If not, you will need to devise new activities.

Resources.   If you are actually going to teach this course-unit (perhaps on teaching practice, if you are a student teacher), you will need to list what resources you will need, and work out where you will obtain them. If you are intending to take children out on a visit, you will also need to decide what preliminary planning will be necessary.

Concept-based planning

Concept-based planning is not profoundly different from content-based planning. In this case, however, the starting-point is not a body of knowledge but a concept or principle, or perhaps a group of inter-related concepts. Since it is unusual for a concept to be of importance in more than one subject, this approach is usually strongly subject-centred. Sometimes teachers committed to an integrated approach plan an interdisciplinary course under a heading such as 'Water' or 'War and violence' or 'Power'. Usually such interdisciplinary planning is not concept-based but content-based, since 'Water', for example, is likely to refer to a loosely related collection of knowledge of various kinds, as does 'Trees in the wood' in the content map reproduced above. 'Power' may be a useful concept in history; it has, however, a different meaning in geography, and it is entirely different from 'energy' in physics. To link them together in an interdisciplinary course seems to me merely confusing: I am not recommending such an approach, though this is not intended to imply that all interdisciplinary courses are confused.

   In some subject-areas, concept-based planning is not suitable until a very advanced stage. In literature, art and music, course-units based on concepts such as 'imagery', 'chiaroscuro', or 'sonata form' would only be suitable towards the end of a child's schooling, and then

11

perhaps only for some pupils. In science or geography, however, concept-based planning is perfectly suited to younger children, so long as they meet the concepts through experiences and activities suited to their level of development and existing knowledge, so that the new learning can be embedded in their previous experience.

Task 1.3 Concept-based planning

1.3.1 Plan a course-unit based upon one of the following concepts: 'probability', 'population', 'energy', 'political power', 'role and status'. (If none of these concepts suit your pupils or the subject you teach, please choose one that is suitable.) The purpose of the unit is to enable your pupils to use the concept as an instrument in their own thinking. With younger children this does not necessarily imply that they should learn the technical name of the concept, though there is every reason why they should talk about it in their own terms. (If you do choose a concept for yourself, you may find it useful to note the warning given above in relation to 'water', that not every word or phrase refers to a theoretical principle suited to this approach.)

1.3.2 Plan a course-unit in which you present to pupils an interrelated group of concepts from a subject-area you are familiar with. (An example from geography would be: population density, population growth, land use, zoning, conurbation, amenities.) The purpose of the unit would be to have your pupils familiar enough with the concepts to use them in their thinking.

The method for concept-based planning which follows is a variant of the sequence suggested for the content-based approach.

Concept-analysis. Decide whether there are any preliminary ideas that need to be taught, or at least revised, before the main concept is presented. (For example, the technical concept 'work' in physics depends, amongst other things, on the pupil's grasp of the concept 'mass'.) If in a larger unit you are to teach several interrelated concepts you will probably find it useful to represent these and their relationships diagrammatically. (Methods for carrying out a detailed analysis of a concept or a group of concepts is given in the section that begins on p. 82.)

12

Activities.   Jot down briefly all the ideas you can think of for experiences and activities that would help your pupils to grasp the concepts you have mapped out. There is much to be said for choosing a range of activities that embody the concept in different situations and in different forms. (For example, 'air pressure' can be met in a bicycle pump and inner tube, in an imploded can, on a mountain top, and so on.)

Sequencing.   The activities should be put into a sequence partly determined by their logical relationships, and partly by the ease with which the pupils will make sense of them. The activities related to each concept can be put together in something similar to a content map, in which each arrow from the central box will show a sequence of activities all directed to the understanding of the same concept.

Skills-based planning

The next group of planning tasks relates to learning in which the mastery of skills is given precedence over the grasping of concepts and the learning of knowledge. This is the familiar distinction between 'knowing how' and 'knowing what'. In science, for example, although many teachers see their task in terms of content, others place as great an emphasis upon cognitive skills such as observing, hypothesising, testing or interpreting. In mathematics, the content is likely to be made up of skills: it will therefore be impossible to separate the one from the other. When a mathematics teacher thinks of commutativity he or she is likely to think of it as a set of interrelated processes, rather than as a concept. In other curriculum-areas, such as craft, the early stages of reading, and physical education, a variety of skills will often play a dominant role in planning. Skills-based planning is appropriate whenever you judge that the learning of skills is the primary purpose of the unit, and that the content to which the skills are applied is of only secondary importance.

Task 1.4 Skills-based planning

1.4.1   Plan a course-unit for children just approaching readiness for reading. What discriminations and skills show that a child is ready to be taught to read? Make a list of these, or find a list in a book on the teaching of reading (such as Brennan, 1978).

1.4.1 The course should consist of a series of activities designed to
contd help children to make the discriminations and to practise the
       skills; it is not intended to include the teaching of reading proper.
1.4.2 Plan a course-unit in map-reading. List the skills used by an
       adult in reading a map. Delete any that are likely to be beyond
       the intellectual grasp of most of the children in the class. Devise
       activities that will enable pupils to practise the skills and dis-
       criminations, and put them into an appropriate sequence.
1.4.3 Plan an introductory course-unit in history for secondary-
       school pupils. You can do this best by listing the main pro-
       cedures used by historians in their work. Plan activities that
       will enable your pupils to experience these procedures *at
       their level*.
1.4.4 Plan a course-unit in a craft area, such as work with clay not
       using a wheel, or an introduction to the use of the cold chisel
       and file. In craft you have the option of starting your planning
       with (i) a set of skills to be learnt, or (ii) a problem to be
       solved. Here it is suggested that you begin planning by listing
       the skills that you want pupils to learn, and then seeking one
       or more pieces of work that would introduce these skills at an
       appropriate level. You will also need to decide whether you
       present the skills as worth learning in their own right, or allow
       the need for them to become manifest during attempts to solve
       a problem.
1.4.5 Plan a course-unit in physical education intended to practise
       a range of skills that require gymnasium apparatus. Your
       starting-point may well be the range of apparatus available, as
       well as the likely ability of your pupils to use it. List the skills
       that can be practised with the apparatus, and plan a programme
       of activities such that all the skills are practised regularly yet
       without the danger of staleness from excessive repetition of
       the same activity.
1.4.6 Plan a course-unit in mathematics introducing pupils either
       (i) to index notation as a preliminary to later work on logar-
       ithms, or (ii) to solving simultaneous equations graphically.

As the nature of skills varies profoundly from one curriculum area to
another, the following method for skills-based planning can only be
roughly appropriate to any one task; some steps will need to be modified, and others possibly omitted altogether.

Choice of skills.· The first step must be to list the skills. Where these are not traditional, they may require thoughtful analysis, as in the case of determining the competences that constitute reading readiness, or the range of skills that are used by historians. At this stage, too, it is useful to decide whether you wish your pupils merely to have experience of using the skills, or whether it will be necessary for them to gain mastery of some or all of them. In craft work, it may be advantageous if the skills can be combined in the making of an artefact, and this is likely to influence the choice of skills.

Match with pupils. Are there any pre-skills that must be taught or brought back into use before pupils can reasonably be expected to utilise the target skills? It may also be necessary to go through the list to ensure that none of the skills are too difficult for the age and ability of the pupils: there is no reason why pupils should not first carry out skills at a low level of achievement, but total failure is not educationally useful.

Content. In many cases you will need to decide what content the skills are to be applied to. While this is not an issue in mathematics or physical education, in history or science the particular historical or scientific topics to be dealt with are likely to be as important as the skills which are to be used in exploring those topics.

Resources. The choice of skills often determines what equipment will be needed. In a subject such as geography or history, however, the collection and production of suitable documentary or other resources for the practice of skills will constitute a major part of the planning.

Presentation and feedback. It is essential in a skills-based unit that learners be provided with a clear model of each skill, so that they know what they are aiming at. If they are to evaluate their own performance in order progressively to modify and improve it, they will need access to appropriate criteria. The criteria will not necessarily be formal: it may be the ability to criticise their own execution of a long jump based upon awareness of motor activity. Without access to appropriate criteria, pupils can engage only in vague trial and error, and wait for hints from the teacher. It should be noted that the presentation of psycho-motor skills in solely verbal terms may be worse than unhelpful: as Bruner (1966) says, the teacher's words may make no contact with the learner's muscles.

Using the skills. In planning patterns of practice and feedback it is first necessary to know which skills are to be mastered, and which the pupils need only be familiar with. With some motor skills in physical education, for example, it may be useful to break down some skills into subskills, practise each subskill separately, put them together, and finally practise the whole sequence until it becomes automatic. But such detail is only necessary to ensure mastery. In any case a varied pattern of practice for alternating skills is necessary to avoid boredom.

It must also be decided whether the skills are to be practised as 'dummy runs' (the term is James Britton's, 1970) or applied to useful tasks. In woodwork the cutting of joints 'for practice' has been largely abandoned in favour of teaching joints as the need arises in making something useful. Similarly, in the teaching of reading, the sooner the skills can be used for reading something the learner wants to know about the better. The continual repetition of a skill for no visible purpose defeats its own end.

When skills produce written work, feedback is less of a problem than with motor skills. Ideally there should be a sliding scale of evaluation so that each pupil is aiming just a little ahead of where he has reached, but this is easy to achieve only with very small classes.

Problem-based planning

The starting-point for this planning is the teacher's selection of a problem that the pupils themselves will be able to solve. Underlying such a teaching strategy is the pedagogical principle of increasing the pupils' responsibility for developing their own understanding. At best, the problem-solving and the discussion that arises from it provide learners with indirect access to important concepts and the opportunity to apply skills to more complex and realistic tasks than repetitive exercises permit. The teacher therefore selects the problem in the light of the conceptual issues it will raise, and the range of skills involved, for guided problem-solving though indirect is not a random method of teaching. Thus the approach is particularly appropriate in subjects such as mathematics and science, in which cognitive processes —

and sometimes motor skills — become a means of access to underlying conceptual principles.

In the tasks that follow, particular problems are outlined in case you wish to use them; you may, however, prefer to invent a problem that fits your own concerns, in order to make the experience of planning more realistic. It is particularly important when planning problem-based units to consider what your role as teacher will be, what range of materials will be available, how you can best help those pupils who are uncertain, what kind of questions will encourage them to think for themselves, and how you will keep an eye on everyone's progress while they are working.

Task 1.5 Problem-based planning

1.5.1 Plan a course-unit in which pupils will design a set of signs that can be set up in a particular school for the direction of visitors. You will need to plan how you can best communicate to your pupils the necessity for a preliminary analysis of the visitors who come to the school, their likely purposes and points of entrance to the school, and the most useful information and positioning of signs. At a more mundane level you will need to predict what materials they will wish to use. (Guidance about such planning can be found in Shaw and Reeve, 1978.)

1.5.2 Plan a course-unit in mathematics intended to introduce primary-school children to multiplication. You should include a variety of tasks, games and problems involving the building-up, comparison and breaking-down of rectangles, both with mathematical apparatus and with more informal materials. The problems should be designed to give the children intuitive insight into the conceptual basis of multiplication, but should lead also to representing in symbolic form what they have done by manipulating objects.

1.5.3 Plan a course-unit in science, in which pupils solve a practical problem which has theoretical implications. One example of such a problem is the task of purifying a mixture of rock-salt and sand. In devising and trying out ways of purifying the salt, pupils should discuss the work with one another and the teacher, and have the opportunity of gaining a better understanding of concepts such as 'mixture', 'dissolve', 'evaporate' and 'condense'. They should, moreover, be able to practise certain elementary skills. (Methods of basing classwork on

1.5.3   this problem are discussed in detail in the Nuffield Combined
contd   Science Project, 1970, *Teachers' Guide I*, pp. 77-85.) However,
you may prefer to choose your own problem rather than use
this familiar one.

1.5.4   Plan a short course-unit (perhaps no more than one lesson) in
which pupils discuss the meaning of a poem. In this approach it
is the interpretation of the poem that provides the pupils with
a problem which they are to seek a joint solution for during
discussion in small groups. Practical decisions to be made in
planning the unit include how your pupils are to be organised
into groups, what initial presentation (if any) of the poem is
appropriate, whether you will provide guiding questions or
leave the task open to your pupils, and how to integrate the
various discussions at the end of the unit. You may also wish to
consider the possibility of setting up further activities arising
from the poem.

Here is a poem that you could use with some pupils, but you
may prefer to choose one for yourself.

The Meadow Mouse   Theodore Roethke (1957)
In a shoe-box stuffed in an old nylon stocking
Sleeps the baby mouse I found in the meadow,
Where he trembled and shook beneath a stick
Till I caught him up by the tail and brought him in,
Cradled in my hand,
A little quaker, the whole body of him trembling,
His absurd whiskers sticking out like a cartoon-mouse,
His feet like small leaves,
Little lizard-feet,
Whitish and spread wide when he tried to struggle away,
Wriggling like a miniscule puppy.

Now he's eaten his three kinds of cheese and drunk from his
    bottle-cap water-trough —
So much he just lies in one corner,
His tail curled under him, his belly big
As his head; his bat-like ears
Twitching, tilting toward the least sound.
Do I imagine he no longer trembles
When I come close to him?
He seems no longer to tremble.

1.5.4
contd

But this morning the shoe-box house on the back porch is
empty.
Where has he gone, my meadow mouse,
My thumb of a child that nuzzled in my palm? —
To run under the hawk's wing,
Under the eye of the great owl watching from the elm-tree,
To live by courtesy of the shrike, the snake, the tom-cat.
I think of the nestling fallen into the deep grass,
The turtle gasping in the dusty rubble of the highway,
The paralytic stunned in the tub, and the water rising, —
All things innocent, hapless, forsaken.

1.5.5 Plan a problem-based course-unit in drama. This task makes the assumption that your pupils have already had considerable experience of mime carried out individually and in pairs, and are ready for more complex work in small groups. I suggest that the best way of setting them a problem is to give them a situation or a series of incidents to represent in the form of a mime. For younger children, a short folk-tale with some variety of incident and feeling would be suitable. For older pupils it might be preferable to invent a situation in a contemporary setting; a political leader whose government has been violently overthrown faces the decision whether to stay at the risk of his life or to accede to his family's wish to escape into exile . . . and so on. Since most children's first impulse will be to launch into unconsidered improvisation, part of your task in planning will be to work out how to induce them to become reflective and analytical in their approach to the representation, in short to treat the task as a problem.

1.5.6 Plan a course-unit based on *The Mystery of Mark Pullen* from the materials devised by the Schools Council History 13-16 Project (1976) (see Appendix A). The published kit is intended to enable 13-year-old students to have first-hand experience of carrying out the central interpretive processes of history. It contains papers supposedly found on the body of a young man discovered lying by the roadside; the pupils' task is to work out from the papers who he is and how he came to be there. (The materials could also probably be used with younger children who are competent readers.) How will you organise your class so that their use of these materials gives them insight into the nature of the historian's task?

1.5.7   Plan a problem-based course-unit in the area of history, geography, environmental studies or social studies, similar in nature
to the history task outlined above. In this case it will be necessary for you to devise the problem and prepare whatever
materials will be needed. In history this might be a matter of
collecting or devising documents which present a historical
situation in which a decision had to be made: the problem is
for pupils to analyse the various motives which might influence
that decision. In geography a problem might be set based upon
the planning of a transport system for a new town: the pupils
would not only be required to make a plan but to justify the
decisions taken. A more general social issue would be to plan for
the expenditure of a sum of money on facilities for elderly
people in a particular district. In all of these cases it will be
necessary: (i) to make a variety of information available in the
form of documents, maps, statistics and diagrams; (ii) to formulate the precise task that your pupils are to undertake; (iii) to
plan the sequence of events, grouping and resources necessary
for the work; and (iv) to decide upon your own role during
the work.

1.5.8   Plan a problem-based unit in design. The principle in this case
is to give your pupils a set of specifications, and the choice of
materials and methods for making a device that satisfies those
specifications. An example of this would be a set of specifications for a washbasin unit to carry toothbrushes, tooth mug and
toothpaste. Your task is (i) to work out an original set of
specifications, taking into account the competences of your
pupils and the materials available; and (ii) to plan how you will
present and discuss the specifications, and how you will support
and check your pupils' designs to ensure that the materials
and methods chosen are appropriate. Finally, you might consider whether the problem-solving might contribute to your
pupils' understanding of general principles in design, and how
you could best encourage this.

Hints of a method for problem-based planning have been included in
the tasks themselves. The general method that follows will need adaptation for different subject-areas: a method for all occasions fits none of
them precisely.

Choosing a problem. Criteria which you might keep in mind when choosing or constructing a problem include:

(*a*) the concepts that might become available in the course of considering and discussing the problem;

(*b*) the skills that might be practised when analysing the problem and planning a solution;

(*c*) the skills that might be practised when carrying out a possible solution;

(*d*) your pupils' capabilities (which may be greater than you suppose);

(*e*) your pupils' interests and concerns;

(*f*) the materials and equipment available, and other practical constraints such as timetabling.

The problem is thus seen as a means to further ends which may in part be planned for.

Setting the problem. In some cases this will constitute a substantial proportion of the task, since it will be necessary to collect or write any documentary materials on which the problem is based. In any case it will be necessary to word the problem with care, especially when the problem consists of a set of specifications to which your pupils must work.

Conceptual analysis. Having chosen the problem it will be important for you to analyse – for yourself, not for your pupils – what conceptual learning is to arise from it. (This may not be appropriate in some areas such as physical education.) On this analysis will depend your decisions about classroom activities, and your own role in them.

Sequence of activities. At this stage you should decide whether you want preliminary discussions, whether pupils should work individually or in groups, and whether at the end of the unit the various lines of thought and methods tried are to be made available for consideration by all your pupils. You will also need to decide what your own role will be in these activities, and particularly how you will take part in the discussion and evaluation of proposed solutions.

Resources. In some cases it will be necessary to provide materials and equipment, and this may need careful planning in advance if you wish your pupils to be able to try out various solutions. In science

21

this amounts to ensuring that your pupils know what range of apparatus is available in the laboratory, and how to use it. On the other hand, you may wish the alternative to appear only during preliminary discussion, which greatly simplifies the provision of equipment, though it deprives your pupils of the full experience of problem-solving. In this latter case you can have appropriate apparatus ready but out of sight; if you have it out on the benches, you curtail the process of problem-solving for any but the most unobservant of pupils. Similar considerations apply in craft and design, and indeed in any area where materials or apparatus are used in problem-solving.

Interest-based planning

This approach is based upon the principle that children learn best what they wish to learn. It would be naïve merely to ask young children what they want to do: interest has to be created. Therefore the essence of this approach is (i) to provide a common experience intended to provoke interest and to challenge questions; (ii) to hold a discussion that will help pupils to see what options are open to them, since without this they will be at the mercy of their own first thoughts or of peer-group pressures; and (iii) to teach new skills as the pupils find that they need them. It is a challenging programme for any teacher.

Task 1.6 Interest-based planning

1.6.1 Plan a course-unit consisting of a class visit and of interest-based work arising from it. For example, a group of pupils might be taken to a stream, a building site, a farm or a factory. (There is the possibility that a visit arranged primarily for content-based purposes might also form the basis for interest-based activities, perhaps with another teacher.)

It will be useful to make a list of issues likely to arise from the visit, if possible on the basis of a preliminary visit without the children. (A group of college students planning a course-unit of this kind could usefully make such a visit together in order to combine their ideas about possible issues and activities.) This list will enable you to help your pupils — unobtrusively if possible — to see what options are available and what media might be used. It will also be useful in planning for

1.6.1 any resources that may be necessary, such as access to books.
contd   Finally, you need to consider how you will organise the discussion and choice of activities, and how you will advise and
supervise your pupils when they carry them out.

1.6.2 Plan a course-unit consisting of a presentation to the class and
of interest-based work arising from it. The presentation may be
dramatic, or based on readings and documents, literary or non-
literary; it may use film or other visual elements, or music; it
may include any or all of these. The preparation of this presentation will constitute a large part of this task; apart from this,
the requirements of this task are similar to those outlined for
Task 1.6.1.

1.6.3 Your class is in the middle of an interest-based course-unit such
as those outlined in Tasks 1.6.1 and 1.6.2, when you find that
you will have to be away from school for the several weeks
during which they will complete it. Your place during that time
will be taken by a temporary teacher whom you will not be able
to meet. You therefore need to write a long letter to him or
her, to explain what the pupils have been doing, including the
purposes of the unit, how it was set up, what individual pupils
have done so far, and the kinds of support that you have been
giving to them.

The method for interest-based planning necessarily begins with the
choice of visit or presentation.

Starting-point.   Your choice of a place to visit, or of a topic and means
of presentation will depend upon your judgment of:

1 areas of experience likely to provoke interest in your pupils;
2 the potential of power of the experience offered (for example,
   by a professional Theatre in Education group; or by a visit to a steel
   works);
3 the range of useful activities likely to arise from it.

Presentation.   Since the success of the unit is likely to depend on the
success of the visit or presentation, the latter need to be carefully prepared. Preparation of the visit includes predicting a range of possibilities
for pupils to follow, so that you tactfully direct attention during the
visit. If you attempt to direct attention by giving your pupils the kind
of questionnaire/worksheet often used during a visit, you risk defeating

your own ends, unless you design a questionnaire that provokes your pupils into generating questions and seeing possibilities for themselves.

Activities. It is essential to spend time in discussing with your pupils the range of possible topics, and the activities which they might undertake, the purpose of this being indirectly to display the possibilities for their consideration.

Materials and equipment. You will need to consider in advance what materials and equipment will be required, and whether your pupils know how to use them.

Skills. It will also be valuable to consider what your role is to be once your pupils have embarked upon various activities. Many will require advice. Some of them may attempt tasks that require skills that you will have to teach to them, while at the same time keeping an eye on the rest of the class. It will be particularly important to see that those who want to gather information do not simply copy extracts from books verbatim; they will need to be taught to skim, extract material, make notes, interrelate ideas from various sources, to use advanced inquiry skills in fact. This is not, however, to be seen as a distraction from the main business of teaching, since one of the great virtues claimed for interest-based work is the possibility of teaching skills, especially the skills of inquiry, to pupils when they want to learn them. But to achieve this demands both planning and skill from the teacher.

As a conclusion to this section on informal methods of planning, it may be useful to consider if there are elements that all kinds of planning have in common, whether they are based on content, concepts, skills, problems or interests. The methods of planning which have been suggested in this section have directed attention to various criteria and concerns:

1 content;
2 concepts that inform the content;
3 skills, both cognitive and psycho-motor;
4 the competences and interests of pupils;
5 the choice and sequencing of activities;
6 resources and equipment;
7 the teacher's roles.

As we moved from one basis of planning to another, the relative importance of each of these varied, and some disappeared altogether. What have not been mentioned are the value systems which underlie all of these; values will be dealt with in a later section.

It should by now be plain that the basis which teachers choose for their planning is likely to vary not only from subject to subject but even within a subject, according to the view that the teacher takes of the nature of the subject and how it is learnt. Let us take history, for example: history is usually seen as a content-based subject, yet recently there have been attempts to base it upon a range of skills and key concepts, while it is also possible to plan history courses on the basis of problem-solving or of pupils' interests. Physical education, in contrast, lends itself most readily to skills-based planning, and mathematics to skills-based or problem-based approaches.

Planning by objectives

We turn now to planning by objectives. Here, too, the distinction between the different bases of planning will be useful, since it will help to explain why objectives are more useful in some curricular subjects than in others. It is perhaps proper to make it clear that I myself am not by any means convinced that planning by writing lists of specific objectives is the best way of preparing a course. The more informal methods of planning discussed in the previous section often seem closer to teachers' intuitively held preferences for ways of thinking about their work. Nevertheless, there have been strong arguments advanced for planning by objectives, so there seems every reason for teachers to understand what is meant by 'objectives' and (even more) to attempt to use them, so that they can choose how they plan on the grounds of informed first-hand experience. Thus the remainder of this chapter takes planning by objectives very seriously as a practical possibility so that the reader can come to his own conclusions.

When the word 'objectives' is used in this book, it refers to statements of what the pupils are intended to learn from the course. 'What the pupils are intended to learn' may seem at first no more than a simple list of items of information, the 'content' of the course. To take an example from history, the content might be aspects of life in England during the time of Elizabeth I. But a moment's reflection shows that content alone does not take us far enough. What do you

25

want your pupils to be able to do with this content? Will the memorising of information be all you want? Probably not. Do you want them to be able to sketch a half-timbered house? Do you want them to be able to make up a tale about farmhouse life during that period? Perhaps you want them to understand what they have read and heard, but what does 'understand' mean? Do you want them to be able to explain why epidemics were rife in Elizabethan towns? Do you want them (if they are older pupils) to learn to interpret original documents, or to compare one account with another? Are you wanting them to have sympathetic insight into Elizabeth's personal and political manoeuvring? The possibilities seem almost endless. Thus it is not enough merely to state the content with which the unit is concerned; it is essential to decide what skills and processes the children are to carry out, since upon this inevitably depends your choice of activities for the children during lessons.

If you want to foster sympathetic insight into Elizabethan lives then the activities must include not only relevant information but discussion of people's concerns, perhaps the reading of stories and dramatic improvisation. Similarly, if you want your pupils to be able to compare original documents you will need to give them the opportunity to do just this.

It was Ralph Tyler (1949), an American curriculum evaluator, who urged that an objective should specify (i) the content to be learnt, and (ii) the processes and skills that the learners are to engage in and develop *in dealing* with that content. Tyler's emphasis is valuable in that it reminds us that what our pupils learn is determined not only by what information we present to them but by what we ask them to do with it. Indeed the latter may often prove to be more important. In the example from history used above, one appropriate objective might be: 'Pupils will be able to write an account of daily life in a typical Elizabethan farmhouse, showing sympathetic insight into the concerns and experiences of the people living there.' This objective indicates the *content*: knowledge of country life in Elizabethan times. It also implies the *processes*: pupils will need to have sympathetic insight into the subjective experiences of people, and be able to embody this insight into a narrative. This latter will become important at the stage of choosing learning activities: the teacher would choose to read stories or first-hand accounts from the period, perhaps have children discuss or re-enact some of these, and require them to write about it. Thus the process element in the objective plays an important role in directing the detailed planning of classroom activities.

Most important of all, such an objective indicates what pupils will be able to *do* after completing the course-unit: in this case they will be able to *write* an account and in doing this they will *show sympathetic insight*. By indicating what the pupils should be able to do, an objective makes it much easier to tell whether the unit has achieved this purpose. It is this emphasis upon stating what pupils will be able to do that is at the heart of the debate about the value of objectives in curriculum planning, a debate that has continued in the United States for more than a generation. Thus when you use the term 'objective' you will do well to reserve it for statements about what pupils will be able to do. This will distinguish objectives from statements solely concerned with teachers' intentions or with information to be remembered or concepts to be understood, like many of the 'aims' in Task 1.1.3.

There is, however, a practical problem in carrying out Tyler's recommendation. One of a teacher's purposes might be to encourage pupils to look critically at what they write. Does this mean that, according to Tyler, this purpose would need to be represented by a separate objective (somewhere in the teacher's lesson notes perhaps) every time any child was expected to write? This would be absurd. In this case it seems more appropriate to write an objective that concentrates on *process* and omits *content*: 'Pupils will habitually re-read what they have written in order to check that they have expressed their intentions fully and in a manner appropriate to the audience they envisage.' Such an objective would apply to all pieces of writing, and avoid the absurdity of repetition for each different item of content. It is interesting to note that the Science 5-13 Project chose to use objectives that similarly expressed processes in science, which could thus be applied to any content. (See examples in Appendix B.)

It is probably clear, however, from the previous section, that there are areas of the curriculum in which it does not make sense to talk about 'both content and process'. In some approaches to mathematics or physical education, in the early stages of reading and in some aspects of craft work, the purpose of teaching is predominantly the learning of skills. Thus if we see skills as 'process' goals, it would not be untrue to say that in these areas the content is composed of processes. In any case to attempt to separate the two is not helpful. This is likely to be true in any curriculum-area whenever it is skills that matter irrespective of what subject-matter they are applied to. A teacher of mathematics may have in mind a general concept such as 'equivalence' when he starts planning a unit, but when he decides upon the details of what will go on in lessons it will be in terms of particular processes such as learning to plot pairs of numbers on a graph. A teacher of physical education, too, may find it useful to specify in detail what skills the children are to learn, and plan a course-unit so that each of the skills is practised regularly.

The next set of tasks is concerned with using objectives for skills-based planning, in the sense that this phrase was used in the previous section.

Task 1.7 Writing objectives in skills-based planning

1.7.1 Take any of the tasks in 1.4 and specify as a set of objectives the skills to be mastered, that is, in terms of what the pupils will be able to *do* by the end of the unit.

1.7.2 A group of young children has reached the stage in their reading when you consider it appropriate to do some systematic teaching of phonics. Write out as a list of objectives what the children should be able to do at the end of the unit. (You will need to use verbs such as 'recognise', 'discriminate', 'imitate', 'combine' in specifying what they will be able to do.)

1.7.3 You are to teach physical education lessons to a new class who have little or no previous experience of work in a gymnasium. Make the first step towards planning their first term's course by listing in the form of objectives the skills that you wish them to have mastered by the end of term.

1.7.4 Take an area of mathematical knowledge (such as 'commutativity', 'equivalence' . . .) and list in the form of objectives a range of processes which would contribute to your pupils' understanding of that area of knowledge.

1.7.5 As part of a craft and design circuit you will be receiving a group of 11-year-old boys and girls for a six-week 'taster' course in metalwork. In order to choose a programme of activities for them you need first to decide what skills they will be able to experience in so short a course. For this purpose make a list of these skills in the form of objectives. ('At the end of the course the children will be able to . . .')

1.7.6 In some secondary schools and colleges of further education there is concern that older pupils should have adequate language skills to carry out the demands of other subjects being

1.7.6 studied. Interview a number of teachers of different subjects
contd about the language abilities they require of older pupils (15 or
16-year-olds perhaps) and analyse their replies. Omit any
requirements that are too vague to be acted upon, or which
really depend on the students' understanding of the specialist
subject-matter. Express those requirements that remain in the
form of objectives. (This task could be carried out as a group
exercise by college of education students.)

All of the above tasks imply skills-based planning. We now turn to
concept-based tasks in which it will be necessary to observe Tyler's
injunction for writers of objectives to specify both content and process.
Tyler (1949) suggests that in doing this one should use a matrix which
allows one easily to relate processes to content; it should be emphasised,
however, that this is unlikely to be useful in skills-based planning. Tyler's
proposal amounts to using the following sequence in writing objectives.

(i) Analyse your content into subheadings (topics), and list these on
the left-hand side of a sheet of paper. (See Figure 1.2 for an
example of this.)

(ii) Categorise the processes and skills that you wish your pupils to
practise. Your list may be made up of several different kinds of
categories. Items in the list may be (*a*) specific skills, such as
measuring, or using a microscope; (*b*) cognitive processes, such
as explaining, hypothesising, planning; (*c*) communication activities such as discussing, writing a report, presenting a case, or
taking notes; (*d*) general skills, such as reading a map or interpreting documents. Which of these you choose to emphasise in
your planning will vary from subject to subject and be part of
your responsibility as a teacher.

(iii) Divide the sheet of paper into a suitable number of vertical
columns, and write at the head of each of the columns the
name of a category from your list.

(iv) You are now in a position to decide which skills and processes
your pupils can usefully practice when dealing with each topic.
Write any objectives that specify both the topic and the process,
or perhaps more than one process. You will find it useful to
number each of the objectives so that each objective can be
recorded on the matrix by entering the appropriate number
in the cell(s) to which the objective applies.

(v)   When you have written a number of objectives and recorded them
on the matrix, you will be able to see at a glance which topics
you are emphasising, and which skills are receiving most practice.
(A similar matrix can also be used to analyse the emphases in an
ongoing course, either planned by you or by someone else.)

An example may make this sequence clearer. (i) Let us imagine that
you are teaching environmental studies to an older middle-school class,
and that you have decided to focus a term's work upon the study of a
village that is easily accessible. First, you analyse the content into
topics, such as: buildings; farming: other occupations; transport;
administration. (ii) You now consider what kinds of activities would
be suitable for your pupils, at this stage not choosing particular activities but general categories. Your list might include: making maps and
sketches; representing numerical information in graphical form; writing
reports; collecting information by observation and inquiry; collecting
information from a library; collaborating in group discussion. (iii)
Your matrix will look like Figure 1.2.

(iv) You can now decide which of these processes you wish your
pupils to engage in while working on the first topic, 'buildings'. One
of your objectives might run like this: 'Objective no. 4: The pupils
will be able to gather information about housing in the village and
represent it through maps, sketches of houses, and block graphs.'
You can then indicate the coverage of this objective by entering the
number four (as I have done in Figure 1.2) in the three cells of the
matrix to which it applies.

(v) You will probably write other objectives related to buildings,
and enter their numbers also on the matrix. Some of them may fall
into the same cells as no. 4 appears in. Then you would go on and
write similar objectives for the other four topics, the advantage of
using the matrix being that it simplifies the process of keeping check
on your planning to see that you are not omitting or overemphasising
any content or any processes. When the writing of objectives is completed the planning of activities for the unit is straightforward, since
they are already implied by the objectives. (It will be noted that this is
essentially an alternative method of content-based planning to that
outlined on p. 8.)

The tasks that follow involve drafting objectives that could be used
in content-based planning. Tyler's matrix is likely to be useful only in
Task 1.8.2.

Content	1 Collecting information by observation and inquiry	2 Collecting information from a library	3 Making maps and sketches	4 Collaborating in group discussion	5 Representing numerical information in graphical form	6 Writing reports
					Processes	
A Buildings	4		4		4	
B Farming						
C Other occupations						
D Transport						
E Administration						

Figure 1.2 *Tyler's matrix*

Task 1.8 Writing objectives in content-based planning

1.8.1 It is assumed that you will have completed one or more parts of Tasks 1.2 and 1.3. Look again at the planning that you carried out in response to one of these tasks, and attempt to rephrase in the form of objectives your decisions about content and process.

1.8.2 Choose a body of knowledge that you are likely to teach (for example, on school practice, if you are a student in training). Analyse the content to be studied and the skills to be practised, as has been suggested above. Construct Tyler's matrix, using your own headings. Write a set of objectives for the course-unit, and enter each objective upon the matrix. Calculate the relative emphasis you have placed on each topic and on each process by summing across the rows and down the columns.

1.8.3 The Schools Council's project 'Geography for the Young School Leaver' (1974) gave this list as the 'objectives' for one of its course-units.

>**Objectives**
>*Ideas*
>There are usually marked differences between residential areas within a city. These may be seen as:
>   (i) differences in age, design, density, quality, cost and tenure of housing;
>   (ii) differences in quality of environment;
>   (iii) differences in provision of amenities;
>   (iv) differences in socio-economic characteristics.
>The residential needs in an area vary from one individual to another. There may be similarities according to age, sex, family status, etc.
>Many residential areas provide environments inadequate for present-day needs.
>It is important that in planning residential areas due thought be given to the environmental needs of all members of the community.
>
>*Skills*
>Analysis of oblique air photographs.
>Reading and analysis of Ordnance Survey maps.
>Analysis of statistical data and diagrams.

1.8.3
contd

Discussion, encouraged by the use of photo-sheets and the interpretation of extracts and statistical data.
Creative writing.

Values and attitudes
A concern with the quality of the environment of residential areas.
An appreciation of the problems which individuals face in inadequate residential areas.
A consideration of some of the dilemmas which face the planners of residential areas.

Rewrite these as objectives in the sense we are using here. If there are any aspects which cannot be shown in the form of objectives, it will be useful for you to consider why it is so. You may also find that in writing the objectives you have to make decisions that are left open in the project's version: why is this so?

For some years there has been a dispute about how specific objectives need to be. Let us take as an example some objectives of an elementary course in reading. Two of these might be: 'The pupils will be able to recognise and say aloud the words in Book Two of the reading scheme used', and 'The pupils will be able to read aloud the sentences in Book Two with sufficient fluency to show that they are understanding them as sentences and not just as separate words.' Two more objectives of the same imaginary course might be: 'The pupils will be able to listen with enjoyment to a variety of suitable stories read aloud to them', and 'The pupils will be able to show insight into the stories by making drawings or by continuing the narrative orally.'

Although these objectives make explicit some of the overall goals of the course, and indicate clearly what strategies are to be used, they do not break down into highly specific details either the complex skills of deciphering print, or the still more complex abilities of understanding and responding to a story. Yet for many teachers these objectives, along with others, would prove explicit enough for practical purposes. With children who are having difficulty in learning to read — perhaps in a special school or a remedial unit — it may prove necessary to break down into details the subskills involved, so that the teacher can plan to re-enforce them by systematic practice. Thus it might be necessary to specify for a particular backward reader that the next stage of his work should be aimed at objectives such as: 'To discriminate "d" from "b", and "q" from "p" '; 'To recognise the consonant digraphs', since these very explicit objectives would help the teachers involved to plan a suitable series of learning activities for him. It must be emphasised that such detailed objectives, useful in his case, would often be quite unnecessary.

It is Robert Mager (1962) who has probably taken the most extreme position in advocating the writing of highly specific objectives. In his view, an objective must, in order to be satisfactory, meet three criteria.

To describe terminal behaviour (what the learner will be DOING):
(a) Identify and name the overall behaviour act
(b) Define the important conditions under which the behaviour is to occur
(c) Define the criteria of acceptable performance.

An example that meets Mager's criteria would be: (*a*) to name the working parts of a diesel engine (*b*) when given a conventional diagram with these parts indicated (*c*) with 95 per cent accuracy. Mager's overall intention is to minimise ambiguity in the framing of objectives. For this reason he lists words that are unacceptable because they are open to a wide range of interpretations, and those which are preferable because they refer to identifiable external actions rather than to states of mind.

Words open to many interpretations	Words open to fewer interpretations
to know	to write
to understand	to recite
to *really* understand	to identify
to appreciate	to differentiate
to *fully* appreciate	to solve
to grasp the significance of	to construct
to enjoy	to list
to believe	to compare
to have faith in	to contrast

Another American writer, N.E. Gronlund (1978), has put forward a persuasive argument for explicit objectives. He points out that, although 'learn symbols on a weather map' indicates what is to be learnt, it does not make clear the outcomes of that learning in terms of what students will be able to do. Possible outcomes would include:

recalls the symbols used on a weather map;
identifies the symbols on a weather map;
interprets a weather map (using the symbols);
constructs a weather map (using the symbols);
predicts weather from a weather map (using the symbols).

The last three of these, which require the student to use the symbols, imply much more complex (and perhaps more valuable) learning than merely recalling the symbols. Thus the teacher's effort to make objectives more specific may amount to asking himself to be clearer about what his goals exactly are.

Mager's position (1962) is undoubtedly open to criticism: actions such as listing or construction are *not* the same as knowing and understanding. Many of the goals pursued by teachers cannot be broken down into a list of visible and unambiguous behaviours. Moreover, there is all the difference in the world between carrying out tasks in the classroom and grasping the principle underlying those tasks sufficiently to use them in daily life. Objectives that propose learning outcomes in terms of specific visible behaviours have traditionally been called 'behavioural objectives'. For some purposes they are useful; for others they may specify component skills yet miss the essence of the intended learning.

Task 1.9 Analysing objectives according to Mager's criteria

1.9.1   Attempt to write two objectives which *do* fulfil Mager's requirements.

(*a*) One objective should be suited to skills-based planning, perhaps a skill in craft, physical education, or the teaching of reading.

(*b*) The second objective should be suited to a course in literature, the appreciation of art or music, moral education or social studies.

When you have done this, I suggest that you consider the following issues:

(i) Was it easier to fulfil Mager's criteria in writing one

1.9.1   objective than in writing the other? If so, why was it?
contd (ii) What problems would you have faced if the task had
         required you to write behavioural objectives in the course
         of interest-based planning?
     (iii) Under what circumstances are highly specific behavioural
         objectives likely to be useful in planning? When would
         they be least helpful? (You may find that there is more
         than one consideration relevant to this.)
1.9.2 The purpose of this task is to help you to analyse and reflect
     upon objectives that you yourself have written. Take a set of
     your own objectives, perhaps written in response to Task
     1.8.2, and test each of them against the following criteria.
     (a) Is the objective framed as a statement of what pupils will
         be able to do at the end of the course?
     (b) In describing pupils' intended behaviour, have you used a
         verb that is specific enough to merit a place in Mager's
         list of 'Words open to fewer interpretations' (see p. 34)?
     (c) Have you specified both content and process? (In some
         cases this will not be an appropriate question.)
     (d) Have you indicated the conditions under which the be-
         haviour is to take place? (Mager's criterion (b), see the list
         on p. 34.)
     (e) Have you laid down what level of performance is required?
     (f) Many of your objectives will probably fail to meet some or
         all of these criteria. Consider in each case whether you can
         justify this.
     (g) Choose some of your objectives to which Mager's criteria
         would be appropriate, and rewrite them in a form which he
         would find acceptable.

Not everyone working in the field of curriculum development accepts
Mager's views; indeed, in the United Kingdom the main stream of
thought and practice runs against behavioural objectives. Nor do those
who favour the use of objectives necessarily advocate such highly
specific ones; an interesting example of this is the approach adopted by
the Schools Council Science 5-13 Project (Ennever and Harlen, 1972).
They made it a matter of project policy not to produce highly prepared materials, but to put the onus of planning upon the teachers
who used their booklets. They suggest topics, and a wide range of
activities, and provide a method by which teachers can plan their

courses using these. (The sequence is not unlike the method suggested above for content-based planning.)

They take the view that in choosing objectives for their science teaching, teachers in primary and middle schools should use two main criteria: (i) the developmental level reached by their pupils; and (ii) the cognitive abilities, skills and attitudes which they are to learn. For the first, the project uses a Piagetian approach, and adopts three stages, of which the first is subdivided.

Project stage	*Piaget's developmental level*
Stage 1(*a*)	Transition from intuition to concrete operations
Stage 1(*b*)	Concrete operations: early stage
Stage 2	Concrete operations: later stage
Stage 3	Transition to stage of abstract thinking

Teachers using this approach are to recognise the developmental level of their pupils and adopt objectives so that the learning experiences offered to them matches their stage of development. You will see from this that it is an unusual and ambitious approach.

Just as we did in discussing Tyler's matrix, the project authors next considered what kinds of learning teachers might wish to encourage, and came up with the following very inclusive list, not of objectives but of categories into which objectives in science might fall. Implicitly the project was saying to teachers: 'If you do not have objectives in all of these areas then you should consider whether you can justify this omission to yourself.' These are the categories:

0/1 attitudes, interests and aesthetic awareness;
2 observing, exploring and ordering observations;
3 developing basic concepts and logical thinking;
4 posing questions and devising experiments or investigations to answer them;
5/6 acquiring knowledge and learning skills;
7 communicating;
8 appreciating patterns and relationships;
9 interpreting findings critically.

Within each of the categories the project suggests a set of objectives suited to each developmental stage. For example, at stage 1(*b*) the following objectives are suggested within category 3, 'developing basic concepts and logical thinking':

> Ability to predict the effect of certain changes through observation of similar changes.
> Formation of the notions of the horizontal and the vertical.
> Development of concepts of conservation of length and substance.
> Awareness of the meaning of speed and of its relation to distance covered.

Within this same category children at other developmental stages have other objectives: for example, one of the objectives for stage 3 in this category is: 'Ability to extend reasoning beyond the actual to the possible.' Similarly, for pupils at stage 1(*b*) objectives are suggested for each of the other categories. For example, under category 7 'communicating' one finds:

> Ability to tabulate information and use tables.
> Familiarity with names of living things and non-living materials.

And so on, until for almost every category and every stage of development there is a set of objectives.

Task 1.10 Using objectives from the Schools Council Science 5-13 Project

1.10.1   You will find the whole of the Schools Council Science 5-13 Project system of objectives reprinted here as Appendix B. Take a group of pupils whom you have taught, choose a developmental stage likely to be appropriate for most of them and select from *all the categories* a set of objectives that would be appropriate to a course in science for this group.

1.10.2   Consider how the 'Science 5-13' objectives match with some of the criteria we have discussed. Do they all answer to Tyler's criterion that an objective should specify content as well as process? Are they as specific as Mager and others would require? Which of them use verbs that Mager would not approve of? Why do you think their authors have chosen to do so?

1.10.3   Use the 'Science 5-13' objectives to plan a course-unit in science. You will be able to follow the planning model (on

1.10.3   p.29) for concept-based planning, but you will need to add
contd   at an early stage the need to estimate your pupils' developmental levels. ('Levels' in the plural because they may *not* all
be at the same stage.) Then, the process of analysing first
concepts and then skills will be much simpler, since all you
will need to do will be to select appropriate objectives from
all of the categories. Nevertheless, you will still have the
task of deciding what activities are likely to help your pupils
to achieve the objectives, and those activities will naturally
also depend on the subject-matter you have chosen.

It will have been noticed that the 'Science 5-13' objectives differ from
strictly behavioural objectives in being considerably less specific. Even
in category 3, 'developing basic concepts and logical thinking', an
objective such as 'awareness of the meaning of speed and of its relation
to distance covered' leaves much undecided. In teaching for such an
objective, the teacher will have to decide such matters as (*a*) whether
to have the children carry out practical experiments in the classroom,
and if so (*b*) what apparatus will be appropriate, (*c*) how far calculation is a necessary part of understanding speed at that developmental
stage, and so on. Such objectives fall far short of Mager's criteria
(1962). Many do not meet even Tyler's requirements (1949). Cognitive objectives, such as 'ability to extend reasoning beyond the actual
to the possible', specify only the process and not the content. However, it should be remembered that the purpose of objectives is to aid
planning and teaching, so that the final criterion is usefulness. The
'Science 5-13' objectives are intended as a checklist to help teachers
keep their basic aims in mind: it is for the teacher to choose content
and methods within that framework.

Explicit planning, including the writing of objectives, is likely to be
useful when you need to communicate with other people, such as
colleagues with whom you are collaborating closely. It is particularly
effective for communications between teachers and examiners; an
examiner who has one of Mager's objectives in front of him has little
problem in devising a test that fits it. Indeed this seems to have been
one origin of the campaign for behavioural objectives that occurred in
the United States in the 1950s and 1960s. On the other hand, writing
objectives is very time-consuming, and for many teaching purposes
it would be uneconomical of time and effort to plan in such detail.
Nevertheless, part of teachers' professional responsibility is to reflect

upon their own teaching and improve it, and it is a good deal more possible to carry out such reflection if one has written plans and records to look back upon and reconsider. At what level of specificity can this realistically be done? Elliott Eisner (1969), a thoughtful critic of behavioural objectives, once calculated that a four-year primary-school course would require approximately 25,000 objectives. Such detail would be neither useful nor possible, yet some planning — and later evaluation — is essential. You will have discovered in doing the 1.9 tasks that specific behavioural objectives are a bad fit whenever the pupils' contribution to learning is of primary importance. They are more applicable when one can lay down exactly a visible and simple skill to be mastered, such as jumping over a bar. Nevertheless, we need to plan even lessons in dramatic improvisation, or in painting, or in writing an imaginative response to historical information, as in the example drawn from Elizabethan history. How can such courses best be planned? Is it better to use the informal methods based on content, concepts, problems and interests which were presented in the previous section, or to use more specific objectives, as has been illustrated in this section. It is for you to decide both the method you will use and the level of specificity that is necessary: only experience of planning will tell.

Task 1.11 Critical analysis of objectives

1.11 The following objectives come from different sources, and are constructed in different ways. Consider each of them in turn from the point of view of their likely usefulness to teachers and others. (Take into consideration the fact that some may be intended for subject-areas or age-groups of pupils whom you do not expect to teach and also that some may be intended for whole courses, whereas others are only for planning a lesson.) The following questions are intended to suggest issues that might be relevant, though you may be able to think of others.

(a) How specific is the objective? Is it too general to be helpful? Is it in some way too specific?

(b) Is the objective framed in such a way that it would help a teacher to choose classroom-learning activities?

(c) Is the objective framed in such a way that it would help

1.11
contd

an examiner to write a test item to find out whether the
objective has been achieved?

(d) Is the objective framed in such a way that it would
help teachers who are discussing the overall goals of a
course?

(e) Does the objective indicate an important goal or merely
one that can be easily observed?

(f) How might the objective be expressed in a more helpful
way?

Objectives

1.11.1   Given an aerial photograph of a terrain including a city, the
student classifies the city as a population and transport centre
by describing and referring to appropriate features on the
photograph.

1.11.2   To study the fundamental geographical features of countries
of the world, and to indicate the influence of these features
on development of industry and occupations of the inhabi-
tants.

1.11.3   The child should know how to think and solve problems
mathematically using the appropriate basic concepts of, for
example, the number system and place value, shape, spatial
relationships, sets, symmetry, and the appropriate language.

1.11.4   Awareness of the impact of man's activities on other living
things.

1.11.5   The ability to evaluate popular health beliefs critically.

1.11.6   Following his learning experiences the student shows he *likes*
literature because he (a) voluntarily secures books to read;
(b) discusses with others what he has read; (c) suggests that
others read books he has enjoyed; (d) voluntarily spends free
time reading.

1.11.7   To develop the ability to organise ideas in reading.

1.11.8   Given an English sonnet, the student will be able to classify
it (as either Shakespearean, Miltonic or Petrarchan) correctly, within five minutes without the help of reference materials.

1.11.9   A student who is socially co-operative:

(a) treats other personalities as intrinsically valuable and
never merely as means to his own ends;

1.11.9   (*b*) works to make himself useful in a social group;
contd   (*c*) contributes constructively in group discussions, projects, etc.;
          (*d*) is intelligent rather than blind in his loyalties;
          (*e*) is tolerant of other groups, other races, etc.;
          (*f*) reveals 'good sportsmanship' by his actions;
          (*g*) does not allow prejudice to control his attitudes in considering problems of underdeveloped groups;
          (*h*) understands and practises the standard codes and mores of his group.

1.11.10 Ability to formulate hypotheses not dependent upon direct observation.

1.11.11 Given a detailed set of facts, the student states valid generalisations that he had not been given previously, and when asked provides the sources and limitations of the generalisations. An example of facts and an acceptable generalisation is: *facts given*: religious practices of Aztecs before and after the arrival of the Spaniards; *generalisation*: the Aztecs adapted many of the religious practices of the Spaniards, but kept many of their own.

1.11.12 Uses critical thinking skills in reading:

          (*a*) distinguishes between facts and opinions;
          (*b*) distinguishes between facts and inferences;
          (*c*) identifies cause-effect relations;
          (*d*) identifies errors in reasoning;
          (*e*) distinguishes between relevant and irrelevant arguments;
          (*f*) distinguishes between warranted and unwarranted generalisations;
          (*g*) formulates valid conclusions from written materials;
          (*h*) specifies assumptions needed to make conclusions true.

1.11.13 The following objective is taken at random from a set intended to guide teachers of blind pupils to help them to achieve the skills necessary for independent everyday life. For each objective the author suggests an appropriate teaching technique. (This example is particularly useful in attempting to answer the question: under what circumstances may extremely specific and detailed objectives be justifiable?)

1.11.13 **Title**
contd Demonstrating the seating of self at a table, desk, etc.

Objective
When presented with a chair which is drawn up to a table, desk, etc., the student will demonstrate the ability to pull out the chair, seat himself and bring himself and the chair towards the table, desk, etc. This will be done in accordance with the following criteria:
1 locating the back of the chair without disturbing surrounding items;
2 by bringing the chair out from under the table — no further than arm's length;
3 by seating himself without disturbing surrounding items;
4 without the student's body being in contact with the table, desk, etc., when seated.

Technique
The student will use one hand to locate the back of the chair. He will place the right side of the body to the left side of the chair and bring the left hand forward to locate the front edge of the table. With the right hand, the student will pull the chair out from under the table, until the left front leg of the chair is even with the right foot. He will remove the right hand from the chair and bring it alongside the left hand. Both hands should now be in contact with the front edge of the table.

The student will take one step forward toward the table and bring the body in contact with the front edge. He will move his right leg to the right, in front of the chair seat and bring the left leg over to meet the right. Making sure that the backs of both legs are touching the chair seat, he will lower his body down to the seat.

The student will place slightly cupped hands on either side of the hips and locate the under side of the seat. He will raise his body slightly from the chair, exercising pressure on the feet, and with cupped hands bring the chair forward until the body almost touches the table.

1.11.14 The objectives of this unit are that pupils should acquire:

1.11.14 contd
1 knowledge of the composition of the air and that air is a mixture;
2 knowledge that burning is the result of the reaction of substances with oxygen;
. . .
8 ability to apply the above knowledge to some problem situations;
9 awareness of the need for controls in assessing the results of many experiments;
10 awareness of the importance of the gases of the air in industry.

1.11.15 The student has the ability to solve problems in mathematics.

1 He identifies the question to be answered in the problem situation.
2 He selects relevant information needed to solve the problem.
3 He relates the problem to analogous situations which supply clues or solutions.
4 He draws a flow diagram of the relationships and processes involved.
. . .
7 He applies his knowledge of mathematical concepts and processes to everyday situations.
8 He uses ideas about measurement in a construction project such as building a model.
etc.

Some of the sharpest critics of behavioural objectives have argued that their use distorts the curriculum by directing teachers' attention towards goals that can be expressed in behavioural terms and away from those that cannot. For example, in history it is easy to write a highly specific behavioural objective about pupils' ability to write down the main terms of the Great Reform Bill of 1831, but this may be of considerably less importance than enabling older pupils to understand the various social pressures that combined to bring about parliamentary reform. There have been attempts to write objectives for history along the lines of 'Students will be able to write down the four main causes of the success of movements for parliamentary reform during the period 1831-84', yet this must be seen as a perversion of history. History, like other subjects, provides a field for alternative interpretations: to reduce historical discussion of the age of reforms to a list of unproblematic 'causes' is to misrepresent the nature of history. Even more difficult is to write behavioural objectives which are not concerned with the understanding of particular historical episodes but with general historical processes such as interpreting a range of source documents, relating them to one another, identifying contradictions and omissions, evaluating their authors' attitudes and reliability, and integrating all this into an account which includes qualifications and uncertainties. Goals like these can only be expressed as behavioural objectives by linking them to a particular set of documents and by predetermining how these documents should be interrelated and interpreted. The danger of such a process is of a kind of *reductio ad absurdum*: the teacher's attention may be directed away from the interrelated complex of historical skills towards getting children to come up with a 'right answer'. The proponents of behavioural objectives may well retort that it is better for a history teacher to teach some historical information successfully than to aim at ambitious but vaguely defined goals, and achieve nothing. It must be for the reader to decide in each piece of planning what level of specificity is appropriate. In the foregoing paragraphs the alternatives have been put in an extreme form with behavioural objectives in the Mager manner at one end, and general — and very ambitious — aims at the other; clearly these extremes do not exhaust the possibilities.

The tasks that follow require you to consider the validity of various sets of objectives, keeping in mind what has been said in the previous paragraph.

Task 1.12 Considering the face validity of sets of objectives

1.12 Choose a set of behavioural objectives, perhaps those published by a project or prepared by teachers in a school, and consider whether they adequately represent the area of knowledge they are concerned with, or whether the objectives direct attention to less important aspects of the subject or even — as in the historical example discussed above — misrepresent the nature of the subject. (It is suggested that you

1.12	should find examples suited to your own teaching experience.
contd	Only a few examples can be included here, and they may not
	be closely relevant to your interests.)
1.12.1	The following is a set of objectives prepared by English teachers

1.12.1 The following is a set of objectives prepared by English teachers in an American high school for their 13-year-old pupils. It is concerned with reading only, other sets of objectives relate to writing, oral work, and language study. Discuss how well this set of objectives represents what you consider to be proper goals in reading for children of that age.

Reading

A   A student will demonstrate an active interest in reading by:
1   reading more books at the end of the year than at the beginning on a voluntary basis;
2   reaching out gradually for more sophisticated books;
3   reacting either in writing or discussion to what he is reading.

B   A student will decode a piece of writing successfully as evidenced by:
1   an accurate oral reading of it;
2   answering questions about the facts in it;
3   writing a brief summary of it.

C   Given the stimulus of a creative form (art, film, dance, poster, TV, collage, music, prose, poetry, drama, *et al.*), the student will in writing or discussion:
1   identify the setting;
2   demonstrate through oral reading his ability to distinguish between dialogue and stage directions in a play;
3   identify the protagonist and antagonist of a work;
4   identify the type of conflict present in the work;
5   explain why a character acts or talks as he does and provide details from the text or production to support his explanation;
6   generalize about a character and explain his understanding by referring to the actions, reactions, dialogue, descriptions, and inner thoughts which the author or actor has used in characterization;

1.12.1 C
contd

7 interpret the work (particularly character and conflict) by drawing parallels or finding similarities in
his own personal experience;

8 identify a stereotyped character;

9 locate an image and tell the sense to which it
appeals;

10 translate the situations and characters of fiction
into plausible and consistent dramatic presentation
(oral or written) by:
 (a) acting and speaking in ways appropriate to the
 character portrayed;
 (b) listening and responding to others in ways
 appropriate to the character portrayed (not
 applicable for writing);

11 translate a character into a new situation, keeping
his new words and actions consistent with his 'old'
character;

12 understand the universality of adolescent and adult
problems by recognizing and evaluating the
problems and problem solutions of characters in
literature;

13 suggest alternative solutions and evaluate the effects
these would have on the story or character;

14 identify theme by choosing the most accurate statement of theme from several provided by the
teacher.

D A student will display a tolerance for the values, appearance, language and life styles of people in literature and
life different from himself by:

1 refraining from stereotyping about the life styles of
others;

2 refraining from derogatory remarks.

1.12.2 The Scottish Integrated Science course puts forward its goals
at four levels (Scottish Central Council on Science, 1977):
 (a) aims;
 (b) course objectives (for the whole two-year course);
 (c) section objectives;
 (d) lesson objectives (linked with worksheets).
A distinction is made between objectives for less able pupils

1.12.2
contd

and those for average and more able pupils.

For this task you are asked to consider the aims, the course objectives, the section objectives for one of the fifteen sections, and finally the lesson objectives for one part of that section. The materials are intended to be used during the first two years of secondary education.

Aims

The purpose of science teaching in the first two years of the secondary school (S1 and S2) is to assist pupils towards:

(*a*) a better understanding of themselves and the empirical world around them;

(*b*) an improvement in their communicating skills;

(*c*) an ability to solve problem situations and think scientifically;

(*d*) the development of some attitudes which are required for good personal and social relationships;

(*e*) an awareness of the culture which is science.

Course objectives

For less able pupils

Band I

A1 interest and enjoyment in science;

A2 awareness of the contribution of science to everyday life.

Band II

A3 an objective attitude towards experimental evidence;

A4 an ability to seek information effectively;

A5 an ability to assess observations and draw conclusions;

A6 an ability to describe information, observations and conclusions in their own words;

A7 an ability to think and act creatively to a limited extent;

A8 an acceptance of the value of co-operating with others in scientific investigation.

Band III

A9 knowledge of some facts and concepts concerning themselves and their environment;

1.12.2
contd

A10 knowledge of the use of appropriate instruments in scientific experiments;

A11 a scientific vocabulary for normal communication needs;

A12 comprehension of some basic concepts in science so that they can be used in familiar situations;

A13 some simple science-based practical skills.

For average and most able pupils

Band I

B1 interest and enjoyment in science;

B2 awareness of the contribution of science to the economic and social life of the community;

B3 awareness of the relationship of science to other aspects of the curriculum;

B4 an acceptance of the value of co-operating with others in scientific investigation;

B5 an objective attitude towards experimental evidence.

Band II

B6 knowledge of some facts and concepts concerning themselves and their environment;

B7 knowledge of the use of appropriate instruments in scientific experiments;

B8 an adequate scientific vocabulary;

B9 an ability to communicate using this vocabulary;

B10 an ability to seek information effectively;

B11 comprehension of some basic concepts in science so that they can be used in familiar situations;

B12 ability to select relevant knowledge and apply it in new situations;

B13 ability to analyse data and draw conclusions;

B14 ability to think and act creatively in science.

Band III

B15 some simple science-based practical skills;

B16 some experimental techniques involving several skills.

1.12.2
contd

Section objectives (Section 4: A model of matter)

The less able pupils should acquire:

1 knowledge that there are three states of matter — solid, liquid and gas;

2 knowledge that matter is made up of tiny particles;

3 knowledge that the particles are moving;

4 knowledge that there are spaces between the particles;

5 some knowledge of the expansion of solids, liquids and gases;

6 some knowledge of gas pressure;

7 knowledge of the use of the words element, atom, compound, molecule;

8 some simple experimental techniques.

In addition the average and above average pupils should acquire:

9 knowledge of a model of the states of matter using kinetic theory;

10 information about some instruments;

11 some elementary information about the periodic table;

12 awareness of involvement of energy in making and breaking compounds;

In addition the most able pupils should acquire:

13 ability to predict behaviour of matter using a kinetic model and to test the predictions experimentally.

In addition to being given these objectives, teachers using the materials are told that the section is concerned with the following 'basic concepts': matter as particles, particle spacing, particle movement, gas pressure, expansion, element, compound, atom, molecule. They are also told that in the section these 'processes' are stressed: classifying, inferring (or deducing), predicting and hypothesis testing.

Lesson objectives (atoms, elements, compounds, molecules)

After the activities the less able pupils should be able to:

1 describe the reaction of iron and sulphur and the electrolysis of copper chloride;

2 state that elements can join together to form compounds;

1.12.2
contd

3 state that the properties of a compound are different from those of its constituent elements;
4 state that compounds can be broken down to give the constituent elements.

After the activities the average and above average pupils should be able to:

5 state that an atom is very small;
6 define a molecule as a group of atoms;
7 state that elements are made up of atoms (molecules);
8 state that, in a particular element, all the atoms (molecules) are identical, whereas the atoms (molecules) of different elements are not identical;
9 recognize the periodic table as a list of all known elements of which there are about 100;
10 state that certain elements combine to form compounds with properties altogether different from the constituent elements;
11 state that energy changes are involved in the making and breaking of compounds.

(It should be noted that less able pupils use different worksheets from those assigned to average and above average pupils.)

1.12.3 The Schools Council project on History, Geography and Social Science for pupils of 8-13 years of age proposed the following set of objectives for that curriculum area as a whole. See Blyth *et al.* (1976) for a valuable discussion of the use and limitations of objectives.

Skills
Intellectual
1 The ability to find information from a variety of sources, in a variety of ways.
2 The ability to communicate findings through an appropriate medium.
3 The ability to interpret pictures, charts, graphs, maps, etc.
4 The ability to evaluate information.
5 The ability to organise information through concepts and generalisations.

| 1.12.3 contd | 6 | The ability to formulate and test hypotheses and generalisations. |

Social
1 The ability to participate within small groups.
2 An awareness of significant groups within the community and the wider society.
3 A developing understanding of how individuals relate to such groups.
4 A willingness to consider participating constructively in the activities associated with these groups.
5 The ability to exercise empathy (i.e. the capacity to imagine accurately what it might be like to be someone else).

Physical
1 The ability to manipulate equipment.
2 The ability to manipulate equipment to find and communicate information.
3 The ability to explore the expressive powers of the human body to communicate ideas and feelings.
4 The ability to plan and execute expressive activities to communicate ideas and feelings.

Personal qualities
Interests, attitudes, values
1 The fostering of curiosity through the encouragement of questions.
2 The fostering of a wariness of overcommitment to one framework of explanation and the possible distortion of facts and the omission of evidence.
3 The fostering of a willingness to explore personal attitudes and values to relate these to other people's.
4 The encouraging of an openness to the possibility of change in attitudes and values.
5 The encouragement of worthwhile and developing interests in human affairs.

The project also proposes the following 'key concepts' for courses in this area: communication, power, values and beliefs,

1.12.3 conflict/consensus, similarity/difference, continuity/change,
contd causality.

1.12.4 The next set of objectives was prepared for a course in communication studies in a college of further education (Dewsbury and Batley Technical and Art College, undated). The
students for whom the course is intended would recently have
left secondary school with only moderate qualifications in
CSE and GCE and would have embarked on a technical
apprenticeship in a factory or workshop. The communication studies course is intended to equip them for communication
in their work, in technical courses in the college, and in their
daily lives.

1 Receives and interprets oral messages

1.1 Follows oral instruction and/or directions accurately.

1.2 Participates effectively in group discussions.

1.3 Extracts information from an oral situation:
(*a*) a face-to-face situation;
(*b*) a non-face-to-face situation.

1.4 Interprets and abstracts ideas in an oral situation:
(*a*) a face-to-face situation;
(*b*) a non-face-to-face situation.

1.5 Appraises student performance in discussion:
(*a*) recognises 'blocking' tactics in small group
discussion;
(*b*) recognises departure from point under discussion.

2 Expresses himself orally in a range of situations

2.1 Relates a short story or personal opinion.

2.2 Contributes to discussion/debate in group situations.

2.3 Explains the setting up/workings of simple apparatus.

2.4 Gives explicit instructions in:
(*a*) face-to-face situations;
(*b*) non-face-to-face situations.

2.5 Responds appropriately in situations requiring prescribed roles.

2.6 Discusses leisure-time reading with other students and
with the teacher.

1.12.4
contd

3 Extracts information from written communication in both verbal and non-verbal forms

3.1 Summarises a given text.

3.2 Summarises the main arguments of a given text.

3.3 Carries out written instructions.

3.4 Finds specific information by reference to books and periodicals.

3.5 Establishes a set of priorities when researching materials.

3.6 Carries out a survey.

3.7 Interprets the results of a survey.

3.8 Explains the advantages of using such alternative modes of communication as maps, statistics, photographs.

3.9 Uses such forms of communication in appropriate situation.

3.10 Converts information from one form of presentation to another.

4 Expresses himself in writing with and without diagrams both explicitly and accurately

4.1 Practises relevant basic technical skills.

  4.1.1 Punctuates acceptably when writing prose, using commas, full stops, capital letters and inverted commas.

  4.1.2 Uses paragraphs where appropriate.

  4.1.3 Joins simple sentences into more fluent and complex sentence structures.

  4.1.4 Breaks excessively long or complex sentences into simpler more manageable sentences.

  4.1.5 Writes legibly.

  4.1.6 Uses acceptable spelling.

4.2 Organises thoughts in patterns which make them readily accessible to the reader.

  4.2.1 Identifies sources of ambiguity or confusion in written English.

  4.2.2 Identifies repetitious language in selected contexts.

  4.2.3 Relates 4.2.1 and 4.2.2 to his own written work.

1.12.4 contd

4.2.4 Identifies jargon in selected contexts, and substitutes clearer, simpler language.

4.3 Communicates effectively in prescribed contexts relevant to everyday and work needs.

4.3.1 Completes forms, questionnaires and work-sheets in a manner appropriate to the context.

4.3.2 Writes clear instructions.

4.3.3 Applies conventions to letter writing.

4.3.4 Records first hand observations.

4.3.5 Expresses quantifiable information in appropriate table, chart or graph form.

4.3.6 Converts quantified information into clear prose.

4.3.7 Preserves information in graphic form using diagrams, drawings.

4.3.8 Completes research assignments on topics of interest.

4.3.9 Presents research findings in report format (see 4.3.8).

4.4 Writes expressively about personal interests.

4.4.1 Expresses subjectively-held opinions in clear, reasoned prose.

4.4.2 Explores aspects of personal experience by writing about them.

4.4.3 Uses language emotively in imaginative writing.

4.5 Evaluates written expression according to variety of criteria e.g. grammatical, aesthetic, psychological — recognising the importance of each.

4.5.1 Practises checking of own written work when completed to eliminate or correct all avoidable errors.

4.5.2 Recognises the importance of extensive reading as an aid to effective written expression.

4.5.3 Recognises emotive language and the uses to which it is put (e.g. in the mass media).

5 Acquires the understanding and skill necessary to apply thinking techniques in a variety of situations

5.1 Names various thinking techniques.

5.2 Identifies which technique might be used in a

55

1.12.4		particular situation.
contd	5.3	Explains the difference between various techniques.

5.4 Describes the limitations the techniques are designed to counteract.

5.5 Uses the techniques in relevant situations.

5.6 Combines different techniques where appropriate.

5.7 Devises problems for colleagues to solve using appropriate techniques.

5.8 Provides solutions to problems he devises.

5.9 Solves problems devised by classmates.

5.10 Identifies statements without evidence.

5.11 Identifies uses of emotive words and phrases in arguments.

5.12 Distinguishes between fact and opinion.

5.13 Distinguishes between inferences and assumptions.

5.14 Identifies cause-effect relationships.

5.15 Distinguishes between warranted and unwarranted generalisations.

5.16 Distinguishes between relevant and irrelevant arguments.

5.17 Specifies assumptions to make conclusions true.

5.18 Organises ideas about particular problems.

5.19 Plans an individual assignment.

5.20 Completes an individual assignment.

5.21 Evaluates different theories about specific problems.

5.22 Defends opinion in a rational way.

5.23 Uncovers logical inconsistencies.

6 Acquires a range of study skills

6.1 Acquires note making techniques.

    6.1.1 Knows procedure for making notes from oral or written sources.

    6.1.2 Understands and applies note making techniques.

        (*a*) Recognises situations where note making techniques are applicable.

        (*b*) Practises techniques.

        (*c*) Discriminates between various note making techniques.

        (*d*) Demonstrates correct usage of techniques

1.12.4		in a variety of situations.
contd	6.2	Demonstrates effective use of dictionary/index.

      6.2.1 Locates given words in a dictionary or index.

      6.2.2 Locates appropriate reference from index.

      6.2.3 Selects correct definition from dictionary display.

      6.2.4 Identifies correct pronunciation of a given entry.

      6.2.5 Identifies parts of speech when checking an entry.

      6.2.6 Names appendices in dictionary.

      6.2.7 Uses appendices to find specific information.

    6.3 Demonstrates effective use of library.

      6.3.1 Describes Dewey decimal classification system.

      6.3.2 States purpose of classification system.

      6.3.3 Names different parts of the catalogue.

      6.3.4 States purpose of library catalogue.

      6.3.5 Names different sections of library stock.

      6.3.6 Names different types of reference book.

      6.3.7 Differentiates between different parts of the library catalogue.

      6.3.8 Explains difference between reference stock and loan stock.

      6.3.9 Explains how to borrow a book.

      6.3.10 Explains how to locate a book in the library.

      6.3.11 Differentiates between the types of information contained in various kinds of reference book.

      6.3.12 Completes a teacher or student designed assignment requiring information from book stock.

      6.3.13 Designs a library assignment requiring information retrieval from book stock.

      6.3.14 Completes a teacher or student designed assignment on library organisation.

This is a suitable point, before moving on to the detailed planning of lessons, to summarise the disputed issues that have so far been mentioned. We first considered ways of planning that did not necessitate the use of objectives, in which content, skills, concepts, problems and interests were given more or less emphasis according to the nature of the subject-matter and the pedagogical style of the teacher. The advocates of objectives insist that planning should be in terms of what the pupils will be able to do. This seems to be of considerable value when knowledge or skills to be learnt can be predicted in advance, and the pupils' contribution is expected to be relatively small. The two approaches can thus be combined (for example) when planning is based on a body of skills. Another disputed issue is the level of specificity required, whether in objectives or other forms of planning. This seems to relate to whether it is necessary (or possible) to break down the learning into very small steps in order to help the learner. Advocates of objectives disagree amongst themselves over various aspects of specificity, including whether objectives should specify only processes and skills or make explicit the content also.

Critics of planning by objectives argue that there is some danger thereby of misrepresenting the nature of learning and of what is to be learnt. Certainly it is easier to express in the form of a behavioural objective a concern with recollecting information than with understanding it, and easier to express a simple skill than a more complex one that involves the pupil in making a judgment about priorities. Most of all, it is hard, if not impossible, to capture in the form of objectives the underlying values and principles that shape a teacher's methods of presentation and response to pupils' contributions to lessons. What is here in question is the way in which teachers can best take responsibility for their own actions, how they can best reflect upon the principles that underlie those actions and make them available to others. Is it best done through objectives − statements of what pupils will be able to do − or are there other ways of taking responsibility? Elliott Eisner − amongst others − has pointed out (1969) that in planning by objectives the teacher implicitly claims to predict what the student's 'response' will be to the 'stimulus' provided by a lesson. He argues that objectives are only appropriate to those aspects of learning where the learner's role is to be no more than reproduction of what is presented to him, and that something different is required whenever the learner is expected to make an active contribution. Creative work in art, or writing stories or autobiography cannot be judged solely in terms of predicted objectives; their value must be assessed retrospectively on the basis of principles appropriate to what the learner has attempted to do. How far pupils' contributions to other areas such as physical education or science could properly be considered 'active' or 'creative' is a matter of dispute. Eisner proposes what he calls 'expressive objectives'. 'An expressive objective,' he writes, 'describes an educational encounter: it identifies a situation in which children are to work, a problem with which they are to cope, a task in which they are to engage; but it does not specify what from that encounter, situation, problem or task they are to learn.' He gives as examples:

1 To examine and appraise the significance of *The Old Man and the Sea*.
2 To develop a three-dimensional form through the use of wire and wood.
3 To visit the zoo and discuss what was of interest there.

It will be observed that expressive objectives are not objectives at all in the sense we have used the word. They specify the activity which the learners will engage in — and therefore the situation which the teacher must set up — rather than the new competence or knowledge that will be learnt. In this respect it is closer to teachers' traditional ways of planning. Most important of all, it recognises the learner's contribution to his own learning, and does not treat him as a passive receiver.

Lawrence Stenhouse's approach to curriculum planning (1975) is intended, like Eisner's, to offer an alternative to planning by objectives but focuses rather upon the modes of learning appropriate to different kinds of knowledge. His view is that the area of knowledge to be taught carries with it implicit principles of procedure which govern learning — and therefore teaching — in that subject. For example, if a science teacher sees science as essentially concerned with making predictions about the physical world and testing these experimentally, then this will furnish him with a set of procedural principles that can guide both his teaching programme and his evaluation of the success of that programme. Thus science would provide him with issues to be explored, methods for doing so, and ways of discussing results which included a conceptual framework. All these would seem to fall within the idea of 'procedural principles'. It should, however, be noted that not all science teachers will necessarily agree what principles are appropriate to science procedures. (See Task 1.13.2 on p. 62 for Stenhouse's own example of a set of procedural principles.)

Stenhouse's approach offers a method by which teachers can take deliberate responsibility for their work, which nevertheless does not involve behavioural objectives. It is not dissimilar to Eisner's approach, but (in my view) it is more theoretically satisfactory because it derives procedural principles from views about the nature of different kinds of subject-matter.

Curriculum theorists of the 1950s, such as Benjamin Bloom (1956), seem to have had ambitions to generate a neutral technique which might be applied to any curriculum-planning. It is now clear that these ambitions were misplaced. The methods we adopt for planning need to be matched to the kind of teaching we are doing: the same teacher in a primary school might use quite different methods to plan a lesson in which she wanted to teach a new procedure in arithmetic from another in which she wished her pupils to explore ways of expressing 'power' through clay modelling. In the first case she can specify in advance exactly what she wants the children to learn, and in the form of specific behavioural objectives if she so wishes. In the other she will equally wish to plan in advance the starting episode in which she presents the idea of 'power', but, thereafter, she will want her pupils to generate their own ideas, and to be free to capitalise on any of these in her teaching. The principles on which this second lesson are based may or may not be made explicit, but they will shape both the way she teaches and her judgment of her pupils' work. These are only two cases but they are intended to represent a much wider diversity of kinds of learning. The different approaches to planning so far suggested are intended to give you a range of methods to choose from so you can match your planning to the nature of what you are to teach.

Principles of procedure

This consideration leads us to an issue not so far mentioned. No curriculum-planning is neutral: every curriculum is imbued with values. These values embody a view of the kind of people we wish our pupils to become, and implicit in that is a view of the kind of society that such people could live in. As Eisner (1969) once wrote when dismissing the idea of neutral curriculum-planning, 'Under the rug of technique there lies an image of man.' Yet in none of our discussions so far have underlying values been mentioned, though it is true that general aims may at times embody them. Some of these values may apply to the whole curriculum of a school; a primary-school headteacher may see the communication of moral values to be a major purpose of his school; a secondary-school headteacher may claim that encouraging self-responsibility is an aim of the school. In Ashton *et al.* (1975a) 'acquire moral values' was ranked third in importance amongst a list of aims by a sample of primary-school teachers. Other values may not be expressed as aims but as general pedagogical principles; teachers of younger or less able children may act on the principle of presenting new concepts to their pupils in the form of practical activities before expecting them to discuss and understand the ideas. Particular subject-areas may have their own specific values: a teacher of initial reading skills may have views about when children are 'ready' for phonics; a secondary-school English teacher may believe that in helping pupils to respond to literature it is important to find ways of enabling them to relate what they read to analogous areas of their own experience. Values of this kind cannot be expressed as behavioural objectives, though they can be seen as principles of procedure. They are of considerable importance, since they play a major part at the point when teachers decide what they will actually do, and tell their pupils to do, during lessons. Our model of curriculum-planning, whether or not based upon objectives, needs to contain these stages:

(*a*) Formulation of principles of procedure:
  (i) those general to the whole curriculum for the pupils in question;
  (ii) those related to particular subject-matter.
(*b*) The utilisation of these principles in choosing activities, and in guiding the teacher's moment-by-moment participation in lessons.

The tasks at this point are not concerned with general school values, which are dealt with in the section 'The content of the curriculum' (especially pp. 104-9 and 157-75).

Task 1.13 Procedural principles

1.13.1 Write a list of principles that would inform your teaching of a particular group of pupils. You might choose, for example, a group of younger primary-school pupils operating mainly at Piaget's level of 'concrete operations' (that is at Stages 1(*b*) and 2 in the scheme set out on p. 37). Or you might write a list for teaching a particular subject to a remedial class in a

1.13.1
contd
secondary school and contrast this with another list for an examination group of older pupils. Students in initial training could be asked to interview teachers in their practice schools to elicit from them the (possibly implicit) principles on which their teaching of a particular class is based. In either case, lists can be compared, and the reasons for discrepancies in teachers' approaches to the same or similar groups can be discussed.

1.13.2   At the commencement of the Humanities Curriculum Project, Lawrence Stenhouse (1969) enunciated the following principles of procedure to be carried out in the teaching in secondary schools of social issues that are 'controversial', in that there is no consensus in our society about what is the proper view to take.

(a)   If the non-involved are to be involved, we must deal with things that interest them and which they choose.

(b)   If we reject directed curriculum we must also reject directed methods of teaching, i.e. we must become neutral chairman in a classroom.

(c)   Things which interest adolescents are likely to be politically and socially controversial, e.g. sex, family relations, law, race relations.

(d)   Such topics can only be handled educatively by being considered rationally, without bias.

(e)   Unbiased treatment requires a retiring, non-directive role for the teacher, linking with (b).

(f)   Non-directive teaching involves direct 'evidence' in the form of documentary materials rather than information fed in by the teacher.

It will have been observed that Stenhouse's argument proceeds from the characteristics of the subject-matter to the procedural principles, while taking the students into account. It is possible to move similarly from the nature of response to literature or the nature of historical investigation or the nature of science to appropriate sets of principles of procedure. These principles are likely to deal both with what children are to do in learning and what teachers need to do in order to encourage this to happen.

1.13.2   This task involves choosing an area of learning — a 'subject', or
contd   (as with the Humanities Curriculum Project) a more nebulous
         area — and setting out a list of procedural principles. It should
         be possible to show, as Stenhouse has done, how the principles
         derive from the nature of the area, from the knowledge and
         procedures which characterise the subject. (If a group is
         carrying out the task it will be useful to compare principles
         put forward both for the same subjects, and for different
         ones.) It will probably be necessary to take into consideration
         the age of the pupils for whom the course is intended.

Planning for diversity: branching schemes

Much published writing about curriculum-planning seems to assume
classes of children all working together on the same task prepared
previously by the teacher. This is not an assumption that I wish to
make, even though it may well be true that lessons in both primary
and secondary schools are still predominantly of this kind, in spite
of the many criticisms that have been levelled at this way of organising them. I have taken care to include in an earlier section some
work on interest-based planning which, in its nature, should lead to
a diversity of work within the same class. I have also included a brief
reference to group work, in which a small number of children control
the progress of their own work, even if it is only for a short period of
discussion before rejoining the whole group. In such cases as these it is
more difficult for the teacher to decide in advance what strategies to
use. Whatever ideas the children come up with are likely to determine
what suggestions the teacher needs to have at his or her fingertips,
and what resources need to be available. Not all teachers are happy
to cope with such an infinity of possible demands upon their knowledge and skill, and some may therefore wish to plan diverse activities
for pupils in advance. This diversity may represent no more than a
range of options to enable pupils to choose; or it may be a way of
sharing out the work so that when pupils 'report back' there will be a
wider range of topics and ideas for the class to consider; or it may be a
way of coping with a range of ability in the same group.

   This section is concerned with ways of planning for diversity. The
options may be offered to pupils for them to choose, or they may be
assigned by the teacher to particular individuals or groups, or they may

be part of a sequential scheme. Two problems in particular need to be dealt with: some children may work much faster than others, and may therefore be able to explore a topic in greater depth; other children may have more difficulty in coming to terms with new skills or new ways of thinking, and therefore need more practice in applying them, perhaps to a variety of situations. We can follow Lawton in referring to these concerns as 'depth' — often called 'enrichment' in the United States — and 'breadth', and ask the question: how can we plan a programme so that it provides either extra depth or extra breadth for those pupils who need it?

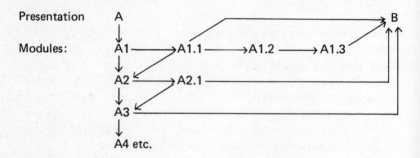

Figure 1.3 *A branching scheme of modules (adapted from Lawton)*

It is Denis Lawton (1975) who suggests a way of doing this by the use of a branching scheme. Let us suppose that in planning a term's work we have arrived at a list of topics appropriate for the class in question. For topic A we have put aside a sequence of lessons, and have a notion of the kinds of activity that would be appropriate. Our task is to plan for a mixed-ability class in such a way that all the pupils have an opportunity to get some insight into the topic and to exercise skills related to it, and also to provide greater depth of study for some of the more able students, and greater breadth of study for some others. Lawton suggests diagrammatically how this might be done; Figure 1.3 is in some respects different from his, however. (A1, A1.1, A2 and so on refer to separate learning tasks or 'modules' which various pupils are to undertake.) The diagram is intended to indicate that all pupils will share an initial presentation of the topic (A), and that all will carry out the core module (A1) which, in Lawton's words 'will include the content and ideas thought to be essential common learning for all pupils'. He adds that 'other pupils will be able to go to greater depth' (A2, A3, etc.) before proceeding to the next topic. Others may move from A1 to A1.1 and so on. 'An essential aspect of the common curriculum is that it must cater for a wide variety of interests and abilities.'

The whole class could then move on at the same time to topic B, and share the opening presentation. Topic B, too, could provide similar opportunities for greater depth and breadth by providing different routes through the tasks for different pupils. Lawton acknowledges that such diversity 'means an enormous amount of preparatory work for teachers', but maintains that this is essential if the curriculum is to offer access to a common culture to all pupils, whatever their academic abilities.

In practice this might result in a five-step pattern of work on a topic, which is here superimposed upon the three lesson stages proposed in the subsection on pp. 73-6, 'Structure of lessons'.

(*a*)	Opening stage	1	The starting-point, or initial presentation to the class.
(*b*)	Development stage	2	A core module, which all pupils would complete.
		3	Route-planning.
		4	Individual work on other modules, including feedback from teachers.
(*c*)	Synthesis stage	5	Sharing and rounding off the work.

Starting-point

The opening stage is often called the 'key lesson' in schools in England. It is likely to involve both presentation and elicitation, as explained on p. 74. Its function is to present the new topic to pupils, and to encourage them to retrieve from memory their existing understanding and knowledge of the topic – to start them thinking, in fact.

The core module

There will almost always be at least one task for all pupils to complete, as a way of developing the ideas presented to them and giving them common ground, whatever their abilities and interests. This I have given the inelegant but unambiguous name of 'core module': it is represented in the diagram as 'A1'. It is important that every pupil's work on this is quickly evaluated, since on this will depend the route he or she is to take through the range of tasks available.

Route-planning

The next step in the development stage consists in planning each pupil's route. There is much to be said to decisions about what should be done over and above the core module to arise from a combination of advice from the teacher and the pupil's preferences. The teacher must see to it that enough information is gained from the pupil's performance on the core module to determine whether what should follow is further practice, or tasks that are different in kind but no more demanding, or further work which will lead into more difficult aspects of the same topic. The pupil will have views about what will be of interest, and may have ideas about what he or she is capable of, though on some occasions the teacher may decide to overrule his judgment. It is likely that pupils will take different lengths of time to complete the core module, and this will allow the teacher to consult with each about the route he is to take through the other tasks, deciding in conjunction rather than imposing by fiat. It may even be possible with older pupils to discuss and agree upon a sequence of objectives to be attained as Gagné and Briggs (1979) suggest.

Individual work

As a result of this planning, each pupil will be able to work alone (or in some cases with one or two other pupils) at a sequence of tasks chosen with and for him. In the diagram these sequences are represented by:

(*a*) A1 → A2 → A3 → A4. This pupil works quickly and can cope with a range of different tasks each making a new demand. Such a sequence of modules can be said to provide 'enrichment' or 'depth'.

(*b*) A1 → A1.1 → A1.2 → A1.3. This pupil works quickly but proves to need a range of varied tasks that reinforce and extend the contents of module A1. This sequence can be said to offer breadth of study.

(c)   A1 → A1.1. This pupil works slowly and is able to complete only the core module and one other before the work comes to an end.

(d)   A1 → A2 → A2.1. This pupil has been able to move on to A2, but is carrying out a further module related in content to A2, either because of his own choice or because the teacher has advised him to do so. Further sequences can be invented if enough modules are available.

(e)   A1 → A1.1 → A2 → A2.2.

(f)   A1 → A2 → A4 → A2.2. Such combinations as this are possible so long as each module is independent of others, that is, does not depend upon knowledge or skills built up in previous modules.

There is much to be said for providing some form of feedback at the end of each module, both in order to inform and encourage the learner, and to enable the teacher to adjust the sequence of tasks should they prove too difficult or otherwise unsuitable. Such feedback may sometimes involve an informal test, but often will be no more than an opportunity for the teacher to look through the completed work and discuss it with the pupil.

Synthesis stage

Part of Lawton's purpose in proposing this kind of planning is to ensure that all pupils, however limited their academic ability, should have some access to the same range of topics and learning experiences. For this reason all pupils complete the core module. I would add to Lawton's prescription another device to ensure that all have the opportunity to gain insight into one another's work by arranging an occasion for the display, sharing and discussion of work done individually. This stage gives an incentive to careful written work by providing a wider audience than the teacher alone, encourages interest in other aspects of the work, and allows an opportunity for teacher and pupils to recapitulate more explicitly the principles underlying the work done, and to discuss its general applicability.

Most teachers will have come across so-called individualised instructions in the form of 'reading laboratories' or worksheet-based mathematics schemes, and these are indeed versions of what is being suggested here. Their fault is often that in order to provide 'self-evaluation' — which means that pupils can check for themselves whether they have the right answers — such schemes often unduly restrict the range of activities required, leaving only those which can be marked right or wrong. This can result in an inadequate version of reading comprehension, or a mathematics that puts emphasis on products rather than processes. For this reason I am not emphasising 'self-evaluation' in this sense of the word. In my view it is the teacher who can best provide feedback, by individual or group discussion of the work that has been done, by reading and commenting on written work as fully as time allows, and by arranging for occasions when a sample of work is considered by the whole class.

Preparing a set of units that can be used in this manner is too time-consuming to be attempted by one teacher working alone, so the task that follows is intended for groups, not individuals. It is probable that a group of teachers who plan a branching scheme for their pupils will not invent afresh all of the tasks. They are likely to have some ideas of their own that will lead to writing new modules, but they are also likely to search in textbooks, in workcards, in any available materials in school or library for activities which are appropriate in content and level, and so can be adapted to become part of the scheme.

Task 1.14 Planning for mixed ability

1.14 The task is to plan in conjunction with a group of colleagues a set of modules all related to one topic, arranged in such a way that all pupils will have access to a core of material and also will be able to carry out further work appropriate to their understanding and interests. The topic may be focused upon a specific issue — such as mathematical sets or a geographical study of the development of towns across time — or it may be general and even interdisciplinary — such as 'Conflict' as an issue in social studies, or 'Fuels and power' which might involve work in science, mathematics and social studies, especially geography.

Notes to Task 1.14
The notes that follow propose a method for setting about this task.

The starting-point for the planning of this scheme can be a body of content, a set of concepts or of skills, a problem, or the interests of a class of pupils: since the implications of beginning with one or other of these has been already discussed (pp. 5-25), this aspect of planning will not be dealt with here. This is therefore taken for granted in the suggested procedures.

1   Choose the topic, taking into account the time to be spent on the work, the general aims of the course, and the pupils' abilities and likely interests.

2   Decide on the range of learning required. This may take the form of a set of objectives. It may alternatively take the form of a content map (p. 10) along with a list of skills and activities which the pupils are to engage in, in which case it will be valuable to lay out content and activities in the form of Tyler's matrix (p. 31). (Activities may include discussion, reading at various levels of difficulty, practical work, library-based inquiry, measurement, survey work and interviewing, practising skills, preparing written presentations, making diagrams and models, recording tape-slide sequences, and so on. It is important to see to it that there is a diversity of activities, especially for those pupils who will be experiencing several modules intended to reinforce a limited range of understanding or skills.)

3   Collect activities for potential modules, writing them afresh or adapting them from textbooks, published worksheets, colleagues' suggestions, and so on. (It may prove convenient for each member of the group to concentrate upon one kind of activity, or upon one aspect of the topic.)

4   This is the crucial stage, since it involves reviewing and considering critically the whole body of activities collected, selecting those which are to be used in the modules, and arranging them, as in Lawton's model, into sequences. Amongst the decisions to be made are the following.

   (*a*) Select the content of the core module, that is, the activity or activities which it is essential for all pupils to engage in (module A1).

   (*b*) Select groups of 'depth' or 'enrichment' activities, those which lead pupils out from the core issues into different and possibly more demanding aspects of the topic. (These are represented as A1, A2, A3 in the diagram.)

(*c*) Select 'breadth' tasks which offer a variety of activities to support, consolidate and generalise the 'core'. (These are represented as A1.1, A1.2, A1.3 in the diagram.) It will also be possible to plan 'breadth' tasks that allow a pupil to spend longer on one of the enrichment activities: for example, having completed the core and another module (A2), a pupil may express such interest in A3 that he should have available other activities (A3.1, A3.2, etc.) related to it.

5 This survey having been carried out, it will be possible to see where there are gaps in the scheme. Thus the next stage includes writing new modules to fill the gaps, and revising and adapting some of the existing activities so that they fit the requirements of the scheme more exactly.

6 The last group of decisions are primarily concerned with organisation and teaching.

(*a*) At this stage it will be necessary to choose the starting-point which all pupils will share, which might be a 'key lesson' or a film, or a visit.

(*b*) At the same time some policy for what has been called 'elicitation' (p. 74) will be required.

(*c*) Once the pupils begin work on the modules their work will have to be recorded and monitored. The latter is important not only because of the need for feedback and encouragement, but because it will be the basis for advising and negotiating with pupils about the route which each is to take through the scheme. This tutorial work will have to be planned in advance.

(*d*) It will be necessary to display to pupils — and to colleagues — the array of modules, and the possible routes through them, since this will in most cases be the basis for tutorial discussion and choice. The scheme as a whole can usefully be displayed as a wall-sheet, with alternative routes indicated. The individual modules can also be displayed publicly on the walls, or can be typed on sets of cards or on sheets of paper in files. It is best not to rely on teachers' oral presentation.

(*e*) Some of the modules will require materials, books, apparatus and specialist advice from teachers, and it will be necessary to indicate to pupils how they are to obtain these.

(*f*) The display and discussion which completes the topic must finally be arranged. This is of considerable importance, as a means of·giving the pupils some access to ideas and activities that they themselves have not been engaged in, thus helping to place what they have learnt into a wider context.

Factors affecting planning

It is not easy to find books which offer help with the final stage of course-planning in which one has to move from objectives (or some other form of statements about content and processes) to plans for what the teacher and the pupils will actually do in lessons. Books that recommend planning by objective are particularly weak in this respect, perhaps because specific objectives, which are very helpful to the tester, leave many decisions about teaching still to be made. Edwards (1977) who gives a good deal of advice about the criteria for selection objectives, nevertheless fails to offer any useful examples; Gagné and Briggs (1979) give only one example, though it is a useful one. The book which is most successful in showing exactly how planning can be done, and which includes plentiful illustrations, is *A Teacher's Handbook to Elementary Social Studies*, prepared by a team led by the late Hilda Taba (1967). As the title indicates, the book is primarily concerned with the teaching of humanities subjects to children of primary-school age. The mode of planning advocated there would be capable of some adaptation, but would not be suited to the teaching of mathematics, motor skills or reading. An illustration of Taba's approach is given at the end of this chapter; in the meantime we shall approach detailed planning first at a general level by identifying the different kinds of consideration that might influence the choice of classroom activities. Figure 1.4 suggests what these considerations are likely to be.

Subject-matter

The approach adopted here is related to the previous sections of this book, so it will be assumed that before you begin to plan in detail you will already have produced whichever of the following are appropriate:

(*a*)   a content map (see p. 10);
(*b*)   an analysis of concepts to be learnt (p. 11);
(*c*)   a list of skills (p. 13).

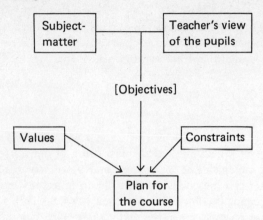

Figure 1.4 *Factors affecting the planning of a course*

View of the pupils

What you plan for your pupils necessarily depends on making some
assumptions about what they know and can do. Sometimes it is possible to find this out systematically, but usually teachers depend more
upon impressions of their pupils derived from previous lessons and from
other classes of similar age and status, though this may be very misleading. Implicit in any planning must be views about:

(*a*) the pupils' present knowledge and understanding of the subject-
matter;
(*b*) their mastery of relevant skills;
(*c*) their general developmental level;
(*d*) their likely interest in the subject.

As Bruner (1966) has pointed out, the form in which new knowledge
is to be presented to pupils should be related to their developmental
stage, and so should the kinds of activity that they are to engage in.

Since the teacher is almost always uncertain about one or all of
these, it seems important to include in lesson-planning some episode
at the beginning which will give an opportunity of finding more about
the pupils' starting-points. This will be dealt with later under the
heading of 'Elicitation'.

Values

Since these were dealt with in the previous section, all that is needed here is a set of headings that can act as a reminder:

(*a*) the general purposes and values of the school;
(*b*) the teacher's general pedagogical principles;
(*c*) procedural principles derived from the subject-matter.

Constraints

All planning must include a realistic appraisal of what is possible. At the very least it is necessary to take into account how much time is available, what equipment, including books, can be obtained, and the suitability of the room. In practice a far wider range of constraints becomes relevant as soon as one plans to take pupils out of the classroom or to collaborate with other teachers. Since all of these depend upon particular courses and upon particular schools there seems little point in attempting to systematise them here.

By now it will be clear why it is that there is so little that is helpful to the teacher who wishes to plan systematically. Not only do different kinds of subject-matter demand radically different approaches, but these have to be related to views about pupils, to educational and pedagogical values, and to the constraints of a particular school. Experienced teachers no doubt carry out intuitively this complex inter-relating of alternative criteria. However, both they and probationer teachers who have yet to build up such intuitions will benefit from approaching planning in a more systematic and reflective way.

Structure of lessons

In order to think systematically about what activities to plan for, and how to order them in a lesson, we need some view of the structure of lessons, and what the alternatives are. There are no agreed models for the structure of lessons: the model put forward here is chosen in order to facilitate planning. It has three stages that will be discussed in turn: an *opening stage*, which includes both the presentation of the topic or skills, and the elicitation from pupils of their existing understanding and competences; a *development stage*, which may be subdivided into a number of episodes; and a *synthesis stage*. Although these three stages are here applied to a lesson, they might equally be the structure of part of a lesson, or of several lessons planned as a unit. The reader is asked to keep this in mind whenever the planning of 'a lesson' is mentioned.

Opening stage. This comprises two processes which may be carried out together or separately.

(*a*) 'Presentation'. The teacher indicates to the pupils the topic, or skills, or area of experience that the lesson is to be concerned with. (The psychologist Ausubel (1966) stresses the importance of giving pupils 'advance organisers' so that new experience can take its place in relation to existing ways of understanding.) This stage may also include the presentation of information, or the giving of a demonstration, or the reading of a story, or the making of a visit, all of these being intended to focus the children's attention, to get them thinking, to give them preliminary information, or to generate interest. At this stage, too, the teacher may wish to link the new topic or activity with previous work.

(*b*) 'Elicitation'. The teacher has two reasons for wanting children to contribute to an early stage of the lesson: it is important to have them active from the start, trying out tasks, raising questions, putting into words what they already know, and offering suggestions and predictions. It is also valuable, however, to get some insight into what they already know and can do; the importance of this insight in planning has already been mentioned. Nevertheless, this latter must not be allowed to obscure the former function of elicitation, the involvement of children in the purposes and issues of a lesson so that their existing competences are ready to be brought to the new learning. To sum up, elicitation is concerned with the expression of pupils' existing understanding or competence, partly as information to the teacher, partly to engage their interest, and most of all to encourage them to recall relevant information, ideas and skills in preparation for the next stages.

Development stage. This is likely to be not one stage but a series of stages, according to the range of activities thought to be necessary. In subject-areas such as mathematics or craft, the development may be a matter of practising a skill, or applying a method to a widening range of purposes. Later in the development stage there may be problems set which require the application of skills to quite different tasks, and their integration with other skills. In content-based areas such as the sciences or the arts and social studies, the development stage may similarly include a range of activities that includes observing, categorising, interpreting and generalising. Here, too, the sequence may include problem-solving, or at the very least the testing of predictions by planning and carrying out practical investigations. Although we have stressed elicitation in the opening stage, it is equally appropriate throughout the development stage: here, however, the main purposes of requiring pupils to talk or write about what they are doing are to encourage reflexive learning and to give the teacher opportunities to let the children know in what respects their learning is going well, and in what respects they need to change their strategies. Thus discussion, with and without the teacher, is likely to be important throughout the development stage. During the planning of the development stage the focus is upon the learners, since it is through their activities that they will get insight into what is to be learnt and master the necessary skills. (See also pp. 65-7 for a discussion of the development stage in individually planned courses.)

Synthesis stage. Learning can never truly be completed yet it seems more satisfying (at least to the teacher) if each piece of work can be rounded off. Besides, there is some evidence that the generalisation of learning so that it can be applied in unfamiliar contexts is facilitated if general principles are made explicit, though ideally it should be the learner and not the teacher who makes the explicit formulation. In skill-based learning this is a matter of combining subskills and applying them to complex tasks, rather than of putting understanding into words, though even here this may have importance for older pupils. In most areas of the curriculum the synthesis stage will be mainly a matter of giving a clear shape to the various learnings that have gone on during the development, recapitulating main issues, formulating general principles, noting uncertainties and exceptions, even perhaps considering unsolved issues. This may be done partly by teacher-led discussion, but with older pupils a written synthesis becomes increasingly important to clarify learning, and to make it available for future reference. In some cases this may include transferring the learning to a different medium, such as when groups prepare a wall display to represent their several contributions to the work of the class.

Course-planning

These three stages can be summarised thus.

Opening stage

(*a*) Presentation: focus on topic or skills;
materials and experiences;
link with previous work.

(*b*) Elicitation: pupils express existing understanding and competences:
to link new work with their concerns;
to recall relevant knowledge and skills;
to initiate thinking and prediction;
to inform the teacher about their starting-points.

Development stage (may include repeated episodes)

Practising skills;
Observing and categorising;
Making hypotheses;
Planning and carrying out practical work;
Applying skills and insights to a wider range of situations;
Exploring in spoken, written or visual media the issues being dealt with.

Synthesis stage

Combining subskills and applying them;
Recapitulating main issues;
Formulating general principles;
Noting uncertainties and unanswered questions;
Expressing understanding through different media;
Recording for future reference.

Selection and ordering of activities

Although in the foregoing I have proposed a detailed structure for lesson-planning, and have suggested some of the activities that exemplify the several parts of that structure, this has not included any principles which might guide the selection of activities; so it is to that that I now turn. The first two criteria relate to larger issues already discussed in the section on factors affecting the planning of a course.

First, the form in which the subject-matter is presented, and the kinds of activity required of pupils, should match (*a*) their developmental level, and (b) their present knowledge and understanding of the subject-matter. (The scheme devised for the Science 5-13 Project, which has been described already on p. 37, shows how (a) might be considered for younger children.)

Second, the activities chosen should embody (a) the goals and values of the school, and (b) procedural principles appropriate to the subject-matter. On the latter would be based the decisions to utilise in particular episodes of a lesson an expository of a discovery strategy. (These will be discussed below.)

The third principle states that the choice and sequence of activities should be based upon analysis of the steps required to achieve learning, and thus upon a model of learning appropriate to the subject-matter. Thus in teaching children to read, the combining of digraphs into words necessitates the recognition of the digraphs, the pronunciation of spoken equivalents, as well as their incorporation into a spoken word. In learning to play a game, it may or may not be appropriate to practise skills separately before playing the game. To understand the concept of heat it is necessary for children to have some grasp of differences of temperature, and of the spreading of heat through a body, and of a number of other phenomena which are not so much prerequisites to understanding heat as parts of that concept itself. In a later section we will present a method of analysing concepts and processes to determine which are presupposed by others. At this point it is necessary to observe (a) that models of learning are to an extent arbitrary, and (b) that psychologists as distinguished as Bruner and Gagné differ about whether teaching should begin with the whole concept and break it down into parts, or begin with the parts and build them up into a whole.

Fourth, however such disputes are to be settled, in practice it may be necessary to use the model of learning to produce what Taba called 'bite-sized increments' of knowledge. Older and more able children may make leaps of insight, especially when dealing with matters within their first-hand experience; other children may need the learning broken down into small steps that can easily be mastered in turn, particularly when — as in remedial work with literacy and numeracy — the child has had the discouragement of previous failures.

Fifth, learners should be given practice in the precise activity they are required to learn: activities should match objectives. If children are to learn to read poetry aloud or carry out experiments to test hypotheses, then they must eventually read poems and do experiments.

Watching the teacher carry out experiments, and joining in choral speaking led by the teacher may be useful preliminaries but they are not the activity itself. Schooling lies to one side of the main stream of living; in school it is easier to provide for dummy runs than for the real experience. If we want to teach adolescents to carry out interviews it is useful to simulate interviews in the classroom and essential to help children to reflect upon what they need to know, and what questions will elicit it, but in the end they will have to go out and do some interviewing for themselves. In sum, learners benefit from preliminary practice and planning and simulations, but in the end they need to undertake the full complexity of the activity itself.

The sixth criterion stresses that activities should be varied, some spoken and some written, some individual and some done in groups, some using visual data, some requiring manipulation, and so on. This is partly because children vary in their preferred mode of learning, but, in particular, so that learning may be reinforced without their becoming bored, this being particularly important in the case of less able children who may require extensive repetition. In these cases, they are applying what they have learned to tasks very similar to those which were first presented to them. To take an example that applies to more able children, in geography a series of pieces of work all related to describing, analysing and interpreting the movement of people through different transport networks will serve to consolidate skills and aid the generalising of underlying concepts. Bruner (1966) stresses the importance of choosing activities which encourage generalisation, since information that has not been built into an existing structure is quickly forgotten. (This seems to correspond to the process that Piaget calls 'assimilation'.)

Yet, as the seventh principle states, assimilation alone is not enough. In many areas of learning it is important to give the learner the opportunity of coping with examples that *do not fit* his existing view of things. The temperature of water rises when one heats it, but at a certain point it stops rising even though the heating continues. Hamlet has every justification for killing Claudius, but does not do so even when the opportunity offers. In their very different ways both of these demand of the learner a reconsideration of the framework itself within which the phenomenon is to be explained. Problem-solving requires us to reconsider not only the problem but the various potential solutions that are at our disposal. It is important to provide opportunities for this, because life does not offer us only tasks which fit our existing skills and understanding, but many others which require rapid adaptation and improvisation. (This corresponds to Piaget's 'accommodation'.)

As the eighth point, the role of discussion and writing activities needs careful consideration. Putting ideas into words helps a pupil to relate new knowledge to what he already knows — which may not be available without some prompting and searching — and encourages reflection and assimilation. Which mode of verbalising is most appropriate? Class discussion can be controlled by the teacher but usually involves only a small proportion of the children; small-group discussion involves everyone but is outside the teacher's control; writing can be monitored by the teacher but inhibits children who cannot write fluently. Each mode can thus be used for different purposes. Another important consideration is the choice between 'exploratory' and 'presentational' talking and writing. In presentational writing the pupils are concerned to produce a 'final draft' within the framework prescribed by the teacher, whereas in 'exploratory' talking or writing they have more opportunity to sort out their own thinking in response to new ideas and experiences.

Finally, recent work in psychology has made it clear that coping with problems embedded in a familiar context is very much easier than dealing with analogous problems in unfamiliar contexts. Donaldson (1976) illustrates how children who cannot think out a problem stated abstractly or in terms of an unfamiliar situation may be able to solve a logically identical problem if it is expressed in terms of objects, relationships and processes which they are familiar with. This might be taken to imply, for example, that children should discuss parent-child conflict in their own families before considering it elsewhere. Bruner (1966), however, argues to the contrary that the very unfamiliarity of parent-child conflict in (for example) seagulls puts the children in a better position to reflect upon their own experience. Whichever view we take, the 'embeddedness' of the tasks which we give to our pupils is clearly to be taken into account when planning. One relevant aspect is that the learners can contribute much more to the thinking when the issue discussed is embedded in their own first-hand experience, rather than distant in time and place. On the other hand, unfamiliar experience, just because it *is* unfamiliar, may challenge the learner to reflect on what has previously been taken for granted; and a range of unfamiliar but analogous examples may provide a good basis for generalisation. These two considerations are only apparently in contradiction: either may in one context or another guide the choice of learning activities.

Here is a summary of these principles for convenience of reference:

1   pupils' abilities and knowledge;
2   values and procedural principles;
3   prerequisite concepts and skills;
4   'bite-sized increments';
5   learning through simulation or the activity itself;
6   varied activities;
7   problems;
8   discussion and writing, exploratory or presentational;
9   familiar and unfamiliar experiences.

The tasks which follow offer practice in applying some of these principles to the selection and ordering of activities.

Task 1.15 Using principles to guide the selection of learning activities

1.15.1   (Principle 1) The following is a set of science activities suggested for low-ability children in the first years of secondary education. Please turn to the developmental scheme for science prepared by the Science 5-13 Project (Appendix B) and assign each of these activities to one of the three main developmental stages. Is this the order in which the children should experience them, or do other considerations apply?

Energy
Making as many different sounds as possible.
Transmitting sound through solids, liquids and gases.
Judging the loudness and pitch of sounds.
Understanding the processing of energy sources in heat engines.
Estimating and measuring temperature.
Finding good and bad conductors of heat.
Constructing a flow diagram to show how the energy of the sun reaches living things.
Classifying conductors and insulators of electricity.
Experiencing changes in the form of energy (for example, winding up the spring of a clockwork motor).
Burning paper by using a hand lens in sunlight.

1.15.2   (Principle 5) You want your pupils to practise the following:

1.15.2
contd
Getting information from reference works (including non-academic ones such as timetables and maps);

writing letters to give and obtain information from adults;

taking responsibility for planning activities;

talking to adults whom they have not met before;

working together in groups.

Plan a series of activities which will enable them (*a*) to practise these in simulated form, and eventually (*b*) to put them all together in carrying out a scheme they have planned. You will probably need to begin by choosing an out-of-school venture which can give point to all of these, or perhaps by offering a range of possibilities to your pupils.

1.15.3
(Principle 6) You are teaching elementary French in a primary school, and you wish your pupils to practise using these forms:

> Qu'est-ce que c'est?
>
> C'est un/une . . .
>
> Non, ce n'est pas un/une . . .

using a very limited range of nouns. Devise a range of activities including group games that will enable pupils to practise them without becoming bored.

1.15.4
(Principle 9) You are planning a course-unit in social and environmental studies for children of 10-12 years of age, and intend to centre it upon the dual principle that man's way of life is both a response to the natural environment and an imposition upon it. Work out two alternative sets of opening activities lasting not more than three lessons, of which the first starts with familiar aspects of the local environment, and the second starts with an unfamiliar and contrasting social environment. Discuss the pros and cons of the two ways of beginning the unit.

1.15.5
As a basis for choosing learning activities, the following set of principles 'on which most psychologists would agree' have been put forward by D.K. Wheeler (1967). How far do they correspond with the list of criteria that I have put forward? What are the implications of the differences between the two sets of principles? What does Wheeler include that I have omitted, and what would a teacher have to do to put them into effect? (What could be done about nos. 7 and 11?) Do the two sets point towards two different styles of teaching?

1.15.5
contd

1 Learning is an active process in which the learner must be involved.
2 Learning proceeds more effectively if, as well as being an active participant, the learner understands what he is learning.
3 Learning is considerably affected by individual goals, values and motives.
4 Frequent repetition of response to a class of situations is important in learning skills.
5 Immediate reinforcement promotes learning. Cognitive feedback is most effective when time-lapse is minimal.
6 The wider the range of experiences presented to the learner, the more likely are generalization and discrimination to occur.
7 Behaviour is a function of the learner's perceptions.
8 Similar situations may elicit different reactions from different learners.
9 While transfer does occur, it is usually much less than people think. What there is may usually be attributed to similarities between the tasks involved. Both likenesses between situations and possibilities of transfer should be pointed out specifically.
10 Group atmosphere affects both learning product and accrued satisfaction.
11 Individual differences affect learning. Such differences are both biogenic and socio-cultural.
12 All learnings are multiple. Though focus may be on one particular (desired) outcome, other learnings take place simultaneously.

Putting activities into sequence

This section begins with a task.

Task 1.16 Putting activities into sequence

1.16.1 This task can best be carried out by teachers or students working in small groups. There follows below a list of activities connected with the topic 'Houses' and suitable for a class of

1.16.1   primary-school children. Each group should put the activities
contd   into a suitable sequence that might constitute a course-unit
lasting several weeks. (Activities can be omitted from the
list and others added, if the participants see fit.) The groups
should then meet to discuss the principles on which each
has based its sequence; that is, the purpose of the task is not
so much to design a unit as to reflect upon the principles,
implicit or explicit, that have informed the solutions severally
put forward by the groups.

Learning activities related to 'Houses'
1 Visit the loft of the school building to see timbers.
2 Walk round the area in which the school is built.
3 Visit a building site.
4 Discuss the houses they live in, and others they know.
5 Discuss kinds of houses, terraces, flats, semi-detached, etc.
6 Draw shapes of roofs, windows, gutters, chimneys, etc.
7 Make models of houses.
8 Read about the materials and processes involved in building houses.
9 Compare measurements of drawings, models, real houses.
10 Make block diagrams of the distributions of kinds of houses.
11 Calculate the properties of rectangular solids.
12 Write about 'The houses I pass on my way to school'.
13 Write about the materials used in building houses.
14 Write about 'The kind of house I'd like to live in'.
15 Listen to a talk by an electrician about wiring houses.

Hilda Taba (1963) wrote that there are four strategic principles for
putting activities into an appropriate sequence for learning.

1 Beginning with simple tasks and moving towards more complex
ones (though it is not always clear which are which).
2 Analysis of the knowledge or skills that are needed before it will
be possible to learn new knowledge or skills.
3 Beginning with the whole, and moving on to the parts. (This might
contradict the two previous principles.)
4 Chronological sequence. (This seems likely to be useful in history,
but not elsewhere.)

Another possibility which Taba did not mention specifically she nevertheless used in some of her own curriculum planning.

5   Moving from the familiar to the unfamiliar (or vice versa).

One version of this is to begin by giving pupils mathematical calculations close to the original example presented by the teacher, and then moving gradually towards diverse situations which require what is learnt to be modified and generalised (the process of 'accommodation', in fact), that is, towards problem-solving. Taba's first two principles seem very similar, and we shall give our attention to the second, the analysis of content.

The American psychologist, R.M. Gagné (1975), has put forward a method of analysis into what he calls 'learning structures', that will be appropriate to our purposes. Gagné intends the method to be used to analyse the prerequisites of knowledge and understanding in subjects such as physics or mathematics, but we shall find that it can be adapted for use with skills. First, we will illustrate the method with an example taken from physics. Suppose one wished to teach the concept of 'density', what are the prerequisite concepts out of which children can build up so complex a concept? 'Density' in fact depends upon the interrelating of concepts of weight and volume; Gagné's view is that there is little point in giving pupils activities illustrating 'density', until they have some grasp of 'weight' and 'volume'. On what does the concept of 'weight' depend? One answer might be that it depends on the concept of 'displacement' plus some grasp of a unit of weight such as 'grams'. Similarly, one can break down the concept of 'volume', generating a hierarchy like this:

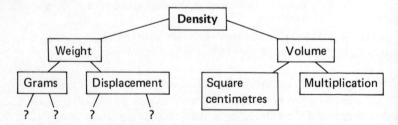

Figure 1.5   *A learning structure for 'density'*

One can go on in the next row to ask what knowledge constitutes a prerequisite for understanding 'grams', 'displacement', and so on.

Gagné's contention is that we should start at the bottom of the hierarchy, find whether our pupils have grasped the lowest level of concepts, and if not begin by teaching them, or at least by revising them.

Figures 1.6-1.8 show three learning structures prepared by teachers; it will be immediately obvious that these are less abstract than the learning structure for density, more closely linked to what children do. Figure 1.6 is intended for low-ability pupils in a special school, and sets out what they need to know and to be able to do in order to take part in swimming as a leisure activity. As with other learning structures, the base lines are necessarily incomplete.

The next learning structure is concerned with sewing a line of stitches, and would be suited to a very young child making his or her first acquaintance with these skills (see Figure 1.7).

The last example of a learning structure is intended for secondary-school pupils aged about fourteen years, and is concerned with teaching children how to maintain a healthy body (Figure 1.8).

It will have been noticed that these last three learning structures (Figures 1.6-1.8), unlike the one concerned with density (Figure 1.5), are not simply analyses of concepts into subconcepts, but include skills such as 'hold and use scissors', knowledge such as 'to specify the sources of the six classes of food', and areas of social awareness such as 'hygiene' which is more a matter of attitude and values than of knowledge. In spite of their differences they all exemplify how analysis into a learning structure can be used to decide what subactivities should take place as part of a larger course-unit. Indeed, this kind of analysis can now be seen to be implicit in the content maps (discussed on pp. 6-11). The next set of tasks relates to the making of learning structures, and their use in the choosing and sequencing of activities for pupils.

Task 1.16 contd Putting activities into sequence

1.16.2   In this task you are invited to look critically at the four learning structures (Figures 1.5-1.8).

(a) Do they deal exhaustively with prerequisite ideas and skills?

(b) How far do they appear to be general, and how far based on a view of particular children's needs and competences?

(c) Do you find them too detailed, not detailed enough, or about right?

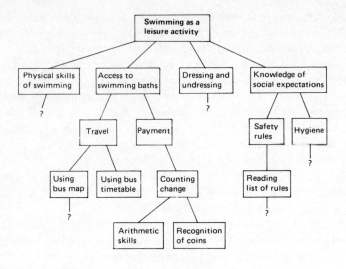

Figure 1.6 *Learning structure for swimming as a leisure activity*

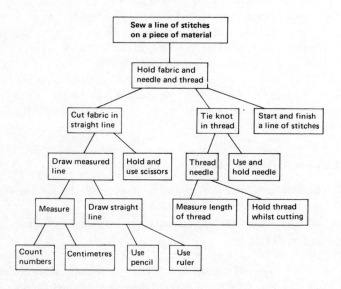

Figure 1.7 *Learning structure for sewing a line of stitches*

86

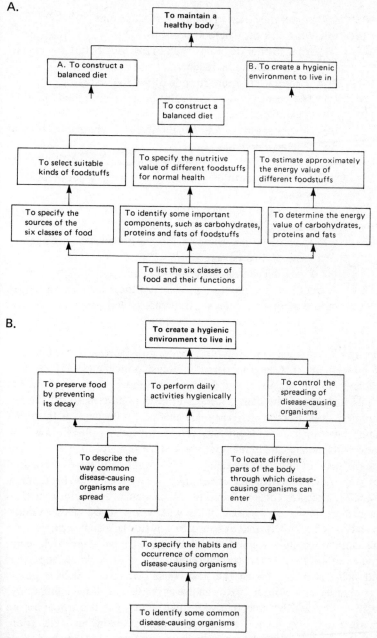

Figure 1.8 *Learning structure to maintain a healthy body*

1.16.2 (*d*) Would they help in planning a course-unit?
contd   (*e*) What changes would improve them?
       (*f*) What further decisions need to be made before the course-unit is ready to be taught?

1.16.3 Plan a learning structure for one of the following.
       (*a*) The construction of a useful object from a material such as wood or plastic.
       (*b*) Understanding fractional numbers (or the equivalence of ordered pairs).
       (*c*) Going shopping (for younger or less able pupils).
       (*d*) A course entitled 'Man, the only language-speaking animal'.
       (*e*) Orienteering (or rock climbing).
       (*f*) A visit to a local folk museum.
       (*g*) A prepared presentation (books in hand) of the opening scene of Shakespeare's *Julius Caesar*.
       (*h*) Preparing and serving a winter salad.

1.16.4 A question for you to consider: are these learning structures independent of particular students, or did you find that you had to take the students into account?

Having written a learning structure, we are now faced with the question of how to use it. Gagné's original strategic principle (1975) was that teaching should begin at the bottom and move upwards: how can pupils understand the complex ideas until they have mastered the less complex ones from which they are made up? Bruner, on the other hand, favours moving from the top downwards (1966): how can pupils understand and remember the details if they do not see what system they fit into? For example, if we want to present to children the way of life of a neolithic community, do we start by giving them an overall impression, or by focusing on particular techniques such as shellfish-gathering or scraping skins with stone tools? This example (which is mine, not Bruner's) seems to suit Bruner's approach, whereas the density example seemed to suit Gagné's. Bruner's approach seems to be appropriate whenever children have existing knowledge that will help them understand the new: their own lives will have points of similarity and contrast with the lives lived in a neolithic community, so that they will be able to make some sense of it as a whole before focusing first upon major issues such as food-gathering and cultivation, and then upon particular techniques used. Does the same principle apply in dealing with a concept such as density? Is there a case for discussing with children their understanding of why a heavy lump of timber floats and yet a tiny iron nail sinks, before going on to check their grasp of volume and weight? I think there is. Nevertheless, it is important at the same time for the teacher to have analysed what concepts are prerequisites to understanding density, for then he/she knows what kind of examples to present, and what ideas to discuss, if his/her pupils prove to be confused about the timber and the nail. Thus the strict version of Gagné's learning structure, the precise analysis of a concept, while a helpful adjunct to planning, should not be treated as a rigid rule.

The issue that has just been discussed is not unrelated to the choice between expository and discovery strategies in teaching, a choice that all teachers are continually compelled to make. In the *expository strategy* we begin by expounding a principle, or demonstrating a process or skill, or giving information, and then go on to require pupils to apply the principle, to carry out the process, to practise the skill, or to use the information. In the expository strategy the teacher controls all the rules of the game; the pupils' task is to apply them. On the other hand, in the *discovery strategy* we begin by setting a problem, and if we give information it is so that pupils can interpret it for themselves; then we require pupils to suggest and try out processes to solve the problem, in the belief that by so doing they will develop skills and gain insight into principles. Indeed, the main purpose of the discovery strategy is to see to it that the pupils have access to the rules of the game, so that what they learn is not mere rote knowledge but part of their thinking. The rationale of the expository strategy is that pupils do not know where they are going and cannot be expected to invent the whole of man's knowledge for themselves. The rationale of the discovery strategy is that people do not learn very effectively answers to questions they have never asked, or skills for doing things they do not wish to do. Both rationales make sense; fortunately we do not have to choose between them once for all, but can choose one or the other as the occasion demands. It seems that Gagné's bottom-upward approach will be a better match for an expository strategy, Bruner's top-downwards approach a better match for the discovery strategy (which does *not* mean throwing children in at the deep end to sink or swim).

In any piece of curriculum-planning a choice has to be made whether to adopt an expository or a discovery strategy. There is no reason why different approaches should not be adopted in different parts of a unit. Even within the presentation section of a lesson, a teacher may wish to use an expository strategy in reviewing what has been done in previous lessons before shifting to a discovery strategy in asking the pupils for predictions as a way of getting them to think about the new issue he/she is about to introduce them to.

One other strategic choice in planning activities needs to be dealt with, and this is the familiarity of the material to the children. Bruner is scornful of what he calls 'the friendly postman' approach to social studies; he prefers to begin 'Man, a Course of Study' with Eskimos and baboon troops so as to throw into contrast the nature of social life in industrial societies. The friendly postman fails to challenge the children's taken-for-granted world; exposing one's elderly relatives to death in the cold does. The argument is persuasive. But change the postman to a policeman, and — with adolescents at least — a discussion of everyday life moves rapidly into the deepest issues of authority and power in our society. We may, in fact, find that for some purposes the children's experience is precisely where we can best start. (To be fair to Bruner, he clearly intends to return there from his distant starting-points.) Thus we have here another strategic choice that has to be made in planning.

You may feel that having given you a firm guideline in Gagné's learning structures, I proceeded immediately to snatch it away by discussing nebulous strategic principles such as the discovery strategy, top-downwards, and beginning with the familiar (or the unfamiliar). This should reinforce what was said earlier: curriculum-planning can never be a neutral technique, since it is always based on complex judgments about values, about what matters for people, that is.

Task 1.16 contd Putting activities into sequence

1.16.5 Choose a topic or an activity similar to those listed in Task 1.16.3 and prepare a learning structure for it. On the basis of that, choose and put into order a sequence of activities that would serve to introduce a group of children (of a particular age) to this topic or activity. In so doing you may find it helpful to take into consideration some of the following issues:

(a) prerequisite concepts and skills;

(b) the appropriateness of a 'top-downwards' or a 'bottom-

1.16.5   upwards' strategy;
contd   (*c*) the appropriateness of an exposition or a discovery strategy;
          (*d*) the appropriateness of starting with the familiar or the unfamiliar;
          (*e*) the possibility of carrying out the final activity:
              (i)   in simulated form;
              (ii)   in real life (perhaps outside the school).

(Some of these will probably not be relevant to the particular task which you set yourself.)

Planning: the whole sequence

Our next concern is to put together everything that has so far been discussed. This implies that matters which have been dealt with in detail will receive no more than a mention, and a reference to the pages where they have already been discussed, so that you can look back for help in carrying out the planning. The planning sequence is represented here as five main steps, some of which may be sub-divided.

1   Analyse the content to be taught
    (*a*) Analyse the concepts to be learnt
    (*b*) Analyse the skills and abilities to be developed
2   Consider the capabilities and interests of the pupils
    (*a*) Consult the pupils
3   Combine the above in a general plan
4   Select learning activities
    (*a*) Make decisions about strategies
    (*b*) Consider procedural principles suited to the subject-matter
5   Revise the activities and put them into sequence
    (*a*) Analyse for balance
    (*b*) Consider the different stages of a lesson

Analyse the content to be taught

In the first section we were concerned with different emphases in planning, according to whether the planning began with content, concepts, skills, problems or interests (pp. 7-25). That can now be seen as a rougher version of the procedure recommended here. In this more explicit approach it is still open to you to choose which starting-point is more suitable. Gagné's 'learning structure' analysis (pp. 84-8) now provides a more sophisticated way of analysing concepts or skills. Nevertheless, as I pointed out earlier, there will be some kinds of subject-matter for which it is not appropriate to analyse either.

Consider the capabilities and interests of the pupils

For the most part teachers do this intuitively, though the scheme devised by the Science 5-13 Project (Appendix B) shows that it would be possible to consider developmental stages more systematically. In interest-based planning (pp. 22-5) the teacher deals with this by involving pupils in the discussion of subject-matter and issues.

Combine in a general plan

This is the stage at which objectives will be written if they are held to be necessary. Where objectives are not being written, the general plan at this stage will look like the so-called 'objectives' written for the Geography for the Young School Leaver Project (see p. 32).

Select learning activities

This stage and the two that follow depend upon some decisions having been made about underlying strategies, using the principles discussed above (pp. 76-80). Some of these strategies will amount to 'procedural principles' derived from the nature of the subject-matter being taught (see pp. 59-61).

Revise the activities and put them into sequence

It is important at this stage to use Tyler's matrix (p. 31) to check that the activities give proper weight to each area of content and each kind of skill. This is not to imply that all should be equal: the purpose of the matrix is to enable you to reflect on the implications of the choices made so far. It will also be necessary to take into account the stages in the structure of a 'lesson' (discussed on pp. 73-6).

There now follows an example of a plan made by Taba and her associates (1967) for the teaching of social studies to children of primary-school age in a part of California. You will see that it includes:

(a) activities for pupils ('students'), divided into opener, development, conclusion in a way similar to that recommended here;
(b) notes to teachers about the strategies that should inform their teaching;
(c) suggested questions to focus pupils' attention;
(d) indication of cognitive processes aimed at (for example, inferring and generalising);
(e) notes of books and other resources that will be needed.

This plan naturally does not exactly reflect the approach recommended in this book, but it is close enough to show what a completed plan might look like — at least in the area of social studies — though it should be borne in mind that this plan was prepared by one group of teachers for other teachers, many of whom had played little or no part in their development. A plan prepared by a teacher for his or her own use would probably look rather different.

TABLE 1.3 *Sequence of learning activities (four communities around the world)*

Unit III
Main idea: Interaction between a people and their physical environment influences the way in which they meet their needs.
Organising idea: The desert people modify their behavior and their environment in order to make a living.

Notes to the teacher	Learning activities

People everywhere have developed some patterns of living that are related to their environment. The following sequence deals with the nomadic life as one way in which some desert people handle the problem of water scarcity.

Opener

Keep the record you make of the students' statements	Let the children who have crossed a desert or who have seen deserts on TV or

93

Notes to the teacher	*Learning activities*

and their papers. They will be used in the Conclusion.

in the movies tell what they think they know about deserts.
Record the statements of the students.
Ask the students to write a paper on the subject:
Could anyone live in the desert?
Examine the papers to see whether any of the students suggest that one response to climate is for people to modify their behavior.

Development
Formulating hypotheses
Students should be encouraged to suggest possible explanations for or predictions in unfamiliar situations.
Faulty hypotheses should not be corrected at the point at which they are given, but once additional information has been gathered, they should be checked.
Keep the record of the reasons for the journeys of the nomad. The children will check it in Activity 6.

1 Display a picture of a camel caravan and ask:
What reason do you suppose these people might have for moving?

If no large study print is available, display *All About the Desert* (Epstein), pp. 22-23, and *The True Book of Deserts* (Posell), pp. 14-15.
All About the Desert is not a reference for students but the illustrations are useful.
Record the reasons the children offer for the journeys of the nomad.

In Activity 18 the students will be formally presented with these points as study questions to which they will seek answers in their research.

2 Read *Sons of the Desert* (Gidal) to the class as an introduction which provides some basic knowledge about the life of the Bedouin. Do not spend time on minor details. Rather, emphasize the major points which will be used for comparing the life of the Bedouin nomads with that of other cultures.

Intake of information

How they get their food
How they get their housing
How they get their clothing
What tools they use
How they travel from place to place

Notes to the teacher	*Learning activities*

How they get their water

Map skills

3 Using the map in the front fly leaf of *Sons of the Desert* (Gidal), help the children locate the travels of the characters in the story.

Since the emphasis of this unit is on the Bedouin of the Middle Eastern deserts, the other desert areas of the world will not be identified until Activity 28. *Evaluation* procedures described in Unit I, Activity 6 (located following Optional Activity 8), could be used here.
Encourage students to raise questions.

4 Have the children locate the deserts of the Middle East on the world map in Unit I.
Have the students relate the location of the deserts of the Middle East to the location of Hudson Bay area where the Central Eskimo lives. Ask: In what direction are the deserts from the Arctic?

5 Tell the children they are going to see a filmstrip about desert nomads. Ask: What ideas do you think are important to watch for?
Many of the ideas eight-year-olds will give will be quite specific. A few children will reach a higher level of abstraction. Note the range of these typical third grade responses:
Whether they have tents
Who get to eat first at mealtime
What rules they have
The way they make a living.
Show the filmstrip *Ahmed and Adah of the Desert Lands*. If the filmstrip is not available, read 'Tent People' from *At Home Around the World* (Goetz), pp. 135-8.
As further intake of information read *Achmed, Boy of the Negev* (Russcol).

It is important that children learn to check their hypotheses once they have more information. It is equally important for

6 Ask the children:
Why did Fayez in *Sons of the Desert* (Gidal) move?
What reason did the people we just learned about (in Activity 5) have

95

Notes to the teacher	*Learning activities*

them to learn that frequently there is more than one cause for an event.

for moving?
Refer again to the pictures shown and the record of reasons for the journeys of the nomad from Activity 1. Have the children check their hypotheses at this time. Ask:
(1) Were the reasons correct that you gave as to why these people might be moving?
(2) Do you have any additional reasons to add now?

Do not put a title on the chart, as that will be an essential part of Activity 8.

7 Develop on the chalkboard a chart of reasons for moving. Help the children recall the reasons the Eskimo hunter moved and the reasons the desert nomad moves.

Recall of information

Add to the chart a list of reasons the children think their own parents have had for moving. For example:

Organizing information

Desert nomad	Eskimo hunter	*Our family*
The search for water They travel to better pastures	They go where hunting is good They travel to trading posts	Daddy has a new job We need a bigger home

Or

The children will produce better results if they work on the assignment in pairs and then share their products.

Let the children work in pairs for a few minutes, listing reasons for the moves of either the Eskimo hunter or the desert nomad. Then let each pair meet with another pair and combine their lists. They may select one person to report for the group. After the contributions have been charted on the chalkboard, let the whole class

Notes to the teacher	*Learning activities*

give reasons their own families, or
families they know, move.

Evaluation procedures
described in Unit I,
Activity 28 (located
following that activity).

8 Have the students suggest a title for
the chart. If you wish to use this
exercise to evaluate their work, ask
each to write out his own title for the
chart and turn it in.

It is usually easier for
children to see differences
than for them to see
similarities.

Inferring and generalizing

9 Have the children contrast the reasons
the different groups of people have
for moving. Encourage them to refer
to the chart (Activity 7).
Suggested question sequence:
(1) What differences do you see in
the reasons that these three
groups of people have for moving?
(2) Why do you suppose there are
these differences?
(3) How are people's reasons for
moving alike?
(4) What can you say about the
reasons people move?
If there are many more reasons listed
under 'our family' than in the other
two columns, ask the children why
they think there are. It may lead to
the idea that we know more about
ourselves than we do about others.

One important realization
the children may reach is
that different people may
feel differently about a
similar event.

10 Let the children explore the way
people might feel about moving. They
should understand that it is the
nomad's way of life to change his
camp, and that nomad children get
quite excited about the prospect of
another move.
Our feelings *might* be different
because our way of life differs.

*Attitudes, feelings and
values*

Suggested question sequence:
(1) How do you think Fayez felt
when his father told the family
they would move on the next day?

97

Notes to the teacher	*Learning activities*

(2) Why do you suppose he felt that way?

(3) What other way might he have felt?

(4) How do you think his father or mother felt?

(5) Have you ever moved?

(6) How did you feel when you moved?

(7) Why do you think you feel the way you do about moving?

(8) What does this tell you about people?

Activities 11-36 deal with the physical environment of the Negev, modifications the Bedouin makes in his environment, and additional modifications he makes in his behavior.

Conclusion

Put the diagram shown below on the chalkboard. Tell the children that the arrows mean 'have something to do with.' Have each child make two pupil-response cards (preferably of different colors), one saying 'With People' and the other saying 'Without People'.

The pupil-response cards should have the same response written on both sides of the cards, so the children may read it as they hold it up for the teacher to read.

Tell the children they are to decide whether the events listed would happen only if people were there. Then when you read the items each child is to hold up the card that says what he thinks, and you will tally their responses.

Notes to the teacher	Learning activities		
		With people	Without people
	Water (have something to do with) Trees → An oasis		
	Heavy rainfall Hard dry earth → Floods		
	Little rainfall Need for water → Wells		
	Herds of camels Herds of goats → Items sold in the market		
	Strong winds (have something to do with) Sand → Hot air → Long, loose robes		
	Water Good soil → Farming		

Inferring and generalizing	After the exercise has been completed ask: What ideas do you get from what you see? Continue questioning until the children have had an opportunity to make a number of statements about the nomad's relationship to his environment.
Checking an inference	Direct the students' attention to their mural. Let them point out the number of items they would have to remove if there were no people in the desert.
If students are asked to re-write their paper, analysis of first and second attempts using at least some of the	Display the record made in the Opener of the children's ideas about desert. Also give each student his paper written in the Opener. Ask how many have changed

Notes to the teacher	*Learning activities*
criteria described in Unit I Activities 21 and 35, can be extremely valuable in *evaluating* growth on the part of the individuals and the total class.	their minds about what they wrote or thought they knew and now could do a better job.

Task 1.17 Final planning task

1.17 The only possible task, as a culmination of all this, is to invite you to plan in detail a unit which you yourself will teach, going through all the stages which have been recommended. I suggest that you should record each decision you make at each stage, and the grounds on which you made it, so you can reconsider them later, or discuss them with others.

This completes the part of this book which is concerned with the planning of courses. The next chapter deals with the content of the curriculum as a whole, and how choices of content can be justified. In the third chapter we shall turn to the evaluation of curricula.

Chapter 2

The content of the curriculum

We now turn from the planning of courses to the curriculum as a whole, from the point of view both of the range of learning that a pupil should experience during his or her school career, and of the school's problems in organising a range of curricula. Both lead to questions such as these. By what criteria can one way of organising the curriculum be preferred to another? How can particular emphases be justified, or particular inclusions or omissions? What is the nature of school subjects and how do they differ from one another? What is gained and lost if a school integrates or groups subjects in this manner or that? What view should be taken of schools' claims to offer a social and personal education to their pupils, over and above the academic curriculum? Is the so-called 'hidden curriculum' part of curriculum at all?

The school curriculum has been described by Lawton (1975) and others as 'a selection from the culture', and it is true that schools could not possibly teach all the knowledge and skills that are professed by every group in our society. The formula 'selection from the culture' has, however, the disadvantage of failing to remind us that schools reinterpret knowledge as well as select it. Nevertheless, it is useful to consider the school curriculum as a selection from all available knowledge, beliefs, skills, values and habits, but in justifying one particular selection we must take seriously the possibility that it is an arbitrary selection, sanctioned only by convenience and tradition. There seem to be two strategies for justifying the range of studies offered to children: one seeks to justify the curriculum in terms of the intrinsic logical structure of knowledge and the other in terms of its likely usefulness in pupils' future lives. We shall first consider the form strategy.

101

Paul Hirst, amongst others, has argued (1974) that man's culture has developed through history a number of distinct and different ways of arriving at knowledge and validating it. He calls these 'forms of knowledge' and has identified seven of them:

(i)   Empirical knowledge in the physical and social sciences
(ii)   Mental or personal knowledge involving explanations of human behaviour in terms of intentions, will, hopes, belief, etc.
(iii) Mathematical knowledge
(iv)   Aesthetic knowledge
(v)   Religious knowledge
(vi)   Moral knowledge
(vii) Philosophical knowledge

Hirst argues (1974) that these forms of knowledge, though historical products of man's cultural development, can be distinguished from one another on purely logical grounds, irrespective of whether they are or are not organised as separate 'subjects' in schools or universities.

The forms of knowledge are linked to the overall structure of the curriculum through the following argument: since schooling is intended to give all young people access to the resources of their culture, then they should all have experience of each of the seven forms of knowledge. Denis Lawton (1975) has detached himself from this argument — perhaps partly in jest — by hinting that it is equivalent to saying that everyone should climb Everest because it is there. He himself would place more emphasis on social utility, though it is not entirely clear how he would demonstrate the social utility of particular bodies of knowledge. One irony of the curriculum is that, since in most countries of the world education is the main means of selecting pupils for different levels of employment, any curriculum content used in public examinations appears to have social utility, especially in the eyes of the pupils, whose future depends on it, and of their parents. Of course, this is quite different from valuing knowledge or skills because they contribute to industrial productivity or because they enhance people's lives.

Denis Lawton has suggested that the school curriculum might conveniently be organised in five disciplines or faculties and one inter-disciplinary area:

(i)   Mathematics
(ii) The physical and biological sciences
(iii) Humanities and social sciences (including history, geography, classical studies, literature, film and TV, and religious studies)
(iv) The expressive and creative arts
(v)   Moral education
(vi) Interdisciplinary work

It should be noted that whereas Hirst's categories are intended to represent logical differences between forms of knowledge, Lawton's headings are proposals for organisational arrangements. Nevertheless, the two lists have a good deal in common. Lawton's proposal that there should be institutional arrangements that ensure that pupils engage in studies that overlap the boundaries of disciplines is an interesting one, which does not conflict with Hirst's views, since the latter has made it clear that his analysis of the 'forms' does not preclude pedagogical decisions to teach them in an integrated way.

This rapid summary of two points of view on the whole curriculum naturally conceals great complexity beneath a deceptive surface. It is not our business here to probe this complexity, though references to Hirst's and Lawton's work are given in the appropriate place. We shall put aside the continuing debate about the validity of these categories and address ourselves to the question: if they are valid, what follows for the curriculum?

Task 2.1 Applying Hirst's and Lawton's frameworks to the curriculum

2.1.1   Hirst has always insisted that his analysis has implications for what should appear in the curriculum but not for how it should be taught nor in what combinations. With this in mind, does his set of seven categories have any implications for the curriculum of a secondary school? Does it demand any changes? Most secondary schools offer options: can these be justified?

2.1.2   Does Hirst's analysis have any relevance to the curriculum of a primary school, or a special school? Would it help to solve questions of curriculum priorities?

2.1.3   Lawton's proposals are organisational, though partly based on Hirst's and other analyses. Consider the implications of adopting them in a middle or secondary school. What advantages might there be and what disadvantages?

The content of the curriculum

2.1.4 Should each area of the curriculum receive equal balance, and if so, why? Is there any reason why some should not be omitted altogether? What would be the implications of leaving the choice to pupils? On what criteria should decisions about the whole curriculum be based?

Aims for the whole school

The Schools Council project 'The Aims of Primary Education' (Ashton *et al.*, 1975a) arranged a series of meetings for several hundred teachers at which they discussed their aims, and arrived finally at a list of 72 aims which made sense to them. These aims are listed in Appendix C; they form the basis of the next four tasks. (It should be noted that in the appendix the aims have been listed in random order.) The tasks are probably best approached as group activities, though they can be carried out individually by students. When the Schools Council project presented these aims to teachers they reminded them that they were concerned with what children *in the middle range of ability* should achieve *at the end of their primary education* and suggested that they should consider them in terms of children in their own schools.

Task 2.2 Considering the aims of primary education

2.2.1 Choose from the list the twelve aims which you think most important for children of a particular age (which need not be at the end of primary education). Justify your choice of these and omission of others that you regard as almost equally important. What implications might your choice have (*a*) for the relative emphasis on one part of the curriculum rather than another; (*b*) for the way in which the school day and week is organised; (*c*) for the pattern of learning activities and social relationships in the classroom.

2.2.2 One headteacher of a school for juniors and infants made his own selection from the list of aims, and wrote:

> **Choice and structuring of aims and objectives**
> The aim that I chose to illustrate, which seems to me to be one of the most important was:
> 22 The child should be developing the ability to make

2.2.2
contd

reasoned judgments and choices based on the interpretation and evaluation of relevant information.

The aim having been chosen, there at once sprang to mind the fact that there was another aim that was inextricably intertwined with it:

23 The child should be developing a critical and discriminating attitude towards his experiences; for example, of the mass media.

Having chosen these two qualities as the nucleus of the aims I then clustered around them six skill-aims (not necessarily in order of importance) which were essential to the realisation of the primary aim.

10 The child should be able to listen with concentration and understanding.

11 The child should be able to read fluently and accurately (at a minimum reading age of eleven).

12 The child should be able to read with understanding material appropriate to his age-group and interests.

15 The child should know how to observe carefully, accurately and with sensitivity.

16 The child should be developing the skills of acquiring knowledge and information from written material; for example, summarising, taking notes accurately, the use of libraries.

17 The child should know how to acquire information other than by reading: for example, by asking questions, by experimenting, from watching television.

Around this central complex of aims there were others that were, at least partially, intimately concerned with the aim both in its original statement and in at least some of its associates. Aim no. 19 dealing with mathematical ability and skill in thinking is an obvious example.

Having evoked this complex of aims it was now apparent that around these again there were knowledge-aims which could not be ignored.

1 The child should have a wide vocabulary.

4 The child should have a general knowledge of his local environment in some of the following aspects: historical, geographical, natural, economic and social.

5 The child should have a wide general (not subject-based)

2.2.2
contd
    knowledge of times and places beyond his immediate experience.

7 The child should know some simple scientific procedures and some basic scientific concepts; for example, properties of materials, the nature and significance of changes in living things.

Whilst in this process of selecting and structuring I realised that I was supporting and clarifying the original statement of the aim and that my choice was being conditioned practically by the need to translate it eventually into the reality of a living school.

This headteacher has explained which aims he wishes to emphasise and how he groups them in his mind.

(a) How far do you agree or disagree with his emphases? Can you justify his omission of the other sixty aims, which implicitly relegates them to a lower status?

(b) On what basis can one decide about curriculum priorities? Is there a more valid basis than tradition or one's own preferences?

(c) What does his choice of aims commit him to in organising his school, in planning a curriculum, in preparing a timetable and syllabuses, and in appointing staff? Does his choice in fact commit him to anything? You can see his own views on how these aims should be put into effect by reading Ashton, Kneen and Davies (1975b, pp. 55-8).

2.2.3 Some of the 72 aims do not relate to particular curricular areas but, if put into effect, would influence the whole life of the school. Decide which these are and what would have to be done if they were to be made effective.

2.2.4 This task can be carried out in relation to a first, junior or middle school. Consider the aims which remain after the general ones referred to in Task 2.2.3 have been extracted. These remaining aims refer directly to the curriculum.

(a) Gather them into suitable categories, omitting any that seem of little importance.

(b) What is the nature of each of your categories? How much weight should be placed on each of them? Which are most important? How have you come to this conclusion? On what criteria are your judgments based?

2.2.4   (c)   Decide how this weighting should be represented in the
contd   programme for a class, or indeed in a whole school, either
            by timetabling or by some other method of controlling
            emphasis. You may find it useful to consider the distinc-
            tion made by the Schools Council project team between
            aims concerned with knowledge, with skills and with
            qualities. See Ashton, Kneen and Davies (1975b, pp. 17-23)
            for the developmental areas into which the team grouped
            the aims.

2.2.5 This task is as appropriate for secondary teachers as for primary.
       Besides asking a large number of teachers to rate the importance
       of each of the 72 aims, the project team asked some subordin-
       ate questions, of which two are given below.

         A   Below are two fundamental purposes of primary educa-
             tion. Would you please indicate the relative weight you
             would give to each by sharing 5 points between the two
             statements. If you wish you can give 5 to one and 0 to
             the other.
             Please put the number you give to each statement in the
             appropriate box. Please use only whole numbers to make
             up the total of 5.
             1   The purpose of primary education is to begin to
                 equip the child with skills and attitudes which will
                 enable him to take his place effectively and compe-
                 tently in society, fitting him to make a choice of
                 an occupational role and to live harmoniously in
                 his community.   ☐
             2   The purpose of primary education is to foster the
                 development of the child's individuality and inde-
                 pendence enabling him to discover his own talents
                 and interests, find a full enjoyment of life in his
                 own way and arrive at his own attitudes towards
                 society.   ☐
         B   Primary education is concerned with various aspects of
             the child's development.
             Please indicate which you consider are:
             (a)   the two *most important* of these aspects by putting
                 an M in each of the two appropriate boxes;
             (b)   the two *least important* of these aspects by putting

2.2.5
contd

an L in each of the two appropriate boxes.

aesthetic	
emotional/personal	
intellectual	
moral	
physical	
social	
spiritual/religious	

These questionnaire items can be used as a basis for discussion by asking each member of the group to complete them in advance, and collating the results in time for the discussion. Members of the group can first be asked to justify the choices they made in item B. When this discussion has run its course, the members can be presented with an analysis of their choices, made in preparation for this part of the discussion (see Table 2.1).

TABLE 2.1   *Analysis of choices made in item B*

	Members who chose societal purpose		Members who chose individual purpose	
	Chosen as most important	*Chosen as least important*	*Chosen as most important*	*Chosen as least important*
Aesthetic				
Emotional/personal				
Intellectual				
Moral				
Physical				
Social				
Spiritual/religious				

The purpose of this analysis is to aid discussion of the hypothesis that teachers' rating of the importance of curriculum-areas is related to an underlying leaning towards societal or individual purposes. It would be useful to have available the

2.2.5 results of the Schools Council study for introduction into a
contd later stage of the discussion (see Ashton *et al.*, 1975a, p. 72).

A final focus for this activity would be to consider the
implications of such value differences for curriculum-planning
in schools. How can planning be carried on so as to accommodate differences in values from one teacher to another? If
teachers differ profoundly, is it a responsible solution to leave
each of them with individual responsibility for their pupils'
studies? Can professional autonomy be reconciled with educational justice? What should a headteacher do about balance in
the curriculum?

Subjects of the curriculum

It would be unrealistic to discuss the content of the school curriculum
without giving attention to the way in which the curriculum — especially in middle and secondary schools — is normally divided into
subjects. To understand a school's curriculum it is important both to
consider what teachers and other subject specialists say is the nature
of a subject, its boundaries and central concerns, and in comparison
with this to find out what actually goes on in lessons. We must also
give attention to subjects as groups of people with common beliefs and
interests, who are likely to collaborate in order to advance those interests. And this will bring us to the idea of integration, since this is
relevant both to what is taught and to the subject as an interest group.

It has already been indicated that Paul Hirst's writings about knowledge have not been directly concerned with subjects, but with more
abstract entities called 'forms of knowledge', which may or may not
relate to school subjects. (The seven forms are listed above on p. 102).
A form of knowledge in Hirst's definition consists of:

1   concepts proper to that 'form';
2   a logical network of relationships linking those concepts;
3   tests for truth — ways of determining the validity of a statement
    which are unique to the 'form'.

Hirst (1974) has illustrated the kinds of concept that he has in mind
in the first part of his definition; the 'form' concerned with empirical
knowledge, for example, depends upon concepts such as 'space', 'time',
'causality', and these essential or 'categorial' concepts give rise to·

109

'substantive' concepts such as 'photosynthesis' or 'atom'. Similarly, the form concerned with moral knowledge is based upon the categorial concepts 'good', 'right' and 'ought', and it has developed substantive concepts such as 'theft', 'pride' and 'humanity'. (It seems that without the *categorial* concepts the particular form of knowledge could hardly exist, whereas the existence of the *substantive* concepts is contingent upon particular historical contexts.)

Hirst has made it clear that we are not to expect school subjects to correspond to forms of knowledge. Some subjects he calls 'fields' because they contain within them a mixture of several 'forms': geography, for example, appears to combine empirical knowledge like that of physics with knowledge based on purposes and values as in history. In his later writings, Hirst suggests that subjects as they are taught in school — and indeed in universities — are all likely to contain divergent elements, and thus to qualify for the name of 'field'. 'Subjects of infinite variety may be composed under one banner', he writes.

What else might be part of a school subject, over and above the conceptual frameworks and tests for truth that Hirst directs attention to? Is there anything that he has omitted? Certainly there will be skills: indeed Hirst included skills in an earlier version of his definition of 'forms'. The role of physical skills in the various crafts, in physical education and in art and music is obvious enough, but physical skills recur elsewhere too. Let us not forget the importance of handling a pencil in early literacy, the use of mathematical instruments in several subjects, or practical laboratory skills in science. Judgment, too, has to be learnt. Pupils have to learn what constitutes an acceptable explanation, what can be taken for granted and what must be made explicit, what is relevant and what irrelevant, what constitutes a reasonable level of accuracy in subjects demanding measurement, and what constitutes 'sounding right' or 'looking right' in the arts and language studies. Such 'judgments' are probably based upon unstated criteria which pupils pick up intuitively from their teachers; it is indeed a kind of knowledge, but knowledge which is usually not made explicit in the form of propositions, which the teachers themselves may hardly be aware of, and which is learnt by pupils taking part in skilled purposive action.

One aspect of judgment is aesthetic judgment; his treatment of artistic experience is probably the least satisfactory aspect of Hirst's theory. He treats aesthetics as a form of knowledge but his critics, including Pring (1976a), have argued that works of art are not propositions. Indeed, we do not normally respond to a work of art such as a painting by believing or disbelieving it — as we might a statement in science or history — but by experiencing, re-enacting, interpreting, enjoying or evaluating it. To reduce all this to 'knowing that' is to misrepresent the nature of art.

What else is omitted in Hirst's stress upon knowledge that can be expressed as propositions that are either true or false? Teachers number attitudes and values amongst their aims. If a biology teacher believes that the study of biology fosters an appreciation of living things, is this appreciation part of the subject, biology? Though Hirst's definition would treat appreciation as an inessential accompaniment to biological knowledge, excluded by definition from the 'form' appropriate to the empirical sciences, from the teacher's viewpoint it is nevertheless part of the subject. Thus Hirst's treatment of knowledge, which excludes everything except propositions that may be true or false, constitutes a deep-seated challenge to most teachers' everyday way of thinking about the curriculum. Alternatively, it could be argued that Hirst's approach to knowledge is so abstract, so distant from the real world in which teaching takes place, that his logical analysis, though interesting, does not carry with it any obligation to teach differently. The weaknesses of Hirst's position are discussed by Richard Pring (1976a, ch. 2). For the practical purposes of curriculum analysis and planning it is undoubtedly necessary to take a view of curriculum that includes not only knowledge but skilled action upon the world, and such action includes skills, judgment, appreciation and purpose.

The foregoing is intended as a preliminary to the analysis of particular subjects in order to gain insight into what they consist of. Although it is secondary teachers who frequently see subjects as of central importance, they are also part of the primary-school teacher's world. Even in a school where the 'integrated day' holds sway, the teacher will be able to talk about young children's progress in 'number work' or in 'reading'. Thus all teachers may at times need to ask themselves precisely what a curriculum-area consists of, whether it be 'reading' for young children or 'science' in a middle school, or 'physics' in an upper school.

In any subject, or area of the curriculum, we can ask ourselves what the main activities are that are proper to that subject, or what one does in order to be a participant in it, either as an acolyte or as an expert. Let us take 'drama' as the subject in question, a subject which may prove on inspection to be neither simple or typical. A participant in

111

drama will presumably act, either in plays or in improvisations. Does it make any difference whether it is before an audience or not? Some people write plays: they too must surely be participants in drama. Other people participate by producing plays or designing sets and making them. Are these activities an essential part of drama or merely a support to play-writing and to acting? Dramatic critics do none of these things, but base their claim to expertise on their ability to analyse and evaluate plays and acting. Are they, too, no more than hangers-on? Questions such as these are highly controversial, even though they seem superficially to be no more than questions about how to use the word 'drama', a matter for conventional agreement. If the questions are answered they lead to defining and drawing a boundary round activities considered essential to drama, and this will be the first step in our analysis. If they are answered by someone in authority the answers may make a difference not only to the content of courses but to the status and careers of various specialists: no wonder that disagreements about the meaning of such words are hotly debated. A second step in the analysis of drama would be to take the concept 'acting' and analyse the knowledge and skills required by actors. (It would be a great deal more difficult to specify the knowledge and skills required by playwrights.) These two steps would constitute a method for constructing an account of a subject based upon participants' activities instead of upon a logical analysis of the knowledge proper to the subject and nothing else.

Tasks 2.3-2.3.4 include analyses of a particular subject. Even if you are not a specialist teacher you will be able to carry out some of the tasks in terms of a subject that you studied in college.

Task 2.3 Analysing a school subject

2.3   Carry out the following analyses of a subject that you know well. The questions are intended merely as a guide; they may be a poor fit to particular subjects.

2.3.1 If the subject you have chosen is based on knowledge, carry out a Hirstian analysis. This would include specifying some of its central concepts, discussing how they relate to one another, and showing what tests for truth are used. This will enable you to consider how close it is to a 'form of knowledge' in Hirst's sense. (You may find it useful to consult A. Brent, 1978, as parts of Chapter 3 would offer a basis for this task.)

2.3.2 On the basis of your answer to the previous task, how coherent and homogeneous is the body of knowledge you are dealing with? Do the concepts form a tightly interlinked network, or are they only loosely related? Are there separate networks within the subject? Does it depend on other forms of knowledge, such as mathematics? Did you find that one 'test of truth' was used, or several? Is it, like geography, a 'field' that combines the characteristics of several 'forms'? If so what holds the subject together in spite of this diversity? Do the logical subdivisions correspond to different groups of people each recommending their own version of the subject?

2.3.3 Alternatively, you can adopt a less idealised approach to the subject. (i) What are the essential activities which together constitute taking part in the subject? (This is the first step in the analysis suggested above.) At the same time you might make a note of those related activities which you considered but rejected as inessential.

(ii) What skills are required in each of the activities you have specified in answer to (i)? You may find that you have never asked yourself this question before, in spite of having often used the skills. I suggest that you should try not to fall back on the conventional phrases that you would use when talking with other specialists, but spell out your meaning so explicitly that a non-specialist could understand. You could even show it to a non-specialist. This task can be surprisingly difficult but is well worth doing; for a very sophisticated analysis of history along similar lines to these, see Coltham and Fines (1971).

2.3.4 What part is played by judgment in the subject you are analysing? Does aesthetic appreciation play any part in it? How can one tell the difference between a merely competent piece of work in the subject and a piece that is brilliant? What criteria would you judge it by? What conventional practices and rules of thumb mark the experienced participant off from the beginner? Are there any purposes and values that every teacher teaching the subject would be likely to share? And finally, how important are all these things? Are they essential to the subject or mere excrescences?

It is easy to fall into the habit of talking as if the particular subject that one is interested in has reached its definitive form with one's own generation, yet this is unlikely to be the case, since each subject seems to have gone through a historical evolution that shows no sign of halting. It is difficult to get access to this process of change since we cannot go back and experience the lessons of twenty or fifty years ago, and there is a sad shortage of accounts by contemporary observers. Several methods, none entirely satisfactory, can be suggested, and these constitute the next group of tasks.

Task 2.4 Analysing a school subject

2.4.1   Go to a journal concerned with the teaching of your subject. (In science this might be *School Science Review*, in English *Use of English*, and so on.)

First, look through last year's issues and note all the articles concerned with either (*a*) the content of the subject, or (*b*) teaching methods and learning activities. If you wish, it would be possible to confine your attention to a particular aspect — practical work in science, for example — or to concentrate on the subject at primary level. Read through all the relevant articles, making notes that will enable you to build up a picture of what is currently being recommended in the subject, and what issues are seen as controversial. Of course, one cannot take this picture to represent exactly what is going on in classrooms, since journal articles frequently present a somewhat idealised account of teaching in the interest of persuading others to adopt the writer's purposes and methods.

More difficult is to look beyond what is said in the articles to discover what is not said, what is so universally taken for granted in conversation or writing that it never gets on the agenda as an issue. (For example, in the 1940s and 1950s school geography was descriptive and regional; this was not a matter of debate, but of the nature of geography. It took a major theoretical upheaval in the subject to generate an alternative hypothetico-deductive approach, but for many years the possibility of an alternative was not conceived of nor conceivable.) It is easier to see what is taken for granted in subjects other than one's own, since part of learning to be a specialist is taking over the current agenda which tacitly determines what is taken for granted and what is open to debate.

Next, turn to the articles published in the journal at some

2.4.1 earlier period, perhaps twenty years before, and carry out a
contd similar analysis. It may prove easier to identify what was then
taken for granted, particularly if any issue has since become the
subject of debate. The eventual purpose of this task is to compare the two views of the subject and to trace the direction of
change.

2.4.2 A similar study can be carried out for a subject at secondary
level by analysing examination papers and syllabuses, and
examiners' reports, again comparing the pictures of the subject
at two different points in time. The results of this approach
may contrast sharply with the picture of the subject drawn from
'enlightened' articles in journals, yet for those older pupils who
take examinations this latter approach may give a more realistic picture of where the emphases fall in the teaching of a
subject.

2.4.3 You may feel that neither examination papers nor journal
articles give a fair picture of the realities of teaching a subject.
The only alternative is to interview teachers and if possible to
see them teaching, read their schemes of work, look through
pupils' written work, and to join in while pupils are working and
talk with them. Though time-consuming, such a study gives the
most complete view of a curriculum in action. It is difficult to
suggest focal issues for such a study, since issues differ from
subject to subject. (General advice about studies of curriculum
in action can be found on pp. 197-209 in Chapter 3.)

The above attempts to discover the state of a subject *de facto* should
not be confused with statements about what the subject *ought* to be.
If you have attempted any of the 2.3 group of tasks you may have
found yourself divided between describing what you know to be taught
in schools and what you think ought to be taught. An issue that has
recently come to the fore in curriculum study is the reason why there is
often a gap between teachers' ideal view of their teaching and what
they in fact do, a gap that many teachers are uneasily aware of. It
would be interesting to identify what concerns, constraints and pressures cause this to be so.

We have considered school subjects as bodies of knowledge that can
be analysed logically, and as groups of skills, judgments, attitudes and
values that can be described and identified. A subject can also be seen
as a group of human beings who have common interests and purposes,

and who collaborate to advance those purposes. In a secondary school, subject departments inevitably compete with one another for resources — money for books and equipment, time on the timetable, rooms — and also for pupils and graded posts. To understand subjects it is important to consider them both as bodies of knowledge and as groups of people with a common interest in advancing the claims of the subject. Both aspects of a subject are profoundly relevant to understanding what happens when there is an attempt to integrate, for example.

Task 2.5 Some social functions of school subjects

2.5.1   Here is an account of subjects written from the point of view of a sociologist of education, Frank Musgrove (1968).

> Within a school and within the wider society subjects are communities of people, competing and collaborating with one another, defining and defending their boundaries, demanding allegiance from their members and conferring a sense of identity upon them. They are bureaucracies, hierarchically organized, determining conditions of senior membership, establishing criteria for recruitment to different levels, disciplining their members through marks of recognition like honorary fellowships and admission to exclusive inner councils. Even innovation which appears to be essentially intellectual in character can be usefully examined as the outcome of social interaction and the elaboration of new rôles within the organization . . .
>
> We need to recognize . . . the function of subjects, particularly at their more advanced levels, in conferring a sense of identity. In middle and late adolescence, identification with a school subject must increasingly take the place of identification with an occupation. (Often, of course, but by no means invariably, the school subject has vocational implications.) The school curriculum teaches a pupil the kind of person he is.

(*a*)   Consider some examples drawn from your experience of subject teachers 'defending their boundaries', as Musgrove puts it. What are some likely results of this for the curriculum?

2.5.1   (*b*)   Musgrove writes of subjects 'conferring a sense of identity'.
contd   At what point in their education are *pupils* likely to
identify themselves with a particular subject? Is this true
of all boys and girls alike? When a pupil does identify himself or herself with one subject what happens to all the
others?

       (*c*)   In the first of the two paragraphs Musgrove seems to be
saying that subjects confer a sense of identity on teachers
too. Is this true, and if so what follows? What is the likely
effect on curriculum and curriculum change if a majority
of secondary-school teachers base both their career prospects and their sense of identity upon a curriculum subject?

       (*d*)   Are there any similar processes of commitment to subject-
areas in primary schools? What kinds of specialisation do
occur? Do these generate groups of people within the
school with different interests, or are staffs more homogeneous than in secondary schools? What is likely to be the
effect on curriculum-planning of (i) a homogeneous staff
of teachers with a general commitment to primary education; (ii) a staff divided into subgroups, each with a strong
commitment to a subject, and to the teaching of that
subject?

2.5.2   The purpose of this task is to explore some of the characteristics believed to differentiate school subjects. In order to do
this I shall ask you to rate a number of subjects for their possession of three qualities. You should award each subject from
one to five points according to whether they are low or high
in the quality in question. The qualities are as follows.

Classification.

This is a technical term which refers to the degree of separateness of this subject from others, including whether elements
from other subjects play a part in it, and whether integration
with other subjects can easily be carried out.

Framing.

This term refers to the degree of separateness of this subject
from everyday life, including whether it relates closely to the
everyday concerns of learners, and whether the informal know-
how of people who are not specialists in the subject would help
them to join in its thinking.

117

2.5.2   Status.

contd   Is the subject thought by teachers as a whole to be of high importance? (See Tasks 2.5.3 and 2.5.4 which are also concerned with status.)

Your ratings of each subject on a five-point scale can be entered under each of these headings in a table (see Table 2.2).

TABLE 2.2   *Teachers' ratings of subjects for their possession of the qualities: classification, framing and status*

Subject	Classification	Framing	Status
English			
Physics			
Geography			
General science			
Environmental studies			
Domestic science			
Another subject*			

* If you are a specialist teacher, please add your own subject here if it does not appear in the list.

The concepts 'classification' and 'framing' can be used in various ways to throw light on the role played by subjects in the organisation and control of curricular knowledge. These two concepts are drawn from a paper by Basil Bernstein (1971). The reader is invited to read the paper in order to check that the definitions given here do not misrepresent the concepts. You can test the following ideas against your own rating of the subjects in the table, or better still compare them with other people's.

(a) Bernstein says that classification and framing vary independently of one another. Does this seem to be true, or are those subjects which are very separate from one another also separate from everyday knowledge?

(b) Does either classification or framing seem to be related to

2.5.2
contd
the status of a subject? For example, do subjects which are closely and obviously related to the concerns of everyday life seem to be of high or low status?

(c) If several students are working together it would be enlightening to have the questions answered separately from the point of view of teachers in primary schools and in secondary schools. It is not unlikely that their answers to questions (a) and (b) will be quite different. Why is this so?

What makes one body of knowledge come to be more highly valued than another? Is science intrinsically superior to the humanities, or vice versa? Some people seem to think so, but it is hard to justify this on any grounds that the other party would appreciate. Is the study of Latin superior to crafts such as woodwork or cookery? The classical languages once characterised the curriculum followed by upper-class boys, but this is no argument for its intrinsic superiority. Philosophers of education such as Peters and Hirst have argued for the superiority of knowledge over skills, since they see the development of knowledge as the centre of human advancement. It might be suggested that it is the usefulness of knowledge that makes it valuable, but is this so? Many people save money and gain a certain pleasure from carrying out repairs and decorations in their own houses. Similarly, cookery is a part of everybody's daily life. Yet neither of these areas of handicrafts is a highly valued part of the curriculum, though the skills and knowledge necessary are undoubtedly very useful. (If one is in any doubt about a subject's status one can ask whether all students follow courses in it, and if not, which pupils do follow this subject.)

An alternative explanation for the relative value attributed to different bodies of knowledge would be that since knowledge — usually in written form — is used for testing success at school, those kinds of knowledge that are (a) obtainable only in schools, and are (b) open to pencil-and-paper testing are likely to be the most highly valued ones. The implication would be that practical know-how and intuitive ways of seeing things, which can be learnt from engaging in out-of-school activities in company with other people, would be little valued in schools, irrespective of its value in living. Is this explanation supported by experience? For example, are the same kinds of knowledge valued highly in primary as in secondary education? If not, this requires explanation.

119

TABLE 2.3 *Grades of post and grouped main subjects of study of full-time secondary teachers (as a percentage)*

Post	Education including physical education	Technical and handicraft	Agricultural and rural science	Science and mathematics	Geography, social science and commerce	Home economics	Language and literature	Arts and history	Music, drama and visual arts	All
Headteachers	1.19	0.87	2.70	4.89	5.96	–	7.44	7.18	1.85	5.02
	1.68	–	–	3.03	3.14	0.54	3.71	2.93	0.90	2.53
Deputy heads and heads of depts	28.56	27.52	26.10	39.19	34.43	–	37.49	34.35	29.27	34.66
	20.44	24.99	6.88	28.77	22.01	23.74	27.93	26.06	23.07	25.93
Graded posts	36.53	34.07	39.15	29.55	30.05	–	29.55	29.44	31.37	30.40
	30.52	24.99	17.20	26.27	27.64	25.55	27.61	28.08	25.68	26.18
Other assistant teachers	33.80	37.49	31.95	26.24	29.54	–	25.50	28.98	37.50	29.92
	47.04	50.00	75.68	41.94	47.42	50.39	40.69	42.52	50.37	45.36
Totals N =	841	1373	222	2964	1577	–	2392	1769	1189	9250
N =	712	28	58	1321	765	1107	1911	986	1110	6135

If the reader is at a loss to determine the status of a subject, here are some indicators.

(a) Do other teachers see it as 'hard' or 'easy'?
(b) How much of a pupil's time is spent on this subject in comparison with others?
(c) Is the headteacher willing to interrupt lessons in that subject in order to release pupils for other activities?

Task 2.5 contd Some social functions of school subjects

2.5.3 Add further indicators of the status of subjects to the above list.
2.5.4 The information in Table 2.3 was extracted by Dennis Warwick from the Department of Education and Science publication *Statistics of Education* (1968) and shows the percentages of secondary teachers who, having studied particular subjects at college or university, had by 1965 become headteachers, deputy heads or heads of departments, had received graded posts, or had remained ungraded (see Warwick, 1974.) In each cell of the table, the upper number refers to men and the number below it to women teachers.
    (a) If you are ambitious for promotion in secondary schools in England and Wales what subject should you study? Is it the same for the opposite sex? How do you account for the differences between subjects?
    (b) What effects (if any) are the preferences implied in these figures likely to have upon the curriculum, including pupils' choices and the competition for resources?

Integrating the curriculum

Since the early 1960s there has been lively discussion in schools — at least in the United Kingdom — about whether all or various parts of the curriculum should be integrated, and about the merits of different ways of doing this. Sometimes it has been asserted that subject boundaries are entirely arbitrary, the results of chance development during history; this approach rejects as irrelevant the kind of logical analysis which Hirst's forms of knowledge exemplify. Other advocates of integration accept that there are logical differences between kinds of knowledge, but put forward arguments for organising some parts of the curriculum in ways that cut across subject boundaries. Hirst has indicated that in his view the demonstration that there are logical differences between forms of knowledge should not be interpreted as in itself an argument against integrated curricula: his analysis is concerned with the goals of education, whereas decisions about the means of attaining these goals — including the way the curriculum is organised — must be based as much upon pedagogical considerations as upon those related to the nature of knowledge.

Integration in schools has two aspects, one concerned with the organising of knowledge and the other with the organising of time. Many primary schools set out to offer to their pupils an 'integrated day'. This kind of integration is certainly concerned with time: children can, if the teacher permits, pursue a piece of work for hours or even days until it is completed. Yet an integrated day does not necessarily imply the integration of knowledge, since it is possible for each piece of work to be concerned with one area of the curriculum, one perhaps involving the reading of a story, another a practical inquiry into a scientific matter, and so on. Nevertheless, an integrated day does make it possible for teachers to integrate knowledge if they wish to do so.

Attempts to integrate knowledge in secondary schools have tended not to be far-reaching. Frequently they have amounted to no more than amalgamating the chemical, physical and biological sciences into one science, or a group of arts subjects into something called 'humanities'. Such integration has frequently not included older secondary pupils preparing for higher-status examinations such as GCE O and A levels, and has thus been confined to younger pupils or to those whose level of achievement makes them unlikely to be GCE candidates. Thus integrated curricula have often been seen as of lower status, suited only to those pupils incapable of the full rigours of academic study. An interesting exception to this is to be found in the Schools Council Integrated Science Project's course. The provision of an O-level examination explicitly linked to the Integrated Science Project course has made it possible to offer an integrated science course to more able pupils, though this course remains the object of suspicion and opposition from many teachers, parents and university scientists.

In appraising proposals for integration it is important to be clear what faults have been attributed to the traditional organisation of the curriculum in subjects, since it is these faults that integration is to alleviate. Richard Pring (1976b) has listed eleven criticisms that have been made of the subjects curriculum. Particularly important items from his list are given below.

(*a*) Insufficient account is taken of the interests of the pupils, and thus of what motivates them.
(*b*) Insufficient account is taken of their previous experiences, level of understanding, local environment and community.
(*d*) There is inability to accommodate practical and interdisciplinary concerns such as careers advice, sex education or current affairs.
(*g*) Links between subject-matters are not made, and there is little support of one subject by another.

The first two of these arguments took on a particular importance in 1972 when the raising of the school-leaving age faced teachers with large numbers of older pupils whose earlier school experiences had often not left them with a great enthusiasm for the traditional curriculum. Integrated courses, especially in humanities, made it possible to offer to these pupils courses which looked different from the subjects they had previously studied, and to involve them in a wider range of activities which appeared to be related to their probable concerns after leaving school. Thus integrated courses seemed to offer to secondary teachers a promising way of dealing with the pressing problem of older pupils' attitudes to school.

The other two arguments quoted above − (*d*) and (*g*) − can help us to understand the movement which produced the Schools Council Integrated Science Project course. Its advocates hold that the division of science into physics, chemistry and biology exaggerates differences between them, failing to do justice either to the conceptual links between the sciences or to the scientific method which they have in common. Moreover, some science teachers have come to believe that to teach science without dealing with the social and moral implications of topics such as nuclear fission or environmental pollution would be to misrepresent the world in an irresponsible fashion. To bring moral issues into the physical sciences is integration indeed, and it still remains to be seen how far even the innovative science teachers who adopted the Integrated Science Project have succeeded in integrating two such diverse forms of knowledge. This example, however, admirably illustrates the 'practical and interdisciplinary concerns' that the subject curriculum has often failed to accommodate.

It is far from easy to conduct a discussion of integration solely in terms of the benefits and losses of interrelating subject-matter. The way a teacher thinks about the curriculum is inevitably influenced by what he or she has studied, by the conversation of other teachers with similar concerns, and by the activities upon which his or her self-respect depends. The arguments brought forward to support or oppose integration will inevitably be deeply involved in their proponents' past experience and future hopes. We must keep this in mind when a secondary-school chemistry teacher says that he does not know enough biology to teach third-year integrated science. Something similar will be true of the opinions of any primary or middle-school teacher who takes over all the French teaching, or accepts special responsibility for the planning of mathematics, or takes a pride in success with withdrawal groups for remedial reading. This does not, of course, invalidate their opinions. It is well to listen for unspoken assumptions and commitments in all educational debate; in discussions of integrated curricula it is particularly important.

Richard Pring (1976a) suggests that there are four distinct kinds of ways of integrating curricula. They are presented here with a commentary which partly summarises Pring's analysis, and partly makes points of my own (with which he may not agree).

Integration in correlating distinct subject-matters

When integration of this kind takes place, it is taken for granted that the two subjects are different and separate from one another. Nevertheless, one may, in part, depend upon another. One cannot go far in science, for example, without using mathematics, even if it is no more complex than counting examples of a phenomenon. A large part of the curriculum depends upon the use of language. Pring mentions other examples, one being the technological knowledge that is needed for an understanding of urbanisation.

Integration through themes, topics and ideas

At first glance this seems an intellectually ambitious form of integration, since it seems to necessitate a search for principles and concepts which are not bound to one subject but are inclusive enough to unite diverse subject-matters and thus offer alternative ways of organising knowledge. Such overarching principles are not easy to find, and many integrated curricula settle for a looser linking of subject-matter on a less rigorous basis. Topic headings that have been used include: Power, Water, Christmas, Colour, and Contrasts. A topic such as Christmas seems likely to offer no more than an occasion to link a range of different activities — painting, acting, writing, reading, music-making, and so on — without uniting them at the conceptual level. There is nothing wrong with this — teachers clearly find such topics convenient — but we must not confuse this with integration in a more profound sense. Is 'power' in history the same as 'power' in technology? If not, can power be seen as an overarching principle? 'Contrasts' might indeed be applied to any body of knowledge, but what would be gained by putting side by side contrasts from history, art, physical science and literature? This can be no serious proposal for integrating subject-matters. One begins to wonder whether overarching principles can be found, or whether all such integration is merely a loose assembly of materials, ideas and activities beneath a convenient heading.

Sometimes secondary schools display a variant of this which might be called 'co-ordination' rather than 'integration'. After a key lesson on a topic, such as Industry, pupils divide into classes and are taught by specialist teachers who give them quite separate lessons on topics related to the key lesson, such as the history of local industry, the geographical dispersal of industry through the world, mathematics based upon industrial data, and art work related to industrial scenes. In a case like this there is likely to be little or no attempt to find common ground beyond the tenuous link provided by the concept 'industry'.

The discussion of this second category suggested by Pring has brought us to the point where we can subdivide it into three versions: (*a*) activities and material loosely linked by a topic; (*b*) specialisms co-ordinated by a common topic but taught separately; (*c*) subject-matter closely integrated through overarching principles (if they exist).

Integration in practical thinking

Pring explains: 'There are areas of practical living (e.g. relations between the sexes, living in a multiracial society, making sense of violence and war, living within a democracy) which require understanding and judgment as well as values', so this kind of integration

125

seems particularly well-based in theory. It has already been mentioned that in some parts of the course developed by the Schools Council Integrated Science Project, social and moral issues are explored in relation to the scientific and technological knowledge upon which understanding of these issues depends; this well illustrates this third category of integration.

Integration in the learner's own interested inquiry

This fourth kind of integration has played an important role in the rationale put forward to justify the integrated day in infant and junior schools, and has been taken up in a modified form by the advocates of interdisciplinary inquiry in middle and secondary schools. The underlying idea is that the activities which a child is most likely to learn from are those which arise from the concerns which give shape to his current view of the world, the problems he regards as important and the questions he wants answered. As his view of the world is unlikely to be split up into forms of knowledge – except in the retrospective analysis of philosophers – the issues he pursues will be interdisciplinary, and lead to the development of general intellectual and other abilities relevant to a range of subject-matter. So runs the argument; the truth of it would require empirical investigation, for no philosopher can tell us this on the basis of a logical analysis alone.

It may be noted, however, that these issues chosen by the boy or girl would presumably be integrated, if they were integrated, in precisely the same manner as the 'integration in practical thinking' which has just been described. The difference between the two seems more a matter of who decides than of the basis upon which integration takes place.

It seems important that practising teachers should be aware of differences between various versions of curriculum integration that may be under discussion in their schools. To analyse proposals for integration it is possible to use Pring's categories, though I am here proposing some modifications.

1 Integration in correlating distinct subject-matters.
2 Integration through themes, topics or ideas:
    (*a*) through loose focus of activities on a topic;
    (*b*) separate specialisms co-ordinated by a common topic;

(c) subject-matters closely integrated through overarching principles.
3   Integration in practical thinking.
4   Integration in the learner's interested inquiry.
5   Integration in name only, subject-matter remaining effectively separate.

Many of the tasks which follow are designed to give experience of using these categories. In practice you will find that the division between each of them is far from clear-cut, so you will need to make your own decision how to apply them in particular cases.

Task 2.6 Differentiating forms of curriculum integration

2.6.1   When you go to observe teaching in a classroom which is said to exemplify an 'integrated day' make a note of all the activities in which you see pupils engaged. Go through the notes later in order to decide: (i) which activities cross subject boundaries and which do not (or Hirst's forms of knowledge — p. 102 — can be used instead of subjects); and (ii) what links have been made by the teacher between one area of knowledge and another.

2.6.2   Collect the themes that are customarily used by teachers in a number of schools, including if possible primary, middle and secondary schools. Using the list based on Pring, decide into which category each theme seems likely to fall. In some cases you will need further information before you can decide. Why is this?

2.6.3   If you turn to Appendix D you will find a scheme of work for use in a secondary school, entitled 'The 97 bus'. The questions that follow here are intended to guide you in considering the value of the scheme.
   (a) For what pupils does this scheme seem to be intended? Is this relevant to understanding and evaluating it?
   (b) How far is the content intended to be integrated?
   (c) Can you identify any overarching principles?
   (d) What role are the pupils' interests to play in selecting the material to be studied?
   (e) Is the subject-matter held together by a practical social issue?

127

2.6.3 (f) Which of Pring's categories best describes this proposal?

contd (g) Is there anything in the course that could not find a place in geography or environmental studies, or some other subject of the curriculum?

(h) What virtues and faults do you find in this proposal?

2.6.4 There now follows a group of four extracts which outline activities, courses or approaches which involve some degree of integration, all intended for secondary-school pupils. The first of these is a summary of all the curriculum units which the Schools Council Integrated Studies Project (1972) at the University of Keele planned to publish in order to exemplify their views about integrated courses. As far as you can tell from this (deliberately) limited information, what kind or kinds of integration are proposed? (It would be useful thereafter to consider the same question in the light of the published materials, if copies can be obtained.)

TABLE 2.4 *Schools Council Integrated Studies Project: Curriculum units*

First stage units: published
(Suitable for use in middle schools, but specifically aimed at the first three years of secondary schools.)

Title	Subject interest	Outline
Exploration man	Whole range of 'humanities'	This unit has a double interest: people finding out, and finding out about people. It begins by asking pupils to use senses to explore the immediate environment and to learn about themselves and other people. This leads to looking at different school subjects as specific tools of enquiry. Finally possible ways of grouping subjects and using them co-operatively are considered. The stress is on concrete examples and pupils' own activities.

Title	Subject interest	Outline
Communicating with others	Expressive arts	The unit explores the range of ways by which men can communicate with each other (words, gestures and sound, form, line, colour), and continually relates human expression to the different social contexts in which it takes place. Among the issues raised are: problems of communication; children's own development of language; the history of writing, and the inter-relation of the arts in an historical period. Stress is placed on pupils undertaking linguistic fieldwork.

Living together	Social sciences	This unit aims at developing pupils' insights into man's social organisation through comparisons between four different communities:
		    Their own — a 20th century industrialised society
		2 Two island societies:
		    (*a*) the inhabitants of Tristan da Cunha
		    (*b*) the Dayaks of Borneo
		3 Imperial China — an 'historical civilisation'
		In each case, comparisons are focussed on homes, family, education, law and order, work and leisure, beliefs. Throughout there is a concern to introduce pupils to the basic concepts and working methods of the social sciences.

Second stage units
(Suitable for use in the fourth form, but also of value in senior forms as well as in colleges of further education.)

Title	Subject interest	Outline
Development in West Africa	Any subjects which can illuminate the life of another society	This unit brings a number of explanatory frameworks to the understanding of a complex society very different in its values and life-styles from the pupils' own, as well as its history and ecology. The theme of 'development' relates West Africa to the problems facing the 'Third World'. Most of the support material focusses on Ghana and Nigeria.
Groups in society	Centred in the social sciences, but exploits a number of bridging out opportunities	This unit scrutinises the problem of groups which are disturbingly different from the society of which they are part, whether in ideas or in their life-styles. After exploring the situation in modern Britain, the unit focusses on a number of case studies, for example: Gypsies; Jews and their history; American examples.
Man made man	A wide range of opportunities, especially for the arts and technology	This unit is based on a double consideration: (a) Man is continually re-making and recording his own image in an attempt to understand the human situation. (b) Man has a growing ability to manipulate the materials of his environment and to extend and amplify his capacities. These themes are seen to interlink, and are explored through a range of image-

Title	Subject interest	Outline
		clusters, e.g. The Hero and the Enemy, The Masks of God, Man and Machine.

2.6.5   These paragraphs are extracted from an early article by Lawrence Stenhouse about the intentions of the Humanities Curriculum Project (1968). Taken in conjunction with the principles of procedure listed in Task 1.13.2 (p. 62) it should enable you to identify the kind of integration that the project was committed to.

> If we wish students to be able adequately to meet important human issues, these issues must themselves be the stuff of the curriculum. We must deal in areas where complex and informed decisions ought to be made by almost everyone. Such topics as family relationships, relations between the sexes, the position of adolescents in society, problems of war and peace and racial prejudice seem immediately to establish a claim to attention. Others, such as law and order, power and ambition, living in cities or human dereliction, though perhaps less compelling, seem to offer rich possibilities. Topics such as transport, water or local government seem difficult to justify in a humanities curriculum; they are derived from a different logic, perhaps that associated with the teaching of the conventional school subjects across disciplines on a project or enquiry base. Moreover, they raise too few issues of value, and deal rather in facts and techniques.
>
> Areas of study should have an internal logical coherence, and should not be based on casual associations. Thus, the juxtaposition of political power and power as energy in the physical sense is unsatisfactory, as is the association of irrigation, boiling kettles, swimming and water on the knee in a unit on 'water'. Themes should probably seem inevitable, rather than clever. All areas of study selected for a humanities course should lead students not only to a consideration

131

2.6.5
contd
of human behaviour in an objective frame of reference, but also to an imaginative sympathy with subjective human experience.

Given the enquiry base, and the difficulties it presents, we believe that the best chance of developing a core tradition of disciplined teaching lies in the exploration of the possibilities opened up by a type of discussion which is not so much an exchange of views as an interpretation of evidence. We start therefore from a model of the classroom situation in which the input of information comes not through the teacher, but through materials which demand critical interpretation. We hope that the close interpretation of evidence can strengthen and stiffen discussion so as to provide a group experience which is a firm centre for an enquiry-based approach. That established, we can explore the possibilities offered by individual and group investigations which feed into discussion, and various types of pupils' work which can develop out of it.

Collection of material will be selected and edited for the use of development schools. The collections will include factual prose, maps, statistical tables, diagrams, fictional prose, poetry, drama, photographs, reproductions of paintings, cartoons and tape-recordings. Such collections will constitute banks of material on which the teachers can draw as they embark upon this style of teaching; but they are banks which ask for further deposits of materials found by the teachers themselves. They will provide the teacher with resources for experimentation, opening up a range of possibilities rather than confining.

2.6.6 These five 'model' examination questions were used to inform secondary pupils about the kind of work they would be involved in if they chose a CSE course called 'environmental studies'. What does the nature of this area of study seem to be?

Question 1
(a) Give examples to show that lead mining was once an important industry in the Dales, using sketches to help

2.6.6
contd

your answer.

(b) How was the lead mined? How was it prepared? How was it smelted?

(c) On the map provided mark areas of production.

(d) What kind of mining or quarrying is important today? Choose one type of quarrying and explain the methods used, the type of stone quarried and the uses it is put to.

(e) On the map mark the position of two important quarries.

Question 2

Explain carefully with diagrams:

(a) *either*

a method of surveying a cave or mine;

or

a method of surveying a piece of open country which you cannot cross on foot.

(b) What is meant by triangulation? What is the practical application of triangulation to the Ordnance Survey?

Question 3

Here is a set of figures from the weather station.

Figures

Barometer
Maximum temperature
Minimum temperature
Humidity
Rainfall
Cloud type
Cloud cover

(a) Give all the information you can about the weather for this day, including a guess at what kind of pressure conditions are general over Britain.

(b) What time of year is it (give reasons)?

(c) What sort of forecast would you give for a short time ahead?

(d) What contrasts would you notice if you left S— to go and live in:

(i) Bridlington;

(ii) Penzance?

2.6.6
contd

Question 4

What headings would you use in setting out a farm study?
Write a brief account of the layout and economy of a farm
known to you, giving an idea of the relative importance of
crops, pasture and livestock of all types.
Would it make sense to turn farms in certain parts of the
Dales into recreation parks for city dwellers?

Question 5

How would you set about the study of settlement in a small
area? Give examples.
What importance do we give to the words *form* and *function*?
How was our part of the Dales settled?
What contribution did each group of settlers make?

2.6.7 The following piece of work appears in a textbook. Does it seem
to be part of an integrated course, and if so what is the nature of
the integration?

Fluoride ions and dental health

In the first half of this century an interesting pattern was
observed in the United States and the United Kingdom.
Dentists had discovered that children born and brought up
in areas where the local water supply contained small
amounts of dissolved calcium fluoride had 50 to 60 per cent
less tooth decay than those brought up in areas where the
water contained hardly any dissolved calcium fluoride.
Although calcium fluoride is almost insoluble in water that
which does dissolve forms the ions of calcium and fluoride.
It was found that as little as one part per million of fluoride
ions in the water was sufficient to produce the pattern.

In 1953 a long-term investigation was started in the cities
of Tiel and Culemborg in the Netherlands. The aim was to
test the pattern. For 10½ years fluoride was added to the
water supply of Tiel but not to that of Culemborg. Before,
during and after this investigation the amount of tooth
decay in children of 11 to 15 years of age was measured.
What results would you expect? Do the results of the investigation confirm your prediction? What was the purpose of
including Culemborg in the study?

134

2.6.7
contd

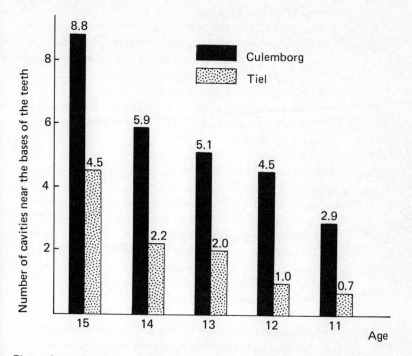

Figure 2.1   *Comparison of amount of tooth decay in children living in Tiel and Culemborg, Netherlands*

In Britain three areas have been studied in a similar way — Watford, Kilmarnock and a part of Anglesey. After five years of fluoridation of the water supply the percentage of children who had ten or more decayed teeth at the age of five was reduced from 15 per cent to 2 per cent.

Studies all over the world have had similar results. In 1962, on the basis of these studies, the then Ministry of Health recommended to all Local Authorities that they should add fluoride ions to the water supply if the levels were naturally very small.

In many areas, however, this provoked considerable outcry from the public and local councillors. These are some of the reasons:

2.6.7
contd

1 Concern that fluoridation may cause ill-health.
2 Concern that fluoridation causes flecks of white on the enamel surface of teeth.
3 Concern that fluoridation is 'mass medication' with a loss of personal liberty by compelling people to have fluoride and concern that decisions of such matters should be left to individuals and not taken on their behalf.

The following answers have been given:

1 There is no evidence despite extensive research that fluorides are a cause of ill-health. The following remarks have been made:

> All the established evidence supports the safety of fluoridation although, from the very nature of the problems . . . we can never prove that there are no harmful effects whatever. The evidence does show, however, that if there are any undesirable effects they must be very rare and very mild or they would have been detected by now. . . . The unquestionable benefits of fluoridation greatly outweigh the . . . possibility of mild and rare harmful effects.

2 Fluoridation (sufficient to produce a significant reduction in tooth decay) can produce some white flecks in the enamel of teeth. Surveys suggest, however, that in non-fluoride areas problems with the enamel surface of the teeth were far more widespread than in fluoride areas.
3 In any community should there be a small sacrifice of personal liberty for the general good?

What are your views and feelings?

2.6.8 Try to invent a framework for integrating diverse subject-matter which would genuinely provide overarching principles.

2.6.9 Curriculum theory can itself be seen as an integrated curriculum, in that its advocates have sought to help teachers to take informed action by utilising conceptual schemes from psychology, philosophy and sociology. Refer to a standard text (for example, Stenhouse, or Kelly, or Lawton *et al.*) and consider what kind of integration has been achieved. For example, what overarching principles, if any, are currently in use by curriculum theorists?

2.6.10 Nine biology teachers in nine secondary schools were asked whether their older pupils could cope with the mathematics needed by new approaches to biology (Norris, 1973). One teacher said that they could; the others mentioned difficulties in the following areas.

TABLE 2.5 *Topics of mathematics presenting difficulty to pupils studying a new biology course*

Topic	Number of teachers mentioning difficult topic
Graphs	1
Ratio	4
Percentage	4
Negative numbers	3
Rate of change	3
Area	5
Power notations	1
Basic manipulative skills	6

(a) Does this amount to a case for changing the mathematics course, or for changing the biology course, or neither?

(b) Whose business is it to teach the mathematics needed for biology, or for that matter the English needed for biology? On what basis can you decide?

(c) Do these questions relate to integration or not?

2.6.11 Basil Bernstein (1971) in a much-quoted paper distinguishes a 'collection code' — the organisation of the curriculum in traditional subjects — from an 'integrated code'. In the following passage he is considering the organisational consequences of these codes, and especially the difference they make to the distribution of power.

Where knowledge is regulated through a collection code, the knowledge is organized and distributed through a series

137

2.6.11
contd

of well-insulated subject hierarchies. Such a structure points to oligarchic control of the institution, through formal and informal meetings of heads of department with the head or principal of the institution. Thus, senior staff will have strong horizontal work relationships (that is, with their peers in other subject hierarchies) and strong vertical work relationships within their own department. However, junior staff are likely to have only vertical (within the subject hierarchy) allegiances and work relationships.

The allegiances of junior staff are vertical rather than horizontal for the following reasons. First, staff have been socialized into strong subject loyalty and through this into specific identities. These specific identities are continuously strengthened through social interactions within the department and through the insulation between departments. Second, the departments are often in a competitive relationship for strategic teaching resources. Third, preferment within the subject hierarchy often rests with its expansion. Horizontal relationships of junior staff (particularly where there is no effective participatory administrative structure) is likely to be limited to non-task based contacts. There may well be discussion of control problems ('X of 3b is a — how do you deal with him?' or 'I can't get X to write a paper'). Thus the collection code within the framework of oligarchic control creates for senior staff strong horizontal and vertical based relationships, whereas the work relationships of junior staff are likely to be vertical and the horizontal relationships limited to non-work-based contacts. This is a type of organizational system which encourages gossip, intrigue and a conspiracy theory of the workings of the organization, as both the administration and the acts of teaching are invisible to the majority of staff.

Now the integrated code will require teachers of different subjects to enter into social relationships with each other which will arise not simply out of non-task areas, but out of a shared, co-operative, educational task. The centre of gravity of the relationship between teachers will undergo a radical shift. Thus, instead of teachers and lecturers being divided and insulated by allegiances to

2.6.11
contd
subject hierarchies, the conditions for their unification exists through a common work situation. I suggest that this changed basis of the relationships, between teachers or between lecturers, may tend to weaken the separate hierarchies of collection. These new work-based horizontal relationships between teachers and between lecturers may alter both the structure and distribution of power regulated by the collection code. Further, the administration and specific acts of teaching are likely to shift from the relative invisibility to visibility.

(a) Does this account correspond to your experience in schools?
(b) What difference does it make to these processes if it is a primary, middle or secondary school?
(c) Why does Bernstein place such emphasis on 'visibility'?
(d) How are shifts of power over the curriculum likely to show themselves?
(e) Which kinds of integration are likely to offer a serious challenge to the 'subject hierarchies' and which not?

2.6.12 **A simulation exercise in curriculum-planning**
This exercise was originally planned for a course attended by secondary-school heads of department. It can be adapted for use by teachers in primary or middle schools if course members take on the role of teachers responsible for particular curriculum-areas, and write as if advising colleagues about what contribution that area could make to integrated work.

You have been appointed as a senior member of staff to a new mixed comprehensive 13-16 high school (1,400 pupils). You will represent your subject/faculty area on a planning committee that is about to meet to make basic proposals for the first-year curriculum which is to be 'diagnostic' without that term having been clearly defined. Your headmaster has laid down the following structure for that year. Half of the time available (20 periods) will be devoted to work in six 'faculties': mathematics, science, social and humane studies, English and languages, design and craft, physical education. This part of the curriculum will be planned by each faculty separately, and is not part of this exercise. The remainder of

2.6.12
contd
the time (20 periods) is to be devoted to what the headmaster calls 'shared time'. He has provided you with the list of principles which you will find below, and invited each member of the planning committee to draft a short informal set of notes about how that member's faculty wishes to have the shared time organised, and what content, skills, and general objectives they would wish to have represented in it. (The headmaster has also made it known that he thinks that schools have not so far made flexible enough application of the possible uses of resource materials.) These sets of notes will be circulated to other members of the planning committee to be read before the first meeting, and will form the bases for your initial negotiations.

The following principles are laid down by the headmaster.

1 A variety of teaching-learning relationships and forms of organisation should be provided.

2 Any learning materials should encourage a range of activities, skills and cognitive and other processes.

3 Basic skills and essential knowledge learnt in 'faculty' time should be used and applied in 'shared' time.

4 Tasks provided should have intrinsic interest and relevance to the environment of the school.

5 The goals of each piece of work should be made explicit to pupils, or by the pupils.

6 The learning activities offered to each pupil should match his or her personal needs and welfare.

In the simulation, you are required to write in advance a set of notes (about 350 words) for circulation which represents the initial contribution of your subject/faculty to the discussion. When you have read one another's notes, you will then constitute the committee which is to make the first steps in planning. You should aim by the end of the discussion to have arrived at sufficient consensus to prepare an overhead-projector transparency that will present to the headmaster and to the rest of the first-year staff the essential structure of your provisional proposals.

Analysing a school's curriculum documents

We now turn back to the curriculum of the school as a whole. It is useful to collect from a school all the documents which embody some kind of statement about the curriculum. When asked to find such documents teachers often doubt whether such things exist and then find a wide range of them. Syllabuses first spring to mind, but there is also the school timetable, various advisory and discussion documents addressed by the head or another senior teacher to colleagues, brochures, letters and information sheets addressed to parents especially when curriculum choices need to be made, examination papers, checklists and tests for monitoring achievement. Documents of this kind can be analysed in order to draw forth the declared intentions of teachers in the school, though they sometimes give other unintended information to the attentive reader.

The materials for the next task comprise a set of syllabuses drawn up by senior teachers in a middle school for children of 9-13 years; these are reproduced as Appendix E. I suggest that in reading these syllabuses you should imagine that you have just been appointed to the school as a teacher of general subjects to the 10 to 11-year-old age-group. You have been sent this bundle of syllabuses so that during the holiday before you take up the post you can familiarise yourself with school policies and carry out some preliminary planning. The questions that follow suggest some of the issues that might occur to you while reading the syllabuses with the need to plan your first month's lessons in mind. You will probably be expected to teach in most, if not all, parts of the curriculum.

Task 2.7 Analysing a school's curriculum documents

2.7.1 (a) How is this middle school's curriculum structured?
      (b) Which of the syllabuses contain each of the following:
          a statement of general aims?
          a list of topics or content to be covered?
          a set of objectives?
          a list of skills to be mastered?
          learning activities and/or teaching methods?
          methods for monitoring and evaluation?
      (c) How useful would you expect to find the statements of
          general aims in planning lessons? What would they help

2.7.1   you to decide?

contd (*d*) The English, religious education and history teachers have chosen distinctly different methods of presenting curricula. Which would you expect to find more helpful. Why is this?

(*e*) Why do so few of the syllabuses specify teaching methods or suggest learning activities? Why do you think some teachers have chosen to do so and some not? Where suggestions have been made, do you think they would prove useful to a teacher new to the school?

(*f*) What is the purpose or purposes of a syllabus anyway? Which of these syllabuses would fulfil these purposes? Which seems to do it best?

(*g*) What is your overall impression of the school and its curriculum on the basis of this admittedly quite inadequate evidence? Have you done well in accepting a post there?

2.7.2   Collect all the current syllabuses from a school — perhaps the one in which you are teaching permanently or on teaching practice — and carry out an analysis based on the questions in Task 2.7.1.

2.7.3   Collect from a school all the curriculum-related documents other than syllabuses and read through them noting any evidence you can find about the school's view of teaching and the curriculum, and the relative importance of various aspects of these.

Life skills as a basis for the curriculum

If one talks with a number of teachers from different kinds of schools about the curriculum it rapidly becomes clear that they differ from one another not only in their relative emphasis on education for conformity as against independence, but also — quite separately from this — in the relative emphasis which they place upon academic knowledge and the skills needed in everyday life. At the 'academic' end of the scale, teachers would give priority to learning in subject-areas, while at the other end there would be a greater emphasis on the skills, attitudes, information and know-how that are likely to be useful in everyday life. Of course, there is learning which is both academic and clearly relevant to everyday life: learning to read is both a necessary ability for academic purposes and highly prized in our very literate society. Nevertheless, in some other parts of the curriculum, academic and everyday goals may appear to be mutually exclusive. For example, 15-year-olds who are due to leave school at the end of the year with minimal qualifications are likely to perceive history, English literature and even mathematics as irrelevant to their concerns. They may value typewriting or handicraft more highly, but even this is likely to depend on job opportunities in the area. Similarly, in special education — and probably in relation to the curriculum for remedial classes too — there has been a long-standing debate about the relative importance to be given to literacy and numeracy as against the goal of helping young people of low academic ability to be competent and self-sufficient in their everyday lives. The former emphasis leads to a great deal of repetitive practice for pupils who already have a history of failure; the latter to spending school time on activities such as catching buses or doing shopping.

I have presented the conformity-independence dimension and the academic-everyday dimension as if they were simply characteristic of teachers' attitudes and quite independent of what school the teachers work in, or which courses they teach. Nevertheless, it is very likely that teachers' attitudes relate quite closely to the particular groups of pupils that they are concerned with, or the subjects that they teach. A secondary-school teacher concerned mainly with the teaching of less able older pupils may over the years move away from emphasising the importance of the knowledge that he himself learnt in college towards an insistence that the curriculum should be 'relevant' to pupils' concerns. This change can come quite naturally as he comes to see the issue through his pupils' eyes, and finds out what curriculum content helps him to manage classes of unenthusiastic young people. Whether or not this is the way in which teachers' perspectives take shape, it is undoubtedly true that those who plan the curriculum have to make decisions which eventually determine how much emphasis is placed upon life skills or upon more obviously academic goals.

If one takes the view that schooling should prepare children for their future lives — and this is perhaps the most frequent justification for schooling — what one does about it is not obvious. No particular curriculum prescription is entailed by this view, since its meaning depends upon the answer to a second question about the kinds of lives that pupils will lead. The truth is that in no individual case can we answer this question. Indeed, it could be argued that no teacher *should* try to answer the question for any particular pupil, since by predicting a particular future the teacher probably makes it more likely to occur. A child may not be doing very well in school at the moment, but can we be sure that there will not come a time when he needs French or German? Another child may show no interest in science, yet no one, not her parents nor the teacher who knows her well, can say that there will never be a time when a grounding in science will not be of value to her. And this utilitarian argument ignores the further possibility that some day these children may wish to learn languages or science purely for pleasure; certainly many people in later life take up interests in music or art. In sum, it appears improper to base a curriculum upon a prediction of a child's future way of life, yet at the same time many teachers find themselves doing just this. The dilemma is at its most crucial when a school proposes a 'community curriculum', a curriculum that is focused upon the concerns and way of life of the working-class community from which the pupils come and in which, it is thought, they are likely to spend their adult lives.

If it is improper to base a curriculum upon predictions of the future lives of individuals or groups of pupils, it may nevertheless be possible to identify skills, knowledge and attitudes that all pupils will need because they will all be living in an industrialised, Western, English-speaking community. In the 1930s and 1940s there were a number of attempts in the United States to analyse the life skills needed by all members of the community in order to base a curriculum upon them. For various reasons they made little mark in this country, and they have since been largely discredited in the United States. Such an approach is directly in conflict with the subject curriculum, which is supported by tradition and the examination system, and thus plays an important part in directing young people to their future careers. It is difficult to demonstrate that a life skill such as 'shows sensitivity to the needs of others' has been achieved as a result of schooling. The emphasis on life skills is said to have led, on the one hand, to vague courses in 'social adjustment' — whatever that is — and, on the other, to courses pursuing no more than a list of practical skills such as telephoning or form-filling. Both were criticised for triviality and for being intellectually undemanding, and fell beneath the attack of those who in the 1950s demanded higher academic standards.

Task 2.8 Basing a curriculum on 'life skills'

2.8.1 Rather than merely looking at other people's lists of life skills you will understand the problems raised in formulating a list if you attempt to make one for yourself, preferably in collaboration with other teachers. The task is to analyse all the skills, knowledge, habits and attitudes that you believe to be needed by all members of our society. You will probably find it best to begin with general headings indicating areas of life, and then to break these down into particular items, which can if you wish be stated in the form of objectives. (It may be best to agree the headings as a group and then to distribute the work within each heading amongst members of the group.)

2.8.2 (This task follows logically from the previous one.) Did you find it possible to find cultural practices and values that run right across the society? If you were working with other teachers did they choose the same practices and values as you did? Can one arrive at an agreed list?

Is there any knowledge that is essential rather than just helpful? Is knowledge part of life skills?

Did you take subcultures into account, both those based on social class and those based on ethnic groups? Does everybody need to know how to set a table for a formal meal? Or is this not the level of skill we should be discussing? How do you decide? (How much do you really know about subcultures other than your own?)

Is it the responsibility of schools to shape children's habits and attitudes, if those the teacher believes to be proper differ from those of the children's homes?

Finally, you might ask yourself whether this approach seems a useful way of reconsidering the organisation of the whole curriculum for the level of schooling you are interested in.

2.8.3 Postman and Weingartner (1969) suggest the following list of questions as the basis for a curriculum. They probably did not intend that children should literally be asked these questions — though many of them *could* be used with older secondary pupils — but that they should suggest a line of thought about the curriculum as a whole. (Though at first glance the bias seems to be towards secondary education, the questions raise issues relevant also to the primary-school curriculum.)

2.8.3
contd

What do you worry about most?

What are the causes of your worries?

Can any of your worries be eliminated? How?

Which of them might you deal with first? How do you decide?

Are there other people with the same problems? How do you know? How can you find out?

If you had an important idea that you wanted to let everyone (in the world) know about, how might you go about letting them know?

What bothers you most about adults? Why?

How do you want to be similar to or different from adults you know when you become an adult?

What, if anything, seems to you to be worth dying for? How did you come to believe this?

What seems worth living for? How did you come to believe this?

At the present moment, what would you most like to be — or be able to do? Why?

What would you have to know in order to be able to do it?

What would you have to do in order to get to know it?

How can you tell 'good guys' from 'bad guys'?

How can 'good' be distinguished from 'evil'?

What kind of person would you most like to be? How might you get to be this kind of person?

At the present moment, what would you most like to be doing? Five years from now? Ten years from now? Why?

What might you have to do to realise these hopes? What might you have to give up in order to do some or all of these things?

When you hear or read or observe something how do you know what it means?

Where does meaning 'come from'?

What does 'meaning' mean?

How can you tell what something 'is' or whether it is?

Where do words come from?

Where do symbols come from? Why do symbols change?

Where does knowledge come from?

What do you think are some of man's most important ideas? Where did they come from? Why? How? Now what?

2.8.3 What's a 'good idea'?
contd How do you know when a good or live idea becomes a bad
or dead idea?
Which of man's ideas would we be better off forgetting? How
do you decide?
What is 'progress'?
What is 'change'?
What are the most obvious causes of change? What are the
least apparent?
What conditions are necessary in order for change to occur?
What kinds of change are going on right now? Which are
important?
How are they similar to or different from other changes
that have occurred?
What are the relationships between new ideas and change?
Where do *new* ideas come from? How come? So what?
If you wanted to stop one of the changes going on now
(pick one), how would you go about it? What consequences
would you have to consider?
Of the important changes going on in our society, which
should be encouraged and which resisted? Why? How?
What are the most important changes that have occurred in
the past ten years? twenty years? fifty years? In the last
year? In the last six months? Last month? What will be the
most important changes next month? Next year? Next
decade? How can you tell? So what?
What would you change if you could? How might you go
about it? Of those changes which are going to occur, which
would you stop if you could? Why? How? So what?
Who do you think has the most important things to say
today? To whom? How? Why?
What are the dumbest and most dangerous ideas that are
'popular' today? Why do you think so? Where did these
ideas come from?
What are the conditions necessary for life to survive? Plants?
Animals? Humans?
Which of these conditions are necessary for all life?
Which ones for plants? Which ones for animals? Which ones
for humans?
What are the greatest threats to all forms of life? To plants?

2.8.3
contd

To animals? To humans?

What are some of the 'strategies' living things use to survive? Which unique to plants? Which unique to animals? Which unique to humans?

What kinds of human survival strategies are (1) similar to those of animals and plants; (2) different from animals and plants?

What does man's language permit him to develop as survival strategies that animals cannot develop?

How might man's survival activities be different from what they are if he did not have language?

What other 'languages' does man have besides those consisting of words?

What functions do these 'languages' serve? Why and how do they originate?

Can you invent a new one? How might you start?

What would happen, what difference would it make, what would man *not* be able to do if he had no number (mathematical) languages?

How many symbol systems does man have? How come? So what?

What are some good symbols? Some bad?

What good symbols could we use that we do not have?

What bad symbols do we have that we'd be better off without?

What's worth knowing? How do you decide? What are some ways to go about getting to know what's worth knowing?

(a) Why do you think that Postman and Weingartner have chosen to present their ideas about the curriculum in the form of questions?

(b) Try subdividing the questions into groups according to what they seem to be concerned with. What categories seem to fit? Do they surprise you?

(c) In what respects would the ideas behind these questions indeed lead to a different curriculum from that we know today?

(d) Are there any reasons why this policy could not or should not be put into effect?

One of the most thorough attempts to outline life skills was carried out during the 1950s by two American educators called H. Goldstein and D.M. Seigle (1971), and first published as *The Illinois Plan for Special Education of Exceptional Children* with the subtitle 'A curriculum guide for teachers of the educable mentally handicapped'. The authors identify ten 'life functions', but they are also concerned with the claims of academic learning, so they list not only life functions but also 'areas of knowledge'.

TABLE 2.6 *Goldstein and Seigle's life functions and areas of knowledge*

Life functions	Areas of knowledge
Citizenship	Arithmetic
Communicating	Fine arts
Home and family	Language arts
Leisure time	Physical education*
Management of materials and money	Practical arts
Occupational adequacy	Science*
Physical and mental health*	Social relationships*
Safety*	
Social adjustment	
Travel	

Note: The asterisks are explained below.

Each of the life functions is broken down into subheadings; 'citizenship', for example, is divided into 'the co-operating citizen' and 'the contributing citizen', and both of these are further subdivided. The 'home and family' category is broken down in even more detail.

Family relationships

co-operation
contributing
family values
    ancestors (grandparents)
    customs, traditions
    holidays and special occasions

Areas of family living

home-making skills

financing a family
   earning
   spending
   saving
starting a family
   dating
   marriage
   sex education
having a family
   reproduction
   parental care
   child care
   health
enjoying a family
   recreation
   work
community relationship
   neighbours
   school
   businesses
   churches
   social services

Sources of help for family problems

family service agencies
medical and health agencies
churches

Some overlap with other categories seems to be unavoidable; home and family, for example, seems to overlap with 'citizenship' and 'management of materials and money'.

Goldstein and Seigle are not merely concerned to categorise, however; they go on to offer detailed curriculum advice with separate sections for teaching pupils at primary, intermediate and advanced levels. At each of these levels they suggest a series of what they call 'motivating activities' appropriate to raising issues relevant to that particular life function. Then they link each of these activities with pieces of work that fall within the areas of knowledge (listed on p. 149). That is, they are concerned that learning activities should both be relevant to the various life functions and also contribute to the

TABLE 2.7 *Curriculum advice for the home and family section of Goldstein and Seigle's scheme at primary level*

Motivating activities	Language arts	Arithmetic	Unit activities	Fine and practical arts
Show film about co-operation in the home Introduce family of dolls	Discussion: Family in film Individual family members Child's own family Ways of being co-operative Ways of being help-ful Ways to be happy	Comparison: Size Age Time: Recognition of clock showing family schedule, i.e. time to get up, to eat, to watch TV, go to school, to go to bed Hour and half-hour	Social relationships: Family helpers in home Science: Animal families	Construct animals from clay, spools, papier mâché Role playing, i.e. being mother, father, brother, sister Illustrate family activities through cutting, painting, pasting
Play birthday record	Discussion: Birthdays Different ways to celebrate birthdays Giving gifts Read: Birthday chart	Recognition of numbers: Pupils' ages Time: Month Day	Physical education: Play party games Health: Mental health aspects of the happy family	Have birthday party and prepare refresh-ments and decorations Make gifts such as bracelet, birthday cards
Read story about holiday, i.e., Christmas, Easter, Thanksgiving	Discussion: Traditional ways of celebrating holidays and events Own family's way of celebrating	Calendar: Season, months, dates	Social relationships: Unit on family fun related to holidays	

TABLE 2.8 *Curriculum advice for the home and family section of Goldstein and Seigle's scheme at intermediate level*

Motivating activities	Language arts	Arithmetic	Unit activities	Fine and practical arts
Reports on kinds of tasks done in and around home Film on household tasks	Discussion: Tasks around the home which pupils do Helping with household tasks as a contribution to the family Remuneration for task at home	Time: Budgeting time for work and play Fractions: Needed in cooking and sewing, i.e. ½ cup, ¼ inch Banking: Keep record of savings	Social relationships: Areas of responsibilities in household tasks of various members of the family Science: Developing habits of cleanliness as related to tasks around the house	Learn and practise home-making skills which may be carried over into the home, i.e. cooking, cleaning, sewing
Report on after-school and Saturday job in the community Films or pictures or talks about family responsibility	Discussion: Ways of earning money Using earnings wisely Part-time work as a means of preparing for a job in adulthood Responsibilities of parents, of children Write and spell: Words in units Write: Stories explaining pictures in notebooks	Compute: Simple budget Money: Identify coins Make change for one pound Problems: Relative to earning, spending and saving	Social relationships: Opportunities for employment in the community as related to life function on management of money and materials Health: Mental health factors related to living within financial means	Make note or scrap-books of pictures illustrating job in the community of interest to pupils

TABLE 2.8 *Home and family (Intermediate contd)*

Motivating activities	Language arts	Arithmetic	Unit activities	Fine and practical arts
Display of baby pictures	Discussion:	Measurement:	Social relationships:	Make a scrapbook of pictures illustrating toys, games, clothing, etc, for baby or young child
Report of the arrival of a new baby in the family	Acceptance and responsibilities in connection with a new sibling in the home	Make a growth chart for a baby or younger child	Family life in relation to physical and financial care	Make a notebook of your family — stories pictures, photographs
Stories about family life	Helping with the new baby	Table of weight Linear measure	Science:	Take trips to learn facilities in the community
Film on activities in the family	Financial responsibilities connected with an additional family member	Fractions: One-half One-quarter	Growth and care of young animal, i.e. a pet which can be brought into the classroom	
	Ways of working and playing with the family		Health:	
	Visiting relatives		Differences in diet as related to age and size	
	Family relationships in relation to school, church, neighbours, and business and community services		Mental health factors in adjusting to a new family member	
	Read:		Mental health factors in having satisfactory community relationships	
	Books about family life			
	Spell:			
	Common words related to units			
	Names in family			

153

TABLE 2.9 *Curriculum advice for the home and family section of Goldstein and Seigle's scheme at advanced level*

Motivating activities	Language arts	Arithmetic	Unit activities	Fine and practical arts
Display of electrical cord, sockets, broken chairs and household equipment needing repair Display of window cleaner	Discussion: Value of being able to make home repairs Ways to repair household items Read: Directions in connection with repairs Spelling: Common household terms	Measurement: Use of ruler Comparison: Cost of making own repair with hiring repair done Cost of repairs versus replacement of new equipment Compute: Costs of tools and materials for home repairs Vocabulary: Measurement terms Compare: Hourly wage rates	Science: Construct simple electrical circuit	Wash windows Repair electrical cords and sockets Collect and catalogue materials and tools used in home repair

TABLE 2.9 *Home and family (Advanced contd)*

Motivating activities	Language arts	Arithmetic	Unit activities	Fine and practical arts
Reports of job experiences Posters of people at work Films on community jobs Trip to bank, store or factory	Discussion: Different types of work Read: Want ads in local papers Stories about people earning their living in different ways Literature relative to banking Write: Lists of jobs open to boys and girls Budget items in budget book	Compute: Time and pay Pay cheque and deductions Problems: Relative to social security benefits Vocabulary: Concepts in savings Monetary terms Banking: Use of bank book Current account Savings account Deposit slips	Social relationships: Personal inventory Earning power Wise and economical buying (compare quality and price) Compare income and living cost Health: Mental health factors in saving for time of need or emergency	Scrapbook of pictures illustrating kinds of jobs Collect and display materials on preparing for job interviews Actual job experience around school or part-time in community

The content of the curriculum

development of skills and knowledge within traditional school subjects. In practice, the areas of knowledge reduce to four, which are represented as columns in the examples in Tables 2.7-2.9. The four are:

Language arts;
Arithmetic;
Fine and practical arts;
Unit activities.

('Unit activities' include social relationships, science, physical education, health and safety – all those marked with an asterisk on p. 149.)

The three examples shown in Tables 2.7-2.9 are drawn from the home and family section of Goldstein and Seigle's scheme, and illustrate how this topic is treated at the three levels. (It must be emphasised that in each case this represents only a small proportion of the activities suggested for that level.)

Task 2.8 contd   Basing a curriculum on 'life skills'

2.8.4   Do you find Goldstein and Seigle's categories of life functions and areas of knowledge acceptable? If not, what changes would you wish to make?

2.8.5   Do you think that this way of linking motivating activities with work in language, mathematics and so on would be helpful to you in your teaching? (The best way of setting about answering this would seem to be to try out some of these suggestions with the class that you are teaching, even though the proposals were originally intended for pupils of very low ability.)

2.8.6   Choose either another of Goldstein and Seigle's life functions (such as occupational adequacy or leisure time), or one of the categories which you yourself selected when working on Task 2.8.1. Develop a set of activities within this category in the way they have done. The purpose would be to select 'motivating activities' so that each of them can be used as a basis for work in language, mathematics, art and craft, and in the areas that are grouped together as 'unit activities'. This kind of planning can be used at various levels to relate academic learning to life skills: it need not be confined to pupils of low ability. (This might provide a method of planning within Lawton's field of 'interdisciplinary work'.)

156

Moral aspects of the curriculum

It is not unusual to find teachers who link the idea of social education
with moral education, though the relationship between the two is far
from simple. It is clearly appropriate for schools to teach the knowledge and skills which will eventually enable pupils to take a full part in
adult life. Is it equally clear that schools should attempt to establish
habits of conformity, or to persuade pupils to accept particular senti-
ments and values, and live by them? Many teachers would reply un-
hesitatingly that this *is* part of the school's duty. Others would hold
that this is the business of the home. Of the former teachers, some
take a wide view of their moral and cultural responsibilities, from an
insistence on truthfulness to the use of cutlery. Some teachers of
older pupils limit their ethical responsibility to the development of
pupils' moral autonomy, and seek to achieve this through discussions in
which alternative moral viewpoints are considered. Yet other teachers
would regard this as an abdication of their responsibility to communicate by precept and example the highest values that our culture provides: such a view has an impressive lineage that passes through
Matthew Arnold, that distinguished member of HM Inspectorate.
Teachers of younger children might in any case judge that their pupils
are not old enough to reflect upon their own behaviour and that they
should therefore be trained in good habits until they are old enough to
take responsibility for themselves. Enough has been said to show that
consensus about moral and social education cannot be expected from
the teaching profession. For this very reason it is important to give
careful attention to this aspect of the curriculum in order to clarify
what responsibility a school is assuming, and to see to it that what is
being done matches those responsibilities.

Task 2.9 Considering a school's policy for 'discipline and social training'

2.9   The document which follows was written as a guide for teachers
      by the headteacher of a junior school for children of 8-11 years
      of age.

   Discipline and social training
      The superiority of the adult over the child is a matter of
      length and width of experience and not of moral quality.
      Few children are so unreasonable or unmanageable by

157

2.9
contd

nature as not to respond to the calmly exercised control of
an intelligent teacher who has their best interests at heart.

(1937 Handbook of Suggestions)

A child's power to make decisions for himself cannot
grow under constant coercion from without but only
from the compulsion that comes from within.

(Primary education)

It is necessary, in view of the emotional overtones which
have gathered round the word 'discipline' to re-define it.
Discipline is the art of being a disciple. The essence of
discipleship is the willingness of the disciple, and the essence
of true discipline is the willing co-operation of the child.

It follows, therefore, that the ultimate aim is to obtain
this willing co-operation from everyone. This does not imply
that the children should be unrestricted and uncontrolled
until this is obtained. The community and, more particularly, the school demands certain standards. Behaviour which
interferes with the work of others, which is harmful to other
children, or which is dangerous, morally, physically, or
mentally to the child himself cannot be allowed. Fortunately,
almost all children wish to be accepted by their fellows, and
are most willing to conform to the standard of behaviour of
the rest.

Our aim of developing independence of thought and
action in our children is in no way incompatible with this.
Freedom of conduct as individuals must go hand in hand
with an awareness of the needs of the group. The danger we
are likely to fall into lies in emphasising one at the expense
of the other.

We must not lose sight of the fact that children have
different needs. Many with good backgrounds will present
no problems at all. Some less fortunate children will need to
develop all sorts of habits and patterns of behaviour which
are already present in the majority. To this end, since the
needs of the community demand it, cleanliness, tidiness,
unselfishness, co-operation, and good manners must be encouraged; and, as always, the example set by the teacher himself is likely to be the most effective way of doing this.

2.9
contd
Reason and persuasion should be effective in producing good discipline in almost every case. Punishment, of any sort, should be used as a last resort and should be regarded, almost, as an admission of defeat. The teacher's power of anticipation are the best safeguard against its use.

Cleanliness
1 *Occasional* comment on the good appearance of the whole class, or private comment, similarly, to individuals.
2 *Occasional* inspection of hands, nails, knees, shoes and books.
3 Private comment on unclean hands, etc., and suggesting immediate washing.
4 Washing hands before dinner, needlework, etc., or whenever necessary (e.g. after art and craft).
5 Protection of clothing when engaged in activities which are 'dirty'.
6 *No* adverse comment to the child about the state of his clothing unless you know that he is responsible for it. Children do not, normally, decide what they wear.

Tidiness
1 Insistence on materials, books, etc. being returned tidily to their proper place.
2 Efficient tidying of the room after 'messy' lessons.
3 Anti-litter campaigns in playground and classrooms.
4 *Occasional* desk inspections, but it is not necessary to lay down a strict pattern in which the contents should be arranged.

Unselfishness
1 Encouragement of 'sharing' materials and books.
2 Encouragement of thought for others — the sick, the unhappy, etc. Allow children to help others.
3 Inclusion of all children in the group — careful attention to 'isolates'.
4 *Occasional* acceptance by the teacher of offers to sweets from the children — even if they are not eaten.

2.9   *Co-operation*
contd   1 Allow children to co-operate in work — even in the
           traditionally individual fields (e.g. arithmetic).
        2 Give plenty of opportunities for working in groups to a
           common end.
        3 Allow the class, occasionally, to decide what they will do.
        4 Allot duties to children, or groups, in turn.
        5 Explain the reasons for disturbance in routine.

Good manners
1 Insist on mannerly behaviour in class and school, but
   avoid being pedantic. It is not necessary for a child to
   say: 'Excuse me' every time he passes a teacher, nor is
   there need for him to stand to speak. The ordinary
   courtesies towards his fellows and adults should, however, be demanded.
2 The dinner table gives us an admirable opportunity for
   influencing table manners. It should be used fully.
3 The teacher must treat his children with the courtesy
   he expects from them.

General
1 The responsibilities of the teachers in this field must
   extend outside the classroom and to all the children in the
   school.
2 The term 'in loco parentis' should be always borne in
   mind. Our pupils should be treated as we would wish our
   own children to be.

2.9.1   How far are the suggestions given by this headteacher concerned
        with morality and how far with matters of a different kind?
        What are these other matters? Do you think that all of the
        matters mentioned should be the school's responsibility? On
        what basis can one decide?
2.9.2   The author of the document says in the introduction that the
        school has the aims of 'developing independence of thought and
        action' and of helping pupils to 'an awareness of the needs of
        the group'. Do the suggestions appear to offer useful ways of
        pursuing these aims? In general, what seems to be the relation-
        ship between the introductory paragraphs and the suggestions?

2.9.3 Consider the implications of using two terms 'discipline' and 'social training'. The headteacher offers a paraphrase of 'discipline': how close is this to the way in which the word is usually used by teachers? When is the term 'training' appropriate and when not?

2.9.4 Draft an alternative document that removes any attitudes, values or emphases that you do not approve of in the one quoted.

In clarifying our thinking about moral aspects of the curriculum we shall turn first to a philosopher and then to a psychologist, remembering, however, that in each case their views are open to debate and criticism. John Wilson and his colleagues of the Farmington Trust Research Unit (1967) have contributed valuably to our understanding by an analysis of moral behaviour into the six elements which they believe to be necessary parts of it. What follows is my paraphrase of what Wilson has written, though I have retained the idiosyncratic names which he has given them by abbreviating appropriate Greek words.

Phil. It is necessary to see other people as having equal rights to one's own.

Emp. In order to act morally one has to be capable of sympathetic insight into people's feelings and motives, including one's own.

Gig. This element in moral action refers to the possession of relevant information: we cannot act with full moral responsibility unless we are fully informed about the situation and the likely outcomes of our actions.

Dik. Moral action entails the possession of moral principles that guide behaviour: habitual unreflective behaviour is not moral. These principles must be rational in the sense of being consistently and logically applied.

Phron. This element concerns the possession of principles that refer to ourselves.

Krat. Moral judgments alone are not enough: Krat. refers to the will to put them into effect.

I shall group these into three pairs in order to discuss their relevance to the curriculum, since the three pairs are likely to differ in this respect.

(*a*) Gig. and Emp. refer to our understanding of the situation,

161

including people's feelings and motives. All parts of the curriculum, particularly humanities and social studies, are likely to contribute to our understanding of the social world in which our actions take effect. Some subjects, such as literature, would lay claim to throw particular light upon other people's viewpoints. These aspects of moral education are unlikely to generate controversy.

(*b*) Dik. and Phron. refer to the possession of principles on which moral action can be based. This provokes the question whether in a plural culture it is the business of state schools to lay down moral principles for pupils. It is necessary to answer the question in two parts. Since no one is likely to dispute the underlying moral law that rights and responsibilities apply to all men and women, there is no reason why any moral principles that follow from this — truthfulness, justice, care for others' health, lives and liberty — should not be presented to all pupils. In practice we do not usually disagree about these general principles but we do disagree about their application to particular circumstances, because of different interpretations of the situation, different views about what principles apply, and different priorities given to one principle as compared to another. Thus in moral education it can be argued that to stress moral principles is only a preliminary, and that the central task for the teacher is to help pupils to understand the contexts of moral dilemmas, and how various principles apply to them. At this point teachers' views are likely to diverge; some will be contented to help pupils to achieve such understanding without urging a particular viewpoint; other teachers, committed to a particular ethical stance, whether on political or religious grounds, find such a *laissez-faire* view untenable, and even immoral. It is thus difficult to consider the learning of moral principles in separation from the understanding of motives and situations, that is, in separation from Gig. and Emp.

(*c*) Phil. and Krat. are more loosely interrelated than the other two pairs. Our willingness to act on our principles (Krat.) is partly dependent on allowing to others the rights which we ourselves would claim (Phil.). It seems unlikely, however, that the school curriculum can directly affect the will to put moral judgments into effect. If school does influence this it is likely to be through the whole of the child's social experience at school, including the values which he perceives his teachers and fellow pupils to be acting upon, and his own sense of being treated as a moral agent in a morally consistent institution. In my view, exhortation and compulsion are unlikely to create Krat. and still less Phil. but not all teachers would agree. It is the whole moral environment provided by the school that is likely to be important, and not any specific curricular provisions.

Task 2.10 Using theoretical categories to consider moral education

2.10   This task is intended to help you to see the implications of Wilson's way of analysing moral action. It is based on this imaginary situation: you are invigilating an internal school test or examination for a colleague with whom you are not on good terms, and who is known to be extremely severe upon children who offend against his rather strict code. You notice a pupil surreptitiously copying from a slip of paper, possibly cheating. You know the pupil to come from a difficult home, and yet to have made considerable progress in your lessons showing interest and some ability.

2.10.1   What action should you take, if any? (This can best be decided in discussion with other people.)

2.10.2   Having decided on the action you come to the main point of this task, which is to use Wilson's six categories to analyse the process by which you made the decision. What principles were involved? How did you decide on priorities amongst them? What insight into other people's feelings and motives were relevant? Was there any information that would have helped you to make the decision? What considerations and feelings of your own would be likely to affect whether you in fact did what you judged to be right?

2.10.3   Could a similar task to this, but using a moral dilemma appropriate to a pupil, not to a teacher, be used with your pupils to discuss moral judgments? Would it be possible for them to be taught to use Wilson's categories? (That was not Wilson's intention.) If possible, would it be likely to be useful to them?

In discussing Dik. and Phron. Wilson makes it clear that to possess principles is not enough: they must be applied rationally. The element of reasoning in moral judgment has received a great deal of attention from developmental psychologists, including Piaget and Kohlberg. Kohlberg considers it by now well established that a child's level of cognitive development (as indicated, for instance by his reasoning on typical Piagetian tasks) determines the highest level of moral judgment that he is capable of at that time (Tomlinson, 1980 and 1981). Since moral action depends in part upon moral judgment, moral action is thus indirectly dependent on rationality, which is not to deny that clever people sometimes do wicked things. Unreflective or habitual action, while it is often important and gains approbation, is not strictly moral. Moral action is purposive, and rests on the ability to conceive of alternatives and to envisage their outcomes.

On the basis of a great deal of research into the basis upon which children and adolescents make moral choices, Lawrence Kohlberg has mapped out six levels of moral judgment. (In the interests of brevity, I shall paraphrase his account and omit certain substages and inter-mediate stages which he has postulated.)

Level I Preconventional

Stage 1. At this stage the child's point of view is entirely egocentric. He has no insight into other people's points of view, and follows the rules only in order to avoid punishment. He tends to perceive bad be-haviour in terms of physical damage to persons or property without considering motive.

Stage 2. The child is now aware that other people have interests and purposes that conflict with his, and that in order to get what he wants he will have to concede something to them. His idea of right therefore resembles an exchange that satisfies several persons' immediate interests.

Level II Conventional

Stage 3. At this stage boys or girls are aware of the need to put them-selves in others' shoes. They value 'being good' and see it as living up to what is expected of them, showing concern for others, and being loyal and trustworthy, this often leading to a stereotyped view of good be-haviour.

Stage 4. At this stage the focus of moral awareness shifts away from the viewpoints of other individuals towards the realisation that social stability depends on adherence to rules. The individual's duty is to carry out the obligations proper to his place in the system, and thereby, to contribute to the good of all.

Stage 4½.   This stage – transitional between 4 and 5 – was added later because Kohlberg found (particularly amongst college students) an ethical perspective based upon an 'outsider's' rejection of conventional good behaviour as a basis for morality. It is as if the young man or woman has perceived the limitations of a morality based upon a particular way of life, but has not yet found more general principles that can apply to different societies and different ways of life.

Level III Principled

Stage 5.   Those who reach this stage are aware that values are not absolute but are based upon a common need to find principles upon which conflicting interests can be united. They believe that values, though relative, should be upheld impartially because they are based upon an implicit contractual commitment to other people and to society.

Stage 6.   The very few persons who reach this stage are committed to a rational belief in the validity of universal moral principles. On the basis of these principles they may choose to behave contrary to particular laws or customs which they believe to be invalid, since their commitment to justice and human rights is independent of the values of any particular community.

Kohlberg has made it very clear that social experience plays an important part in moral development, as one would expect from the marked cognitive element in the process. Thus experience at school, including an appropriately planned curriculum, can be expected to contribute to such development. Kohlberg acknowledges that we may operate at a higher level in some areas of moral concern than in others; he has used eleven such areas in his research. (They are listed below in Task 2.11.3.)

The next set of tasks is intended to give the reader the opportunity to test as a basis for curriculum-planning the usefulness of Kohlberg's developmental categories and Wilson's analysis of the components of a moral choice. Kohlberg's categories arise from his interpretation of empirical data, Wilson's from a logical analysis. Both are open to criticism and modification, so in using them as aids to planning we must keep in mind their hypothetical status.

Task 2.11 Using theoretical categories to consider moral education

2.11.1 Our development as moral agents takes place throughout our experience and not merely in lessons planned to encourage moral development. In order to plan a suitable curriculum we need to have some conception of the nature of these experiences, and these can to some extent be deduced from Kohlberg's analysis.

Take Kohlberg's stages in pairs (1 and 2, 2 and 3, etc.) and note what changes in perspective occur between each pair. What kinds of experience would you expect to have contributed to each of these changes in perspective? Could similar experience be provided as part of the school curriculum? In cases where this would be impossible, does it seem likely that opportunities to discuss and reflect upon out-of-school experiences might contribute to moral development? At what stages in our lives is conscious reflection on moral issues likely to be valuable?

Choose one of the changes of perspective between two of Kohlberg's stages and devise activities in and out of the classroom that might encourage that change in perspective.

2.11.2 Kohlberg and some of his associates have taken a practical interest in advising prison authorities that educational experiences might offer to prison inmates opportunities for moral development that they may have missed. For inmates whose moral thinking has reached no higher than stages 1 or 2, they suggest the following kinds of experience.

1 Role-taking opportunities: opportunities, especially through discussion and mediation via stage-sequential interpretation, to see others' point of view.

2 Intellectual stimulation: encouraging logical analysis and reasoning.

3 Responsibility: giving the prison inmate responsibility for making his or her own decisions.

4 Cognitive-moral conflict: small-group discussion of moral and personal dilemmas.

2.11.2 5 Exposure to the next stage up.

contd 6 Living in a community perceived as fair and concerned: prison inmates have often come from environments which are basically and habitually unjust, and 'there is no stimulus to moral thought or action in a low-stage or unjust world'.

The task is to take each of these categories in turn, and to consider whether equivalent experiences could — and should — be provided for schoolchildren. If so, what form might these experiences take?

2.11.3 Kohlberg has used in some of his more recent research the 'value areas' that are listed in the left-hand column of Table 2.10.

TABLE 2.10 *Topics and activities covering different value areas at three age-levels*

Value areas	Age A	Age B	Age C
1 Laws and rules			
2 Conscience			
3 Personal roles of affection			
4 Authority			
5 Civil rights			
6 Contract, trust and justice in exchange			
7 Punishment and justice			
8 Value of life			
9 Property rights and values			
10 Truth			
11 Sex and sexual love			

Although this is not the purpose for which they were intended, it seems possible to use these value areas as the basis for curriculum-planning in moral education. It is clear, however, that one would approach the area of authority (no. 4) in a different way with young children than with adolescents, though the work with older children might well be building on moral perceptions which school activities had contributed to when they were younger. This seems to be a case for a 'spiral

2.11.3
contd
curriculum', in which the same areas are returned to at different points in the child's schooling, in each case using experiences, topics and methods suited to his or her age and level of
development.

In order to begin considering what such a curriculum would
entail, you should select three convenient age-levels (ages A,
B and C in Table 2.10), or, if it seems more useful, three of
Kohlberg's stages. Suitable ages might be 8, 11 and 14 years.
For each value area suggest a topic or activity that would be
suited for age A; then go on and do similarly for B, and C.
(For a group of teachers with experience at different age-levels
these tasks could usefully be distributed.) The topics and
activities can then be entered into the table in the form of a
convenient abbreviation.

You might also consider whether there should be any blank
places in the table, and whether all of the areas are likely to
be teachable.

2.11.4
This task can be carried out individually but is more interesting if it is done by a group.

The team of the Schools Council Moral Education Curriculum Project have produced curriculum materials for older
pupils under the title *Lifeline* (McPhail, 1972). Amongst these
materials are a set of 24 workcards intended to develop sensitivity; they can be used to 'introduce role-play, drama, creative
writing, mime or art work, as well as general discussion'. One
of these workcards gives this topic for discussion: 'A boy or
girl of your own age, with whom you are friendly, appears to
be very upset for some reason unknown to you. What do you
do?'

In order to illustrate how this might be used in class, I
suggest that each member of a group of teachers should answer
this question in terms of a friend of their own age. Then there
should be discussion of the pros and cons of various ways of
dealing with the situation. Finally, it should be useful for the
whole group to consider the scheme in Appendix F, and relate
it to the various viewpoints taken up in the discussion.

2.11.5
Readers will have noticed how remarkably different from one
another are the five analytic schemes that we have used: the
Illinois analysis of life functions (pp. 149-56), John Wilson's
components of moral choice, Lawrence Kohlberg's develop-

2.11.5   mental categories as well as his list of value areas, and Peter
contd   McPhail's scheme for analysing young people's responses to
his questions (Appendix F). It is worth considering how such
differences have come about.

Uncovering the hidden curriculum

During the 1970s the idea of there being a 'hidden' curriculum as well
as an explicit one caught many teachers' imagination, since it seemed to
explain some puzzling aspects of schooling. The idea originated in the
social psychology of small groups: a committee, we are told, has its
official agenda, but also has a hidden agenda concerned with the social
relationships of its members – who is going to dominate the discussion,
who is going to put the establishment point of view, whose anger is
going to express the group's frustrations, and so on. The idea of a
hidden agenda was transferred to schools as a hidden curriculum. What
would children learn over and above the official curriculum about how
to cope with school, how to avoid a question when you do not know
the answer, what constitutes being a good pupil, how far you can risk
giving your real opinion, how you get round rules without being caught,
how you can get fun out of a boring lesson? The list of possible learnings is a long one.

What do they have in common? First, they are all unintended, not
part of any teacher's objectives. Then they all tend to be what one
might call 'social' learning, about what people expect of you, and how
you can best cope with their demands. Some aspects of this hidden
curriculum may be short-term, such as not raising your hand with the
first few or the last few in the class if you do not want to be called on
to answer. But there is also the possibility of long-term learning, such as
some pupils learning that teachers think they are dull and uninteresting
and unlikely to gain much from schooling. Some writers, such as
Jules Henry (1972), have gone so far as to suggest that one of the main
functions of schooling is to prepare the young for some of the less
admirable aspects of our culture: 'It instills the essential cultural night-
mare fear of failure, envy of success, and absurdity.' It is clear from this
view why the hidden curriculum became an urgent issue: if young
people *are* learning this from their schooling we all ought to know
about it; it should not remain hidden.

Some of the social learning in schools is far from hidden. The British public schools of the late nineteenth century set themselves quite deliberately to foster in the boys of a future ruling class the characteristics thought proper to a Christian gentleman. Rather more recently, I can remember when I was very young being instructed very deliberately by a junior-school teacher to say 'Excuse me' whenever I walked in front of her; perhaps I was one of the masses being gentled. Many teachers today, as we have seen, hope that their pupils will gain obliquely from their experiences of school life quite explicit socio-moral habits and attitudes. Of course, not everyone believes that teachers should take on such responsibilities. The point being made here is that they take on these responsibilities deliberately, whereas the social learning that is called 'the hidden curriculum' happens without teachers intending it, and possibly against their will. Once they become aware of it, it is no longer 'hidden'.

It might be argued that the hidden curriculum is nothing to do with curriculum, but is a matter of the social organisation of the school. I do not take that view. It is for teachers to take responsibility for all the learning that takes place while pupils are in their charge, whether it is academic or social. Schools should be organised so that pupils' social experience is beneficial, and for this reason it is important that the hidden curriculum should be uncovered, discussed and analysed.

Writing about those aspects of classroom life that are so familiar that we take them for granted, Philip Jackson (1968) pointed out that the ritualistic and cyclic aspects of the activities carried on in the classroom make it a very homogeneous social context. Each pupil has to 'come to grips with the inevitability of his experience' and must 'develop strategies for dealing with the conflict that frequently arises between his natural desires and interests on the one hand and institutional expectations on the other'.

These institutional expectations all arise from three characteristics of schools which Jackson labels 'crowds, praise, and power'; one might paraphrase this by saying that the essential characteristic of classrooms is that they all contain large numbers of children competing for the attention and approbation of one teacher, who has considerable power to affect their present comfort and future prospects. As a result of this, according to Jackson, students have to learn to wait patiently, to submit to the frustration of their wishes, to be interrupted frequently in what they are doing, and to live amongst a multitude of competing distractions. He urges that we should study how teachers and pupils cope with these facts of school life in order to understand 'how that coping might leave its mark on their reactions to the world in general'.

There has been little explicit research on the hidden curriculum. We do not know except from our first-hand experience what values schools tend to inculcate. Even less do we know how successful they are in doing so, or what differences there are from school to school. Thus the tasks which follow ask you to think about this on the basis of your own experience, and to collect a little evidence of your own, safe in the knowledge that you are (nearly) first in the field.

Task 2.12 The hidden curriculum

2.12.1 We shall begin with an exercise in self-examination. What do *your* pupils have to do to gain your attention and approval? What behaviour do you reward, and what behaviour do you ignore or snub? Do you place great importance on neatness and accuracy, on rapid obedience, on quiet behaviour, on politeness, on originality, on speed of working . . . and so on? Compare some pupils you approve of with some from the same class whom you disapprove of. How do they differ? How far are you influenced by their social behaviour, how far by their speech and appearance, and how far by their academic achievement? (This task could usefully be carried out by a group of teachers, first individually, then by comparing notes, and last by carrying out the next task by working in pairs and interviewing one another's pupils.)

2.12.2 Arrange an informal discussion with a group of pupils — not too many, and preferably not from a class which you are at present teaching — to find out (a) what behaviour and characteristics they believe to be valued by teachers in general, and by particular teachers, and (b) what strategies and devices they use to convey at least the appearance of conformity. (John Holt (1964, 1967) discusses some of these points.)

2.12.3 Does Philip Jackson's account of the demands of life in classrooms correspond with your experience as pupil and as a teacher? What are the rituals that he refers to? What happens to pupils who do not accept the frustration of their wishes, or who do not wait patiently? What part is played in this by teachers' evaluations of pupils, including those momentary judgments which are shown by replying to what a child has

2.12.3 said as against ignoring it, for these too are recognised as
contd evaluations by pupils? Is such evaluation inevitable?

2.12.4 This task can be carried out in a classroom in which you are
observing someone teach, or can be based on an audio or
video recording of a lesson. Make a note of all of the pupils'
contributions to the lesson which gain approval or disapproval
from the teacher. (You will probably find that when a pupil's
answer to a question is received without comment this is
frequently equivalent to a rejection of it.) When the lesson is
over, separate out those incidents that seem to refer primarily
to the content of the lesson — indications whether a pupil's
contribution is true or false, relevant or irrelevant — from
those that refer primarily to general behaviour, such as atten-
tiveness, talking without permission, not working, etc. From
this material you should be able to construct a picture of the
hidden curriculum of that classroom, and make a partial
distinction between those aspects of the pupils' assigned role
which relate to content — such as the relative emphasis upon
memory as against problem-solving — and those aspects which
relate to social order.

2.12.5 The hidden curriculum operates not only in classrooms but in
school assemblies, in corridors, on the games field and so on.
Or are there different hidden curricula for each of these
domains? What are the functions of school assemblies? What
are the functions of public occasions such as open days? (It
will be necessary to consider the hidden functions of such
occasions as well as their acknowledged purposes.) Make a
table of school domains; and list any explicit rules which
differentiate them, such as who has access to the domain at
various times of day. Then list behaviour in each of the
domains which teachers attempt to suppress. Your table will
appear similar to Table 2.11. Try to account for the differences observed. Would all schools share the same pattern?
Will there be differences between primary and secondary
schools? What view of their role in school will pupils be likely
to take away with them?

2.12.6 A group of liberal critics of our education system, notably
Ivan Illich (1971), have been so impressed by the hidden
curriculum that they have called for 'deschooling' to free our
society from its effects. Here is a summary of their version

TABLE 2.11 *The rules and proscribed behaviour in various school domains*

Domain	Explicit rules	Proscribed behaviours
Classroom		
Assembly		
Corridor		
Playground		
Gymnasium		
etc.		

2.12.6
contd

of what the hidden curriculum teaches (Lister, 1974).

Some messages of the hidden curriculum

1 Schooling and education are the same thing.
2 The world is non-educational: the school is unworldly.
3 Learning is the result of teaching.
4 Economically esteemed knowledge is the result of professional teaching.
5 Learning is mastery of the curriculum. The curriculum is a commodity. Schools and teachers package and sell the commodity.
6 Knowledge is divided into packages (subjects/topics). Learning is linear — knowledge comes in sequential curricular and graded exercises. (Curriculum reform is the filling of the curriculum with new packaged courses.)
7 Specialist knowledge is the kind which is most highly esteemed.
8 Other people make all the decisions. (You must accept the environment. You cannot influence — never mind change — it.)
9 Life is a zero-sum game in which individuals and countries compete for scarce resources (university places, petroleum). One man's/one country's gain is another man's/country's loss. Competition, not co-operation, is the essence of 'life', and is therefore 'natural'.

173

2.12.6 10 Individuals and countries can be graded/degraded on a
contd   sliding scale. (IQ/'academic' — 'Newsom' children/
               restricted-elaborated code/'developed' — 'underdeveloped'
               countries.) The 'poor' are incapable of helping themselves
               and need to be helped by those who are 'better off'.
               Philanthropy is thus a 'natural' part of the system.
         11 There is a phase of a person's life when he/she is at 'school
               age'. Education ends when schooling ends. In order to get
               more education we must therefore raise the school-leaving
               age.

The deschoolers are concerned with the possibility of a very
deep-seated effect of schooling upon our whole view of what is
worth knowing and our sense of being able to participate in formulating knowledge (Lister, 1974). Design a piece of research
that might test the truth of these hypotheses. Can it be done?

2.12.7 Since we have only limited evidence, the last task must be
no more than an exchange of opinions and judgments. Was
Jules Henry right to see the hidden curriculum of schools
as a malign assault upon human dignity and autonomy? Is it
true that schools prepare young people to be competitive consumers in an economy based upon consumption and competition? Is it true, as some writers say, that a repressive and
boring regime in schools prepares the less able for repressive
relationships and boring work in later life?

How effective do you think the teaching of the hidden
curriculum is? Who seems to accept its values and who rejects
it? Is it possible to 'play along' in school but remain untouched
outside? How deeply is the role of pupil likely to penetrate a
child's personality during school years?

Is it possible to conceive of a form of compulsory mass
education which does *not* inculcate values such as those we
have discussed? Is the hidden curriculum inevitable in some
such form as we know it today?

The whole curriculum

This is the appropriate moment — at the end of this chapter on the
content of the curriculum — to attempt a plan for the whole of a

school's curriculum. The task that follows (2.13.1) applies to pupils in the middle years of schooling, who might be expected to have a curriculum that has only partially been diversified into subjects. You may, however, prefer to attempt a similar exercise for a primary school or a high school, each of which presents rather different problems.

Task 2.13 Planning the whole curriculum

2.13.1   Imagine that you are planning the overall curriculum for pupils in a middle school or the lower forms of a secondary school. Make a list of the subjects they will study, and allocate time to each of them, assuming a week of 35 periods. Decide whether all will be compulsory or whether there will be options. Justify your categories, your emphases, and your decision about compulsion and choice. (Ideally this task should be carried out in a small group so that each teacher presents his plan to the others and has to justify it in the face of their criticisms.)

Task 2.13.1 assumes that the way the curriculum is organised will not change radically, and that the only changes that occur will be minor rearrangements and shifts of emphasis, that the nature of schooling will remain unchanged. But is this inevitable? Are schools really confined to their present ways of preparing children for their adult lives, or are there alternatives? We have looked briefly at arguments based on accounts of the nature and structure of knowledge, and have seen some alternative views of the curriculum in terms of 'life skills'. We have considered the effects of organising the curriculum in subjects, and some alternatives. Some writers would argue that the very idea of curriculum-planning traps us in the status quo, and Postman and Weingartner's (1969) radical proposal (p. 145) is an attempt to find a way of shaping a curriculum that responds more to the learner's needs than to the teacher's intentions. The final task in this chapter challenges you to find an alternative to our current ways of organising the curriculum.

Task 2.13 contd Planning the whole curriculum

2.13.2   In the nature of the task I cannot offer you any guidelines. I am envisaging some way of organising the curriculum that wholly or in part breaks away from our preconceptions about

175

2.13.2   subjects, faculties, 'kinds of knowledge' and even 'life skills'.
contd   Is it possible to develop genuine alternatives? (When you have
attempted this you may care to go on and discuss the problems that you faced in trying to escape your preconceptions.
Is it merely that we are trapped by what is familiar and taken
for granted? Or is the pattern of curriculum as we know it
inevitable? Or is it only inevitable if we take for granted the
way education is organised, and the functions it performs in
society as a whole?)

Chapter 3

Analysing and evaluating the curriculum

All teachers evaluate the curriculum at least informally: at the end of a lesson, or of time spent with an individual pupil, they have some sense of whether the work has gone well or not. What is this judgment based on? One might guess that several things influence it, including the teacher's awareness that the pupil or pupils were attentive and interested, the extent to which they seemed to be understanding and making appropriate replies to questions, and the quality of any writing or practical work done. Most of the changes which teachers make in their teaching styles or in the content of their teaching are based on evidence no more substantial than this. At times this evidence may be too impressionistic, uneven and unsystematic, so the purpose of this chapter is to suggest a wider range of methods which can be used by teachers in obtaining feedback from their teaching.

Although the final emphasis of this chapter falls upon methods that can be used by teachers themselves, it seems useful to begin by putting this into context by relating it to large-scale evaluation of the kind that demands considerable time and resources. Five determining factors in an evaluation can easily be identified by asking five questions, thus:

Evaluation
1   of what?
2   where?
3   for whom?
4   for what purposes?
5   by whom?

For example, there might be an evaluation (1) of last week's teaching, (2) carried out in the one classroom, (3) purely for the teacher's own use, (4) in order to plan the following week's work, and (5) carried out by the teacher himself.

Task 3.1 Distinguishing kinds of evaluation

3.1   What should be the answers to the five questions when they are applied to the following evaluations?

3.1.1   The Department of Education and Science has set up an Assessment of Performance Unit. An introductory pamphlet (undated) asks: 'How do we measure standards in education? How can we monitor progress?' and later continues:

> The last ten years have seen changes in school organisation and curriculum. We need to be able to monitor the consequences for children's performance in school. We need to know how our schools are serving the changing needs of children and society.

The authors of the pamphlet add:

> It is not necessary to test every pupil, but monitoring performance by sampling in selected age groups in primary and secondary schools will provide a general picture of performance.

The task of constructing and administering tests has been entrusted to the National Foundation for Educational Research and to certain universities, all of them independent of DES control.

3.1.2   The organisers of an experimental course for first-year pupils in a secondary school met with a certain amount of scepticism both within the school and from parents. One might surmise that other specialist teachers saw the integration as potentially threatening to the values they believed in, and possibly likely to draw resources away from their own departments. Some parents wondered whether such an unorthodox organisation of part of the curriculum might affect their children's progress adversely. For this reason the school each year invited

3.1.2   someone from outside — a teacher from another school or a
contd   lecturer in an education department — to spend several days
        observing the course in progress and to write a report on what
        they saw. Analyse this evaluation according to the five questions.
3.1.3   Read the account by Harlen (1973) of the evaluation of the
        Schools Council Science 5-13 Project, and analyse the evaluation
        according to the five questions.

You may have noticed when answering question (4) 'for what purpose?'
that answers tend to fall into two categories. Sometimes information
about the success of a course is sought by teachers or by the members
of a curriculum-development team — themselves often seconded
teachers — solely for the purpose of revising and improving the course.
This kind of evaluation is often called 'formative', probably since it
contributes to the forming or shaping of the curriculum. The result of
formative evaluation is unlikely to be threatening to the teachers,
though it may imply extra work in replanning. The purpose of the
other kind of evaluation is to consider a curriculum as a whole and to
decide whether or not it deserves support. This kind of evaluation,
which is often called 'summative', can be very threatening to teachers
and administrators alike. The allocation of considerable sums of money
may be at stake, and their future careers and standing may depend
upon an outside evaluator's report. Evaluation is, in practice, seldom
purely formative or summative, since there is usually amongst its
motives both the wish to improve a curriculum as well as the wish to
persuade others of its value.

Task 3.2   Formative and summative evaluation

3.2   Consider each of the three cases of evaluation in Task 3.1 from
      the point of view of whether it is primarily formative or sum-
      mative. To what extent — in your opinion — do the answers to
      the other questions depend on the answer to question 4, 'for
      what purpose'? Or, in other words, does the purpose of evalua-
      tion determine its other characteristics?

What kinds of information are likely to be relevant to evaluating a
curriculum? A question like this may seem artificial to a teacher trying
to evaluate his own work, since he is likely to be sharply limited by
what he can get access to during the time available. Nevertheless, it is

useful to consider the full range of information that might be relevant, and the various methods needed to collect different kinds of information. On this basis you will be able to make an informed choice whenever you need to evaluate. For the purpose of displaying the range of possibilities, we shall first move away from the limitations of one teacher with his pupils and consider the strategies open to an evaluator who has been given time to evaluate a whole school programme, or to evaluate the course produced by a curriculum project as it is used in a sample of schools.

Evaluation strategies

When teachers turn their minds to evaluating the success of courses, what first occurs to them is often to test pupils' knowledge. While this may be useful, it is not always possible to carry it out very effectively. Will tests tell us which parts of the course are working well and which not? Will they tell us whether all of our pupils are benefiting equally? (Those pupils with high scores on a test are not necessarily those who have gained most.) Tests *can* be devised to give this information, though it is a complex task. What tests will not do is to tell us *why* one part of the course is not so successful as the rest, or *why* some pupils, classes or schools are gaining much less than others. Moreover there are some aims that are very difficult indeed to test; socio-cognitive aims such as 'display a critical habit of mind' are particularly obscure, partly because they show themselves only over long periods of time, and partly because they are likely to be inhibited by the test itself. The best evidence for such intangible aspects of the curriculum may be to demonstrate that pupils are indeed engaging in classroom activities likely to encourage their development, and perhaps showing hints of them there and then during lessons. In sum, tests of outcomes are useful but are far from exhausting the range of methods available.

What information may be useful, then, in evaluating a curriculum? First, we will consider this in very general terms, as if we were evaluators of a development project, and then narrow our attention to what may be practicable for a teacher in an average classroom. Robert Stake, an American evaluator, has made a helpful distinction between antecedents, transactions and outcomes (1969). The term *antecedents* refers to aspects of the situation that the curriculum is taught in, such as the time available, and the books and other resources provided. *Transactions* refers to what actually happens in lessons, including what is done by both teachers and pupils. *Outcomes* include pupils' achievements and also the effect of the curriculum on their attitudes to the subject, as well as teachers' feelings about teaching the curriculum. An approach that gives attention to antecedents and transactions as well as outcomes will be more likely to give the evaluator the opportunity to answer questions about *why* the curriculum was or was not effective in various circumstances.

At this point it is useful to make a distinction between the *intended* curriculum and the *observed* curriculum. They are not different curricula but the same seen from a different point of view. A group of teachers may get together and plan a new course, deciding together what ground they will cover, what materials they will use and the style of teaching they will adopt. Or a curriculum-development project may plan a course in detail, issuing a guide to teachers that proposes an appropriate teaching style and publishing a sequence of classroom materials. We can call both of these plans an 'intended curriculum'. But when intentions are put into practice they usually change in a smaller or greater degree, especially when they concern groups of young people who may, at times, be something less than fully co-operative. The 'observed curriculum' is what can be seen to happen. We can never know what happens more than in part; in our own lessons we are too busy to get more than an impression of what is going on. The project evaluator can observe lessons, interview teachers and pupils, look at the work done, and thus piece together his version of what actually happens. However, whether or not we are aware of it, there will certainly be gaps between our purposes and our performance, between intention and effect, between intended and observed curriculum.

Robert Stake's second contribution to our thinking about evaluation is to suggest that we can compare intention and effect with respect first to antecedents, then to transactions and then to outcomes. Let us illustrate this with examples. Amongst the various antecedents, the equipment that was supposed to be available for the pupils to use can be compared with what in fact was available. Amongst transactions, we might, for example, check whether the amount of time spent by pupils on individual work corresponded with what had originally been intended. As for outcomes, we come to a very familiar comparison between our objectives for children's learning and what they actually learn. These are, of course, only examples: what antecedents, transactions and outcomes an evaluator looks at depends on what seems important to the course in question. Another evaluator, Michael Scriven (1973) has argued that evaluators should not look at what is intended by the course planners, since some of the most important effects, pleasant or unpleasant, may come quite unplanned. However sensible this 'goal-free evaluation' may seem, evaluators usually cannot spare time to cast their nets at random.

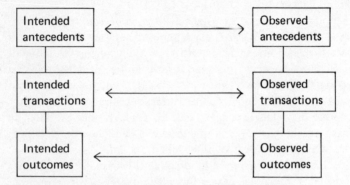

Figure 3.1 *Relationship between the intended and observed curricula as regards antecedents, transactions and outcomes*

Figure 3.1, adapted from Stake, summarises his analysis. Stake has proposed that it is the business of evaluators not only to observe the relation between the intended and the observed curriculum as regards antecedents, transactions and outcomes, but also to consider whether the intended antecedents together with the intended transactions were ever likely on the face of it to lead to the intended outcomes. (The observed antecedents and transactions clearly *did* lead to the observed outcomes.)

The next tasks require you to take up the simulated role of evaluator and to plan the evaluation of a course, and I suggest that you should use Stake's model (Figure 3.1) to guide your planning. An evaluator draws his account of the intended curriculum from whatever documents are available that describe what the course is intended to be. Intended antecedents will include the resources that are supposed to be available, the pupils for whom the course is intended, in sum the organisational context into which the course is to fit. Intended transactions are likely to appear either as a recommended style of teaching or a set of learning activities that are meant to take place. Intended outcomes may or may not take the form of objectives.

The observed curriculum, on the other hand, can only be observed, as the name suggests. There are, however, a wide range of possible sources which can give direct or indirect information about how the course turns out in practice and these are listed in the notes that follow the tasks.

Task 3.3 Simulated evaluation of courses

3.3.1 Evaluating part of a secondary-school curriculum

Two years ago Witherton School embarked on a new programme for the whole of its reception year. For three half-days each week all the 13-year-olds follow a common course called 'social, humane and literary studies', SHALS for short.

Witherton School is a well-established comprehensive school in a small town which is a few miles outside a large city. It has a seven-form entry and a large sixth form. It is well thought of locally, and its established reputation has given senior staff the confidence to encourage curriculum experiment, though with careful preparation of courses and monitoring of how they are put into effect. The SHALS course came out of the discussions of a group of enthusiastic young teachers of arts subjects, supported by a newly appointed deputy head, responsible for curriculum development amongst other things.

Approximately two hundred boys and girls enter upon the SHALS course during the first week of their lives in the high school. The course lasts for two terms, at the end of which there is an examination. After the examination pupils opt for the subjects which they will follow for two years until they sit CSE or GCE examinations. During those two terms the pupils work in mixed-ability classes in all subjects. Unlike SHALS, the rest of the curriculum during those two terms is organised in conventional subject-areas; science, for example, is taught separately as chemistry, physics and biology, and the science teachers bemoan the lack of time available.

The SHALS course is organised in units of a month, so that there are six units in all. The month begins with an extensive 'key session' lasting half a day: a group of three members of staff from different departments prepare presentations on the subject of the unit. Various subjects have been chosen during

183

3.3.1 the two years that the course has run, but the ones so far
contd favoured by the teachers involved include: 'The Family'; 'Witherton — a changing community'; and 'Ships and the sea'. It
is not clear, however, on what basis they favour these. The
same group also prepares classroom materials, boxes of books
and other resources, and lists of follow-up activities. Thus after
the initial presentation the pupils are randomly assigned to
groups, of which there are eight, each supervised by a member
of staff. It is intended that the member of staff, whatever his
or her specialism, should see to it that the pupils first carry out
the suggested activities, and then, when those are completed,
go on to choose relevant and useful individual projects. The unit
ends with an exhibition of a selection of work done by each of
the groups.

The values behind the SHALS course have been made plain
in a document circulated by the deputy headmaster before the
first course began. This document summarised the views
achieved during lengthy discussions between the deputy head
and the three teachers whose enthusiasm had led to the course
being set up. The headmaster had read the document and
approved it on a temporary and trial basis. A local education
authority adviser had also interested himself in the planning,
and had not only found extra funds for buying resources, such
as extra books, but had played some part in persuading the
headmaster. Amongst the values expressed in the document
were the following.

1 Pupils should have an opportunity to study issues that cross
  subject boundaries.
2 Pupils should be encouraged to find problems for themselves
  and work out ways by which they might be solved.
3 Nevertheless, it is important that pupils should practise
  those skills which they would have learnt had they studied
  history, geography, art and English as separate subjects.
4 Besides their individual work, pupils should have the opportunity to take part in discussion both led by a teacher and
  in small groups.

Other values and purposes were also listed. It was emphasised
in the document that pupils should be given the responsibility
of becoming active agents in their own education, in order to
encourage them to think for themselves and to collaborate with

3.3.1 others. The goals of SHALS were — the document concluded —
contd both cognitive and social.

During the second year of the project a local newspaper printed an article on the school which, though on the whole enthusiastic, hinted that some anxiety was felt both inside and outside the school about the SHALS course. This led some of the local education authority advisory staff to press the headmaster to carry out an evaluation of the course, and finance was put aside to release a teacher from another secondary or middle school from teaching for a term to carry out an evaluation of the course and report back to the staff of the school, who would then decide whether to make the report public or to take other action.

As a teacher in a nearby school you have been vaguely aware that Witherton School had organised an integrated humanities course, and when you were approached by an adviser with the invitation to be seconded for a term to act as evaluator, you accepted after consulting your own headteacher. So far you have had no opportunity for anything beyond informal conversations with a Witherton teacher who is a neighbour of yours, and with the local education authority adviser, who was the one who originally supported the project. From these conversations you have derived no more than vague hints and impressions.

Current gossip indicates that there is dissatisfaction amongst several groups of Witherton teachers about SHALS. There is talk of wasted time, of bad behaviour by pupils who have gone outside the school grounds during SHALS periods, of failure to learn any geography or history, and of falling standards in written work. Teachers involved in SHALS are said to think that they have not received adequate support either from the headmaster or from the deputy head, who originally encouraged them, and in particular that they have not been given enough time for joint planning and preparing materials. A particular point of contention seems to be that not all staff timetabled to SHALS are enthusiastic about it: one teacher is reported to have said that he is not going to have 'his' class wasting time on the activities prepared for the current unit. However, all this is gossip at second-hand, so you are wary of taking it at face-value.

3.3.1   Your immediate task is to plan how you will use your term,
contd   which will be the first term of a new SHALS course. Decide
        (i) what information you need and (ii) how you will get it.
        You can count on co-operation from the enthusiasts amongst
        the SHALS teachers, but they are unlikely to spare much time.
        Plan your term so that you have a reasonably clear idea about
        the order and duration of each of your information-gathering
        activities. (See the 'Note on Tasks 3.3.1 and 3.3.2' on pp.
        188-9 for suggestions about how to carry this out.)

3.3.2   **Evaluating part of a primary-school curriculum**
        Humby Lane County Primary School has always been well
        thought of. Drawing its pupils from a socially mixed area on
        the outskirts of a large city, the school had been streamed
        until a new headmistress seven years ago instituted mixed-
        ability grouping throughout. Not all of her fourteen colleagues
        were equally enthusiastic about this reorganisation, and they
        expressed particular uneasiness about the effect of mixed-
        ability grouping upon their teaching of mathematics. Many of
        the teachers began to use commercially produced workcards
        in mathematics, or to prepare their own. The effect of this
        was to generate an extreme diversity in the mathematics cur-
        riculum, so that pupils in different classes experienced both
        different mathematical topics and different styles of teaching.
        After a year or two the effect of this upon continuity became
        apparent, and soon the headmistress began staff discussions
        which eventually led to the adoption of the School Mathe-
        matics Project 7-13, with the intention that pupils should follow
        the same sequence of topics whichever class they were in, and
        receive similar styles of mathematics teaching whichever teacher
        taught them.
            The SMP School Mathematics Project 7-13 curriculum has
        now been in progress for two years, and not everyone is entirely
        satisfied. It is clear from staff-room talk that not all members of
        staff are committed to mixed-ability grouping and that this
        includes in some cases disapproval of the SMP cards. More-
        over, some other teachers who do support mixed-ability group-
        ing nevertheless confess to problems with their classes in using
        the scheme. (It is not clear, however, which classes these are.)
        The headmistress has received a visit from a group of middle-

3.3.2 class parents, including one of the school managers, who believe
contd that their children are not making the progress that they might
have made with more conventional teaching. She is not clear
from what they say whether there is any objective basis for this, or
whether they are responding primarily to the unfamiliarity of
the course. However, the headmistress has been disturbed
enough to consult the local education authority mathematics
adviser. The adviser has suggested that a teacher from another
primary school, who is to be seconded to follow an advanced
diploma course in a nearby university, should undertake an
evaluation of the mathematics curriculum as part of the requirements of the course.

You are, of course, the teacher in question. Your university
tutor has told you that you will have approximately a day a
week for two terms, and a whole fortnight at the end of the first
term, for carrying out the study. You have made one visit to
the school, a visit made easier by the fact that you are already
on friendly terms with two of the teachers who were your
contemporaries at college. One of them, who is something
of an enthusiast for SMP, blames the difficulties upon members
of staff who do not follow the SMP guidelines closely enough,
and hints that if pupils are bored it is because there is not
enough time given to discussion either as a whole class or in
groups. Your other friend is less enthusiastic, saying that some
of her less able pupils have difficulty in using the cards, perhaps
because of reading problems, and complete only one or two
cards on each topic. She also speaks of the difficulty of knowing
where individual pupils have reached and what problems they
are experiencing, and says that if children sometimes waste time
it is because she has not enough time to get round and sort out
their difficulties. She hints at inadequacies in the accommodation and equipment available, but seems unwilling to enlarge on
this. The headmistress says that she is not sure that the SMP
scheme has achieved the continuity she had hoped for, since
some teachers are introducing other written materials into lessons,
and some not. She is also concerned about achieving agreement on
the notation to be taught, and on a consistent scheme for assessing
pupils' progress. These conversations suggest some lines of inquiry, but you resolve that you will regard what has been said as
in need of more objective checking and confirmation.

3.3.2   Humby Lane School has pupils from 7 to 11 years of age,
contd   organised in year-groups of about a hundred pupils in each.
Each year-group is taught in three separate classes, and remains with the same class teacher for English, mathematics
and environmental studies. The headmistress has promised to
give you confidential access to record cards, but you are not
clear how wholeheartedly accommodating some of her colleagues
may prove to be.

Your immediate task is to plan how you are going to carry
out the evaluation. This includes deciding what information you
need — your tutor has shown you Robert Stake's model — and
working out the most likely ways of obtaining it. It will also be
necessary to plan the sequence of your information-gathering
activities on the basis of an estimate of how much time each
will require.

Note on Tasks 3.3.1 and 3.3.2

These tasks can be approached in three stages.

What information do I need? Stake's model will help you to answer
this, since you will need to know what the *intended* antecedents,
transactions and outcomes are. Then you should *observe* as much as
possible of what happens, also in terms of antecedents, transactions
and outcomes.

How can I best obtain this information? You can use the list made in
answer to the first question, and write possible methods against each
item. A checklist of information and methods, which should help you
to decide, is given in Table 3.1. You would not have time to use more
than a proportion of the methods listed, so you will have to select realistically in the light of the time available and the relative importance
of the information.

How long can I spare for each activity and in what order? You may
find it helpful to use a diagram with the time-line marked in weeks as
the basis for planning how you would apportion the time available to
various information-gathering activities. Nevertheless, your final answer
to the task as a whole should be primarily concerned with explaining

TABLE 3.1 *Observed curriculum*

	Kinds of information	*Methods*
Antecedents	Organisational background	Timetable
	Resources	Syllabuses and text-books
	Attitudes of administrators, parents	Interviews
	Examinations available	
	Context in curriculum	Interviews with staff
	Knowledge and skills of pupils	Planning sessions
Transactions (in lessons)	Teachers: Roles adopted	
	Use of time and re-sources	Activity records
	Contact with pupils	Observation of class
	Pupils: Cognitive processes	Self-report by teachers
	Interest and involve-ment	Self-report by pupils
	Use of time	Observation of individuals
Outcomes	Pupils' achievements	Tests and written work
	Pupils' attitudes, inter-pretations	Questionnaires
	Teachers' attitudes, inter-pretations	Interviews
	Effects on other parts of institution	

what you would do and why.

To the tutor. These two tasks have been planned to refer to particular curriculum materials, but they can readily be modified. It may be more appropriate for a particular group of students to consider the problems of adopting a course in their own subject-area. If so, it would be possible, with some changes, to substitute in the secondary-school task a different set of materials, perhaps the Schools Council Integrated Science Project or the Schools Council History 13-16 Project or a series of textbooks, or in the primary-school task the Breakthrough materials or a more traditional reading scheme. A simulation exercise of this kind is particularly useful to prepare students for a visit to a school where the materials are in use, since it will direct students' attention to aspects of the materials in use that they might otherwise take for granted.

Analysing curriculum materials

Most teachers are involved to some extent in the evaluation and selection of curriculum materials. A publisher's representative appears in the staff-room at break and spreads his wares upon a table conveniently near the door. As teachers come in they pause and glance at a textbook or two, and may be drawn into conversation with the representative and ask for specimen copies of some of the books. Indeed, I can remember one or two regrettable occasions when colleagues have bought a set of textbooks on no more detailed inspection than break-time allows. Textbooks that may shape the learning activities of hundreds or even thousands of pupils deserve more careful analysis and choice; the purpose of the next task is to give you an opportunity to carry out a detailed analysis. Perhaps it is more detailed than most teachers would think practicable in the rush of school life; its justification, however, is to direct your attention to aspects of classroom materials that may in future inform your choice, in the hope that, though your examination of potential purchases may in future take up less time than this analysis, it may be no less searching.

In order to help you to look at every relevant aspect of the materials I shall provide a detailed analytical scheme for you to follow. No one scheme, however, can fit all curriculum materials. This scheme is therefore intended to be adapted to fit whatever materials or textbook you are analysing. Omit any questions that seem not to fit, and give varying emphasis to others according to their importance. If you seem already to have answered a question under a previous heading there is no purpose to be served by repeating that part of your answer.

The scheme will fit any materials that include details of what children should do — whether or not this includes classroom texts — and a statement of goals and methods. It can be used to analyse textbooks, either one or a series, and is particularly appropriate to the publications of Schools Council or Nuffield curriculum-development projects, when they include details of classroom activities. It can be used to analyse some curricula developed by individual schools, but only where these include specific recommendations as well as general statements of goals. It is not useful for analysing books that offer advice to teachers without providing detailed plans for pupils' learning activities.

You would be well advised to begin by familiarising yourself with the layout and the general values and procedures of the materials you are going to analyse. Then read carefully through the scheme for the analysis of curriculum materials so that you understand its structure: it begins with an analytical description of the materials, continues with discussion of how they are intended to be used, and ends with an evaluation of various aspects. You are advised to be as objective as possible during the first two parts, putting aside your own values and preferences, and speaking for an imaginary 'typical teacher'. The final part of the evaluation section invites you to write from your own experience and commitment a personal evaluation that constitutes the culmination of the whole. I suggest that you write a continuous essay, yet keep to the main sequence of the scheme. (It may occur to you that what you are doing is carrying out a detailed description of an intended curriculum.)

If you choose a whole course including a great deal of material it will be necessary at various points in the analysis to choose representative sections — a booklet, a chapter, etc. — for more detailed analysis. If you are working in a group, the parts can be shared between you. Some of the analytical description requires you to determine the relative emphasis of one topic as against another, or one learning activity as against another. You will be well advised to devise ways of estimating amounts and emphases, so as to avoid laborious and unproductive counting. It is best to share such tasks with others, and meet to discuss the results.

Task 3.4 Analysis of curriculum materials

3.4   Carry out an analysis of a body of classroom materials. They should include both (i) details of classroom learning activities and (ii) statements of goals and methods. This task can be

3.4
contd

carried out on any scale, from two hours spent on a single chapter in a textbook to several weeks spent on a large and complex body of published materials. The analysis should be structured by the 'Scheme for the analysis of curriculum materials'.

Scheme for the analysis of curriculum materials

The design of the set of questions below owes much to Eraut, Goad and Smith (1974).

A Description
1 Overt characteristics
   (*a*) What do the materials consist of? Are they composed of a series of volumes? Do they include other resources not in book form? To whom are they addressed?
   (*b*) What are their stated aims? (Quote or summarise as appropriate.)
   (*c*) What pupils and educational context are they said to be intended for?
2 Analysis.
   (When teachers' and pupils' materials are separate it may be decided to deal with each in turn, using this set of questions to guide each analysis.)
   (*a*) What content is to be presented to pupils? (Devise a form of analysis appropriate to the particular materials; this might constitute, for example, a list of topics with an estimate of the relative emphasis given to each of them.) What importance is placed on the sequence of the topics? Do any central principles unite them?
   (*b*) What range of learning activities or exercises is provided for pupils? What skills are to be exercised? What relative emphasis is placed upon them? (You may find that the categories and questions on p. 195 will help you with this part of the analysis. You will in any case need to set up categories and estimate frequencies within each of them.)
   (*c*) Are there indications of appropriate tests (as against learning activities) for learners? If so, what knowledge and skills do they emphasise?

3   Analysis of sections. If the materials are too lengthy for detailed
analysis, supplement the above questions by a detailed account of
a typical section, or of two contrasting sections.

  (*a*) What concepts are presented in the section? (This analysis
       might include their level of abstraction, their interrelation-
       ships, and the means by which they are presented, including
       the use of examples and illustrations.)

  (*b*) If the section does not present concepts, what does it do?
       What relative emphases are placed upon knowledge, skills,
       values and attitudes?

  (*c*) How are learning activities (if any) related to content?

4   Underlying assumptions. (This section deals with characteristics
which, though unstated, can be inferred.)

  (*a*) What view of the nature of the subject-matter (or of know-
       ledge in general) appears to underlie these materials?

  (*b*) What conception of teaching and learning in this subject
       seems to underlie these materials? Do they embody a view of
       social relationships in the classroom, or of the part played by
       the pupils in learning?

B   Materials in use

1   Use of the materials

  (*a*) How are the materials intended to be used? (Here the emphasis
       falls on the teacher's use, in contrast to the pupils' use in
       A1(*a*).)

  (*b*) How far are teaching methods made explicit and how far are
       they left to the teacher? What decisions would have to be
       made?

  (*c*) Where could the materials find a place in the whole curricu-
       lum? Would other courses have to precede or follow them?
       How would they relate to parallel courses? Would integrating
       be possible, or duplication of subject-matter?

  (*d*) How do the materials relate to available examinations, or to
       other demands for demonstrable knowledge or skills?

2   Resources

  (*a*) Will special timetabling be necessary?

  (*b*) Are further resources required?

3   Teachers

  (*a*) Do the materials imply a high level of specialist expertise and
       knowledge in the teachers who are to use them?

    (*b*) Will the use of the materials make special demands on teachers'
         time and skills before or during their use?

    (*c*) Will special teacher training be required?

4   Pupils. What preliminary knowledge and skills are required in pupils?

5   Adaptation. What modifications would be likely if the materials were used in non-ideal situations? Would any parts be likely to be changed or omitted? How radically would these affect the nature of the course?

C   Evaluation

1   What objections might be made to the values and purposes which underlie the materials? (Here you should speak for educators in general.) What arguments can be mustered in support of these values? (The following question deals with the means to these ends.)

2   What objections might be made to the materials and methods as means of putting these values and purposes into effect? What practical problems might arise? (Apart from those already mentioned in B3 and B5.)

3   Are there any reports or evaluations of these materials? Were they tried out and modified during writing? What opinions of them have been expressed in informal reviews and reports? Estimate the reliability of these judgments.

4   Would you yourself choose to use these materials? Come to a personal judgment upon the materials, briefly indicating which of the various considerations already mentioned weighed most in your conclusion. (If you are working as a group, each member should write a separate personal judgment.)

Analysing worksheets

Worksheets, whether published or made by the teachers who use them, are widely utilised as a means of diversifying curricula within a class, particularly if it is unstreamed. They are intended to allow children to work at their own speed, and to keep all of them busy while the teacher gives attention to individuals. They have, however, been criticised for failing to encourage pupils to think (especially by requiring much copying from books), for requiring pupils to answer questions with no more than a few words· rather than at length, for isolating pupils who need more discussion with adults, and − in sum − for functioning more as a control device than as means of helping children to learn. The advocates of worksheets retort that worksheets need not be open to these criticisms if they are properly written. There is thus a considerable need for a basis on which to analyse worksheets in order to determine whether they are likely to encourage the kind of learning required.

Some teachers become anxious whether the language used in worksheets is too difficult for pupils. This is indeed one matter to be considered, but only one. Since worksheets are usually intended to encourage pupils to think, it seems important not only to consider what activities pupils are engaged in, but also what cognitive demands those activities are likely to make.

The scheme that follows can also be used for analysing the learning activities proposed in a textbook or other curriculum materials, and thus can function as an adjunct to the first section of the 'Scheme for the analysis of curriculum materials'.

Scheme for the analysis of worksheets

1 Presentation of information. How is the information presented?
(*a*) In written form on the worksheet itself (through specific references to other limited sources *or* to be gathered by pupils through a wider search).
(*b*) Orally:
by the teacher;
by recording, radio, TV.
(*c*) Drawn from pupils' memories.
(*d*) Visually (pictures, maps, models).
(*e*) Demonstration by teacher.
(*f*) Manipulation of materials or apparatus by pupils.
(*g*) To be obtained by inquiry outside school.

2 Pupils' activities. What is the nature of the activities for pupils?
(*a*) Are psycho-motor skills involved?
(*b*) Are value-judgments required?
(*c*) Do the activities demand collaboration or new social roles?
(*d*) What writing is required? Are answers to be 'continuous' or in phrases and single sentences? Is an audience mentioned?

195

(e) Is discussion asked for? What purpose is it to serve? How clear is the task?

(f) Does the work require imaginative projection (for example, into a work of literature or a historical situation)?

3 Cognitive processes. What kinds of thinking are the pupils required to engage in?

Level I   1 Reproducing information from texts with little or no modification.

        2 Recalling.

Level II 3 Measuring and recording numerical data.

        4 Categorising (identifying and naming).

        5 Reading to find specific information.

        6 Applying procedures (for example, calculation).

        7 Describing observations (without interpretation).

        8 Translating from one medium to another (for example, map to verbal).

Level III 9 Summarising information.

        10 Planning (to test hypothesis, etc.).

        11 Narrating (within specifications, imaginative projection, etc.).

        12 Describing (within a frame of reference, but not drawing general conclusions or explanations).

Level IV 13 Interpreting or hypothesising (placing phenomenon in a theoretical framework).

        14 Applying principles (to an unfamiliar type of problem).

        15 Problem-finding (formulating issues to investigate).

4 Context of use

(a) Are the tasks appropriate to the pupils for whom they are intended? Is there any provision for different levels of ability?

(b) Is the language used within the reach of the pupils?

(c) How closely do the tasks set define the content and format of the expected response?

(d) Are alternatives offered? How far are pupils expected to choose or make other decisions?

(e) Are the worksheets self-sufficient or do they imply that other resources will be available?

Notes. These questions may need modification for different kinds of subject-matter. For example, worksheets based on stories or poems will need an alternative scheme to that headed 'cognitive processes'. Often the answer to questions will be 'no'; their purpose is to urge the reader to consider whether this should be so.

Task 3.5 Analysis of worksheets

3.5 Take a set of worksheets — perhaps borrowing them from a school you visit — and analyse them according to the above scheme.

See Appendix G for examples of worksheets for analysis.

Studying a curriculum in action

We now turn from the analysis of classroom materials to what is both more realistic and more difficult, the analysis of what actually goes on in classrooms. In the end our ability to evaluate curriculum, which is part of taking joint responsibility for the schooling we offer to young people, will depend upon our ability to offer realistic accounts of teaching and learning, not in the idealised form in which they appear in curriculum documents, but as they happen in schools. As has already been said, tests of children's achievement do not on their own enable us to evaluate the curriculum; at best they tell us something of what has been learnt, but not how and why.

This empirical study of the curriculum will be approached in three stages. First, there will be discussion of how a group of students working together can carry out a descriptive analysis of the whole curriculum of a school, leading to the writing of a joint case-study. Then we shall turn to the description and evaluation of a particular course; some of the principles put forward in the section concerned with the whole curriculum will also be relevant here. Finally, we consider a number of contrasting schemes for observing classroom teaching.

A case-study of a school

It can be very illuminating to study the curriculum of a single school, particularly if one is able to penetrate beneath the taken-for-granted

197

phrases and beliefs which help teachers to carry out their everyday work, but which do not necessarily represent the whole of the purposes and concerns that shape their actions. We must, of course, share many of these beliefs with them; if we did not we would not be able to understand what was going on in a lesson. But a degree of detachment is essential. That is why it is probably better not to carry out a study like the one about to be proposed in the school in which one is teaching: to detach oneself from one's everyday assumptions would require superhuman efforts. (More closely defined studies in one's own school are another matter.)

A case-study of this kind can vary greatly in scale, from a superficial and possibly misleading single visit to a long-term research inquiry. In suggesting methods for carrying out a study of a school's curriculum I shall assume a group of students who may or may not be experienced teachers, and who are able to spend only a limited time in the school.

What strategy is it best to adopt? There will be relatively objective information to be gathered about the way in which the curriculum is organised in the school; next, it will be necessary to obtain an outline of the aims and values that have been officially adopted for the school; one would also hope to get insight into how the curriculum aims are put into effect. Part of this would be to understand any constraints that teachers feel they work under which affect their teaching. Finally, it would be useful to find out how curriculum decisions are made in that school. Some of these latter kinds of information may require several visits and a good deal of skill and perceptiveness in carrying out the inquiry. There now follows a more detailed breakdown of these kinds of information.

1 Structure of the curriculum.
Common core; differentiation according to streams or bands.
Changes according to pupils' ages: compulsory elements; options; new subjects or activities introduced.
Subdivisions of the timetable (secondary): subjects, faculties, integrated time: relative time spent on each.
Subdivision of the timetable (primary): which activities are timetabled? What structured activities (for example, reading schemes)? What is left to the teacher?

2 Declared aims and values.
School aims: personal and social values.

Aims and values of particular areas of the curriculum.
Preferred teaching-learning procedures.

3 Covert values and constraints.
Which aspects of content or skills are emphasised, if taken over a length
of time.
Typical patterns of lesson organisation and teaching-learning procedures
as they have been observed.
Teachers' explanations of why they diverge from recommended
methods.
Teachers' problems: constraints they are aware of.
Teachers' views of their pupils' characteristics and capabilities.

4 Control of curriculum in the school.
Official assignment of responsibility to individuals or committees.
Structure of departments: structure for pastoral care (if any).
Control of resources, including rooms and time.
Siting and control of learning materials.
Teachers' perception of their own influence on decisions.
Pupils' and parents' participation.

Gaining understanding of the curriculum as a whole is likely to be
a very different matter in a small primary school from what it is in a
large comprehensive high school; in schools without a departmental
structure some of the above headings will not be applicable. In large
schools, the organisation into subject departments, or into the more
inclusive 'faculties' suggested by Lawton (1975), makes it likely that
each department will have available a statement of values, over and
above any statement for the school as a whole. If a group of students
sets out to study the curriculum of a school large enough to have a
departmental organisation, it will be best to organise the work in three
stages. First, the whole group meets the headteacher and other senior
members of staff, such as the deputy head responsible for curriculum
development, if one exists. Then they divide into subgroups to investigate the major departments, while other subgroups might look into
such topics as the effect on children's learning of the arrangements
for access to books and other resources, the interaction between the
pastoral and academic roles of teachers, and the implications of the
school's internal monitoring, testing and examining procedures. Such
a division of responsibility between subgroups naturally implies that

the students will take extensive notes, and after discussion write reports for presentation to the other subgroups. In the final stage, after these reports have been circulated, there needs to be generous time for the whole group to discuss the information gathered and the issues raised by it. Indeed, this last is the prime aim of a case-study of this kind. The curricular issues have more verisimilitude and importance for the students because they have arisen from teachers', administrators' and pupils' accounts of what they do and why. Curriculum is concerned with the realisation of purposes and values within the constraints and pressures of a particular organisational milieu; to understand it requires insight not only into what is done but also into why. That is why a study of the observed curriculum, of curriculum in action, is so important.

Let us consider for a moment what is the nature of a study of curriculum in action. The curriculum analyst's first task is to describe, not judge; to present a representative display of evidence, not to evaluate it. A totally unbiased approach is, of course, impossible: the analyst's description is inevitably based upon preconceptions which cause him to interpret what he sees and hears in this way rather than that, and to treat this piece of evidence as significant rather than another. Nevertheless, for the purpose of description it is important to take up a stance which minimises the effect of one's own values and concerns, by constructing the viewpoint of an informed but uninvolved spectator.

It is essential to detach oneself as far as possible from the taken-for-granted assumptions of the teachers one is talking to, in order to see the familiar events of the classroom not as inevitable but afresh as one amongst many possibilities. For this reason it may be advisable for any student who has a teaching specialism not to study the department of the school concerned with his own subject, since familiarity will tend to blunt freshness of vision.

The first and second stages of the study, I have proposed, should be predominantly descriptive, though with the proviso that the description will include summaries of what teachers have said and perhaps accounts of lessons observed which are necessarily based upon an observer's judgment. At the third stage, when the reports are collated and discussed, it will be appropriate to consider from an explicitly evaluative stance those aspects of the curriculum that the reports describe. What has been observed can often be compared with the school's own declared aims and values; the educational implications of curriculum organisation can be teased out; and an attempt can be made to reconstruct the school's hidden curriculum, those unstated norms and procedures that are covertly communicated to pupils. (It should not be forgotten that the hidden curriculum communicated to one group of pupils may differ from that communicated to others.)

Although there is some information about the curriculum which has a quasi-objective, public status — as, for example, that contained in a school's timetable or the formal requirements laid out in an examination syllabus — this takes us only a short distance towards understanding what is actually taught and learnt in the school. For this reason it is useful to distinguish 'the intended curriculum' from 'the observed curriculum', in the way that has already been discussed. The intended curriculum exists in syllabuses, in lists of objectives and in teachers' formal statements of their values and intentions. The observed curriculum is harder to get access to as it is part of the ongoing life of the school. At best we can hope to piece together a picture of it from observing lessons, talking to teachers about what happens in lessons you have seen, sitting with pupils while they work, looking at what they produce, and so on. Of course, there will usually be considerable correspondence between the intended and the observed curriculum, but human intentions are almost always modified in action. An adequate account of a school's curriculum necessarily includes both what is intended and what is observed to happen.

Nor are we dealing for the most part with objective information. Curriculum is concerned with purposes and their outcomes; people's perceptions of these inevitably differ. A headteacher is likely to place emphases differently from a young probationer; a teacher of young children will pursue different educational goals from a teacher of adolescents; a teacher of English has a different conception of knowledge and learning from a teacher of science. Pupils, too, have their own goals — even though they do not formulate them as specific objectives — so that they see lessons and school as a whole in a different light from their teachers. The outside observer sitting in on a lesson may detect emphases and preferences that the teacher himself is unaware of, though it is always wise to give the teacher the opportunity to comment on and explain the behaviour that has been observed, since the observer may have entirely misunderstood his motives. An understanding of a school's curriculum has therefore to be built up from a range of diverse perspectives, of which the observer's perspective is only one, and fallible. To describe such a diversity of perspectives the

201

investigator needs to cast his net wide. Sources of information might include the following.

Documents. School timetables, syllabuses, letters and information sheets addressed to parents and pupils, and formal examination syllabuses are all valuable resources which can be analysed to give not only information about the curriculum in general but also indications of priorities, values, different emphases for different groups of pupils, and so on.

Formal interviews with teachers. By 'formal' interviews it is implied that the interviewer will follow a schedule of questions; suggestions for such a schedule follow on pp. 207-8.

It is often useful to ask teachers what they would like to do but cannot, since this is likely to elicit from them what they perceive as the institutional and other forces, which shape and constrain how they realise their curricular aims. Amongst the issues that may arise from this starting-point are the presence of interdepartmental rivalries for time, resources and able pupils, the competing interests (in secondary schools) of academic departments and pastoral staff, and the view taken by teachers of pupils and their parents. In this last case the investigator should watch for stereotyped views of pupils' home backgrounds, while carefully avoiding questions such as 'what are the children here like?' which invite stereotyping. It is extremely unlikely that all the homes in a school's catchment area are culturally alike; such stereotypes, however, are sometimes used to justify one curriculum policy or another.

Amongst the issues that might be dealt with during formal and informal conversations with teachers are those related to the control of the curriculum. In a large school there will probably be official machinery for curriculum development, perhaps a committee or a senior member of staff given the responsibility of encouraging and guiding the reconsideration and renewal of curricula. In both smaller and larger schools it is valuable to consider which members of staff have access to information, who can initiate discussions or influence decisions, who sits on committees or allocates resources, including money, accommodation, books and apparatus. It may prove informative to ask teachers from various groups — probationers, teachers of some years' experience, heads of departments and deputy heads, for example — how far they are able to take part in curriculum renewal and influence decisions at various levels. Appropriate strategies include asking about the history of recent attempts at innovation, successful or otherwise, and asking about curriculum changes that a teacher would like to see in the school.

Informal talk with teachers. Teachers may give a more complete insight into their purposes and concerns if it is possible to arrange to talk to them in an informal context, perhaps over a cup of coffee after school. Those investigators who make repeated visits to a school have greater opportunity to achieve more open relationships with teachers. But in any case, when the observer has sat through a lesson, and is therefore able to ask about specific episodes and the reason for handling them as the teacher did, the teacher may give a very different account of his motives from that which he would have given, if asked out of context for an explanation of his goals and methods. The informal chat and joking which teachers engage in when relaxing in the staff-room can also be informative. Such talk frequently acts as a safety-valve for negative and cynical attitudes which would be unlikely to be expressed in an interview. Whether these attitudes play a significant part in shaping teachers' actions is more difficult to decide; to take them at their face value is potentially misleading.

Observation. The purpose of observing lessons is to gain access to the teacher's logic-in-action. When you ask a teacher about his aims you are likely to be given a view of what he would ideally like to achieve, and he may moreover be influenced by a desire to gain your approval, especially if he knows you to be an experienced teacher. In his classroom teaching, however, the aims are likely to be modified by constraints of time and materials, and by exigencies arising from moment-by-moment interaction with pupils, who naturally have minds of their own. He will cope with these constraints and exigencies in terms of an implicit logic-in-action which he himself may not be aware of. This logic can be made available in only two ways: by analysing what the teacher actually does; and by asking him to comment on particular episodes, as has been suggested above. One's task as observer is to detach oneself from the taken-for-granted assumptions that make life in classrooms so familiar, and look beneath them in order to understand the pressures and processes that shape that life. In part, this is a matter of identifying the purposes and constraints that influence the teacher, and in part of reconstructing the messages that classroom events are likely to

203

communicate implicitly to pupils, the messages that constitute the so-called 'hidden curriculum'.

A useful strategy is to consider how far the teacher's declared aims and values are being put into effect. Alternatively, one may observe the use that is being made of published curriculum materials. Nuffield science courses, or the Humanities Curriculum Project materials, for example, include explicit recommendations for their use: the curriculum proposals include prescriptions for learning activities and for styles of teacher-pupil interaction. These can be used as a baseline for observing how far teachers using the materials conform to or diverge from the prescription. (See pp. 212-18 for details of methods that can be used.) It should be emphasised, however, that there should be no presumption that the project prescriptions are in some sense 'the right way of doing it' and any divergent methods 'wrong'. One's interest should be in the nature of the divergence, and the explanation that the teacher gives of it, which may itself need further 'explanation'.

The representativeness of the few lessons observed may be something of a problem. Are they typical of that teacher? Is the teacher typical of the department or of the school? Would there be differences with different groups of pupils? Unless a group of students can spread out and observe lessons taught by various teachers to various classes it will be dangerous to generalise. Nevertheless, even a little observation can confirm or disconfirm impressions formed elsewhere. Observation other than in classrooms can sometimes be of unexpected value. Time spent in a library or resource centre watching how it is used by teachers and pupils is not necessarily wasted, for example.

Interviews with pupils.   Even adolescent pupils are often unreflective about the curriculum and treat it as god-given — as do some teachers, of course — so that direct questioning is unlikely to be fruitful. Most pupils, however, are perceptive about what gains a teacher's approval, even those who seldom earn it, and this can be a source of indirect evidence about the implicit values of different curriculum-areas. What skills and knowledge really matter in a certain teacher's lessons? Is originality or conformity more valued? How much time is spent on practical work? Are pupils forever being reminded of an impending external examination? Which children seemed to be approved of? Why? Such questions can usefully be addressed to less conforming or less 'successful' boys and girls as well as to 'model pupils' who may reflect the publicly acknowledged values of their teachers.

Most teachers readily invite visitors to move about their classrooms and talk to pupils while they are working, and this gives an admirable opportunity to investigate pupils' grasp of the goals and purposes of the work they have been set, their acceptance or rejection of those goals, and what values and abilities that part of the curriculum seems in their eyes to be primarily concerned with.

Text and exercise books.   Textbooks on the shelves are not very informative: it is essential to find out how much and for what purposes they are used. Exercise books and other collections of children's work are more valuable, since they may constitute a kind of summary of work done, or at least they can do so for 'academic' subjects in middle and high schools. A rapid analysis of the contents of three or four exercise books can give information about the range of subject-matter covered during a period of time, and at least an impression of the range of learning activities. This could be misleading, however, if it is not accompanied by questions to the teacher, since some significant work might not be represented there, particularly if the class at times is divided for different kinds or levels of work. In the more practical areas of the curriculum, and with younger children, this source of information is not available and so one must look elsewhere — to teachers' records, to checklists, to workcards — to find what activities have taken place.

Questions for interview schedules

The questions that follow are not intended as a prescription but to form a basis for discussion, and should be used selectively, modified and supplemented according to the characteristics of the school, and the issues which interest the investigators. (It should be noted that some of these questions, particularly in the first section and those addressed to heads of departments, are unlikely to be appropriate in a first or primary school.)

1 Questions for headmasters, their deputies, and co-ordinators of curriculum

Management of curriculum

(*a*) Which parts of the curriculum are common to all the pupils in each age-group? If there are differentiated courses, how are pupils assigned to them?

(*b*) How is the curriculum subdivided? How much time is given to each subdivision? Do any subdivisions require special resources? Are any more important or suited to different pupils?

(*c*) What changes take place in the curriculum as the pupil becomes older? Are options available? Is choice totally free or are there restrictions? What advise is available to pupils?

(*d*) Who is involved in making decisions about (i) the timetable, (ii) the allocation of pupils to classes, groups or courses, (iii) the content of the curriculum? Is there any formal structure concerned with curriculum change?

(*e*) How are the teachers organised into teaching teams? Who takes responsibility for (i) the courses taught and (ii) the pastoral care of pupils?

(*f*) Do you have a policy about monitoring and testing achievement? What records are kept?

Aims and values

(*a*) Are teachers expected to take responsibility for their own curricular goals, or does the school have overall aims? Do you have any documents which explain the school's aims and values?

(*b*) What do you expect of your pupils as members of the school community? What school rules are there? How do you deal with anti-social behaviour? How do you cope with matters such as school assembly or movement about the school?

(*c*) Is there a school policy about teaching methods or teacher-pupil relationships?

Influences and constraints

(*a*) How well do your premises fit the school's needs? Are there parts of the curriculum where lack of resources, etc. prevent desirable development?

(*b*) If you had to recruit entirely new staff would you make any changes of grouping or emphasis?

(*c*) What arrangements do you make for consultation with parents about the curriculum? How much interest do the parents show?

(*d*) Are there any other influences from outside the school which you take into account when planning?

2 Questions for heads of department and others responsible for curriculum areas

(*a*) How do you see the subject-matter which you are responsible for?
Does the subject have goals different from those of other subjects?
Which parts of the subject are most important? How would you
rate in importance (i) the learning of information, (ii) the ability
to think in the way demanded by the subject, (iii) mastering skills,
(iv) developing appropriate attitudes?

(*b*) Are there patterns of teaching and learning which particularly fit
the subject? Is there a departmental policy about teacher-pupil
relationships in the classroom? How important is (i) written
work, (ii) oral discussion, (iii) practical work?

(*c*) Do you think that your subject is receiving its proper share of
time and resources? What arguments would you advance to get
more?

(*d*) How do you make decisions about courses? Who does the detailed
planning?

(*e*) Do you make any arrangements to ensure continuity from one year
to the next, or continuity with other schools?

(*f*) Are textbooks the main learning resources used by the department? What others are used? How are they stored and made
available (i) to teachers, (ii) to pupils?

(*g*) What is the department's policy about external examinations?
What methods are used for monitoring, recording or testing pupils'
progress?

(*h*) How do you regard the possibility of collaborating with other
departments?

3 Questions for other teachers

(*a*) What in your opinion are the main aims of the subject(s) you
teach? Which parts of the subject are most important? How would
you rate in importance (i) the learning of information, (ii) the
ability to think in the way demanded by the subject, (iii) mastering skills, (iv) developing appropriate attitudes?

(*b*) Are there patterns of teaching and learning which you prefer, or
which particularly fit the subject? What relationship with pupils
do you aim for? How important do you take (i) written work,
(ii) oral discussion to be?

(*c*) What or who has most influenced your views on (i) your subject,
(ii) teaching it?

(d) What is your criterion of a successful lesson (or series of lessons)? What would you treat as evidence of this?

(e) What seem to you to be the things most valued in this school? What is expected of pupils? Which is valued more highly, the curriculum or social learning?

(f) Are there any changes in curriculum policy which you would like to have put into effect? How much influence do you have on decisions affecting curriculum (i) within your own lessons, (ii) in the department, (iii) in the school?

(g) How do you find the pupils here? Do you have the support from their parents which you would wish?

(h) What do you see as your pastoral responsibility for pupils? Does it overlap with curriculum in any way?

(i) Have you recently been involved in any attempts to change the curriculum? What happened? What seemed to be the main things supporting or opposing the changes?

4 **Observation in classrooms.** (More detailed suggestions for methods of observation can be found later in this section from p. 219 onwards.)

(a) What patterns of teaching-learning and classroom organisation seem to occur most frequently? What range of activities are the pupils engaged in?

(b) What kind of written work has been done? How has it been 'marked'? What values are implicit in teachers' written comments?

(c) What curriculum materials are in use and how are they used?

(d) What view of knowledge in the subject can be inferred from what the teacher says and does? How do these relate to the teacher's explicit values?

(e) What view of the pupils' capacities can be inferred from what the teacher says and does? How far are pupils expected to join in the thinking?

(f) How far do the pupils appear to accept the values and purposes of the lesson?

5 **Questions for pupils**

(a) What subjects are important? What makes you think so?

(b) Have you been able to choose which subjects you take? Which ones have you chosen? Why have you chosen those? Who helped you to choose?

(*c*) What do you have to do to be good at school work? (Or in a particular subject?) What gets the best marks? What does your teacher think is the most important thing in . . . ? Are other teachers different?

(*d*) Does the teacher expect you to do a lot in these lessons? Do you understand what you are supposed to be doing? Is the teacher interested in what you say and do?

The next group of tasks arises from the foregoing discussion of methods of studying curriculum in action.

Task 3.6 Practical study of school curricula

3.6.1 Work out a strategy for studying the curriculum in a school, which can be a primary, a middle or a high school. What range of issues will you be interested in? Who will you ask to talk to? What are the main questions that you would like to have answered? What will you look out for? How will you report your findings?

3.6.2 This task is particularly suited to students in initial training, especially when the size of the group precludes a joint visit to a school. It is necessary for the tutor in charge of the course to approach a school and invite the headteacher and some colleagues to visit the college to be interviewed about the school curriculum. The students then work in groups to prepare sets of questions appropriate to the headteacher, deputy head or other member of staff whom they are to interview, and these sets are compared and modified. The actual interviews are probably best carried out in the groups that have planned them, one member acting as spokesman, but it would be equally possible to carry out all of the interviews in front of the whole group. All students would take notes and bring back issues and observations for discussion at a later meeting when the teachers were not present. Indeed it is possible to prepare a report which can later be sent to the visiting teachers in order to hold up a mirror that will show them the version of their curriculum that they presented.

3.6.3 This task is appropriate to an individual or group who are able to make only a single brief visit to a school. Using the methods described earlier in this section they would seek to describe the

3.6.3   overt curriculum arrangements made by the school, and the
contd   staff's declared aims, methods and emphases, as far as this could
        be done in the time available.

3.6.4   When a number of visits is possible the group can attempt not
        only a description of overt aims and methods — the intended
        curriculum — but can compare this with what they can observe
        of the curriculum as it is realised by teachers and pupils in
        classrooms and elsewhere, as has already been described.

3.6.5   The preceding task can be combined with a study of the way in
        which the school controls its curricula, and of the working of
        the provisions that are made for curriculum change, or this can
        be carried out as a separate study, perhaps in schools using
        contrasting methods.

3.6.6   Consider critically the methods of inquiry that have been sug-
        gested in this section. What are they likely to find out and what
        may they miss? What misconception or misinterpretations might
        they give rise to? Give particular critical attention to the sets of
        questions, and the strategies for interviewing.

Evaluating a course

The principles relevant to a study of curriculum in action have already
been discussed in relation to the case-study of a school (pp. 197-209).
The case-study of a school differs from evaluating a course not only
in that it concerns the whole curriculum but also in that its purpose is
not explicitly evaluative. The two are more alike, however, than might
at first appear, since an evaluator, when he is gathering information,
should see his task as that of creating an unbiased description: thus
what has been said (on p. 200) about the curriculum analyst's task
and stance applies equally to the curriculum evaluator. Indeed, Robert
Stake (1969) has questioned whether the evaluator should undertake
to go beyond description: it can certainly be argued that the making
of judgments based on that description should be left to the teachers
and administrators concerned. If one takes that view, then curriculum
analysis and evaluation become one and the same thing. However,
we are here concerned with describing and evaluating one course in
action, and not the whole curriculum of a school.

In describing a course in action it is useful to have a statement of the
intended curriculum that can act as a baseline for one's observations. If

the course is based on published materials they will provide statements about content, learning activities and teaching style with which to compare what you observe. If no public materials are used, there may be a school syllabus, or one can interview the teacher to find out what he or she is setting out to do. In any case, the value of beginning with a statement of the intended curriculum is that any divergence by the teacher from the intentions is thereby thrown into relief. One would not wish to treat the teacher as wrong; indeed such divergences are an excellent basis for future discussion with the teacher (though one has to use some tact to avoid sounding as if one is accusing the teacher of diverging). This strategy is particularly valuable in helping one to see teaching afresh; we are all so familiar with classrooms that it is not easy to see what teachers do as needing explanation, as being only one choice amongst various possibilities.

Task 3.7 Planning an evaluation

3.7   Let us imagine that the teachers involved in a secondary school's first-year experimental course wish to find out how successful it is, partly for their own purposes and partly to persuade their colleagues that all is well. (i) Analyse the statements made in their policy documents (see Appendix H) in order to draw from them a list of the principles of procedure which are intended to guide teaching and learning in the course. Since no content is specified for the course, any evaluation will have to concentrate on skills and processes. (ii) Imagine that you have been invited to spend five days as an observer of the course, and to report back to the teachers upon their success in carrying out those principles. Work out how you will gather information about each of the principles of procedure you have listed, taking into consideration the short time you are to spend in the school.

The next task (3.8) can be carried out in various ways; this would depend in part on the time available and on the teachers' willingness to take the visitor(s) into their confidence. In order to give the reader some practical insight into one possible way of carrying out such a task, there now follows an account of how one group of teachers attempted it. They were experienced teachers from middle and high schools who had been seconded to follow an advanced diploma course. Only one or two had taught science; the point of the activity was

211

the analysis, not the science. This was the task they had been set.

Descriptive analysis of a science curriculum

Aims
(*a*) To give a user's view of a unit of the Nuffield Combined Sciences course;
(*b*) to describe the ways in which different teachers interpret the unit in action;
(*c*) to identify the constraints which influence the way in which the guiding principles of the course are carried out.

First, they went to the Nuffield Combined Sciences materials (1970) in order to draw procedural principles from them. From the introduction they made notes that ran like this.

Procedural principles of the course
1 The pupils will:
   (*a*) work in pairs, helping one another;
   (*b*) have ready access to apparatus and materials.
2 The teacher will:
   (*a*) give hints and information to individuals and groups;
   (*b*) allow pupils to try out their own ideas;
   (*c*) give pupils time to learn from mistakes.
3 Pupils will be encouraged to:
   (*a*) formulate hypotheses;
   (*b*) suggest methods and design experiments;
   (*c*) modify hypotheses in the light of experiments;
   (*d*) realise that a final answer cannot come from one or two experiments;
   (*e*) show a critical attitude to wider issues.

These principles, drawn from several pages in the introduction to the published materials, laid down the general teaching strategy for which those materials had been planned.

The next step was to turn to the particular section of the materials which was to be used in the schools to be visited. On this occasion, the section, intended for pupils of about 10 years of age, was concerned with some of the properties of water. The pupils were to work

212

in small groups on tasks and problems related to water, observing and carrying out miniature practical inquiries. This section of the materials begins with advice to teachers, and from this it was possible to draw objectives specifically related to these activities. For example, for one group of tasks it was made clear that the main cognitive goals were that pupils should understand the following concepts:

(*a*) the 'skin' on water;
(*b*) absorbent as against repellent surfaces;
(*c*) submerging as different from wetting;
(*d*) and they should also know the role of detergents in washing.

Similar lists of goals were drawn from other activities in this section.

These lists of goals, along with the list of procedural principles, furnished the group of teachers with the guidelines for planning the visits to several schools. In each of these schools a teacher was planning to use in a series of lessons the section of the Nuffield course concerned with water. The purpose of the visits was to throw light on the process by which intended curriculum becomes observed curriculum; the students expected that there would be differences not only between the guidelines and what they saw in one teacher's lessons, but also between the interpretation that different teachers placed on the materials and therefore between how they were used.

The students were to make their visits to the schools in subgroups of twos and threes, so that it was necessary to agree in advance what information would be looked for, in order to make comparison possible from one school to another — or rather from one science teacher to another. It was agreed that each subgroup should:

(*a*) Tape-record the teacher's presentation(s) to the whole class, and any further teacher-class discussion, for later analysis.
(*b*) One member should, with the teacher's permission, follow him/her during practical work, trying to record or note down the discussions with groups of pupils.
(*c*) The other members of the subgroup should stay with a particular group of pupils and try to get insight into their view of what they were doing and what it meant. This would include notes on apparatus and the children's manipulation of it.
(*d*) Interview the teacher, one member asking questions and the others making notes. After discussion and several drafts the group of students agreed upon the following questions for the interview.

(In the event they added further questions which arose from what they had seen in the lessons.)

Interview with the teacher
I   1 What facilities do you have for science teaching?
     2 How much time do you have?
II 1 What range of subjects do you teach?
     2 Was science your main subject at college?
III 1 Does this lesson depend upon work done previously?
     2 What do you see as the main aims of science teaching at this stage?
     3 Why do you use Nuffield Combined Sciences?
     4 What changes do you have to make to fit the course to your particular situation?
     5 Do you think that written work is valuable in science?
     6 Have you any way of finding out what they have learnt?
IV What do you see as the main problem in this work?

After the visits had been made, the subgroups of students analysed and summarised what they had found in each school so that the information could be passed round in draft form. The observation of pupils working together was reported informally in a quasi-anecdoted style, but an attempt was made to analyse more formally the presentations made by the three teachers. After discussion, the following categories were arrived at; these were intended to make it possible to describe every utterance that the teachers made in discussion with the full class, and arose from attempts to analyse transcriptions from the tape-recordings.

A schedule for the analysis of teacher's moves
1 *Statements*
   (*a*) Summarises what has gone before.
   (*b*) Identifies a problem or topic.
   (*c*) General explanation of scientific principles.
   (*d*) Particular descriptions of events or objects.
   (*e*) Evaluation of pupils' contributions (including threats or reprimands).
   (*f*) Other (including hints and reminders).
2 *Commands*
   (*a*) Instructions to carry out learning tasks.

(*b*) Classroom order (instructions for behaviour not connected with learning.)

(*c*) Other.

3 *Questions*

(*a*) Method (asks for method of achieving an end).

(*b*) Evaluation (asks pupils to evaluate suggestion).

(*c*) Hypothesis (asks to construct outcome of action).

(*d*) Explanation (asks for explanation of phenomenon or statement).

(*e*) Naming (asks for identification or name).

(*f*) Description (asks for description or narration).

(*g*) Definition (asks for definition of term).

(*h*) Evidence (requires support for assertion).

(*i*) Completion (requires completion of sentence).

Note: Count repetitions as the same question, even when reworded, *unless* one reply has been accepted, and an alternative asked for. Interpret utterances by their implicit functions, not their forms. For example, 'I can see a boy who's playing about' is more likely to be a command than a statement.

The final report was a conflation of the draft reports from the three subgroups. It was organised in these sections and subsections.

(*a*) The place of science in the curriculum:
time available; accommodation and resources; the integration of sciences; relation to other subjects.

(*b*) The teachers' views of science and science teaching:
aims; the part played by writing and talking; evaluation; problems; attitudes to Nuffield Combined Science; procedural principles.

(*c*) Patterns of teaching and learning:
grouping; ways of sequencing and ordering activities; making issues explicit; analysis of the teachers' contributions.

Some of the flavour of the report may be gathered from these quotations from sections (*b*) and (*c*).

Aims. All four teachers agreed that middle-school science involves developing powers of observation, skills in using equipment, and skills in recording in a careful logical manner the results of experimentation. These skills seemed to be given first importance, and the development of scientific thinking was seldom mentioned. One teacher spoke of 'the development of reasoning powers', though this applied to 'scientifically minded' pupils only. Her main aim in teaching science to the other pupils was to develop greater literacy and numeracy. Another teacher implied that he valued the grasping of scientific concepts when he criticised the Nuffield Combined Science presentation of 'the skin on water' as misleading. Another said that subjects of inquiry should be easily observed in the environment and not depend upon sophisticated apparatus as they had when she was a pupil.

Procedural principles. The subsection on procedural principles began with a table. Table 3.2 is only the first part of the table; each of the 'guiding principles' in the table are commented upon below.

TABLE 3.2 *Results of observations on the procedural principles of the course at three schools*

	Guiding principles	School I	School II	School III
1	Pupils will work in pairs	No	Yes, for some, others in threes	Yes
2	Have ready access to apparatus and materials	Yes (supplied)	Yes (supplied)	Yes (supplied)
3	Teacher should give hints to groups	No	Yes, on some occasions	Yes
4	Pupils will be allowed to try their own ideas	Limited	No, or very, very limited	Limited
5	Time given to permit learning from mistakes	No	No	Limited opportunities to make mistakes

(1) Although the curriculum guide recommends that children work in pairs, School I preferred pupils to conduct experiments individually under the teacher's supervision. (Further details of grouping will be found in the next section.)

(2) There appeared to be no lack of the curriculum guide's required apparatus and materials in any of the schools. However,

the term 'ready access to materials' used in the guide was interpreted by the three schools as a suggestion that the pupils should be
supplied with those items they would need rather than that they
should be able to assemble them on their own initiative.

(3) The guide's suggestion that hints to groups might be preferred to 'class announcements' received the full range of responses.
In School I, where class teaching alternated with individual pupils
conducting experiments, no opportunity was given for the teacher
to give hints to groups. School II gave hints, but also frequently
asked pupils to pause and listen as a class to general instructions or
to points of interest. School III spent the early part of its lesson
revising as a class the procedure discussed on a previous occasion,
and then conducted the practical experimentation with very few
interruptions for class announcements and relied upon teacher/
small-group interaction and 'drift' to influence the direction of the
pupils' work.

(4) The question of whether or not pupils were allowed to try
their own ideas is difficult to determine, since this would depend
upon the scope which was given by the experiments themselves.
The observers felt that in all three schools the pupils did make some
contribution but that on the whole the procedures were closely
teacher-controlled.

(5) There did appear at School III to be some opportunity for
the pupils to learn from mistakes, but this statement is qualified
by the point (made under 4) that the scope for making significant
mistakes was limited. In both School I and School II the pressures
(i) of time and (ii) to get the 'right' answer written up inhibited
the accomplishment of learning from, though not the production
of, mistakes.

Ways of sequencing and organising activities. The informal description
of classroom activities can be illustrated with the following extract that
refers to one school only. The sequence of the lesson was as follows:

(a) The test tubes were half full of water and pupils had to observe
the shape of the meniscus.
(b) Pupils had to fill the test tubes to the top and with a teat
pipette fill it to the brim and observe the shape of the meniscus.
(c) Various children were asked to go to the board and draw what
they had observed.

217

(*d*) Pupils had to observe the shapes of drops of water forming from a teat pipette.

(*e*) Drops of water were put on various surfaces, for example, leaves, cotton wool, absorbent and non-absorbent surfaces.

(*f*) Water with detergent was poured from a test tube on to various surfaces, and pupils had to observe its behaviour.

The teacher gave detailed instructions on how the experiment was to be carried out. The teacher demonstrated, and the pupils followed her example:

T. I want you to take . . . keep your voice down, we don't like a lot of noise. Those of you who have been here before, what do we call this?

P. A pipette.

T. A pipette, and this is called a teat pipette because it has the little rubber on the top. Put it into the water . . .

P. This one?

T. Squeeze the air out of it. Pipette in the water and let the water be sucked up into it. Right? Now, I want you . . . Uh! into your beaker, not your test tube, dear, Anthony!

(In a second lesson with less able children a substantial part of the time was spent in directing the children to draw in their books a tabular format for the recording of results.)

You will have noticed that, though the tone of the report implies detached description without comment, the authors have selected evidence which throws into relief the differences between the teachers' classroom procedures and the procedural principles of the Nuffield Combined Science approach. The purpose of describing this piece of work at such length is to offer you a framework upon which the next task can be organised.

Task 3.8 Practical study of the use made of curriculum materials

3.8 Select part of a body of published classroom materials, and abstract from them both the general principles that are intended to guide the teaching of the whole course, and any aims or procedures recommended for the part selected. This, then is

3.8 to be used as a framework for observing the interpretation
contd placed upon that part of the materials when used in the classroom. The study can be carried out with one teacher or more,
according to the time available. The final report should include
accounts of (*a*) the principles drawn from the materials, (*b*) the
teachers' views about the materials and their use, (*c*) the
observed use of the materials by teachers and pupils.

Classroom observation in the evaluation of curriculum

Task 3.6 involved interviewing teachers and observing some of their
lessons. Interviewing has already been discussed in an earlier section
(pp. 205-9); it is now appropriate to say something about lesson
observation, and to do so in a wider context than that of observing how
a teacher interprets some curriculum materials. You may find yourself
in another teacher's lesson for a variety of purposes, and it is possible
to devise various ways of focusing attention. The main problem is to
find ways of looking at something we are very familiar with as if it
were strange. We have to ask Why? about procedures we have taken
for granted since we were children. An obvious method is to formulate
questions beforehand and to look for answers to them. However, the
usefulness of this depends on asking the 'right' questions. For this
reason you may choose to use rather loose questions, unless you are
looking for something in particular, as were the group who were observing how teachers interpreted part of the Nuffield Combined Science
materials.

In much informal lesson observation, for example on school
practice, the observer is in the position of Michael Scriven's goal-free
evaluator (1973), in that he has not received an account of the objectives of the lesson or the principles of procedure that the teacher would
claim to have adopted. In fact for the most part teachers make neither
objectives nor procedural principles explicit to themselves. Thus there
is a wide range of possible focus-points for the observer.

Task 3.9 Informal classroom observation

3.9.1 Imagine that you are sitting in on lessons with a class whom you
will teach in a week's time. You will naturally want to collect
information and impressions that will help you to make your

3.9.1 planning and your actual teaching as appropriate and effective
contd as possible. Make a list of questions that will guide your observation.

3.9.2 You are to observe lessons in which teachers are using published
materials such as a mathematics or reading scheme, or one of
the Nuffield science courses, or the Humanities Curriculum
Project. Read the introduction or teachers' guide to the
materials, and list any principles of procedure which the authors
put forward to guide teachers' use of the materials. Translate
these procedural principles into a list of questions for your use
in observing the lessons. The principles will thus serve as a baseline from which each teacher's use of the materials can be
characterised.

3.9.3 As an experienced teacher you have been asked to take part in
the assessment of a student teacher at the end of his/her school
practice. (i) List in question form what you think you should be
looking for. (ii) Discuss with colleagues whether your list of
questions would form a proper basis for judging teaching.

3.9.4 You have heard a lecture by an educational theorist in which he
asserts persuasively that too much rote-learning and too little
thinking goes on in most lessons. Piqued by this, you tape-
record two of your own lessons, but find that playing back the
recording does not tell you what kinds of thinking are going
on. You decide that before you listen to it again you will make
a list of different kinds of thinking, so that you can note what
kind of thinking each of the questions you asked required your
pupils to engage in. Make a list of the kinds of thinking that you
hope to encourage.

(See Appendix J for two extracts from lessons, which can be
used for various tasks in this section if you happen to be unable
to tape-record a lesson.)

The above tasks were hypothetical, but if you are actually teaching,
whether in your own school or on practice, you can carry out such
an analysis, for there is a great deal to be said for reflecting upon one's
own teaching behaviour. It is one of the characteristics of teaching
that classroom events happen so rapidly, so many pupils requiring
attention, that it is almost impossible for any teacher to reflect there
and then upon what he is doing. Situations are scanned intuitively and
decisions made so quickly that the teacher himself hardly knows on

what grounds they were made. The tape-recorder offers us the unique possibility of being participant and observer of the same events: we can reply and reflect upon our own behaviour. This is potentially a very powerful instrument for the improving of our teaching, since it enables us to say, 'Oh, was I doing that? It would be better if I changed it.' There is much to be said for simply listening to recordings of our own teaching, since we inevitably compare what we hear with our ideal view of teaching. Nevertheless, it is sometimes suggested that a set of questions helps one to review one's teaching more perceptively. You may care to jot down your own ideas about what you might want to know about your teaching before reading the schemes that follow, since they were designed for purposes which you may not share.

Task 3.10 Classroom observation using schedules

3.10.1   Make a list of aspects of your teaching methods that you would like to know more about in order to improve. For example, you might want to know whether the questions you ask require your pupils to think aloud or merely to supply information. Or you might want to find out what strategies you are using when you go round and talk to children individually. Again you might want to consider whether your explanations are clear enough, and whether most of your pupils seem to be grasping your meaning. Then, as a second stage of the task write down what actual behaviour — by yourself or by your pupils — you would need to record in order to find out about this aspect of your teaching. For example, if you are concerned whether or not you are sufficiently encouraging to your pupils you may need to consider how encouragement is communicated. (Some means of encouragement will not show up on an audio recording.)

The six schemes that follow were devised to help with lesson-observation for various purposes and in various contexts. We shall begin with a scheme intended to check whether teachers were carrying out the classroom procedures recommended for using a set of new curriculum materials, continue with schemes intended to aid less formal observation, and turn finally to schemes intended to help teachers to reflect on their own teaching. The schemes vary also in the tightness with which they predetermine what is to be observed. It is impossible to note down everything that we see and hear, and what we think it means too, so selection is necessary, but selection of what? There are three ways of dealing with the dilemma. (*a*) We can decide in advance what we are interested in and make a list of visible behaviours that can be identified. (*b*) We can decide to record certain things, but work also with rather loose headings that will enable us to deal with the unexpected. (*c*) We can observe without having predetermined precisely what we are looking for, and decide what is important when we see it.

Loose questions leave one free to re-interpret them in the light of what one sees, and indeed to invent new questions to deal with unforeseen aspects of the lesson. On the other hand, because they do not direct attention to anything in particular, loose questions are of limited value when a group of observers wants to meet later to compare results, or when one observer wants to compare a number of lessons observed on different occasions. We shall therefore give some consideration to 'tight' as well as to 'loose' questions (or categories) as a guide to observation. I suggest that as you read these schemes you should compare them with what you wrote down in answer to Task 3.9.1.

A African Primary Science Program

The African Primary Science Program recommended to teachers that in science lessons they should adopt the following objectives and strategies (Yoloye, 1977).

Objectives. The African Primary Science Program should aim at developing these characteristics in children.

1   First-hand familiarity with a variety of biological, physical and man-made phenomena in the world around them.
2   Interest in further exploration of the world around them on their own initiative.
3   Ability to find out for themselves — to see problems and to be able to set about resolving them for themselves.
4   Confidence in their own ability to find out for themselves and do things for themselves.
5   Ability to share in a common development of knowledge, through collaborating on problems, telling, listening and discriminating use of second-hand sources.

Strategies. The science programme should have the following characteristics.

1   The focus of study should be on the concrete phenomena themselves.
2   The materials selected should capture and hold the attention and
    interest of children.
3   The materials should reveal that there is not always one right
    answer.
4   Materials should allow opportunities for a variety of different ways
    to find out.
5   The classroom experience should lead to social interaction among
    children.
6   To a large extent, the materials should be simple and familiar.
7   The materials should encourage children to do things on their own,
    in their own ways.

In order to find out how far teachers were in fact following project
policy, the curriculum developers designed three observation schedules.

  (i)   A child-observation checklist.
 (ii)   A class activity sheet (to aid in estimating the time given to indi-
        vidual work, class discussion, etc.).
(iii)   A verbal-interaction schedule (which is reproduced as Figure 3.2).

The authors of this schedule were clear that this kind of record shows
only part of what goes on in the classroom, and that in this case it
focuses only upon certain limited aspects of what teachers say.

   At the end of a period of observation it would be possible to calculate what proportion of a teacher's moves were (c) (close-ended questions), and compare this with the proportion of (e) (giving information
or expressing opinion), and so on for the other categories too. (In
practice, there might be some problem in deciding on the unit being
used. For example, how many units are there in: 'Don't touch the
gauze. It'll get very hot'? None, or one, or two? The observer has to
make a decision about the unit he is using, and be consistent.)

Task 3.10 contd Classroom observation using schedules

3.10.2   Compare the items observed with the lists of objectives and
         strategies. How far can each of the items in the verbal inter-
         action sheet (Figure 3.2) be justified by reference to the
         African Primary Science Program's objectives and strategies?

Date . . . . School . . . .
Class . . . . Unit or lesson . . . . Teacher . . . .

T																		
C																		

T																		
C																		

Recording instructions:
1   Record only teacher-child (T) or child-teacher (C) interactions.
2   Record interactions in the appropriate box in the sequence in which they occur.
3   Indicate the type of interaction by using the symbols a, b, c, d, e, f, or g.
4   When concentrating on teacher talk only, do not bother to categorise child's statement. Indicate a child's statement simply by a dash (−).

a   Direct instruction (e.g. Use only one battery to light the bulb).
b   Open-ended question (seeking information, e.g., What are you making?).
c   Close-ended question (requiring a specific predetermined answer, e.g. What is the boiling point of water?).
d   Suggestion (e.g. There is no torch available; would you like to try a kerosene lamp?).
e   Giving information or expressing opinion.
f   Supportive action (e.g. agreement or approbation).
g   Comment implying that the child's statement is unacceptable (e.g. No; you are wrong; Yes . . . but).

Figure 3.2   *Verbal interaction sheet*

B Analysis of language used in teaching

While carrying out with a group of teachers a study of the language used in various lessons during the first few weeks of secondary schooling I produced the following list of questions. Its purpose was to help the teachers analyse tape-recordings they had made of other teachers' lessons, thus giving us a basis on which to compare them in seminars. It should be noted that whereas the scheme for analysing teachers' questions is sufficiently tightly defined to allow one to count the questions that fall into each category, most of the remaining questions are open and impressionistic, intended to lead to discussion rather than to quantification (Barnes, 1971).

Teachers' questions. Analyse *all* questions asked by the teacher into these categories:

1   factual ('what?' questions):
    (i)   naming;
    (ii)   information;
2   reasoning ('how?' and 'why?' questions):
    (i)   'closed' reasoning – recalled sequences;
    (ii)   'closed' reasoning – not recalled;
    (iii) 'open' reasoning;
    (iv)   observation;
3   'open' questions not calling for reasoning;
4   social:
    (i)   control ('won't you . . . ?' questions);
    (ii)   appeal ('aren't we . . . ?' questions);
    (iii) other.

Naming questions ask pupils to give a name to some phenomenon without requiring them to show insight into its use. *Reasoning* questions require pupils to 'think aloud' – to construct, or reconstruct from memory, a logically organised sequence. *Recall* questions are concerned with summoning up required knowledge from memory. *Closed* questions have only one acceptable answer; whereas to *open* questions a number of different answers would be acceptable. Open questions might be factual in some circumstances: for example, a request for 'any fraction', where the range of choices open to the pupil is unusually wide. (It is necessary to check apparently open questions by examining the teacher's reception of pupils' replies, which may show that he will accept only one reply to a question framed in apparently open terms. Such questions might be called 'pseudo-questions'.) *Observation* questions are intended to include those questions (about phenomena immediately present to the children) which require them to interpret what they perceive. (There may be difficulty in distinguishing some of these from 'naming questions'.) *Control* questions are directed towards imposing the teacher's wishes upon the class. *Appeal* questions, which ask pupils to agree, or share an attitude, or remember an experience, are less directive than control questions: that is, it is possible for children to reject them without necessarily giving offence.

Pupils' participation.
1 Was all speech initiated by the teacher? Note any exchanges initiated by pupils.
   (i)   if these were initiated by questions, were they 'what?', 'how?' or 'why?' questions? Were they directed towards the material studies or towards performing the given tasks?
   (ii) If they were unsolicited statements or comments, how did the teacher deal with them?
2 Were pupils required to express personal responses:
   (i)   of perception?
   (ii) of feeling and attitude?
3 How large a part did pupils take in the lesson? Were any silent throughout? How large a proportion took a continuous part in discussion?
4 What did pupils' contributions show of their success in following the lesson?
5 How did the teacher deal with inappropriate contributions?

The language of instruction.
1 Did the teacher use a linguistic register specific to his subject? Find examples of vocabulary and structures characteristic of the register.
2 Did any pupils attempt to use this register? Was it expected of them?
3 What did the teacher do to mediate between the language and experience of his pupils and the language and concepts of the subject?
4 Did the teacher use forms of language which, though not specific to his subject, might be outside the range of 11-year-olds? Find examples, if any.

Social relationships.
1 How did the relationship between teacher and pupils show itself in language?

2 Were there differences between the language of instruction and the language of relationships? Was the language of relationships intimate or formal? Did it vary during the lesson?

Language and other media.

1 Was language used for any tasks that might have been done better by other means (for example, pictures, practical tasks, demonstrations)?
2 Were pupils expected to verbalise any non-verbal tasks they engaged in?

It is important to realise that this is unlike the African Primary Science Program scheme in that its purpose was not to evaluate a large number of teachers, but to enable a few teachers to gain further insight into their own teaching by analysing other teachers' lessons and discussing the results at length.

C   Teacher's behaviour in the classroom

Walker and Adelman in their book *A Guide to Classroom Observation* (1975) suggest that student teachers might shape their observation of lessons by making a 'lesson profile' that contains (*a*) physical setting, (*b*) pupils, (*c*) teachers, (*d*) resources, (*e*) the lesson, and (*f*) background information on the school. (Interested readers are referred to the book to see how the full profile can be made.) Here we are primarily concerned with (*c*) the teacher's behaviour, and the questions that follow are those which the authors put forward to guide observation of the teacher.

Observing teachers.

1 How do they enter the room, and where do they go first? Do they enter before or after the pupils? Do they make them wait or line up outside?
2 What are the teacher's first posture, gesture and statement; to whom are they addressed?
3 What effects are apparently intended? (Notice tone and loudness of voice, as well as what is said.)
4 How long is it before the lesson proper can begin? What things

have happened up to this point?

5 Does the teacher seem to be a different kind of person inside classroom and out? How?

6 Assess the complexity of vocabulary and grammar used by the teacher. Do they match that used by the pupils in (1) their responses to the teacher, (2) their talk among themselves? The teacher's language may be precise, esoteric, everyday but accurate, or loose. Does the language used by the teacher elucidate the intended meanings or does it hinder them?

7 What does the teacher do when a child asks a question that reveals he has not understood the lesson? Does the teacher's language change at this point? How?

8 Are questions to pupils:
  (*a*) previously worked out?
  (*b*) spontaneous and exploratory?
  (*c*) implying an answer?
  (*d*) by several exchanges leading the pupils to the one answer expected?

9 Does the teacher use analogies? Do they communicate the point to the children?

10 Does the situation seem to be one of mutual communication between teacher and children? How do you assess this?

11 Does the teacher use many negated sentences as compared to positive sentences?

12 Is the teacher's voice being clearly perceived (i.e. do the pupils recognize the pronunciation as understandable even if the observer finds it difficult)?

13 Is the teacher pausing within and between sentences so as to make each clause, phrase, etc. stand out? Does the voice modulation enhance the meanings, or disrupt them?

14 How does the teacher register that the pupil's response is considered incorrect? What is the response of other pupils to the teacher's signal of incorrectness?

15 How does the teacher deal with the unexpected event?

16 In individual learning situations:
  (*a*) does the teacher get to all those needing help?
  (*b*) does the teacher adjust his language and posture from child to child?

17 Does the teacher have particular postures and gestures which signal to the class that he is expecting a major change in activity?

18 How does the teacher use silences to communicate?
19 How does the teacher adjust his talk to different groups of
    children engaged in the same task?

D *Teacher's strategies for self-evaluation in classroom*

Man: A Course of Study is a complex body of curriculum materials
produced in the United States and intended to present anthropological
principles to children of 11 or 12 years of age. (Jerome Bruner was
deeply involved in the production of these materials, and one can
see in them an attempt to test in practice his celebrated hypothesis
that 'any subject can be taught effectively in some intellectually honest
form to any child at any stage of development'.) Once the material
had begun to be used in schools, a group of independent consultants
was asked to carry out an evaluation (Whitla *et al.*, undated). For this
purpose they devised a series of strategies which were to be used by the
teachers using *Man: A Course of Study*, both to get insight into what
children were learning and to monitor their own teaching styles. The
strategies included:

(*a*) interviews with small groups of pupils;
(*b*) lists of questions for pupils (asking them about their own attitudes
       and styles of learning);
(*c*) tests for pupils on the content of the course;
(*d*) creative writing and art work on topics central to the course;
(*e*) classroom observation.

This list of activities may seem to make unrealistic demands on
teachers' time, though three of them would be used in a limited way as
part of most teachers' normal teaching. The suggestions for classroom
observation *by the teacher of his own teaching* that follow below have
been modified from those proposed for *Man: A Course of Study*.

Evaluation.
Factual questions predominate./Opinion questions predominate.
Short answers./Longer answers.
Questions mostly from teacher./Many questions from pupils.
Teacher controls the agenda./Pupils initiate topics.
Less than a third of pupils participate./Most pupils participate.
Student interest low./Student interest high.

Teacher style.
Stands apart from pupils./Stands close to pupils.
Little teacher movement./Much movement by teacher.
Teacher does not draw out pupils./Teacher tries to draw out pupils.
Teacher 'talks down' to pupils./Teacher treats pupils' views seriously.
Teacher dominates./Teacher collaborates.

The evaluators of this course suggest that at some point during the lesson when pupils are working the teacher might spend a minute evaluating himself (1-4 points) on each of these dimensions. A tape-recording might make this a good deal easier, however. (It is only fair to add that the course evaluators point out that this list is only one amongst many possible lists for evaluating teaching.)

E   Scheme for analysing lessons for probationary teachers

The following list was prepared to help teachers during their probationary year. The suggestion was that they should work in pairs, each tape-recording a similar lesson, and then discuss the recordings together.

This is a checklist of questions to guide the teacher's analysis of tape-recordings of his own lessons. It is assumed that the lesson consists of an introductory discussion, followed by individual or group work, and a final discussion. The teacher will have described in advance what his goals are for the lesson, what methods he will use, and what contributions he expects his pupils to be able to make.

Introductory presentation and discussion.
(*a*) Did your pupils appear to understand the starting-point of the lesson? If not, why not?
      If you teach the lesson again, what changes will you make in your presentation?
(*b*) Were your pupils able to contribute from their own understanding and experience?
      Did your questions help them to join in, or did they find some of them difficult to respond to?
      Were you able to get them to make alternative suggestions and to give evidence that supports them.
      What else might have helped them?

Individual or group work.

(*a*) Did your pupils' approach to the individual or group work show
insight into the task?

How did you cope with those who were lost?

Do you now know what their problems were?

(*b*) Were they able to get on with the work, or did they keep asking
for support and advice?

If the latter, how can you in future help them to take more
responsibility?

What problems could be dealt with in advance?

(*c*) What did you say when you approached various groups or individuals?

What purposes did you have in mind in saying this?

Were they able to explain to you what they were doing?

In retrospect which of your comments do you judge most likely
to be helpful?

Final discussion.

(*a*) How did you set up the final discussion? Would you do it again in
the same way?

(*b*) Was there enough time for the main issues to be restated and
emphasised?

If not, how might this be achieved in future?

Did the issues come from your pupils or did you have to tell them?
Does it matter?

Were they able to link the new ideas with things they already
knew?

(*c*) Did most of your pupils seem to have grasped the main issues?

If some still had problems how might you help them in future?

General.

(*a*) Were you able to persuade most of your pupils to join in the
lesson?

Or did you have to do most of the talking?

What might you do in future to get the silent ones to join in the
thinking?

(*b*) What kinds of contribution did pupils make: explanations,
suggested methods, questions, challenges, additional information,
supportive arguments, relevant experience?

How could you set up lessons to get a wider range of participation?

231

(c) What did pupils seem to understand easily and what did they have difficulty with?

How will you help them with the latter when you next teach a lesson on this topic?

Will you begin with a different demonstration, give them other information or tasks, or conduct the discussions differently?

(d) How did you treat pupils' contributions that seemed irrelevant or incomprehensible? Were you able to make use of them, or to turn them aside tactfully?

Would any of these contributions have made better sense if you had had more time to think about them?

(e) How much of the time did you spend in controlling the class, as against teaching? If there was any misbehaviour, what do you think it stemmed from?

Did any of the pupils feel bored because the work was too hard, or too easy, or because they were unoccupied for too long? If so, how can this be avoided in future?

Could any have felt snubbed by anything you said to them?

F Reflections on small-group working and discussions with teacher

A great deal of most teachers' time is spent in moving round the classroom and talking to individual pupils or groups of them about the work they are doing. There have been very few studies of what goes on in these brief exchanges, and little discussion of what teachers should aim for and how they might best achieve the aims. The questions that follow are partly intended to deal with these exchanges, but also offer pointers for reflecting on what groups of pupils say when they are working together on a task in your absence.

1   What range of matters are you discussing with your pupils? Are you mainly concerned with methods or are you asking them to talk about the meaning of what they are doing?

2   Are you succeeding in eliciting your pupils' thinking, so that you understand their idiosyncratic ways of interpreting things, their problems and misconceptions but also their strengths?

3   Can you sit in on a group discussion and gather how the work is progressing without all the group addressing their remarks to you? Do you join in pupils' discussion as a participant rather than

an evaluator?

4   Are your pupils really discussing the meaning of what they are doing? For example, in science are they talking about how their 'experiment' relates to the principle in question, or is their talk mainly at the 'Pass the matches' level?

5   Can they find problems and formulate them, put forward explanatory hypotheses, use evidence to evaluate alternatives, plan lines of action?

6   Can they cope with differences of opinion, share out the jobs to be done, move steadily through a series of tasks, summarise what they have decided, reflect on the nature of what they are doing?

7   Have the topics which they have chosen or you have prescribed led to useful discussion? Did they succeed in raising valuable issues, or would they have benefited from some help in focusing attention? On the other hand, if you gave them questions to consider, were these helpful or constricting, did they lead to the kind of discussion you believe to be valuable?

The tasks that follow refer to these six schemes. See Appendix J for two extracts from lessons, which can be used for various tasks in this section.

Task 3.10 contd   Classroom observation using schedules

3.10.3   Compare the list you made in response to Task 3.9.1 with the six schemes. Modify your own list in the light of other possibilities shown in the schemes. (This can be carried out as a group discussion in order to bring out the uses and limitations of alternative approaches.)

3.10.4   Use one of the schemes during school practice or on another visit to a school. Walker and Adelman's scheme on teacher's behaviour in the classroom (C) is intended for this purpose; both the *Man: A Course of Study* scheme of teacher's strategies for self-evaluation in the classroom (D) and the African Primary Science scheme (A) can be used for a wide range of subject-matters. My own scheme on the analysis of language used in teaching (B) could be used, but it would be impossible to record and categorise all the questions.

3.10.5   (This task is a more elaborate version of 3.10.4.) Two or three students observing the same lesson can use different

3.10.5 schemes, one using a relatively 'tight' scheme such as A,
contd another using a looser scheme such as B or C, and the third
not using a scheme but jotting down whatever interests him.
The purpose of this is to increase one's understanding of the
effect on classroom observation of using different schemes
or none at all.

3.10.6 Tape-record part of one of your own lessons, planning in
advance (*a*) a series of different activities such as those suggested in the preamble to scheme E, and (*b*) the principles
of procedure which are to shape your own contributions to
each part of the lesson. For example, you might decide that
when eliciting your pupils' existing understanding at the
beginning of a lesson you should be encouraging and un-
critical, and not lay down tight criteria of relevance. For the
next stage of the lesson you might choose quite different
principles: the recording will enable you to observe how far
you have been able to switch from one style to another.
Scheme E, which was planned to help in self-monitoring of
this kind, can be tried out, but should be abandoned if it
proves not to fit your needs.

All six schemes – even the science and *Man: A Course of Study* ones
(A and D) – were content-free, in the sense that they could be used in
lessons in which different subject-matters were being taught. On some
occasions, however, one wants to know how particular subject-matter
is being treated in lessons. In a lesson of environmental studies one
might want to know how much time was being spent in explaining
food-chains in general, and how much in dealing with a particular
food-chain on which further work was to be done. Or one might
want to know how much attention was being paid to interpreting
maps, to obtaining information from books, or to constructing maps
by the pupils themselves. If one does want information so closely
linked to particular content, then an observation scheme must be
prepared for that content.

Task 3.10 contd Classroom observation using schedules

3.10.7 Prepare an observation scheme linked to the material in part
of a textbook. Your task is to find ways of observing during
a series of lessons how much time is being spent on each

3.10.7   aspect of the material, and what proportion of the pupils'
contd   time is spent in practising various activities and skills. You
         may also decide to include some way of estimating the level
         of thinking being required of the pupils.

Observing pupils

It will not have escaped readers who teach in infants' schools or in
special schools that all but one of the schemes for classroom observation that we have been using assume that a class of pupils is being
taught as a unit, and working on a shared curriculum. (The exception
is scheme F, of course.) Teachers in these schools, although most of
them occasionally work with the whole group of their pupils, are more
accustomed to thinking of pupils working separately at different speeds
and often on different curricula. Something similar may be true elsewhere in schools: craft and design work in secondary schools is sometimes based upon individual choice within a framework of options.
But all teachers have some work done individually by pupils; some use
group work for certain limited purposes. In either case, part of evaluating the 'transactions' of a curriculum in action must be to find out
what pupils are doing when they are not directly under the teacher's
control.

It is not easy when teaching a class of children to be able to spare
enough time with any one of them to obtain a real insight into any
problems and misunderstandings that are currently hindering his
learning, or to see what next step would best fit his needs. A teacher's
ability to offer appropriate help to individual pupils necessarily depends
on the skill of doing this rapidly, yet many teachers − even experienced
ones − have not developed this skill to any great degree. In effect, they
base their advice to pupils on a general impression of 'the kind of problems children tend to have with this kind of work' rather than on the
particular needs of an individual, and may therefore fail to notice basic
difficulties that ought to be dealt with. This is not to criticise teachers,
but to acknowledge a practical problem inherent in class teaching.
Understanding children's difficulties is, however, a skill that can be
learnt, and many problems in any one area − mathematics, for example −
occur frequently enough to become readily recognisable after they have
been met once or twice. It is for this reason that I am including an exercise in observing an individual pupil in this final part of the subsection

235

on evaluation; no teacher is so experienced that he or she cannot learn more by observing pupils at work and trying to understand how they approach learning tasks.

Task 3.11 Observing individual pupils

3.11 Obtain the permission of another teacher to sit with one pupil during a lesson or a series of lessons. (For student teachers this can convenienlty be arranged during school practice either with an experienced teacher or with another student, perhaps in the latter case teaching and observing alternately.) The child or adolescent is to be observed when carrying out a task that sets him a series of problems, perhaps a mathematics card or some mathematical apparatus, some reading for a child not yet fluent, work based on a textbook or workcard, or involving laboratory equipment. The purpose of the observation is to gain enough insight into the child's existing learning strategies to enable appropriate teaching to be given on another occasion.

(*a*) Sit through the lesson in which the work is explained and the task set, so that you understand something of where the child you have chosen is setting out from.

(*b*) Observe the pupil carefully as he carries out the task, making detailed notes on what he or she says and does, whether right or wrong. (In the teaching of reading this is called 'miscue analysis'; similar methods can be used, however, in observing any learning.) You will need occasionally to ask the child to explain why this or that has been done, but *it is essential to resist the temptation* to teach him or her during the observation time: your task at this stage is to observe and understand.

(*c*) Later review your notes and attempt a provisional account of what the child you have observed can and cannot do. Plan a short piece of individual teaching intended to improve his/her understanding of some aspect of the work, and his/her choice of strategies for dealing with similar tasks.

(*d*) Carry out the individual tuition that you have planned, observing whether your diagnosis appears to have been correct, and whether your teaching does improve the pupil's approach to the work. If necessary carry out informal tests.

Chapter 4

The control of the curriculum

During the last few years a new field of inquiry has been opened up within curriculum studies; I am calling it 'control of the curriculum', though it might equally be called 'curriculum and society' or 'politics of the curriculum'. Typical questions to be addressed within this field would be: where does control of the curriculum lie? How do decisions made in institutions relate to changes of opinion amongst teachers and amongst the general public? What influence do public media such as newspapers have upon what is taught in schools? What part is played by pressure groups, including those composed of industrialists or trade unions? How powerful are official bodies such as the Department of Education and Science or the local education authorities? Is it true that individual schools really control their curricula? Questions such as these ask for replies that are essentially descriptions of how things are. Other questions might have an ethical component and ask what *should* be the case. Who should control the curriculum? Should parents have more influence than they do upon what is taught to their children? Should they be able to choose? Should the Department of Education and Science or the local education authorities establish guidelines for the curriculum that would be binding on all state schools (as in most other countries in the world)? Linked with these ethical questions are hypothetical ones about the probable results of certain actions. What would happen if teachers were given more encouragement and resources to engage in curriculum development based upon their schools? What is likely to be the effect on the curriculum of extensive testing of achievement, whether nationally by such bodies as the Assessment of Performance Unit, or locally by education authorities or by the schools themselves? If the managing

bodies of schools were encouraged to take more responsibility for oversight of the curriculum, what effect would this have? The answers to
the ethical questions depend in part on the answers given to 'what
if . . . ?' questions such as these.

This new field of inquiry raises many important questions that I
shall not be able to deal with in this chapter. (For example, the extent
to which schools show the characteristics of bureaucracies, and the
effect of these characteristics upon teachers' perceptions of their
professional responsibilities, and particularly upon their participation
in curriculum-development activities.) This section will confine its
attention to four groups of issues: relationships between schools on the
one hand and parents or local community representatives on the other,
and the effect of these relationships on the curriculum; increases in
central influence on the curriculum; school-based curriculum development; and accountability.

Curriculum, parents and the community

A central question that might be asked about the curriculum is whether
it is intended to *extend* the culture — the knowledge, assumptions and
preferences — that children bring from their homes, or to *supplant* that
culture, substituting something better. No simple answer is possible.
If school merely reinforced the home it would have little excuse for
existing except as a child-minding service. Yet if the curriculum becomes a head-on challenge to a child's home culture it is unlikely to be
of great benefit. The experience of children from different homes must
be quite different from one another in this respect even when they are
in the same school class. Teachers' aims are often sharply different
from parents' aims.

Earlier in this century a French educationist carried out an informal
study of what people from different walks of life thought their children
ought to be able to do at the end of their schooling; this is reproduced
as Appendix K.

Task 4.1 Parents' involvement in the curriculum

4.1.1   (a)   Read Appendix K. Which items surprise you? Why do you
think they were given support by the French parents? In
what way are they surprising?

4.1.1   (*b*) Which of these abilities, etc. would not normally be part of
contd   the curriculum experienced by a boy or girl who left
             school aged 16? Is there any good reason why they should
             not have had this experience?

      (*c*) Is anything noticeably lacking from the list?

      (*d*) In sum, how do the emphases that can be detected in the
             French parents' answers differ from the typical emphases in
             curriculum in our schools at primary and at secondary levels?

      (*e*) If you were a French educational official, how would you
             justify to these parents the fact that schooling does not
             always fit their expectations? Or were the parents right?

Nearer to home and to our own time, the Schools Council (1968) carried out a more sophisticated survey to find out what school objectives school-leavers thought were important (both when they left and after a few years' experience of the world of work) in comparison with what teachers and headteachers thought important. The results are summarised in Figure 4.1; the length of each line indicates what proportion of the group in question said that a particular objective was 'very important'. The objectives are grouped under four headings: careers; everyday life; self-development; interests and awareness.

Task 4.1 contd Parents' involvement in the curriculum

4.1.2   (*a*) Who tends to agree with whom, amongst pupils, parents,
             teachers and headteachers?

      (*b*) Which of the objectives provoke the most marked differ-
             ences between the groups of people consulted? Which
             of the four headings do these objectives belong with?
             How can these differences of emphasis be accounted for?

      (*c*) Have any substantial changes of viewpoint resulted from
             the 19 and 20-year-olds' experience of the world outside
             school?

      (*d*) In so far as pupils and parents want a different curriculum
             from teachers — and this can only be a half-truth at best —
             how can we decide who is right? Or will it be impossible
             to find principles that can settle this once and for all?

      (*e*) Why do you think that 'poetry' and 'drama' were the only
             curriculum topics asked about? (Why not, for example,
             the physics of heat, or nineteenth-century political history?)

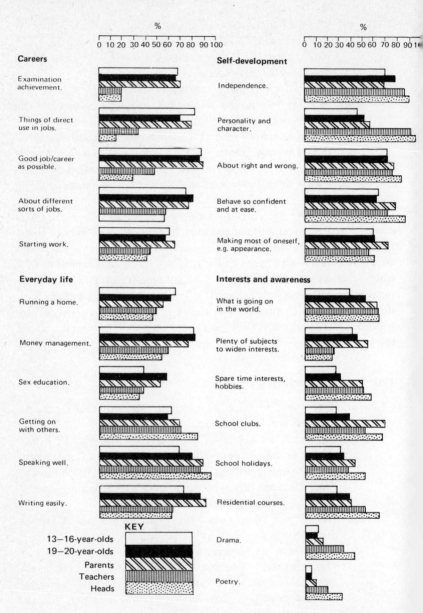

Figure 4.1 *Proportions of 15-year-old leavers, their parents and teachers saying that various school objectives were very important*

Communication between schools and parents has traditionally amounted almost entirely to the schools giving information to parents. When one considers, however, the large part in children's success in school which relates to their parents' attitudes to schooling, this tradition may not be a wise one. It has been suggested that parents might be asked to supply information including:

difficulties children encounter in understanding certain parts of a course;
difficulties that children encounter in preparing homework;
support material, such as reference books, that children use at home;
interest that pupils show in the work;
spontaneous reports by children of what they are doing in school
(Yoloye, 1977).

This may seem, however, a very restricted view of what parents might contribute in a discussion with the school.

Task 4.1 contd Parents' involvement in the curriculum

4.1.3   (a) Suggest other information available from parents that might help a school to improve the appropriateness and effectiveness of school work.
   (b) How can information of this kind best be obtained? Plan a strategy for a whole school.
   (c) When you next meet the parents of some of your pupils, try to get information from them about some of these matters. Jot down at some convenient moment what they have said, and consider what action might be taken in the light of the information.
4.1.4   It is a commonplace of staff-room talk that the parents whom the teachers want to see seldom turn up at parents' evenings.
   (a) Make a list of the reasons why teachers probably want to see these particular parents.
   (b) Why is it that many parents never attend school functions? Consider what they might have to gain and what they might lose from attending.
   (c) Parents' evenings frequently cast the parents in a very passive role, either being told in lecture format about the school, or being told individually by teachers how their

4.1.4
contd
children are getting on and what ought to be done about it. In what ways might parents be enabled to play a more active role in the school? (How 'active' is it to run bazaars in order to collect money for the school fund?)

We have seen that there can be differences of emphasis between teachers and parents about what is most important in the curriculum. Some teachers take the view that they have special professional expertise and individual knowledge of their pupils such that they and no one else has a right to determine the curriculum. It is clear that from the teachers' point of view there are distinct advantages in being relatively free to act independently of parents' wishes: it is difficult enough to manage one's teaching, coping with pupils and colleagues and with various organisational tasks, without having to persuade parents that what one is doing is in their children's best interest. For one thing, parents do not speak with one voice: they may have quite diverse expectations because of different values or because of the schooling that they themselves experienced. And their interests may genuinely conflict, as when some parents press for increased time to be spent in examination work and other parents want a more general education for their children. It is possible to argue that only the professionals can arbitrate between these conflicting interests, at the same time as arguing with equal validity that parents have a right to influence their children's schooling, and indeed that their children will gain far more from school if the parents understand what is going on and approve of it.

Task 4.1 contd   Parents' involvement in the curriculum

4.1.5   (a) Gather together the arguments for and against 'teacher-autonomy' and 'parents' participation'. Is a reconciliation of the two possible? How far are teachers ever truly autonomous? What are they able to decide and what not?

(b) Make a list of the ways in which parents are involved in the life of one school that you know. What other ways might there be of bringing them more fully into the life of the school? How could you see to it that all parents join in, and not only the ones who attend all school occasions?

(c) It is not possible to avoid the central issue of parents' participation in decisions about the curriculum. Take a particular issue that might be controversial, such as the use

4.1.5
contd

of the Initial Teaching Alphabet (ITA) in a first school or the introduction of integrated science or sex education in a secondary school, and plan how parents might be brought into the decision-making. Could this become the basis for a continued consultation about the curriculum, or is it appropriate to bring parents in only over controversial matters?

Schools undoubtedly vary a great deal in the way they approach parents. Appendix L contains materials prepared by schools and sent out to parents; the following tasks are based on these materials.

Task 4.1 contd   Parents' involvement in the curriculum

4.1.6   Extracts A to E in Appendix L all come from documents addressed to parents. They are put together so that you may consider:
   (*a*) the relationship between school and home that is implied by the style in which the readers are addressed;
   (*b*) the variety of social and educational values expressed.

4.1.7   The remainder of Appendix L contains two guides to parents prepared in two middle schools (for children 9-13 years of age) in England. What do you think most parents would want to know about the school their children are about to attend? Do the guides provide this? How much information about the organisation of the curriculum is given? How much about content and teaching methods? Are parents given enough information? How much do they need to know in order to give full support to their children's schooling? How much have they a right to know as the persons finally responsible for bringing up the children?

What impression do you receive from the two guides about each school as a whole, and about each school's attitudes to pupils and their parents?

4.1.8   It has been suggested that every school should produce a detailed prospectus, and that parents should have a free choice amongst schools on the basis of the information thus made available. What do you think schools would put into a prospectus in order to attract pupils? (Perhaps there would be different answers to this according to the age of the pupils.)

243

4.1.8 What would be the likely effect of this upon curriculum, social
contd relationships and the general organisation of schools?

So far we have been considering ways in which parents might be directly
involved in schools, but we must also take into account the possibility
of indirect involvement through parent and community representatives
on the governing bodies of schools. Legal responsibility for school
curricula in England and Wales lies with the local education authorities.
Section 23 of the 1944 Education Act states unambiguously that 'the
secular instruction to be given to the pupils shall . . . be under the
control of the local education authority', and the Secretary of State
for Education should only intervene if he or she can demonstrate that
a local education authority is 'proposing to act unreasonably'. The
omission in the above quotation − indicated by a row of dots − quali-
fies this allocation of responsibility by indicating that some of this
responsibility may be delegated to the governing body or 'managers'
of a school, and this is what normally happens (Auld, 1976). For
example, the Inner London Education Authority in its 1973 guidelines
retains for itself only the responsibility for 'the general educational
character of the school'. The authority makes it perfectly explicit:
'The managers shall, in consultation with the head teacher, exercise
the oversight of the conduct and curriculum of the school' (Gretton
and Jackson, 1976). Other local authorities publish similar, though
not identical, guidelines for governing bodies. Thus the legal position
is clear: the control of curriculum does *not* officially lie with the
teaching profession but with the community, acting through its elected
and appointed representatives on education committees and governing bodies.

In practice governing bodies have seldom taken an active interest
in curriculum, which by default has become the responsibility of the
headteacher and staff. However, during the 1970s a current of public
dissatisfaction with the education system brought with it, amongst
other things, a call for the community in general, and parents in particular, to have more say in curriculum matters by means of their
representation on governing bodies. The Taylor Committee recommended in its report *A New Partnership for Our Schools* (Department
of Education and Science/Welsh Office, 1977) that each school should
have its own governing body, and that these should be composed
equally of nominees of the local authority, elected representatives of
school staffs, elected representatives of parents, and representatives

of interests in the community. Some local authorities are said to have made moves in this direction.

There does seem to be a problem in selecting the curriculum issues that might usefully be debated in an advisory body of the kind proposed in the Taylor Report. It would hardly be appropriate to consult them on which stories to read to the 6-year-olds, or on the order in which mathematical topics should be sequenced in a secondary-school course: these are clearly matters of pedagogical expertise. On the other hand, it would hardly involve the governing body in school thinking about the curriculum if they are used solely as a bench of judges in controversial matters, such as when parents complain that there is too much play and not enough teaching in an infants department, or when a secondary-school English department is accused of giving to their pupils novels in which sexual matters are presented in unsuitable ways.

Task 4.1 contd   School governing bodies and the curriculum

4.1.9   Make a list of topics related to a school curriculum which might form an agenda for two meetings of a governing body. Take into account that they would need to be informed about each topic as well as joining in discussion of policies and decisions. (If you are at present teaching in a school it would be best if you based your list on issues which are genuinely under consideration at the moment.)

4.1.10   You are a member of staff who, because of your particular responsibilities or specialist knowledge, have been asked to attend a governor's meeting to join in the discussion on one of the issues chosen in the previous task. Prepare a brief paper for prior circulation explaining the issue: it should not be more than about six hundred words in length. If the discussion is likely to lead to future action, the paper ought to include what seems to you to be the range of possible actions, and some analysis of pros and cons.

4.1.11   Read the schedule of questions for school self-evaluation (printed as Appendix I). Complete the section related to curriculum using information about whichever school you know best. Imagine that this section of your report is presented to the governing body: what questions and comments do you think it would provoke? (This would probably be best

4.1.11   as a group activity, with all students writing reports, and then
contd   choosing one of them for presentation to the governors. The
          group can then constitute itself as a governing body and,
          simulating particular parental and community interests,
          attempt to construct the comments and responses that the
          report might give rise to in real life.)

So far our discussion of the role of the community in education has
been restricted mainly to parents and their influence on the curriculum.
Many local authorities have set up what they call community schools.
Sometimes this is little more than renaming an existing school; at other
times the building of a new secondary school is linked with other new
provisions such as a local library, sports centre, public hall and so on.
What 'community school' means under these circumstances can vary
widely. At one end of the scale, it means little more than an economical
use of buildings, with evening classes and sports clubs using the facilities
when they are not required by the day school. At the other end of the
scale, there would be an attempt to break down the boundary between
school and community, so that adults came into the school in various
roles, as students, informants, advisers and planners, and teachers and
pupils from the school joined in a wider range of community concerns and activities, including many that would not traditionally have
been counted as education. It seems unlikely that many schools (if
any) have gone so far as this latter extreme suggests.

The following document was prepared early in the life of a new
school and community college to outline what was going to be
attempted (Holroyde, undated).

Community education in the school and community college – Sidney Stringer School and Community College

A community college is created by the coming together of people –
of all the people in the community. They meet for education and
recreation and to work together for their mutual benefit. A college
building is not essential, but helps greatly, and it belongs to the
people in the community.

It may be that we can pick out groups of people in that community, for example.

young people of compulsory school age;

the parents of those young people;
adults and young people over the school-leaving age;
members of recognised and established groups;
professional teachers, community workers, social workers,
health visitors and other officers.

These groups may see themselves as having little to do with each other, but in the community college they work and play together without imposed or self-created boundaries.

It is sensible to base the school in the community college so that school and non-school activities support each other, and extra resources can be put in by combining those normally available to a school with those provided for further education, youth and community.

A community college is not an extension of the school; the school is part of the community college. Listed below are eight features of a community college.

Government.   The government of the community college is the responsibility of the community, and representatives of the groups of people listed in the second paragraph, alongside and outnumbering local education authority representatives, form the governing body. (Many of the education authority representatives are elected members too.)

The governing body decides such things as membership, activities and projects, and has control of all finances other than those which are the statutory responsibility of the local education authority. It carries out the customary responsibilities of the school governors.

Staffing.   On the staff of the community college are professional community and youth workers, in addition to the normal complement of teachers. Many staff are qualified in both community and school work and are able to work in community projects and on the school timetable.

A resource for the community.   The college is likely to be the largest single capital investment made by the local authority in the area, and the expensive buildings and equipment are available to the community in the way the people wish to use them. The services of professional staff are available to provide a life-long education and

247

the recreational programmes that the people want.

Buildings are utilised for many hours each week. Adults may join in with school programmes and school pupils with adult programmes. The school day may be extended to make it easier for adults and pupils to share programmes and facilities together.

The community is a resource.   People from the community contribute to the educational and recreation programmes with whatever skills they can offer, and work alongside the professionals in community projects, playing a leading part if possible.

The area itself, its culture and its people and the everyday situations in it, are a laboratory for learning for the school pupils, and the pupils spend time outside the school building during the school day studying and working in the community.

Shared responsibility for education.   The education of the rising generation is the responsibility of everyone, not just the professional teachers. Parents and other adults are encouraged to take an interest in and influence the curriculum, and, if they are able to, contribute to the programmes.

Parents are encouraged to come freely into school, and staff are encouraged to visit the homes and build working relationships with parents as well as pupils. When parents understand what is happening to their children in school, they can help to educate the children at home.

The curriculum.   The school curriculum is designed so that pupils are helped to understand the contradictions they see around them, whilst being presented with a vision of what life could be. Their present experience and understanding is the starting-point for the school programme.

School is only a small element in the education process and must be seen by pupils to fit into life, and be relevant to their present and to their future. Pupils are made aware of the problems of their area, and the changes that are needed, and are encouraged and trained to help to bring about change.

Community development.   The staff work with residents to overcome specific problems, or to help specific groups of disadvantaged people; and to encourage people who would not normally take advantage of the college resources to do so. The people are helped to understand what facilities and services are available for them and how to use them. Projects are mounted outside the college for the people who will not come to the college.

An agency for change.   The college is in a unique position to mobilise co-operatively all the agencies working in the area; for example, social workers, health visitors, planners, politicians, teachers and residents groups; to commit themselves to deal with the problems of the area, even if to do so conflicts with their functional 'professional' interests. In this way, the college is able to help people to cope with problems which are too big or complex to be solved by individuals or agencies working alone.

Some of the problems that might be expected had already been predicted by the author of the above document. These include the five points mentioned below.

First, there is the difficulty of involving in the government of the community college persons representing a wide range of interests in the community, without putting excessive power in the hands of the most confident and articulate members of society, and into the hands of existing well-organised groups from sports clubs to political parties.

Second, many adults, particularly those who had not themselves been very successful at school, are reluctant to take part not only in classes but in any activities taking place in school buildings.

Third, teachers tend to be anxious about being required to respond to outside pressures, to adopt alternative ways of working – including, for example, teaching mixed groups of young people and adults – and to abandon their traditional control over curriculum.

Then there is pressure on the time, skills and energy of both teachers and community staff who are required to play a variety of roles in daytime and evening activities, some of them apparently more social than educational.

Finally, there is a tacit acceptance of the current curriculum and its assumptions, so that both teachers and non-teaching members of the community may be unsympathetic towards one another's proposals for change.

Task 4.1.12 Community colleges and the public

4.1.12 (a) Discuss the problems outlined in the above notes. What might they mean in practice? What groups might tend to take too much control of resources and why? Why is there a problem of involving the public in the use and management of resources intended for them? What new demands — in terms of unfamiliar roles and skills — might be made of teachers? What kinds of activity might community members want that might challenge teachers' conceptions about what constitutes education? What changes might teachers want to make in the curriculum that might challenge non-teachers' preconceptions?

(b) Imagine that you have been appointed the warden of a new well-equipped community college or centre, incorporating one or more schools. Plan your activities for the first two years, deciding how you will bring members of the public into the new centre, how you will organise the government of its activities, how you will set up the various aspects of its work outlined in the document quoted above. In particular, devise ways of coping with the problems identified in part (a) of this task.

(c) What do you see as the virtues and disadvantages of attempts to break down boundaries between school and community?

Control of the curriculum in England and Wales

In England and Wales it is not easy to say where control of the curriculum lies. The present state of affairs is best thought of as an interplay between two sets of events, administrative decisions and shifts of opinion; we can label these the institutional and ideological domains. We must also take it into account that administrative decisions can be made at four levels: national, local, school and classroom. Moreover, within the ideological domain we can distinguish professional opinion — amongst teachers and others within the educational system — from public opinion about educational matters. This can be represented spatially in a diagram (see Figure 4.2).

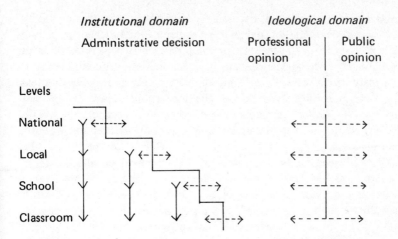

Figure 4.2   *Control of the curriculum at various levels and domains*

In the institutional domain, the unbroken arrows represent administrative decisions made at various levels which influence the school curriculum. For example, decisions about open-plan patterns of school architecture made at national level affect local and school action and eventually influence what teachers do in the classroom. Local decisions — for example, to build middle schools — similarly limit what curriculum choices can be at school and classroom level. Similarly, a headteacher's decisions about the allocation of time, pupils or resources set the conditions within which teachers make their decisions about teaching. Administrative decisions pre-empt the choices that can be made at lower levels: teachers' choices are constrained by the many decisions already made at other levels.

But all this is only within the institutional domain, and the educational system in England and Wales is far from impenetrable by outside opinions, whether of teachers or of vociferous public groups. The broken arrows represent the interplay of opinion. Not only is there interchange at different levels between professionals and public — though perhaps not as much as there ought to be — but the decisions made at different levels are sensitive to public pressure. For example, at national level the Department of Education and Science has been most circumspect in its moves towards proposing a core curriculum, carefully consulting opinion within the profession and outside. Before introducing a new mathematics scheme into the school, a primary-

251

school headteacher would be foolish not to ensure both that he has his colleagues' co-operation and that most parents understand the nature of the change and the reasons for embarking on it. This is the point of including the ideological domain in our model of curriculum control: the institutional domain is highly sensitive to opinion in certain areas of decision-making, even though the professionals have in the past managed to obtain considerable autonomy in controlling the details of curriculum content. Because of this sensitivity, Becher and Maclure, in discussing control of the curriculum (1978), use the phrase 'the politics of acceptability' to represent the way in which major curriculum changes have to be tested against various interest groups to find whether they will be acceptable. (For example, the Schools Council has circulated 'for discussion' several schemes for changes in examinations so as to widen the sixth-form curriculum: in spite of general agreement that some widening would be advantageous each of these schemes has met opposition and been withdrawn.) The politics of acceptability is to be contrasted with the situation in many — probably most — other countries in the world (though not the USA), where major curriculum decisions are seen to be of public concern and therefore to be decided at national level by those elected to represent the public's interests. In England and Wales, control of curriculum is not only diffused through the educational system, but it is also responsive at all levels to some aspects of public opinion.

Task 4.1 contd   Parents' involvement in the curriculum

4.2　　The value of a model like that shown in Figure 4.2 is that it can be the basis for discussion of actual cases, which can be used to test whether the model accounts for, or represents accurately, how the system works in practice. This model of curriculum control in England and Wales can be used in various ways.

4.2.1　Make a copy of the model and show diagrammatically on it the position and influence of each of the following. (This can be done by shading areas and including arrows to indicate influences, perhaps using different colours for each example below.)

　　　The influence of teachers' unions on policy.

　　　Parents' associations.

　　　Individual teacher's decisions.

4.2.1   The DES requirement for plans for secondary reorganisation.
contd   Industrial pressure groups.
         School managers.
         'The Great Debate'.
         Staff meetings.
         Local advisers' funds used as 'pump priming' for curriculum change.
         Schools Council and its various activities.
         (It should be noted that many of these can be interpreted in more than one way, so that their representation in diagrammatic form will give an opportunity for discussion.)

4.2.2   Discuss the overall adequacy of the model. What aspects of actuality are not represented in it? Are any wrongly represented?

4.2.3   How is the diffusion of power likely to affect curriculum adaptability? Will it lead to rapid innovation at national, local and school level, or will it lead to educational conservatism? Would there be advantages in a centralised system in which major decisions about the curriculum were made by the elected government as a matter of public policy? What disadvantages might follow? Show the changes you propose by making alterations or additions to the diagram.

This overview of the distribution of power in the educational system has been a necessary preliminary to a consideration of events during the late 1970s, which can be interpreted as a shift of power, but which nevertheless shows no sign of superseding the model we have been considering. Indeed the initiative for change seems to have come from outside the state education system; criticisms of the Right-wing press and by the pressure group that published the Black Papers (which criticised the supposed progressivism of state education) focused and co-opted a range of public dissatisfaction with schools. It would be misleading to identify this dissatisfaction simply with those parents who believed that comprehensive schools were depriving their children of the level of education they might have received in grammar schools: some parents of less able children were equally out of sympathy with what they believed — wrongly, it now appears — to have been going on in primary schools, the abandonment of determined teaching of reading and mathematics. As a result of this public pressure, the then Labour Prime Minister, James Callaghan, asked the Department of

Education and Science for a report. The report — called by journalists the Yellow Book — was presented to Callaghan in July 1976. Originally intended as an internal document, it was leaked in part to the press and published. The following points illustrate its tone and some of its emphases.

(*a*) The public think that secondary schools 'demand too little work and inadequate standards of performance in formal subjects'.

(*b*) Pupils in secondary schools need more science and technology to 'prepare them for their economic role'.

(*c*) There was a need for a statement of 'generally accepted principles for the composition of the secondary curriculum'.

(*d*) The authors of the report wanted the Prime Minister 'firmly to refute any argument . . . that no one except teachers has any right to any say in what goes on in schools'.

I have chosen these four phrases from the secondary section of the Yellow Book because they point to four issues of central importance in the ensuing debate: (*a*) standards; (*b*) preparation for work; (*c*) a core curriculum that would be binding on all schools; (*d*) the right of non-professionals to influence curriculum.

After receiving this document Mr Callaghan announced in October 1976 that there was to be a Great Debate on education. A series of regional conferences were to take place to which a very wide range of interest groups from outside as well as inside the education system were invited to send representatives. Such conferences could play no great role either in decision-making or in informing the educators or the public of one another's views, but they had the valuable symbolic function of visibly admitting non-professional opinions into the debate. They were succeeded by the publication in July 1977 of a government Green Paper, entitled *Education in Schools: A Consultative Document*, which dealt for the most part with the same issues as had the Yellow Book, though in more cautious terms (Department of Education and Science/Welsh Office, 1977).

(*a*) No clear view about standards was expressed.

(*b*) 'Industry and commerce should be involved in the curriculum planning processes at national and local level' and there was to be provision for other contacts between schools and industry, including arrangements for secondary-school teachers to spend short periods with industrial concerns.

(c) There was a 'need to investigate the part played by a core element' in the curriculum.

(d) Schools, it was asserted, should be accountable for their performance, though no details were given of what might constitute such accountability, except for a reference to the governing bodies of schools.

After the publication of *Education in Schools* the Department of Education and Science circulated local education authorities with a questionnaire about the ways in which they were fulfilling their statutory responsibility for the curricula of schools under their care, and in November 1979 their replies were summarised in *Local Authority Arrangements for the School Curriculum* (Department of Education and Science/Welsh Office, 1979). The intention of the Department of Education and Science is not left in doubt, since we find on the third page: 'Many authorities need to increase their working knowledge of what goes on in their schools, in order to improve their capability to develop and implement more effective approaches to staffing, curriculum development, assessment and the distribution of resources, all of which should be closely related to their curricular policies and the aims of the schools.' A later part of the publication makes it clear that at least three-quarters of all local education authorities had not formulated 'curricular policies', so that the sentence quoted above amounts to an injunction to do so.

During these same years Her Majesty's Inspectors had been carrying out, by means of questionnaires, visits and observation, a thorough survey of a large sample of primary schools and a large sample of secondary schools. They reported their findings as *Primary Education in England* (1978) and *Aspects of Secondary Education in England* (1979). Once again, I will pick out some major aspects of the reports, dealing first with the primary-school one.

(a) No support was given to assertions that standards in basic subjects had been falling. On the contrary, the tests of reading achievement administered during the study gave 'results . . . consistent with a rising trend in reading standards between 1955-1977'.

(b) It seemed that in many schools basic skills in language and mathematics had been emphasised at the expense of their application and use: 'The teaching of skills in isolation . . . does not produce the best results.'

(c) The Inspectors judged that teachers were not always successful

255

in matching learning tasks to children's capabilities, particularly
in choosing books for the more able. On the other hand . . .
'Children in inner city schools are more likely than others to be
underestimated by their teachers and least likely to be given work
that extends their capabilities.'

(*d*) 'Over 40 per cent of the schools had schemes of work in science
but there was little evidence of these programmes being imple-
mented.'

(*e*) 'There is no evidence in the survey to suggest that a narrower
curriculum enabled children to do better in the basic skills or led
to the work being more aptly chosen to suit the capacities of the
children.' The authors then went on to mention art and craft,
history and geography, music and physical education, science,
language, mathematics, and religious and moral education.

The following points are selected from the report on the secondary-
school survey.

(*f*) The large range of options offered in the fourth and fifth years of
many secondary schools does not 'necessarily result in a balanced
programme or one which has coherence for the pupil'. Moreover
'the less able pupils who might be thought most in need of motivation often have least real choice'.

(*g*) There was explicit criticism of certain styles of teaching that are
'widely employed' in secondary schools, including 'heavily directed
teaching, a preponderance of dictated or copied notes, an emphasis on the giving or recall of information, with little room or time
for enquiry or exploration of applications'.

(*h*) The report said that the ablest pupils were 'not always sufficiently
challenged', but made far stronger reference to the less able. 'There
were more widespread indications that the less able commonly had
inappropriate programmes' and that it was those pupils who lie
just below the average in ability who are 'most likely to spend their
time on the more mechanical exercises in writing and computation,
with too little context to evoke interest or relate their learning to
real life'.

(*i*) 'It may be necessary to develop a more explicit rationale of the
curriculum as a whole.' Later, the authors mentioned 'the discussion of policies, their translation into the planning of specific programmes of work in the classroom, their regular assessment and
evaluation'.

(*j*) 'Day-to-day assessment of the work in hand, the diagnosis of difficulties, and regular review of progress are important parts of the educational process.'

(*k*) 'Particularly at risk are those aspects of education which are not simply identified with particular specialist subjects — language development, reading skills at all levels of ability, health education, careers education, social and moral education and . . . preparation of pupils for life in a multi-racial society.'

During the succeeding years the Department of Education and Science has continued to move very cautiously. In January 1980, two documents were issued for discussion, *A Framework for the School Curriculum* (Department of Education and Science/Welsh Office, 1980), and *A View of the Curriculum* (Her Majesty's Inspectors of Schools, 1980). Although there were substantial differences in emphasis, these brief publications expressed similar views on the following topics.

(*a*) Local authorities should have a curricular policy.

(*b*) All schools should 'articulate aims and evaluate achievements'. (The Inspectors went further and recommended 'a careful assessment of children's capabilities', urging 'the exercise of assessment skills by all teachers at all stages'.)

(*c*) A core of essential subjects was recommended, and examples given of appropriate allocations of time to them.

(*d*) Emphasis was placed upon preparation for employment and adult life.

Max Morris, the secretary of the National Union of Teachers, described *A Framework for the School Curriculum* in *The Times Educational Supplement* as 'a compendium of trite banalities'. However, later in the same article he noticed a revolutionary change in the Schools Council's role: 'It is . . . the Council's determination to play its part in devising a curriculum framework, which is the revolutionary change from the old days of non-intervention.' From the NUT point of view the changes taking place were changes not in content but in the location of power.

In selecting points from these and from the other documents discussed above, I have naturally had to omit a great deal, so that the resulting emphases may not correspond to their authors' intentions in all cases. (You are invited to test them against the much more detailed accounts to be found in Becher and Maclure (1978), Kogan (1978) or Lawton (1980), which are in any case highly relevant to the tasks which follow.) It is not difficult to pick out continuing themes that were already visible in the Yellow Book of 1976, though there have been changes of emphasis too which suggest changes in DES policy.

At the same time as all this was going on, another DES initiative was taking shape, which was also a response to public pressures. It was during 1975 that the Assessment of Performance Unit (usually called the APU) was set up within the Department of Education and Science. The APU was set up to 'monitor' children's performance in six 'areas of development' (see Table 4.1). These areas of development were chosen not to be co-terminous with school subjects but to run across boundaries in a manner made familiar by the phrase 'language across the curriculum'. It was intended to be 'performance not knowledge' that would be tested, the content and method of teaching remaining the responsibility of schools. The purpose of the APU was, and is, to describe overall levels of performance: it does not make statements about individual pupils, schools or education authority areas. Their reports do, however, give separate information about regions (southern, midland, and northern England, Wales, and Northern Ireland), location (in metropolitan as against county authorities), size and type of school, and percentage of children taking free meals. (This last is a rough attempt at a measure of social disadvantage.) APU testing takes place at 11 and 15 years of age, but also at 13 years in science. The testing is based on a 'light sampling' procedure, so that a limited proportion of children in the age-group is tested on any one occasion.

TABLE 4.1 *The 'areas of development' in children's performance to be monitored by the Assessment of Performance Unit*

Area of development	First tests	First report published
Mathematics	1978	1980
Language (reading and writing)	1979	1981
Science	1980	1981
Personal and social	Not funded	
Aesthetic	Not funded	
Physical	Not funded	

In order to improve the validity of the tests, a wide range of tasks has been prepared in each area, far more than it would be reasonable to ask any one pupil to attempt. For example, within the language area this has meant that the abilities that constitute 'writing' are represented by a range of different kinds of writing, and not by one or two kinds only, as is common in public examinations. In order to make this possible, the tasks are given to different groups of pupils, so that no one pupil attempts more than a part of them, and the results of the different groups are amalgamated. Since no statements are to be made about individuals, it does not matter that no one person attempts the whole range of tasks.

By 1981, only mathematics, language, science and French had been given funds to begin testing. (It should be noted that the inclusion of French breaches the original proposal that cross-curricular 'areas of development', not school subjects, should be tested, since a foreign language seems more a subject to be learnt than a unique set of processes appropriate to a form of development.) Proposals for testing personal and social development — which appears to include moral, cultural and religious values — met fierce (and in my view well-merited) opposition from the teachers' unions and have been abandoned. Nor does it seem likely that funds will be found for tests of aesthetic and physical development.

The tasks that follow relate to the various events since 1975, including the setting up of the APU. The work of the APU can be interpreted both as part of the events of these years, and as an administrative move of potential importance in its own right. For this reason, you will wish to consider its meaning alongside other recent events; the next set of tasks gives occasion to do this. However, a set of questions (4.4), focused specifically upon the APU, follows immediately after them.

Task 4.3 Interpreting political influences on UK curricula

4.3.1   What do you consider to be the main sources and causes of public pressure on the education system of England and Wales during the 1970s? You will find it useful to consider not only the official publications that I have referred to but also the books referred to on p. 258. (This search can reasonably be shared by students who are working in a group.) It would be relevant to ask yourself how far the events and documents I have mentioned should be thought of as responses to cuts in

4.3.1 public expenditure as well as (or instead of) responses to a
contd debate about standards and priorities. The following four
passages also raise considerations that may be relevant.

(a) In recent years the social environment in a number of
schools with more emphasis on personal development
and less on formal instruction has been diverging from
that encountered in most work situations, where the
need to achieve results in conformity with defined
standards and to do so within fixed time limits calls for
different patterns of behaviour. (Manpower Services
Commission, 1975)

(b) In the last three decades the move to informal methods
in teaching reading and the general use of look-and-say
have had a great effect upon our schools, and I believe
that the poor performance among the children from
Social Classes 4 and 5, referred to in the ILEA and
Aberdeen surveys . . . is directly attributable to this
movement. . . . A disturbing feature of the decline in
reading standards among young children in recent years
is that the new informal methods would appear to be
particularly to the disadvantage of boys. It is note-
worthy in this connection, that in the survey called
Roots of Reading carried out for the NFER by Cane and
Smithers in 1971 we learn that in the twelve working-
class infant departments which were studied, two years
after entering (about age seven), 15% of the girls and
30% of the boys were still unable to read. . . . The
modern tendency for boys to take longer over the reading process than girls confirms my view that informal
methods in reading or in any other school activity are
only suitable for those who do not need disciplinary
pressure to work. (Froome, 1975)

(c) Such bodies as the Confederation of British Industries
maintained that schools were not doing enough to encourage basic skill learning or motivation towards the
applied sciences and arts that might help the manpower
needs of industry and business. It is worth remarking,

4.3.1
contd

however, that there has never been an occasion upon which the employers' federations have not complained about the standards of the schools. In 1977, a knowledgeable Labour peer, Wilfrid Brown, in addressing a University Congregation, could by implication deplore the growth of comprehensive education by declaring the demise of the secondary technical schools to be one of the main contributions to our economic difficulties. (Kogan, 1978)

(d) Working-class parents do not like primary-school progressivism. Nor have they been the most fervent supporters of comprehensive education. Working-class electors, who stand to be the highest beneficiaries of the expansion of higher education, have not been particularly enthusiastic about the growth of a large student proletariat whose ways of life and aspirations they cannot easily reconcile with their own wishes and working lives. If change means a move towards deinstitutionalising education it is by no means clear that the mass of the people are for it. (Kogan, 1978)

4.3.2 Write a summary of what appear to be the main features of the Department of Education and Science policy in response to public pressures since 1975. What changes of emphasis do you detect during these years? How can these be accounted for? Do you think that the two reports by HM Inspectors on primary and secondary schools were likely to increase or damp down public uneasiness and criticism?

4.3.3 Imagine that you have been appointed headteacher of a new school. Write a document for discussion with those of your senior staff already appointed, giving the main policy lines for the management of the curriculum that can be drawn from one or both of HM Inspectors' reports.

4.3.4 What arguments can be brought forward to support or oppose the opinion that the public or its representatives have a right to influence decisions about school curricula? Compare, for example, point (d) quoted above (on p. 254) from the Yellow Book with the following passage which comes from the response published by the National Union of Teachers (1977) to the

4.3.4 Department of Education and Science's *Education in Schools:*
contd *A Consultative Document*.

> It is necessary to distinguish between the natural and legiti-
> mate interest which the local education authority, governors
> and parents have in the curriculum and the responsibility of
> teachers for the day to day education of children. The
> curriculum should relate to the differing needs and back-
> grounds of pupils; teachers should be receptive to ideas and
> advice, but views on the curriculum are often conflicting
> and it is the teacher, who has the experience and detailed
> immediate knowledge of the children, who is in a position
> to evaluate and discriminate. The interpretive work of the
> teacher is the fundamental basis of his professionalism and
> an essential element in the learning process. In the last analy-
> sis the teacher in the school who has day to day contact with
> pupils must be able to exercise professional judgement.

4.3.5 How far do the events of the 1970s amount to an increase in
the central control of education? Lawton (1980), for example,
entitles one of his chapters 'The growing power of the man-
darins', and seems to be referring more to the influence of
permanent officials at the Department of Education and Science
than to the power of the government. What has happened to the
influence of local authorities, once believed to have a third of
the power in a supposed three-cornered equilibrium between
the Department of Education and Science, local authorities and
the teachers' unions? Where does the influence of parents, and
of other members of the community immediately about the
school, make its impact? (See the previous section, pp. 238-50.)
Maclure (1970), discussing the way in which various pressure
groups — employers and trades unions generally, as well as the
teachers' unions — enjoyed representation on national bodies
(for example, the Consultative Committee of the APU), pointed
out that 'all these power groups tend to be centralising forces',
and came to the conclusion that as a result it is 'harder than ever
for the consumers to organise peripheral pressure into a national
force'. You might take into account also the NUT's energetic
opposition to the recommendations of the Taylor Report on
school managing bodies.

4.3.6 *A Framework for the School Curriculum* (Department of Education and Science/Welsh Office, 1980) includes proposed guidelines for the allocation of time to subjects in the curriculum. All children should give at least 10 per cent of their time to English and a similar proportion to mathematics throughout their schooling; indeed, it is suggested that at certain stages (unspecified) the proportion might be considerably greater. Children should begin the study of science in their primary schools and continue until at least 13 years of age, taking at least 10 per cent of their time but not more than 20 per cent. The learning of a foreign language should 'normally begin during the secondary stage' and be allocated 10 per cent of every pupil's time for a period of at least two years. It was also reaffirmed that all children should receive religious education and physical education.

Compare this with the findings of HM Inspectorate reported in *Aspects of Secondary Education in England* (1979). 'In the majority of schools the core was allocated between 14 and 18 periods per week, roughly as follows: English and Mathematics 5 or 6 periods each; 3 or 4 periods of physical education; careers and religious education . . . 1 to 3 periods between them.' One of the tables in the report shows that 62 out of 243 schools (25.5 per cent) gave less than 40 per cent of their time to the core, which would be roughly equivalent to the 'between 14 and 18 periods per week' mentioned in the sentence quoted above, so that 'the majority of schools' seems to mean 'about three-quarters'.

On the basis of these figures, what proportion of secondary schools seems to fall below the proposed guidelines? Why, in your opinion, do ministers of state find it necessary to insist on curriculum guidelines in order to influence this proportion of secondary schools?

The next group of tasks relates to the activities of the Assessment of Performance Unit, and in particular to the likely effects of national monitoring of achievement upon school curricula.

Task 4.4 Assessment of Performance Unit

4.4.1 How much testing goes on at present in schools? The National Foundation for Educational Research reports large and increasing

4.4.1 sales of test materials, especially to primary schools. Interview
contd teachers from as many schools as possible and find out what
tests are given at what ages to how large a proportion of pupils.
(In some schools it may be necessary to ask the headteacher
or the teacher in charge of remedial work in order to gain the
information.) What function or functions do these tests appear
to serve for the schools? How do the teachers justify them?

4.4.2 Dennis Lawton (1980) identifies three kinds of test:
(a) Criterion-referenced tests 'which are designed to find out
whether a part of a taught syllabus has been successfully
learned'.
(b) Diagnostic tests which are 'used to identify strengths and
weaknesses of individual children in a specific area of the
curriculum'.
(c) Norm-referenced tests which 'are designed to show how
well a pupil (or a group of pupils) performs in relation to
a much larger sample — usually a standardised norm'.

These categories will help us to consider the different kinds of
relevance that tests have to the curriculum.
(i) Which kinds of test are likely to be most useful to
teachers in their day-to-day work? Why is that?
(ii) What category do examinations such as GCE O level and
CSE fall into?
(iii) Lawton continues: 'The APU will be developing tests of
the third kind: that is norm-referenced tests essentially
concerned with questions of standards.' If Lawton is
right — and you can check by looking at the examples in
Table 4.1 — how far will the APU tests be useful to
teachers? How might they be used by administrators?

Some earlier APU statements asserted that because of the light sampling
approach the tests would have no 'backwash' effect on teaching (Marjoram, 1977). More recently, however, the APU has been somewhat
more willing to admit to the possibility of backwash, and even to hint
that in some circumstances such backwash might be beneficial. This
typically modest statement comes from the introduction to a booklet
issued in May 1978 to outline plans for the assessment of language
(Department of Education and Science/Assessment of Performance
Unit, 1978).

While the whole APU monitoring exercise has been deliberately designed to minimise any 'backwash' on the curriculum, it must be accepted that assessment procedures may transmit messages to teachers about curricular priorities. Accordingly, it is essential for the APU to produce national forms of assessment that do justice to the intuitive model of writing acted on by most teachers.

(We could substitute for the word 'writing' other curriculum areas such as 'reading', 'mathematics', or 'science'.) Some teachers say that they would not, under any circumstances, be influenced by APU tests; others fear that nervous headteachers will insist on their teaching for the tests. One teacher said to me naively, 'Well, we know that the child-centred stuff is no good and we've got to concentrate on basics, don't we?' One message seems to have reached her, perhaps even without the aid of APU.

In considering the likely impact of the APU tests on schools and their curricula, we must take into account a facility called LEASIB which is part of the National Foundation for Educational Research, the body that has been given responsibility for carrying out all the APU testing except that in science. LEASIB stands for Local Education Authorities and Schools Item Bank. Although it is not part of APU, LEASIB is to provide tests which can be bought by local education authorities and indeed by any schools that can spare the money. These tests will be very similar to the actual APU tests, so that it will be possible to give these tests to children in a school or group of schools and then to relate their scores to national norms laid down by the APU. Of course, something similar is already possible, using the many standardised tests already available from NFER and elsewhere. Some local authorities have been enthusiastic in their support of the APU, however, in the hope of having better (in the sense of 'more valid') tests available for their own use, and those authorities will no doubt make use of LEASIB. Whether they will engage in what is called 'blanket testing' – that is, testing all children in an age-group – or use some method of sampling remains to be seen. Other local authorities do not wish to engage in extensive testing of the norm-referenced kind, and prefer to rely upon informal evaluation of schools by advisers and on school self-assessment, and use existing diagnostic-type tests when it is necessary in order to plan individual curricula for children with handicaps, and so on.

The leaders of the APU have been aware from the first of some of the possible implications of such evaluation of schools, as they were well acquainted with some of the more unfortunate American experiences. To take an example, when an assessment programme was set up in 1969 for schools in the state of Michigan, the state Department of Education undertook not to release data upon individual schools or on local school districts (an American administrative unit much smaller than British local authorities). However, elected representatives on state legislative bodies forced the state Department to release this information, which — we are told — was used to put pressure upon local school districts and even upon individual school principals. Administrators from one school district, disgusted at this, described the test programme as 'politics masquerading as research' and asserted that: 'the conclusions were written before the project was undertaken . . .' (Kearney and Huyser, 1977; Read, 1973). The APU has been at considerable pains to ensure that their results cannot be used as a political lever in this way. However, it would not be impossible for an injudicious local authority — using either existing tests or items from LEASIB — to set off on such a path. That no local education authority has been so rash can be attributed not only to the good sense of senior officers, but also to their not inconsiderable respect for the views of teachers' unions.

It only remains to make available some samples of the work of the APU. There are three ways in which the APU may transmit messages to teachers: (i) by its preliminary statements about what is to be tested, which amount to a model for that area of the curriculum; (ii) by the actual test items used; and (iii) by the reports published. Examples of each of these follow.

The first example comes from the monitoring of achievement in science (Department of Education and Science/Assessment of Performance Unit, undated). It has been decided to group the criteria upon which assessment is based under these headings:

1 using symbolic representations;
2 using apparatus and measuring instruments;
3 observation tasks;
4 interpretation and application;
5 design of investigations;
6 performing investigations.

The APU science team are of the opinion that: 'A pupil's performance may be as much affected by the concept area in which a question is set as by the science activity category.' (That is, the activities listed above.) For this reason they have supplied a list of concepts and knowledge 'as a basis for ensuring an adequate coverage by the tests across these concept areas'. The list is divided into six sections:

A   interaction of living things with their environment;
B   living things and their life processes;
C   force and field;
D   transfer of energy;
E   the classification and structure of matter;
F   chemical interactions.

Each of these is subdivided: for example 'force and field' is subdivided into: C1 movement and deformation; C2 properties of matter; C3 forces at a distance; and C4 the Earth in space. To give you an impression of what the whole list is like, here is the whole of one of these subdivisions.

C3 forces at a distance

Age 11. Magnets attract and repel other magnets and attract magnetic substances.

Age 13. Magnets attract and repel other magnets and attract magnetic substances. The region in which a magnetic effect can be detected is called a magnetic field.
There is a magnetic field surrounding the Earth.
Magnetism is induced in some materials when they are placed in a magnetic field.
An electric current in a coil of wire produces a magnetic field around it.
Some materials can be electrically charged by rubbing them with a different material.
Similarly charged objects repel each other, and oppositely charged objects attract each other. The force between such objects is stronger when the objects are close.

Age 15. Magnets attract and repel other magnets and attract magnetic substances.
The region in which a magnetic effect can be detected is called a magnetic field.

There is a magnetic field surrounding the Earth.

Magnetism is induced in some materials when they are placed in a magnetic field.

An electric current in a conductor produces a magnetic field round it.

There is a force on a current-carrying conductor in a magnetic field so long as the conductor is not parallel to the field.

The force on a current-carrying conductor in a magnetic field increases with the strength of the field and with the current.

Relative motion of a conductor and a magnetic field can be used to produce an electric current.

Electric charges are separated when certain materials are rubbed against one another.

Similarly charged objects repel each other, and oppositely charged objects attract each other. The force between such objects is stronger when the objects are close and when the charges are large.

(The whole list can be obtained on request from the Department of Education and Science.)

The test questions do not test simple recall of these ideas. They are designed to assess the extent to which pupils can use them in a range of situations, including, for example, the interpretation of observation, the design of experiments and in making predictions about or explaining presented events.

Beside this, we can place an equivalent set of specifications for monitoring achievement in writing, which is part of the language 'area of development' (Department of Education and Science/Assessment of Performance Unit, 1978). When 15-year-old pupils are monitored, the writing tasks they are given will fall into some of the following categories.

15.1 Personal response to pictures, music, short quotations from poems or prose, or similar stimuli.

15.2 An autobiographical narrative or anecdote in which the pupil is able to reflect upon the experience recounted.

15.3 A fictional story.

15.4 An objective description or account of a process which the pupil can write from the confidence of personal authority.

15.5 Discussion of an issue of the pupil's own choosing in which he is required to present a point of view and persuade the reader to it.

15.6 An account of how a problem is to be solved or a task to be performed, sometimes with the additional requirement of producing notes or a flow-chart from which the account is then developed.

15.7 Discussion of an issue for which the pupil has himself to produce data and evidence, explore the various arguments, and present his own conclusions.

15.8 Discussion of an issue for which evidence and data are provided and the pupil is required to take account of opposing viewpoints.

There is no list of subject-matter analogous to the science concepts; as in public examinations in English at secondary level, the range of topics for writing has not been specified in advance.

Our examples of test items and reporting must be taken from the mathematics area, since these are the only ones available at the time of writing. The APU publishes a proportion of the test items used in each year, so that these can be discussed in the text; the other items remain confidential so that they can be used again. The first survey published, *Mathematical Development: Primary Survey Report No. 1* (Department of Education and Science/Assessment of Performance Unit, 1980), released test items concerned with a variety of mathematical topics: angles, symmetry, time and temperature, area, numeration, decimals, multiplication, fractions, division, proportionality, equations, sets, and graphs and bar charts. I shall illustrate these with three items concerned with interpreting a calendar, and three with reading a thermometer. (In mathematics, as in science, there are also practical tests which will not be discussed here.) Figure 4.3 comes from the report and shows both the items themselves and the percentage of 11-year-olds who answered each item correctly. The commentary – which I quote below – deals with a group of items concerned with telling the time, as well as the ones shown in Figure 4.3.

Questions testing pupils' knowledge of the clock face and the recording of clock time were answered successfully by between 60 and 80 per cent of the pupils. A group of applications requiring calculations involving time intervals in common situations ranged in facility value between 30 and 60 per cent and, for one item, up to 80 per cent. This last item asked for the time of finish of a TV programme when the starting time and duration of the programme were given. This was a straightforward addition operation with no

Response analysis			Item facility	
a)	Incorrect	5%	92%	**R1**
	Omitted	3%		
b)	Incorrect	15%	78%	
	Omitted	7%		
c)	Incorrect	29%	59%	
	Omitted	12%		
a)	Incorrect	11%	83%	**R2**
	Omitted	6%		
b)	Incorrect 2°	18%	34%	
	Other incorrect	39%		
	Omitted	9%		
c)	Incorrect + 8°C or 8°C	2%	21%	
	Incorrect 11°C-12°C	27%		
	Other incorrect	42%		
	Omitted	8%		

R1

February calendar

February					
Sunday		5	12	19	26
Monday		6	13	20	27
Tuesday		7	14	21	28
Wednesday	1	8	15	22	
Thursday	2	9	16	23	
Friday	3	10	17	24	
Saturday	4	11	18	25	

This is a calendar for the month of February.
On what day of the week is
a) 1 Feb? . . . .
b) 1 March? . . . .
c) Is this calendar for a leap year? . . . .

R2

What is the reading on each of these thermometers

Figure 4.3 *Extract from* Mathematical Development: Primary Survey Report No. 1

270

carrying needed. In contrast the hardest item in this group required the calculation of the time interval between two times, a few minutes on either side of 12 o'clock.

Three of the released items R 1a, b and c, shown in [Figure 4.3] refer to calendar time and it can be seen that 92 per cent of the children could successfully find the first of the month on a calendar (Rla), the same proportion could find a particular date in the body of the table and R1b shows that 78 per cent of the pupils understand the structure of the calendar and are aware that March 1st follows February 28th. 59 per cent answered the leap year question R1c correctly and approximately 50 per cent of the pupils referred to February 29th as an 'extra day' or some equivalent idea to justify their answer.

It is perhaps important to add that there is no further commentary in the report on these items. Nor can we assume that in the next test these released items will be replaced by equivalents which also use a month from the calendar, and diagrams of thermometers.

Task 4.4 contd Assessment of Performance Unit

4.4.3   On the basis of the information given above, do you think that there is any likelihood of a backwash influence from APU tests upon what is included in school work, and upon what aspects are emphasised? If so, what kinds of influence are the tests likely to have on mathematics teaching in primary schools, and on science and English teaching in secondary schools? And is the influence likely to be beneficial or harmful?

4.4.4   However, it is not possible to estimate the likely impact of the monitoring solely on the basis of schemes, tests and reports. So far, the press has taken little note of APU reports, perhaps because nothing in them has provided occasion for surprise or outrage. But what if one report did show falling standards in one area? Most teachers have not yet had experience of APU testing in their schools, but if some local education authorities were to utilise LEASIB and test extensively, this too might alter their sensitivity to the implications of testing. There have recently been moves to compel secondary schools to publish their examination results: could this be extended in some areas to the publication of local test results, or is this unthinkable?

4.4.4 Who is right, the teachers who say APU will have no effect, or
contd   those who fear loss of autonomy? Is it possible at this time to
        make an estimate of the likely impact of the testing upon the
        curriculum?

4.4.5 The Department of Education has given money to a university
        to investigate the impact of APU testing on school curricula.
        Plan a programme for that research, which will last for several
        years. How will you decide what information you need? How
        far can teachers be treated as unbiased witnesses to their own
        teaching behaviour, and what alternative sources of informa-
        tion are there? What sort of evidence is likely to show changes?
        Indeed, how can you decide what kinds of change might occur?

4.4.6 So far, the Department of Education and Science has funded
        tests in mathematics, language (now including spoken language),
        science and French; nothing else. They have decided not to test
        moral, personal or social development. What is the implication
        for those areas of the curriculum so far omitted: social studies,
        history and geography, the aesthetic and physical 'areas of
        development', design and technology? Should they regret that
        they lack the imprimatur of the APU, or be glad to have
        escaped? Spoken language will be included in the tests, in spite
        of some fears about the possibility of valid tests in so intangible
        an area, because it was thought that otherwise it would not
        receive its share of curriculum time in comparison with reading
        and writing. If this argument is valid for spoken language, would
        it not be valid for other omitted areas of the curriculum? This
        raises the general question whether the APU should test every-
        thing in the curriculum to avoid overemphasis on those parts
        which are at present tested. Write a persuasive document as if
        for an APU conference, expounding the claims of an area not
        yet tested, or arguing that testing in another area is improper
        and should either be discontinued or never begun. (You might
        find it useful to choose the area of personal and social develop-
        ment which has already been the subject of heated debate with-
        in the APU, though this would involve deciding exactly what is
        included within that heading.)

4.4.7 It has sometimes been said that the true purpose of the APU is
        to reassure the public in a time of financial shortage that they
        are getting value for money, and that the monitoring cannot in
        its nature be of any use to schools. What is your opinion of this?

School-based curriculum development

Although the APU and the sequence of official publications that we have been considering seem to imply a loss of autonomy by schools, another event points in a different direction. This is the publication by the Schools Council (in August 1979) for the curriculum and examinations of their 'programmes', which are designed to give schools a much greater share of responsibility for curriculum development than had their earlier policies. The Schools Council, funded jointly by the Department of Education and Science and the local authorities, was set up in 1964 to advise schools about curricula. The word 'advise' is highly significant: the role of the Schools Council was (and is) to widen the range of curricular options available to teachers to choose from. The Council has never been given the least authority to enforce its recommendations, so its power has derived solely from its official status and from its ability to fund curriculum development. In earlier years, most of the development projects funded were sited in universities, which set up teams with a status at national level, and the ambition to influence a wide range of teachers.

The present 'programmes', on the other hand, are focused upon local initiatives: the Schools Council appears to have redefined its functions as the encouragement and support of curriculum development in individual schools, groups of schools and by local education authorities. One result of the criticisms of education in the late 1970s has been for the government to take effective control of the Schools Council away from representatives of teachers' unions, who had formerly had a majority of places upon all its committees, and to bring in representatives of various interest groups outside education, including ones from employers' organisations and trades unions. This can be seen as part of the general move to make it clear that the control of the curriculum was no longer to be left in the hands of professional educators. This organisational shift within the Council coincided with the spread of disillusionment at the effects of central projects, which have been set up to produce new methods and perhaps classroom materials and to disseminate these to teachers. (Whether this disillusionment is justified, whether Schools Council projects have had an influence upon schools commensurate with the money expended, is still a matter for debate.) An unsympathetic observer — one still devoted to national projects, perhaps — might well note that the new 'programmes' seem likely to be a good deal less expensive than the old projects — though the Council is still continuing to fund a few of those.

Thus in 1979 the Schools Council, while retaining its responsibility for the oversight of examinations, set up these four programmes.

(i)   Purpose and planning in schools. This programme is concerned with curriculum aims, self-evaluation by schools, curriculum continuity within and between schools, and issues related to specialism in primary schools.

(ii) Helping individual teachers to become more effective.

(iii) Developing the curriculum for a changing world. The programme has four subsections:

  science, mathematics and technology;
  spoken language, reading and study skills;
  social, vocational and personal education;
  topics that run across the curriculum (probably those mentioned by Her Majesty's Inspectors (1979) (see p. 257 above).

(iv) Individual pupils. This programme is concerned with special education, the education of disruptive pupils, gifted pupils and the education of pupils who belong to ethnic minorities.

It will perhaps be easiest to estimate the nature of this change in emphasis if we compare a typical national project with a local initiative that was supported by the Schools Council (as it happens) before their overt change of policy. The project I have chosen at national level is Geography for the Young School Leaver, and the local activity is the Language Development Project which was also supported by Avon Education Authority (Schools Council/Avon Education Authority, 1979). The Geography for the Young School Leaver Project, which began in 1970, might be described as a 'second-wave Schools Council project', since by this time the Council was highly aware of the problems of disseminating the work of project teams. Such second-wave projects deliberately involved teachers at an early stage and set up regional groups to give moral and practical support to participating teachers, while retaining overall control at the centre. Here is a summary of information about the project (Parsons, 1980).

Sponsor   Schools Council.

Grant   £127,300. This includes all additional funds made available to the project up to the time of writing and £600 from Northern Ireland for the period 1976-79 for support and dissemination.

Location   Avery Hill College of Education, 1970-76.

Designated pupils   14-16 average and below average ability pupils (originally).

Period of funding   Development phase 1970-74. For dissemination and support from 1974 to 1976 and on a reduced level 1976-79.

Project team   1970-74 Rex Beddis and Tom Dalton — co-directors (each ½ time). 1974-79 Pamela Bowen and Trevor Higginbottom research officers. Trevor Higginbottom was funded for a further two years full-time to act as national co-ordinator for the project. He is now an adviser with the Sheffield Metropolitan District Education Authority and continues to act as national co-ordinator.

Co-ordinators to support the schools in their locality were appointed during the project trials. 12 regional co-ordinators were appointed at the dissemination stage in 1974 and they continue to operate. LEAs were invited to appoint local co-ordinators. Regional co-ordinators receive expenses and honoraria for their services.

Trials   Pre-trials work was carried out in a small number of schools in the south east London area. Testing of the first pack of materials began in 1971 in 23 schools clustered in five areas of England and Wales. 22 'associate' schools were also involved.

Materials   Three published themes: *Man, Land and Leisure*; *Cities and People*; *People, Place and Work*.

Each published theme contains a teachers' guide; 30 copies of numerous resource sheets for pupils; other audio-visual material. Published by Thomas Nelson & Sons Ltd, from 1974.

Teachers Talking: a magazine about GYSL. The first two issues were produced by the project. Since 1976 it has been published biannually by Nelson, still edited by the project team and containing mostly articles by teachers on the use and development of GYSL.

It is instructive to contrast this with the Schools Council/Avon education authority Language Development Project (1979). Although this began in 1975, well before the 1979 change of policy, it illustrates one kind of local activity that is likely to gain support within the new programmes.

Sponsors   Schools Council and Avon Education Authority.

Grant   Schools Council awarded £7,442; the Avon contribution
was £3,500.

Location   Weston Teachers Centre.

Designated pupils   11-to-16-year-olds.

Period of funding   Avon alone 1973-4; Schools Council and Avon
1975-7.

Project team   The project began when Avon released a teacher for
two terms to go round secondary schools making tape-recordings of
the spoken language used in lessons. As a result of her report, a
submission was made to the Schools Council who jointly with Avon
funded a two-year extension of the study. During those two years
a teacher-director, Geoffrey Eggins, was released for one day a week,
and part-time secretarial help was provided. Eight schools took
part in the project, and it was the representatives from these
schools — all English teachers working in their spare time — who
constituted the project team and wrote the eventual report. Several
academics — of whom I was one — acted as consultants, and an
evaluator was appointed who briefly visited the schools involved
and wrote a descriptive report on the work being done. Informal
support was given by the warden of the teachers' centre and by
Avon advisers.

Materials   It was not the purpose of the project to produce classroom materials but to study the part played by talk in learning, in
order to improve their own teaching. The strategy was to tape-
record pupils carrying out their work, often in small groups, and to
discuss transcriptions of the recordings; during succeeding discussions the participants became progressively more able to define what
they were looking for. Eventually the group wrote and revised
jointly the report which has been published as Schools Council
Working Paper 64 *Learning through Talking 11-16* (Schools Council/
Avon Education Authority, 1979).

Task 4.5 Comparing past and present Schools Council policies

4.5.1 What would you expect to be the differences between national and local projects, if Geography for the Young School Leaver and the Avon Language Development Project are taken to be representative of each of these categories? What would you expect to be different in their aims and their methods? What kinds of people would you expect to find taking an active part in each project? What previous experience would you expect them to have? What would each expect to gain from taking part? In one case the main participants would work full-time on the project; in the other they would do much if not all of the work in their spare time. How would this affect the work of the projects? (If possible you should read at least part of the Geography for the Young School Leaver materials and part of *Learning through Talking*.)

4.5.2 Here are two lists of accounts of curriculum innovation on a local and on a national scale. Read at least one from each list and discuss the advantages and disadvantages of each approach.

Local

Eggleston, J. (1980) *School-based Curriculum Development in Britain* (any chapter).

Watts, J. (1973) 'Countesthorpe: a Case Study' in Taylor, P.H. and Walton, J. (eds) *The Curriculum: Research, Innovation and Change*.

Gross, N. *et al*. (1971) *Implementing Organizational Innovations* (an outsider's view of a primary school innovation that failed).

Schools Council/Avon Education Authority (1979) *Learning through Talking 11-16* (the Avon study outlined above).

Walton, J. and Welton, J. (1976) *Rational Curriculum Planning: Four Case Studies* (Chapter 2, 3 or 4).

National

Stenhouse, L. (1980) *Curriculum Research and Development in Action* (almost any chapter).

Shipman, M. (1974) *Inside a Curriculum Project*.

Rudduck, J. (1976) *Dissemination of Innovation: the Humanities Curriculum Project*.

The control of the curriculum

4.5.2   MacDonald, B. and Walker, R. (1976) *Changing the Curriculum*
contd   (Chapter 4, 'Nuffield Science', or Chapter 5, 'Project Tech-
        nology').
        Centre for Educational Research and Innovation (1975) *Hand-
        book on Curriculum Development* (Chapter 2 contains brief
        accounts of projects from various countries).
        Schools Council (1973) *Pattern and Variation in Curriculum
        Development Projects.*
        Whitehead, D.J. (1980) *The Dissemination of Educational
        Innovations in Britain* (Chapters 2, 6 and 8 deal with the
        project 'History, geography and social studies 8-13').

4.5.3   A group at the University of Sussex has carried out for the
        Schools Council an independent investigation of the 'impact and
        take-up' of the full range of published curriculum-development
        projects from the Schools Council, and of others not financed
        by the Council. They used two main criteria in doing so. Since
        the purpose of the Schools Council is to offer teachers a wider
        range of curriculum options to choose from, the investigators
        argue that a project will have fulfilled part of its function if
        it offers an alternative which teachers are aware of. Thus the
        first criterion which they used to measure the success of a
        project was how large a proportion of the teachers who might
        use what the project had produced knew about it, irrespective
        of whether they chose to use it in the classroom. A second
        criterion was the proportion of those teachers who might use
        what the project had produced that claimed actually to make
        some kind of use of it, though this need not amount to whole-
        sale adoption. Let us consider some of the figures produced
        by the Schools Council Impact and Take-Up Project (1980).
            The following information, for example, was gathered from
        the replies made by the headteachers of primary schools to a
        postal questionnaire. Eight Schools Council projects were
        known or well known to over 40 per cent of them; only ten
        primary projects were known to less than 20 per cent of them.
            Because of the specialisms in secondary schools it was neces-
        sary to consider only those teachers who might reasonably be
        expected to take an interest in a particular project. Six secon-
        dary projects had 'achieved contact' with more than 50 per
        cent of appropriate teachers (86 per cent in one case) and were
        being used by more than 30 per cent of them. Nine secondary

4.5.3 projects, however, had at that time achieved contact with
contd less than 10 per cent of the relevant audience.

Next we turn to information about individual projects
(Tables 4.2 and 4.3); I have chosen some that are much used
and some that are little used.

TABLE 4.2 *Use of projects in primary schools by teachers of the appropriate age-groups*

Project/publication	Some use (%)	Extensive use (%)
Breakthrough to Literacy	32	9
Communication Skills (3-6)	13	2
Nuffield Mathematics (for comparison)	30	5
Environmental Studies	3.5	0.3
Musical Education of Young Children	4	0.5
Development of Scientific and Mathematical Concepts	1	0.2

Note: The above figures were taken from postal questionnaires. When a sample of schools was visited the proportion of teachers found to be using the projects was a little lower in most cases, except Breakthrough where it was higher.

TABLE 4.3 *Use of Schools Council projects by the relevant secondary teachers*

Project/publication	Some use (%)	Extensive use (%)
Cambridge Classics	9	46
Geography for the Young School Leaver	23	16
Careers Education and Guidance	27	10

Note: The above are the three most 'successful' Schools Council projects for secondary schools.

4.5.3 Of course these constitute only a very small proportion of the
contd   projects funded by Schools Council — a glance at the 1979
index of projects suggests that about 120 had been supported
by that date — and they naturally vary greatly in scale and in
the outcomes that were planned for.

There has been some dispute in the press whether the
Schools Council should continue to be supported by the Department of Education and Science and the local authorities. One
way of looking at this is in financial terms: do the educational
benefits of the Council's work justify the costs? It has been
said that the amount of money made available to the Council
in latter years has been equivalent to that spent in running three
comprehensive schools. (This can be compared with the cost
of some 4,700 secondary schools and 21,400 primary schools in
England and Wales.) For example, in 1978-9 the Council received 2½ million pounds (out of a total educational budget
of £7,750 million). Is it possible to come to a conclusion on
the basis of these figures and the selected items from the Impact
and Take-Up Project whether the nation has received value for
money? You should take into consideration that some costs and
benefits will certainly be hidden; for example, it would be hard
to estimate either the cost to teachers' time or the benefit of
meeting other teachers to discuss new materials and new ideas
even if they are not adapted.

If you come to the conclusion that cost-benefit analysis is
not a proper way of assessing the work of the Schools Council,
on what basis can it be judged? Certainly neither the opinions of
journalists — who may not be unbiased — nor staff-room gossip
could give an adequate basis. What other possibilities remain?

4.5.4   In the mid-1970s the Schools Council issued a document intended as a guide to teachers and others who wished to apply
for support for small-scale local curriculum development projects. They suggested that a preliminary letter should contain
the following information (Schools Council, undated).

1 Title of project.
2 Where will the project be based?
3 Age-range of pupils to which the project would relate.
4 Aims of the project.
5 What are the expected results of the project which will

4.5.4
contd
enable other teachers to benefit from it? (e.g. a report on methodology; evaluation report on existing work; pupil material, etc.)

6 What group of teachers will be involved in the project?

7 How long is the project expected to last?

8 Describe briefly how the project will operate.

9 Who will be in charge of the project?
(It may not be possible to name a Director at this stage, but an indication should be given if possible of the kind of person it is hoped might direct the project.)

10 Approximately how much grant is being applied for?
(Absolute accuracy is not expected at this stage; detailed financial estimates will be discussed if the application seems worth while pursuing.)

11 Name and address of LEA [local education authority].

12 With which LEA officer or adviser has the proposal been discussed?

13 Has the LEA indicated that it is likely to support the project if the Council is prepared to make an award?

14 Name and official address of applicant with whom future correspondence should be conducted.

Invent a project that you would be interested to take part in, and work out some of the details. Write a letter to the Schools Council along the lines indicated in the above extract from the information sheet.

On receipt of this letter the applicant would normally be invited to meet an official of the Schools Council, and the discussion would cover:

curricular ideas;
development work conducted to date;
proposed method of operating;
local support available;
how Schools Council support might be used, for example, for staff release to work on the project: for evaluation, etc.;
costing;
personnel or staff;
evaluation;
possible publication;
dissemination.

4.5.4
contd
Make notes in preparation for a meeting with the official, including various alternative possibilities for the scale, manner of working, and outcomes of the project.

4.5.5
Some years ago the following proposal for a local curriculum-development scheme was presented to the Schools Council (Whitehead, 1976). Imagine that you are a member of the committee that decides whether to award £12,000 for this purpose. Discuss what would influence you in making the decision.

Introduction

1   Description of the purposes of the project

This is an attempt at local level to respond to the needs of teachers faced with the problems of teaching science to 11-14-year-olds of wide ability ranges, individually and in small groups. Teachers from five schools are attempting to solve their problems by forming workshop groups to re-organise existing resources from the Nuffield and Schools Council Projects and creating additional resources to meet specific needs.

The outcome of this general attempt to look at what the children and teachers are doing in science will be a co-ordinator's report, which will describe and evaluate the curriculum developments.

2   Originated by

Teachers working as a group at Swindon Curriculum Study Centre, Swindon.

3   To be conducted by

A Group of Teachers co-ordinated by Mr Jack Whitehead, Bath University School of Education.

4   Approximate duration

2 years.

I Proposal

Origin

The proposal originated from a group of science teachers

4.5.5
contd

who formed a workshop group to solve their problems of organising a learning situation for 11-14-year-olds, in mixed ability groups, to engage in scientific activity.

Background

In November a request was made by Jack Whitehead of the University of Bath for £1,000 to support teachers who were producing independent learning schemes for children of all ages and abilities. The Science Adviser to the Council, Dr Burdett, replied that the procedural lines for local development proposals would be clarified in the new year.

Early in January a course was organised at the Swindon Curriculum Development Centre for teachers who had problems with their third year science teaching. The course dealt with the teachers' intentions, forms of assessment and the range of science resources available, for teachers and 11-16-year-olds, from the Nuffield Foundation and Schools Council Projects. Following this course teachers in five comprehensive schools decided to form a workshop group to design, produce, organise and evaluate an individualised learning situation for 11-14-year-olds in mixed ability groups. In the light of Schools Council's concern with local curriculum developments, the teachers decided in April 1974 to request financial aid from the Council. The Round I proposal was submitted with the approval and support of the Chief Education Officer and in June the proposal was placed in the B category.

The LEA has recognised that the work of the project is well under way and are anxious to ensure that it is not hindered during any waiting period which may occur. Limited funds have been made available for the project and these funds are administered by the Curriculum Development Centre.

Research Development and Dissemination

The Research Development and Dissemination model assumes that one must gather together a small number of people who are actively improving their curriculum. They must be given funds and time to be able to develop this curriculum and then actively engage in the dissemination process.

283

4.5.5 *Present situation*
contd The teachers concerned in the project possess a wealth of experience in the use of modern source materials in science, developed for the 11-14 age range. They and many of their colleagues in the locality are involved in the teaching of mixed ability groups in science. They have progressed through a number of stages, beginning with the implementation of the modern schemes as they stand, NCS and SCISP, proceeding to adaptations of these schemes for the mixed ability situation and have now reached the significant stage of writing material of their own, using the feedback of the experience of earlier stages.

The project has reached the point when normal school resources cannot meet the heavy demands of a development programme of this kind; when support from a Centre of Higher Education must be on a regular and systematic basis; when reprographic facilities must be enhanced and when skilled evaluation methods are needed.

The initiation of the project by this local group coincides happily with the wishes of the LEA and Schools Council to provide support for school generated curriculum development and thus support was granted.

II Aims
The aims of the project fall under two headings:
1   Educational aims
The main concern of the teachers is to provide for their pupils meaningful and enjoyable scientific situations which are relevant in the best educational sense. They feel that the best learning situations occur when pupils are encouraged to devise solutions to their own questions.

The educational aims of the project correspond precisely with those of the individualised learning in general, namely:
1   to place the pupil in an active learning situation;
2   to allow the pupil to operate in an atmosphere of success and reward, derived from his own operations;
3   to enrich the natural development processes of children;
4   to promote a situation of pleasing and motivating inter-personal relationships involving pupils and teachers; and, in addition

4.5.5
contd

5 to use the particular qualities of science, its empiricism, its discipline and its imaginative thinking to complete the whole education of children.

The mixed ability situation is often seen as one which creates insoluble problems and yet is a situation which draws attention to learning methods which might well have been used in any class grouping and which have not only been neglected in traditional teaching to a great extent but are also highly efficient and productive.

2 Strategic aims

1 To establish a network of mutual support between teachers, lecturers, advisers, scientists and industrialists.

This aim has been achieved in fact, in Wiltshire, where a contract is already in being between Wiltshire LEA and the University of Bath, to enable lecturers to promote individualised learning in Wiltshire schools. In the project locality, there are extensive connections between schools and local industry and the locality has very strong associations with technological education. There is already very effective co-ordination from the Curriculum Development Centre which has considerable administrative potential.

This particular project is seen as a specimen development, based in schools, but embodying the kind of relationships envisaged in the concept of a Professional Centre.

2 To establish a resources retrieval system.

The concept of group development implies growth and proliferation. The resources produced are a tangible means of demonstrating the value of group development in both the processes and the end product.

Objectives in terms of proposed outcomes

1 The design, production, organisation and evaluation of resources in the learning situation, which are responsive to individuals' enquiries in mixed ability groups.

2 The formulation, expression and criticism of learners' questions about physical phenomena.

The importance of this outcome rests upon the view that the generative act of scientific reasoning is the asking of a question, the creation of an idea or the formulation of an

4.5.5
contd

hypothesis. It is assumed that this process is outside logic but that once an opinion is formed and expressed it can be exposed to criticism. This criticism involves the empirical testing of the logical consequences of the beliefs usually through experimentation.

3 A network of relationships between teachers, lecturers, advisers, scientists and industrialists which are responsive to solving the teachers' problems in the provision of dialogue and material resources.

This outcome has partly been achieved between teachers, lecturers and advisers in Wiltshire and is manifested in the contract negotiated between the Wiltshire Authority and the University of Bath to enable lecturers to promote individualised learning in several Wiltshire schools. Scientists and industrialists are also being requested to comment on the content and relevance of the materials and will help to evaluate the teachers' intentions and learners' scientific activities. These outcomes are being achieved in two phases. In phase I the teachers facing mixed ability groups have changed their classroom organisation for individual and small group teaching. This has included the production of a variety of worksheets with most of the problems 'given' to the pupils.

The outcome of phase II will be the learning situation described in 1, 2 and 3 above and will include a resource retrieval system which, with the teacher, will be responsive to the learners' enquiries.

III The proposed pattern of organisation and operation
The pattern of organisation is centred on the activity of teachers in the workshop group, designing, producing, organising and evaluating the individualised learning schemes for their pupils. These activities are being co-ordinated by a lecturer from the University of Bath. This co-ordination involves the development of closer relationships between advisers, lecturers, scientists and industrialists for the criticism and evaluation of pupils' scientific activity. Meetings are being held at fortnightly intervals in the schools for an on-going dialogue on fundamental goals and criticism of resource materials. The latter are modified and reproduced at the schools or local teachers centres.

4.5.5 **IV Evaluation**

contd This will be a co-operative activity between learners, teachers, lecturers, scientists and industrialists. The teachers will express their intentions verbally, in writing and with practical examples. The learners will be interviewed and video-taped whilst working to detect the state of their scientific activity. The view will be taken that language is inadequate to express a person engaged in scientific activity, it is the kind of phenomena which can only be shown. The evaluation sessions will be dialogues between the above people as they attempt to make available to each other their interpretations of the teachers' intentions and the learners' activities, and the assumptions on which they are based. Records will include written statements, transcripts of interviews and evaluation sessions and video tapes of the learner's activities.

Of course, not all of the new programmes are concerned with helping teachers to look more analytically at their own teaching. Some local projects may produce their own materials, or devise new ways of using and combining existing ones. What is likely, however, is that projects which genuinely arise from teachers themselves are not always going to begin with a clear focus: much of the 'curriculum development' in these cases will be a matter of progressive clarification of the nature of the problem to be solved. Classroom problems are seldom clear-cut; they usually contain a mixture of issues in which debate is likely to be as much directed towards identifying values, formulating purposes and distinguishing concepts as towards discovering the relative merits of different methods. Thus their outcomes may look unimpressive in comparison with the publications of national projects, and there is likely to be a major problem in seeing to it that the benefits gained by participants are available to others. Indeed, this last may be an effort doomed to fail: the virtue of the new pattern may be precisely that it engages participants' idiosyncratic ways of thinking about their teaching, this being by definition difficult to make available to teachers not taking part.

Some writers have expressed scepticism about teachers' ability (or willingness) to initiate and maintain curriculum-development work, especially when day-to-day demands on their time and energy are taken into account. Malcolm Skilbeck (1972) has also suggested that many teachers lack the necessary skills. Although he himself favours school-based curriculum development, he has listed some of the factors likely to discourage it, and these points are drawn from his list:

a sense of low self-esteem and inadequacy in staff;

lack of relevant skills (in analysing objectives, constructing tests, working in planning groups, etc.);

failure of authorities to provide advisory and specialist consultancy services;

lack of interest or conviction in staff, particularly in sustaining change processes over a period of time;

inadequate allocation of resources (time and personnel as well as money);

lack of incentive in teachers to engage in planning and evaluation;

failure to appreciate the subtleties of group interactions when the balance of power in an existing institution is threatened;

tendency for institutions to revert to earlier forms of organisation and control if the pressure for change is not continuous.

A study carried out in the state of Hesse in Germany approached the matter differently by trying to answer the question, 'Which teachers take part in curriculum development?' (Centre for Educational Research and Innovation, 1979). They found out which teachers had attended more than half of the meetings of local groups organised in the course of an attempt to involve teachers in curriculum renewal and in planning co-ordination between schools. (This, of course, may or may not be different from the teachers who would take part in a working party in their own school, or in area meetings organised by other teachers, rather than by advisers or other officials.) Fewer than 20 per cent of teachers attended half of the meetings, but there were no clear-cut characteristics distinguishing them from the other 80 per cent. They tended to come from the 26-40 age-group, not to hold very senior posts in their schools, to come from comprehensive schools rather than selective schools, to have had previous in-service training, to be members of professional associations, and not to be closely dependent on textbooks in their teaching. But these were only tendencies. What clearly differentiated the two groups was that far more of them came from industrial areas than from rural ones. (Unfortunately the report does not indicate whether transport and accessibility might have influenced this.)

But this is only half of the story. In discussing why the Schools

Council Integrated Studies Project was more successful in some schools than others Martyn Shipman (1973) wrote:

> The overall message of these statistics is that the net impact of this curriculum project seemed to depend on the commitment of the teachers involved. This confirms the now common finding that any innovation, means of organisation or teaching method depends for success on the attitudes of the teachers, regardless of the intrinsic merits of the scheme.

Elsewhere Shipman (1974) refers to a school's commitment to a project in terms of:

1 willingness to hold team meetings in school time;
2 willingness to modify timetables for the new curriculum;
3 assignment of senior staff to the innovation;
4 provision of written feedback to a central team;
5 attendance at central meetings;
6 collection of supplementary classroom materials.

(It should be noticed that some of these matters are under the control of senior staff, and some depend on individual teachers.) Shipman was, of course, referring to a curriculum innovation instituted and led from outside the school, so we must be cautious in transferring what he wrote to school-based initiatives.

It is unlikely that curriculum change in a school can often be seen simply as colleagues working together to solve a problem. A new scheme, unless it is confined to one classroom, may bring benefits to some teachers but threaten to deprive others. If a lively group of teachers proposes a new scheme and gains the headteacher's support, it is very likely that the scheme will require changes in timetabling, the allocation of extra funds, perhaps a new department with its own voice in school decisions, and certainly public limelight and the headteacher's approval for the successful leaders. That is, the new scheme will inevitably threaten to take away resources or status (or both) from those teachers who have a vested interest in the status quo. This is one of the reasons why innovations so frequently disappear when their initiators leave the school.

Task 4.5 contd   Analysing school influence on curriculum change

4.5.6   Ernest House (1974) describes the school as 'a combination of various departments and interest groups, all competing for scarce resources. . . . Organisational decisions are based on which coalitions of groups are in ascendancy at the moment — a political process.' Do you find this account persuasive and accurate? Is it the whole truth? How far does it match with your own experience of schools?

New arrangements are costly in teachers' time and energy, requiring attendance at meetings and often the preparation of new teaching materials and discussion of methods. Moreover, every curriculum innovation deskills, as Barry MacDonald (1973) has said; the changed conditions and purposes take away the teacher's reliance on existing routines and compel him or her to work out new methods, an experience which can be very disturbing. All of these factors weigh against radical change, and particularly against change initiated in schools. Yet it might well be argued that it is changes that teachers have initiated that they are most likely to work for, since it is they who experience directly the pressures of the classroom and staff-room and can thus weigh advantages and disadvantages in a manner closed to outsiders.

Task 4.5 contd   Analysing school influence on curriculum change

4.5.7   Consider Skilbeck's list of discouraging factors, the findings of the Hesse study, and Shipman's conclusions. Do you find Skilbeck's points persuasive? How would you explain the Hesse results? Do you think it true that teachers lack the skills needed to engage effectively in curriculum development? What do you take those skills to be?

4.5.8   Why should teachers take part in change? What might they gain from it? What might they lose? This task involved working out an imaginary profit-and-loss account for any teacher who might consider expending time and energy upon curriculum development. Besides differentiating potential gains from potential losses, it is also useful to distinguish intrinsic from extrinsic motives: for example, while the desire to bring the content of a course up to date is intrinsic to the purpose

4.5.8
contd
of educating children, the desire to further one's career, though important to many teachers, is clearly extrinsic to that purpose. You will probably find it useful to lay out your ideas as shown in Figure 4.4.

	Gains	Losses
Intrinsic		
Extrinsic		

Figure 4.4 *The potential gains and losses for a teacher engaged in curriculum development*

4.5.9
This task requires some experience of curriculum development. If you have ever taken part in an attempt to change the curriculum, either in response to ideas and materials from outside or initiated by some of your colleagues, you can utilise your experience on that occasion. Trace the course of the innovation from its first introduction into discussion as a possibility to the point where it either disappeared from view or was incorporated into the normal structure of school life. It will be useful to identify persons and forces which tended to support the change, and to offer explanations of this, as well as those which opposed it. On what grounds was the innovation supported or opposed? What persons stood to gain or lose from it? (The notes that follow Task 4.5.11 may be of some assistance.)

4.5.10
You are a headteacher and have the opportunity to appoint a deputy head who will in effect be a Director of Studies with a particular responsibility for curriculum development. Write a job specification for sending out to potential applicants for the post. Explain what responsibilities the Director of Studies will have, the ways in which he or she will be expected to be involved in curriculum development, and the knowledge, skills and personal qualities that you are looking for.

4.5.11
Take a school that you know well and choose an innovation

4.5.11
contd
that you would like to see introduced into the school. It should be an innovation that will involve different members of staff, rather than a domestic one that you could adopt in your own teaching without affecting others. List those forces in the school that are likely to support the innovation and those likely to oppose it. What support from outside might you look for? How might you minimise the threat to those teachers likely to oppose the change, or how might you draw the sting from their opposition? The framework that follows may help you to give structure to your analysis.

There is no standard model for investigating the forces in a school likely to influence whether an innovation will succeed, so what follows is no more than a tentative checklist that has proved useful to other students.

The innovation itself. The most important aspect of the innovation from this point of view is what has been called its 'divisibility'. Is it a 'domestic' innovation that can be tried out in one or two classrooms without affecting anyone else or is it a large-scale one that affects most or all of the school? (This is important because it increases the risks in case of failure.) In particular, will it cut across departmental divisions?

The other aspect of the innovation that ought to be considered is its complexity. Is it something that teachers will be able to understand and use with little difficulty, or does it involve a major shift of attitudes and methods that would make in-service training advisable?

Values and informal structure. It is obviously of great importance whether an innovation is compatible with the values and preconceptions of the teachers who are to put it into effect. However, teachers like other people are often open to persuasion, and may come to see the innovation differently. Whether they are open to persuasion is likely to depend on various things, including the strength of informal groups amongst the staff, 'the old guard', 'the young radicals', and so on. Successful change will probably offer some benefits to all such groups. A collegial approach in which everyone takes some part in decision-making is useful precisely because it allows some horse-trading to go on, thus ensuring that even if the innovation is not carried through in its original form it does offer something to most of the groups who might otherwise have opposed it.

Leadership style. There is evidence to suggest that in many cases the headteacher's support is a crucial factor. He or she may operate (i) through direct use of power, backing his authority with promises and threats; (ii) through gradual persuasion, gathering together a favourable group of influential members of staff who gradually put indirect pressure on the rest of their colleagues to fall into line; (iii) through discussion and collegial decision-making, abandoning some of his or her own authority to gain the support of staff.

Formal structure. This is more likely to be important in large schools, where there is often a strongly entrenched departmental system, and also a pastoral structure cutting across it. Any changes tend to threaten existing interest groups, either by depriving them of some of their resources and status, or by limiting their freedom to act. Two aspects of structure are likely to be important: the extent to which power is delegated downwards through the vertical hierarchy; and — linked to this — the strength of the barriers between parts of the system, such as between departments or between pastoral and academic responsibilities.

Resources. Change makes great demands on teachers' time and energy — to plan and decide, write materials, make visits, and so on. And other resources too are important, including buildings, equipment and secretarial support. 'Pump-priming' money is often helpful, since otherwise an innovation immediately creates opposition by taking resources from elsewhere in the school.

Outside support. Successful consultation with parents and governors may be important, and various kinds of support from advisers and HM Inspectors is often necessary.

Task 4.5 contd   School-based curriculum development

4.5.12   This is a simulation task in which you are asked to concentrate your attention on the managerial task rather than upon the pros and cons of the innovation itself, which is indeed highly open to debate.

Managing change in a secondary school

You are a deputy headteacher of a seven-form entry compre-

4.5.12
contd

hensive school for boys and girls aged 13-18 years. Your responsibilities include curriculum development, and a new headteacher has asked you to institute innovations in the curriculum for the youngest age-group of pupils, still called 'the third year' as in many other schools.

The headteacher wishes to make an end to streaming in the 'third' year, and to set up what he calls a 'diagnostic course', as a preliminary to the making of subject choices for the following two years. The curriculum of the six middle schools from which you receive pupils varies, but in most cases is subject-based in the traditional manner. Your head-teacher believes, however, that the diagnostic year should present pupils with a curriculum that is (i) integrated across major curriculum-areas, (ii) relevant to their present and future lives, and (iii) partly chosen and planned by each pupil for him or herself. Eight periods of the 35 each week are to be put aside for basic work in English and mathematics, and for physical education, though this does not imply that these subjects will not play a part in the rest of the curriculum. The headmaster says that any remedial help must be part of the scheme, and not draw attention to the pupils receiving it.

Your headmaster seems unwilling to expand upon his three criteria, and wishes his colleagues to make decisions for themselves under your leadership. The school is organised in subject departments, but as the school's academic tradition is not of long standing — it was created ten years ago from two secondary modern schools — most of your colleagues do not seem strongly entrenched. Some indeed are young, liberally inclined, and eager to talk of change. Their elders are, however, more circumspect. There is a deputy headmistress who has held her post since the school began, but no other senior members of staff.

The school building is relatively new and well-equipped, though on a traditional plan. There are adequate physical education and sports facilities and a language laboratory. There is a library, but it is not well-stocked nor well-used, partly because it is run in his spare time by the much over-worked head of the history department, who undertook this responsibility many years before as a young teacher in one of the secondary modern schools.

4.5.12
contd
The headmaster has announced his intention of curtailing subject allocations by one-fifth in order to finance the new scheme. This has not pleased the heads of departments. He has not, however, mentioned any other sources of finance.

The school lies in a small county borough not noted for flexibility nor innovativeness in its educational provisions. The four advisers are mainly concerned with helping the primary and middle schools in the borough. The fathers of pupils belong predominantly to manual trades, especially in mining. The borough has had a history of economic insecurity, and new light industries have not yet made a marked impression on patterns of employment. Your colleagues talk to you about 'social deprivation' and a lack of 'cultural experience'. There are relatively few white-collar jobs in the area, and pupils' job expectations tend to be restricted to the small range locally available. The school has no parent-teacher association.

You have three terms in which to carry out the planning of the course. You yourself will be able to give a substantial part of your time to the task, and the headmaster seems to be willing by various means to release a few colleagues to help for occasional periods.

It is not your business to decide what the course should be — though you have your own opinions. Your task is to decide:

1 what issues should be discussed;
2 what order they should be discussed in;
3 who should be consulted;
4 who should be involved in decision-making at various stages;
5 what preliminary organisational arrangements should be made during the planning year (with the headmaster's permission);
6 any necessary approaches to bodies outside the school;
7 any other actions necessary to prepare for the new curriculum (they may be conditional upon curriculum decisions).

You should produce two documents:

4.5.12   (*a*) A schedule of arrangements for the attention of your
contd   headmaster (and your colleagues?);

        (*b*) a private annotation to remind yourself of the principles
             underlying your strategy.

        (This task can most usefully be carried out by several small groups who can meet at the end to compare strategies.)

4.5.13   One of the programmes chosen by the Schools Council is entitled 'Helping Individual Teachers to Become More Effective'. Suppose you were one of a group of teachers of similar experience and interests who had been given the opportunity to meet once a week as part of this programme, what would it be useful for you to do, and how would you set about it? Your task would be to improve your own and one another's teaching. What aspects might you focus on? What might help you to improve? What resources might be useful? What indeed are the crucial elements in effective teaching? How might you benefit from being in a group rather than on your own? (I certainly do not agree with those teachers who throw their hands in the air and say 'It's all a matter of personality.' Teaching is something that we can learn to do better. This task requires you to consider how.)

4.5.14   What in your view would constitute the most effective form of in-service training for school-based curriculum innovation?

Accountability

It would seem strange to leave the study of curriculum in its social context without mentioning accountability. It is a word that is interpreted in very different ways; one of these ways of interpreting it has already been touched on in the section concerned with the Assessment of Performance Unit. But the national testing of achievement is only one of many possible ways in which schools can 'give an account' of their work. It is very appropriate to turn to accountability immediately after the section on school-based curriculum development, since there is much to be said for school-based approaches to accountability. The central questions are: 'To whom is account to be given?' 'What powers have they to require an account and to respond to it?' 'What aspects of the life of a school are open to accountability?'

A team from the University of Sussex who carried out a study of Accountability in the Middle Years of Schooling have provided the framework which I am going to utilise. They distinguish three possible meanings of the word 'accountability' (Barton *et al.*, 1980).

(*a*) Accountability is sometimes used by teachers to refer to their sense that they have a duty to give information to pupils and parents, which the Sussex researchers call *answerability*.

(*b*) Next there comes professional accountability to colleagues, which they call *responsibility*.

(*c*) Finally, there is contractual accountability to employers, which they call *strict accountability*.

The crucial difference between these three lies in the relationship between the teachers who give the account and the persons they give it to. (*a*) With answerability it is the school that controls the flow of information to parents about their children's progress, allows parents a certain amount of access to teachers and classrooms, and decides how open it will be to questioning. (*b*) In the case of responsibility, however, colleagues may require information because as a group they have agreed to carry out monitoring of standards, curriculum reviews, screening of individual children for diagnostic purposes, and various kinds of record keeping. (*c*) Strict accountability occurs when a local authority or the Department of Education and Science requires schools to carry out testing or to undergo inspection by advisory staff or by HM Inspectorate. It could be argued that all three kinds of accountability procedures are necessary, both for maintaining the normally healthy running of the school system, and for detecting and dealing with problems.

Task 4.6 contd   School accountability

4.6.1   Analyse the accountability procedures of a school that you can get detailed information about. It would be possible, for example, to plan and carry out a group interview of a headteacher on these lines.

(*a*) At the level of *answerability* to pupils and parents;

(i)   what are the school's procedures for the maintenance of a normal flow (and exchange) of information?

(ii)   what arrangements are there for responding to parents' complaints and anxieties, and for dealing with other

4.6.1   special problems?

contd (*b*) At the level of *professional responsibility* shared by colleagues:

     (i)   what arrangements are there within the school for record-keeping and monitoring children's progress, for regular reviews of staffing, curriculum and teaching, and for maintaining relationships with other schools?

     (ii)   how does the school ensure vigilance for signs of crisis, recognise individual children with special needs, and provide diagnosis and remedial help?

 (*c*) At the level of *strict accountability*:

     (i)   what demands for information are made by the governing body and the local authority upon the school, and how are these normally satisfied?

     (ii)   what methods would the local education authority be likely to use if they suspected the existence of major problems in the school?

The Sussex team — on whose report these questions are largely based — stress how important it is that the procedures under (*a*) and (*b*) are widely known, not only to parents but to the community generally, since this is likely to affect the school's credit as an efficient and responsible professional organisation. This leads to another question:

 (*d*) What efforts are made to ensure that these arrangements for accountability are widely known, particularly to parents who may wish to make use of them?

We are now going to turn to several statements about accountability in order to compare them with one another and with the framework derived from the Sussex study. The first comes from the United States, and is taken from an article entitled 'Implementing a results-oriented budgeting system' (Rappaport and Brown, 1971).

> In recent years, the old measures of the quality of a school system have come to be regarded as inadequate. . . . School boards and professional educators are confronted with the reality that the quality of school management must be measured (1) by the increment of progress over present levels of performance and (2) by comparison with the performance of similar districts in terms of

benefits to students. . . . In short, the school must be evaluated in terms of results. . . . It appears to many that the productivity of the investment in public education has actually been declining.

The second is a recommendation from the Green Paper *Education in Schools* (Department of Education and Science/Welsh Office, 1977).

It is an essential ingredient of this partnership [that between the Education Department, the local education authorities and the teachers] that schools should be accountable for their performance: accountable to the local education authority — and those who elect it — as part of the public system of education; accountable through the school governors and managers to the local community that they serve.

And the third is part of the National Union of Teachers' reply to the Green Paper (1977).

Teachers recognise that their role is to secure high standards of literacy and numeracy in order to provide a curriculum as broad as the staffing and facilities of the school permit and to obtain from each pupil the highest possible standards both in academic, cultural and physical pursuits and in social attitudes, values and behaviour. In its work towards these aims, the teaching profession is accountable to society, and the Union would draw attention to the checks and balances written into the Education Acts which give form to this accountability. The Green Paper states that schools should be accountable for their 'performance'. 'Performance', however, is not defined in the Green Paper or indeed in the Education Acts, and it would be misleading if the performance of a school were based simply on examination successes or on other externally assessed levels of performance without taking full account of class sizes, staff levels, environment, capitation, the nature of the school buildings and many other factors. The Union . . . would point out that both in the Green Paper and the Taylor Report there is a failure to recognise that no profession or group can be held accountable if it is not able to exercise full responsibility for the organisation and exercise of professional skill and expertise. Central to the responsibility of the teaching profession is the curriculum.

Task 4.6 contd   School accountability

4.6.2   (*a*) How far do these three statements about accountability seem to be in agreement? What differences can you identify? Where might differences in the authors' intentions be hidden by vagueness and ambiguity of phrasing?

(*b*) Relate each of these statements to the six categories set out in Task 4.6.1. Which category does each fall into? Or alternatively does any of these statements seem to refer to more than one of the categories?

4.6.3   Where would the Assessment of Performance Unit (pp. 258-72) fit into the Sussex analysis? Is it concerned with accountability or with something else?

4.6.4   Jackson and Hayter (1978) in an account of the evaluation of the whole school see evaluation as primarily a matter of providing information to aid the making of decisions. They put forward seven 'decision areas' which relate as much to the different people making decisions as to the nature of the decisions themselves. Here is a summary of their description.

(*a*) Parental choice: information related to choices within the curriculum and to choice of schools.

(*b*) Maintaining standards: the evaluation activities of HM Inspectors in particular.

(*c*) Attributing responsibility: questions relating to whether the public is receiving value for money invested in education. (See Elliott's 'economic evaluation' below.) How is responsibility exercised?

(*d*) Planning development: information relevant to possible development or reorganisation in a school.

(*e*) Understanding the working of an institution: the occasional review of the normal running of the school.

(*f*) Resolving conflict: study of how to deal with problems that threaten the well-being of the school.

(*g*) Pupils' decisions: choice of subjects, optional activities, careers.

Your task is to consider Jackson and Hayter's analysis critically. For example, how acceptable is their view of evaluation as the provision of information to decision-makers? Does the list place its emphases on the most important aspects of evaluation? Is

4.6.4 anything overemphasised, underemphasised, or omitted? Is
contd 'evaluation' the same as 'accountability'? Have we lost our
focus on the study of the curriculum and slipped away into
something else, school management perhaps? Compare this
scheme with the Sussex one in terms of their relative usefulness to teachers and schools.

There have been some attempts to argue that accountability is the
private business of the school itself. This perhaps means confining it
to what the Sussex group calls answerability, and to some of the
procedures that belong in the categories called responsibility; and it
certainly means that the school would keep tight control over any
information gathered. It is true that whenever accountability implies
the evaluation of teaching this is potentially threatening. Ernest House
(1973) says that teachers do not wish to be evaluated, since they have
everything to lose and nothing to gain. What they have to gain, of
course, is the sense of doing a job well and the opportunity of finding
out how they might do it still better, but for many — perhaps most —
teachers this is outweighed by the possibility of being damaged in their
own eyes and that of their colleagues. But such potentially threatening evaluation need play only a marginal role in a school's accountability procedures, probably occurring only amongst the arrangements
referred to as 'monitoring standards', which is part of the 'professional
responsibility' aspect of accountability. (See question (*b*i) in Task
4.6.1 above.) In any case a wise headteacher would ensure that evaluation, when it occurred, was seen as evaluation of joint efforts by staff,
and if comment was required on an individual teacher's work he or she
would make it privately, at least in the first instance. Nevertheless, it
is clear that this aspect of accountability can be threatening, and therefore bulks large in teachers' attitudes to it.

Ernest House may have been excessively pessimistic in his views
about teachers' responses to the evaluation of their work, but this
does lead him to an important insight. As we have seen, the purposes
of accountability are many: they include not only giving an account
to those with the right to receive it — parents, governors, local authorities — but also the monitoring, discussing, reviewing and improving of
the school's work by teachers themselves. It is these self-critical processes, including the evaluation of curricula, which constitute much
of the 'professional responsibility' aspect identified by the Sussex
researchers. House was interested to characterise the kind of information

likely to be most useful to teachers. Would it be the kind of data produced by psychometric tests or by other educational research methods? What is important, according to House (1973), is the match between the conceptual basis of the data and the teacher's 'vocabulary of action', the implicit or explicit beliefs that really control his everyday actions.

> We all live in a concrete world, in a world of metaphor and anecdotes of strong feelings and personal relationships. When I make decisions for myself it is on the basis of this concrete world, not an abstract one. The kind of information a person can act on must be meaningful in terms of personal experience. . . . Communicating scientific findings is not a matter of understanding research terminology; it is a matter of translating the findings to fit the audience's personal experience. Every person has a vocabulary of action in his mind: only when evaluation data roughly correspond to his internal vocabulary does he respond to them.

If House's argument is valid, it follows that teachers are more likely to act upon information planned and gathered on the basis of their own concerns and ways of thinking about their work — their 'vocabulary of action' — than upon information gathered to answer questions asked by other people.

Task 4.6 contd   School accountability

4.6.5   It is not easy to get access to one's own 'vocabulary of action' (nor to anyone else's), since one may genuinely be unaware of some aspects of it. Nevertheless you can start by jotting down everything in your school you think might be improved if you and your colleagues took a cool look at it. Then, add to it anything you know that someone else is dissatisfied with, or anything you have heard colleagues disagreeing about. Have there been any dissatisfactions expressed by pupils or parents? The list you now have should make a good start for the problem-solving side of accountability, but may not deal adequately with the maintenance side. Make a second list of the things you know you and your colleagues *ought* to reconsider now and again, even if they are not causing dissatisfaction. What, for example, ought the governing body to take an interest

4.6.5 in, even if they do not? The best way of improving the list is to
contd get together with other teachers who have made similar lists,
and discuss differences in order to arrive at an agreed list. You
may find it useful to express these concerns and issues in the
form of questions, and to group them in convenient categories.
How is your list different from Jackson and Hayter's list? Why?

The current interest in accountability has led some local authorities
to produce booklets of questions to guide headteachers and their staffs
in planning school self-evaluation. One such booklet, which was produced by Lancashire Education Committee (1980) for use by primary
schools, is printed here as Appendix I. (A similar set of questions
appears in Appendix E, entitled 'Simple statistics'.)

Task 4.6 contd   School accountability

4.6.6 Read Appendix I: 'Primary School Evaluation: A Schedule for
Self Appraisal'.
  (a) To whom does the schedule appear to be addressed?
  (b) If you compare this with the categories in Task 4.6.1, do
  there seem to be any important omissions? You can use
  the list you made in answer to Task 4.6.5 to help you
  test this.
  (c) Attempt to answer all the questions in the 'curriculum'
  section with respect to the school you teach in or a primary school you have access to. Which questions prove
  difficult to answer? If the teachers at the school were to
  set themselves to answer all these questions, what would
  be likely to happen?
  (d) Some evaluation schedules have been criticised for encouraging teachers to gather information without giving
  them any help about how to act on it. Do you think this
  would be a just criticism in this case? What kinds of action
  might be called for, and what kind of advice (if any) would
  help? What do you think the function of schedules like this
  is intended to be?

John Elliott (1979) contrasts what he calls 'social' and 'economic'
evaluation. Testing of the kind done by APU and by some local authorities he calls 'economic', because in his view it sets out to achieve a

once-for-all ('summative') judgment about whether schools are giving value for money. He greatly prefers 'social evaluation', which appears to correspond to 'answerability' together with 'professional responsibility' (sections (*a*) and (*b*) of the Sussex scheme). He justifies his preference thus:

> Determining the social quality of curriculum policies is a difficult and complex affair. Any particular policy will carry a variety of social advantages and disadvantages which are not always easy to detect and weigh up. Moreover, the balance of advantage to disadvantage will vary over time. What looks like on balance an undesirable policy in the short term can turn into a desirable one in the long term, and vice versa. It is not only important to scrutinise the intrinsic qualities of a policy but also its short and long term consequences, including unintended side-effects. Over time its qualities shift and change. The social evaluation of curriculum policies is therefore a matter of piece-meal ongoing social criticism. There can be no absolutely conclusive summative evaluation. There will always be times when the school self-evaluation suggests that on balance existing policies need to be changed and a decision ought to be made. But even at the point of responsible decision one can never be completely sure.

The Sussex group appears to have set out upon the study of accountability with views not entirely dissimilar to those expressed by Elliott, but to have changed them in the course of the work. Here they explain their final position (Barton *et al*., 1980).

> One [preconception] was that the schools probably held the key to some of the more crucial policy choices, and that school-based accountability procedures were likely to be the focal point of our attention. Another was that accountability would transpire to be closely concerned with the development of good public relations, and that we might need to give particular attention to this aspect. . . .
> As our work developed, we found ourselves forced to recognise that we had got each picture out of focus. . . .
> Schools are undeniably important components in educational accountability, but our hope of building up a policy framework on the 'every-school-for-itself' principle was foredoomed. What we at first failed to realise was that, in terms of accountability, the

ruling principle must be that 'no school is an island'. Public reputation presupposes interdependence, not independence — the one school with a bad name contaminates the ninety-nine with a good. So while each must do the best it can in its own cause, the collective interest must in the end be protected by the authority (which is there to guard it) rather than by the schools (who are there to serve it). . . .

As our many interviews and discussions over the past two years have shown, it is also clearly the case that the successful discharge of accountability must involve the education service in more open dialogue, more vigorous publicity, a more conscious promotion of public relations, than has been its practice in the past. But to equate accountability with communication skills, as we were at first inclined to do, would be to overlook a host of other activities which we now recognise as relevant to our theme. They are those activities which concern the internal well-being of the system: the identification and amelioration of problems, the proper exercise of professional responsibilities, the efforts of self-appraisal, the enhancement of existing skills, and many others we have touched on in the course of our report. In the long term, these may turn out to be more important than mere improvements in the techniques of presentation, persuasion, and pacification, for they can have a catalytic effect in the regeneration of morale and self-respect, and hence in winning the respect of others. The best way of all of earning the public confidence is the most direct: namely to be clearly seen as doing a good job.

Task 4.6 contd   School accountability

4.6.7   The final task in this section is to compare these two views of school accountability. (It is probably necessary to read the Sussex passage in conjunction with the analytical scheme in Task 4.6.1.) What do you think Elliott means by 'piece-meal . . . social criticism'? What is the alternative to it that he rejects? What does the Sussex group mean by 'no school is an island', and how is it relevant to accountability? Does Elliott really mean that accountability should be left to the school? What if the school does nothing? (There have been many schools who have showed little aptitude for self-criticism, and still less eagerness to engage in it.) Under what circumstances might external demands on a school to evaluate its own way of life be beneficial?

Chapter 5

Coda: the study of the curriculum

Ever since state education systems were first set up there has naturally been debate about what curricula should be taught in schools. In the United Kingdom, for example, the Taunton Commission proposed in 1868 that there should be three grades of secondary education each with its own curriculum intended for three different social groups, one for the upper middle class, one for the minor professions, and the third for future clerical workers (Schools Enquiry Commission, 1867-8). The content of elementary education was also a subject of dispute: for example, a court decided in 1901 (the Cockerton Judgment) that it was illegal to spend public money on an elementary education that included more advanced study than that specified in the Elementary Code issued in the previous year. Similarly, in the United States and in other European countries there was continuing debate about what the curriculum should include.

Nevertheless, it was not until the second and third decade of this century that this debate began to take shape as a subject of academic study; in 1926 the American National Society for the Study of Education (1927) set their seal on curriculum as a topic by devoting their conference to 'Curriculum making: past and present', but the label 'curriculum theory' seems not to have appeared until some years later.

A very influential publication in the history of curriculum as a subject of academic study is Ralph Tyler's book, *Basic Principles of Curriculum and Instruction* (1949). Tyler's emphasis falls on course-planning and evaluation — which is not surprising since he had during the preceding two decades distinguished himself as an evaluator — and this became for some time the main focus of curriculum studies. Discussion of the curriculum cannot long avoid, however, the basic question about what should be included in a child's schooling, so that justification of the contents of the whole curriculum is at least as important an issue as is the planning of courses. Of recent years, a third area of interest has joined these two, and — at least amongst English writers — seems not unlikely to squeeze the other two into insignificance. Teachers and the curricula do not exist in a social void; the decisions teachers make about what they teach are inevitably situated in particular contexts and times. The way in which teachers and administrators organise the curriculum is not based on abstract logical considerations, but is a response both to the exigencies of the practical situations they find themselves in, and to current ideologies about what knowledge and skills are important. Thus there has grown up within curriculum theory a third area of study that considers the social and political contexts within which curricula take shape, and this includes giving attention to such matters as the effect of the organisational structure of schools on curriculum, the claims of parents and the pupils themselves to a say in what is taught, the competition between alternative ideologies about the nature and purpose of schooling, and the way power is exercised by central or local government agencies, or by pressure groups inside or outside the education system itself. This new approach does not, however, leave the others unchanged. To consider curriculum as a political issue — whether in the macro-politics of the national arena or the micro-politics of the school — throws an entirely different light on curriculum-planning. From this perspective, to treat curriculum-planning as a rational methodology seems not only irrelevant but downright misleading. Teachers seldom talk of their work in terms of aims and values, and when they do they are likely to be giving at least as much attention to negotiating with colleagues and to the *de facto* distribution of power between members of staff. This is why many teachers are sceptical about rational curriculum-planning, in spite of the rumblings from the Department of Education and Science about school goals and their evaluation.

Within the three areas of study which I have outlined in the previous paragraph two themes stand out: 'innovation' becomes a focus of interest because teachers and administrators alike want to know how they can most effectively exert pressure in order to change the curriculum in the direction they wish; and 'evaluation' takes on a new meaning. Indeed one result of the new interest in socio-political contexts and in how the curriculum is controlled is to place evaluation in the centre of curriculum theory. Evaluation, however, is now no

307

longer just a matter of testing the effectiveness of a new course, since in some cases an evaluator's report can be the crucial instrument for establishing or preventing change by its impact on professional and on public opinion, and in other cases evaluation can provide a focus for negotiation between the providers and consumers of education.

Probably the sharpest recent debate — amongst academics rather than amongst teachers — has related to social reproduction, the argument that curriculum selects young people for different careers and socialises them so that they accept whatever the future holds for them as appropriate and inevitable. Considerations of this kind lie behind 'The Great Debate', and the discussions about making the curriculum more relevant to jobs in industry. The idea of a common curriculum has been put forward as an alternative to giving different curricula to different groups of pupils in the manner proposed by the Taunton Commission in the last century. Although both The Great Debate and common curricula appear as topics, this book does not have a section that deals with social reproduction directly, mainly because it is difficult to translate so theoretical an issue into practical tasks.

It would thus be fair to say that curriculum theory as it now exists contains four areas of study:

(*a*) the planning of courses;
(*b*) the organising and justifying of the contents of the whole curriculum;
(*c*) the analysis of the social contexts of curricula, and the management of innovation;
(*d*) the description, analysis and evaluation of curricula.

These are, of course — under different headings and in a different sequence — the areas of study which this book has been concerned with.

It would be misleading to treat this brief account of the shape and nature of curriculum studies as if it were unchallenged and unchallengeable. For example, curriculum theory is certainly not 'theory' in the sense that a philosopher of science would use the word: it is not a body of concepts and relationships that can be defined so unambiguously that it can be used to generate testable predictions about what will happen in schools. The factors affecting real-life learning in schools are so many and inaccessible as to make such a scientific model of curriculum study inappropriate. But, of course, this does not mean that it is not important to try to understand the curriculum, though some people think that it would be better not to use the word 'theory'.

A more profound criticism comes from M.F.D. Young (1971), who hints that curriculum theory has developed as an academic band-wagon, useful to its adherents' careers but unlikely to rock the boat. (I must add that this is my way of expressing it, and not Michael Young's.) He wrote,

> There is an enormous literature in this field which demonstrates the concern of those who have been aptly labelled 'the curriculum mongers' to create and institutionalise an autonomous discipline 'curriculum studies' with its own theory, house journals and professors. Most of the writings . . . is more informative about the writer's perspectives and beliefs than about school curricula.

Young wants an approach to the curriculum that asks more challenging questions about the role played by different curricula in differentiating children from one another and inducing them to accept different views of themselves and their future lives. He rejected much earlier writing on the curriculum because it was based on the implicit question, 'Given that we know our objectives, how can we most efficiently achieve them?' He himself asked: 'But do we know our objectives? Don't we disagree radically about them?' Young's attack on curriculum theory as it was ten years ago played an important part in the shift of some British writers towards an interest in the relationship between curricula and the way in which schools function as part of society as a whole.

Another criticism made more recently by Michael Young (1977) is that curriculum theory has allowed itself to become divorced from the constraints and concerns that teachers actually experience, so that even if the theoretical structures look well they do not describe reality. Writing of teachers' *implicit* understanding of their work he says: 'Teachers have theories of knowledge, teaching and curriculum which . . . are crucially important for the possibilities of change but they lack the abstract elegance of philosophy, the conceptual obscurity of sociology, and the mindless banalities of the curriculum taxonomies.'

Since this book is designed to institute a debate amongst its readers and not to reduce them to silence, it is highly appropriate to end with a group of tasks which invite discussion of curriculum study as a whole.

Task 5.1 Critical consideration of curriculum studies

5.1.1   Is curriculum theory out of touch with classroom realities? Go through the tasks in this book and decide which are realistic and important, and which are irrelevant, remembering that other teachers may have interests and concerns which are different from yours. What curricular concerns important to teachers were omitted?

5.1.2   M.F.D. Young (1977) writes of teachers having 'theories of knowledge, teaching and curriculum'. What are these implicit theories, and why are they crucially important for the possibilities of change? (You will probably need to consult his paper.) How far do you find Young's views acceptable?

5.1.3   Should 'curriculum studies' as an area of academic study continue to exist in colleges and universities? What arguments can be summoned to defend its usefulness? Is it really little more than a career route and an apology for the status quo in schools? Could not all the activities in this book be carried out under other headings?

Appendices

Appendix A

The mystery of Mark Pullen

This appendix is an extract from the Schools Council History 13-16 Project (1976).

History books tell us about people in the past and what they did. They try to record the story of the past as fully and as accurately as possible. But before they can be written, historians have to look for evidence about what happened in the past. Like detectives, they have to look for clues and finds which will help them to piece together a story. An investigation of the 'Mystery of Mark Pullen' will show you some of the ways in which a detective works.

CONTENTS

Police report and map
Notice of Cricket Club meeting
Dental appointment card
Bus timetable
English Literature timetable of tutorials
Note of bank account
Ticket to see Captain Beefheart
NUS Students' Union card
Telephone message
Party invitation
University Rugby Club card
Photograph of girl

POLICE REPORT AND MAP

POLICE REPORT No. 13264/73/GR   **KENT CONSTABULARY**   7.6.75

6th June 1975

I was called in car 1KF at 21.37 hours to investigate a report of a youth being found injured near the A2 road to Dover 2km north of Lydden. It was raining hard, with very low cloud and the incident occurred at a point without any street or house lighting at all; it proved difficult to find. I arrived at 21.50 hours.

Mr. John Edwards had reported finding the youth. He had been walking his dog as he always does between 21.00 and 21.30 hours. On discovering the injured man he ran to his own house, about 500 metres away and telephoned for police and ambulance; he then returned to the scene of the incident and met me as I arrived.

The injured man, who appeared to be about 20 years of age, was lying in a ditch about one metre deep and about two metres from the roadside. His clothing was very wet indeed; I judged that he had been in the ditch for quite some time, perhaps as much as an hour. He was unconscious and was lying on his left side. I could see even in the poor light that his right leg was broken and that he had other injuries on the right side of his body. Mr. Edwards and I could not move him out of the ditch on our own and we did what we could to make him more comfortable, supporting his head and shoulders with a box and a blanket, and covering him with other blankets. The ambulance arrived at 21.56 hours. I noted, as the youth was carried to the ambulance, that he was very well dressed. He was certainly not a vagrant, as I had at first suspected. His clothes, though very wet, appeared clean and far from cheap. I took a wallet from his jacket; the contents of this wallet are enclosed with this report. He had no money at all on his person, but it was not possible to judge at the time whether anyone had been through his pockets before my arrival at the scene.

After the ambulance had left, I studied the roadside and the ditch. The only result of this search which may have had some bearing on the incident was the discovery of some tyre tracks (possibly skid marks) on the grass verge between the road edge and the ditch. These tracks were certainly made by a heavy vehicle, to judge from their width and depth. This vehicle must have steered off the road and then quickly corrected its course. The tracks were about 500mm from the road edge at their farthest point. It was, however, impossible to tell how recent these tracks were as the heavy rain that evening followed a dry spell.

I contacted the hospital to which the youth had been taken and I was told that he had died without regaining consciousness. I postponed further investigation. The diagram overleaf indicates the situation in which the youth was found.

Signed *George Ryder*

Rank and No. *P.C. 517*

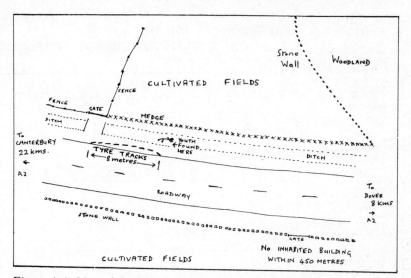

Figure A.1 *Map of the vicinity where the youth was found*

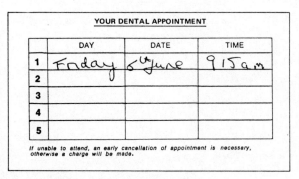

Figure A.2 *Notice of Cricket Club meeting*

Figure A.3 *Dental appointment card*

CANTERBURY · UNIVERSITY   **EAST KENT**   ROAD CAR COMPANY LTD   **SERVICE 32**

Bus Station, St. George's Lane, Watling St., Rose Lane, Parade, High St., St. Peter's St.. The Westgate. (Return—St. Peter's Place, Rheims Way, Wincheap Green, Pin Hill, Rhodaus Town, Watling St., Rose Lane, St. Georges St.) St. Dunstan's St.. Whitstable Rd.. St. Thomas' Hill, University Rd. University, Eliot College Roundabout, Giles Lane, Darwin College.
This Service is restricted to passengers travelling to and from the University and Beverley Farm.

From 8 OCTOBER, 1974

Mondays to Fridays

Bus Station	0745	0840	0847	0940	1040	1140	1222	1250	1315	1340	1440	1540	1610	1640	1740	1840	1940	2023	2135	2150	2235	2335	....
University, Eliot College	0755	0850	0857	0950	1050	1150	1232	1300	1325	1350	1450	1550	1620	1650	1750	1850	1950	2033	2145	2200	2245	2345	....
University, Darwin College	0757	0852	0859	0952	1052	1152	....	1302	1327	1352	1452	1552	1622	1652	1752	1852	1952	2035	....	2202	2247	2347	....

Saturdays

Bus Station	0745	0840	0940	1040	1140	1220	1340	1515	1640	1740	1840	1940	2135	2150	2235	2335	....
University, Eliot College	0755	0850	0950	1050	1150	1230	1350	1525	1650	1750	1850	1950	2145	2200	2245	2345	....
University, Darwin College	0757	0852	0952	1052	1152	1232	1352	1527	1652	1752	1852	1952	....	2202	2247	2347	....

Sundays

			5A□		5□				V	5□			
Bus Station	0940	1220	1400	1515	1640	1740	1840	1940	2110	2135	2150	2235	2335
University, Eliot College	0950	1230	1410	1525	1650	1750	1850	1950	2130	2145	2200	2245	2345
University, Darwin College	0952	1232	....	1527	....	1752	1852	1952	2132	....	2202	2247	2347

Mondays to Fridays

																			5□		▲	b
University, Darwin College	0853	0906	1006	1106	1203	....	1233	1306	1406	1506	1606	1625	1706	....	1735	1806	1906	2006	2038	....	2206	2250	2352
University, Eliot College	0855	0908	1008	1108	1205	1235	1235	1308	1408	1508	1608	1627	1710	1710	1737	1808	1908	2008	2040	2119	2208	2252	2352
Bus Station	0907	0920	1020	1120	1217	1247	1247	1320	1420	1520	1620	1639	1722	1722	1749	1820	1920	2020	2052	2129	2220	2304	0004

Saturdays

										5□		▲	▲
University, Darwin College	0906	1006	1106	1203	1235	1406	1533	1708	1806	1906	2006	....	2206	2250	2350
University, Eliot College	0908	1008	1108	1205	1237	1408	1535	1710	1808	1908	2008	2119	2208	2252	2352
Bus Station	0920	1020	1120	1217	1249	1420	1547	1722	1820	1920	2020	2129	2220	2304	0004

Sundays

		5□		5□						
University, Darwin College	1006	1235	....	1533	....	1806	1906	2006	2206	2250	2350
University, Eliot College	1008	1237	1410	1535	1710	1808	1908	2008	2208	2252	2352
Bus Station	1020	1249	1420	1547	1720	1820	1920	2020	2220	2304	0004

CODE

◆ —Passes near Canterbury East and Canterbury West Railway Stations.
● —Primarily intended for students attending classes at 0900.
★ —Primarily intended for staff commencing duties at 0900.
⊕ —Operates during Term Time only.

5/5A□—Services 5/5A to or from Whitstable via Chestfield and South Street.
V —Operates from Canterbury East Station (Dep. 2103) and via Canterbury West Station (Dep. 2123).
▲ —Extended to Sturry Station during Term Time only.
8/10/72: w

The Services shown are subject to the Company's Conditions of Carriage and Passenger Regulations, details of which may be obtained at any Booking or Enquiry Office, or at the Porter's Lodge of each College at the University.

Figure A.4 *Bus timetable*

ENGLISH LITERATURE   SUMMER TERM 1975

This term we shall study the plays of Shakespeare. Each tutorial will concentrate on one particular play. Tutorials will be held in H22 from 2.30 pm to 4.00 pm on the following dates:

       Friday   25th April
       Friday   2nd May
       Friday   9th May
       Thursday   15th May
       Friday   23rd May
       Friday   30th May
       Friday   6th June
       Friday   13th June

                     J.P.R. CRAIG
            Lecturer in English Studies

Figure A.5 *English Literature timetable of tutorials*

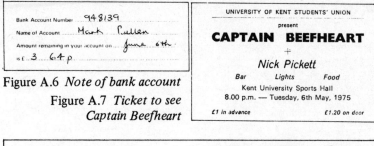

Bank Account Number 948139
Name of Account Mark Pullen
Amount remaining in your account on June 6th :
is £ 3 64 p

Figure A.6 *Note of bank account*

Figure A.7 *Ticket to see Captain Beefheart*

UNIVERSITY OF KENT STUDENTS' UNION

present

CAPTAIN BEEFHEART

+

Nick Pickett

Bar   Lights   Food

Kent University Sports Hall

8.00 p.m. — Tuesday, 6th May, 1975

£1 in advance   £1.20 on door

East Kent Students' Association

This card entitles members of the East Kent Students' Association to attend social functions staged by the constituent organisations of the Association and to participate in the activities of such clubs and societies as are open to students of the Association generally. The constituent organisations of the Association consist at the present time of :

Canterbury College of Art
Canterbury Technical College
Christ Church College of Education
Nonington College of Physical Education
University of Kent at Canterbury
Wye College of Agriculture (London University)
South Kent College of Technology

Holders of this card are entitled to non-voting membership of all non-sporting clubs and societies of the University of Kent Students' Union upon payment of the normal membership fee (for full details, phone Canterbury 65224). Membership of the clubs and societies of other constituent organisations is limited to such clubs and societies, and on such conditions, as may from time to time be advertised. (Contact your Students' Union for details).

The holder of this card is

a full time student member of the

National Union of Students

and the

Students Union
University of Kent, Canterbury

for the academic year 1974-5

№ 477583

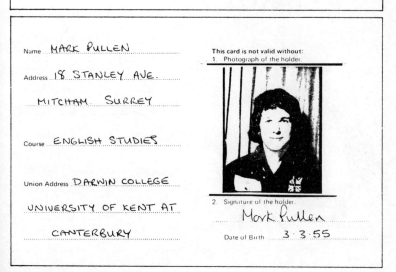

Name MARK PULLEN

Address 18 STANLEY AVE.

MITCHAM SURREY

Course ENGLISH STUDIES

Union Address DARWIN COLLEGE

UNIVERSITY OF KENT AT

CANTERBURY

This card is not valid without:
1. Photograph of the holder.

2. Signature of the holder.

Mark Pullen

Date of Birth 3·3·55

Figure A.8 *NUS Students' Union card*

Telephone Message

Date 6th June 1975
2.10pm.

To MARK PULLEN

From Jeff

Car has broken down again. Can you make your own way to the party tonight? Jeff is sure someone at the party will give you a lift back to Canterbury.

Figure A.9 *Telephone message*

To Mark

There will be 'RED HOT' fun

at Cathy's – 73
Nook Rd Dover

On Friday 6th June

At 9 o'clock

Come and make it sizzle!

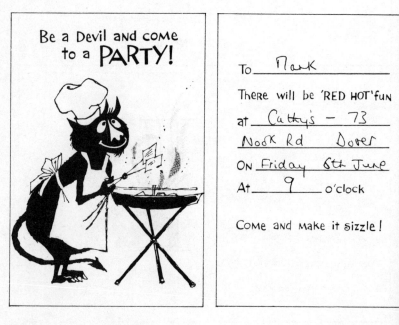

Figure A.10 *Party invitation*

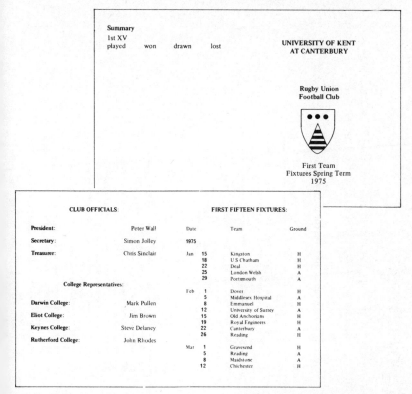

Figure A.11 *University Rugby Club card*

Figure A.12 *Photograph of girl*

319

Appendix B Science 5-13: objectives

These objectives, prepared by the Schools Council Science 5-13 Project (Ennever and Harlen, 1972), are arranged in developmental stages and in nine categories, according to the kind of learning intended. They are not seen as prescriptive, but are available for teachers to select from.

Attitudes, interests and aesthetic awareness

.00/.10

Stage 1
Transition from intuition to concrete operations.
Infants generally.

1.01 Willingness to ask questions
1.02 Willingness to handle both living and non-living material.
1.03 Sensitivity to the need for giving proper care to living things.
1.04 Enjoyment in using all the senses for exploring and discriminating.
1.05 Willingness to collect material for observation or investigation.

Concrete operations.
Early stage.

1.06 Desire to find out things for oneself.
1.07 Willing participation in group work.
1.08 Willing compliance with safety regulations in handling tools and equipment.
1.09 Appreciation of the need to learn the meaning of new words and to use them correctly.
1.11 Awareness that there are various ways of testing out ideas and making observations.
1.12 Interest in comparing and classifying living or non-living things.
1.13 Enjoyment in comparing measurements with estimates.
1.14 Awareness that there are various ways of expressing results and observations.
1.15 Willingness to wait and to keep records in order to observe change in things.
1.16 Enjoyment in exploring the variety of living things in the environment

Stage 2
Concrete
operations.
Later stage.

2.01 Willingness to co-operate with others in science activities.
2.02 Willingness to observe objectively.
2.03 Appreciation of the reasons for safety regulations.
2.04 Enjoyment in examining ambiguity in the use of words.
2.05 Interest in choosing suitable means of expressing results and observations.
2.06 Willingness to assume responsibility for the proper care of living things.
2.07 Willingness to examine critically the results of their own and others' work.
2.08 Preference for putting ideas to test before accepting or rejecting them.
2.09 Appreciation that approximate methods of comparison may be more appropriate than careful measurements.
2.11 Enjoyment in developing methods for solving problems or testing ideas.
2.12 Appreciation of the part that aesthetic qualities of materials play in determining their use.
2.13 Interest in the way discoveries were made in the past.

Stage 3
Transition to
stage of
abstract
thinking.

3.01 Acceptance of responsibility for their own and others' safety in experiments.
3.02 Preference for using words correctly.
3.03 Commitment to the idea of physical cause and effect.
3.04 Recognition of the need to standardise measurements.
3.05 Willingness to examine evidence critically.
3.06 Willingness to consider beforehand the usefulness of the results from a possible experiment.
3.07 Preference for choosing the most appropriate means of expressing results or observations.
3.08 Recognition of the need to acquire new skills.
3.09 Willingness to consider the role of science in everyday life.
3.11 Appreciation of the main principles in the care of living things.
3.12 Willingness to extend methods used in science activities to other fields of experience.

Observing, exploring and ordering observations
.20

1.21 Appreciation of the variety of living things and materials in the environment.
1.22 Awareness of changes which take place as time passes.
1.23 Recognition of common shapes—square, circle, triangle.
1.24 Recognition of regularity in patterns.
1.25 Ability to group things consistently according to chosen or given criteria.

1.26 Awareness of the structure and form of living things.
1.27 Awareness of change of living things and non-living materials.
1.28 Recognition of the action of force.
1.29 Ability to group living and non-living things by observable attributes.
1.29a Ability to distinguish regularity in events and motion.

2.21 Awareness of internal structure in living and non-living things.
2.22 Ability to construct and use keys for identification.
2.23 Recognition of similar and congruent shapes.
2.24 Awareness of symmetry in shapes and structures.
2.25 Ability to classify living things and non-living materials in different ways.
2.26 Ability to visualise objects from different angles and the shape of cross-sections.

Developing basic concepts and logical thinking
.30

1.31 Awareness of the meaning of words which describe various types of quantity.
1.32 Appreciation that things which are different may have features in common.

1.33 Ability to predict the effect of certain changes through observation of similar changes.
1.34 Formation of the notions of the horizontal and the vertical.
1.35 Development of concepts of conservation of length and substance.
1.36 Awareness of the meaning of speed and of its relation to distance covered.

2.31 Appreciation of measurement as division into regular parts and repeated comparison with a unit.
2.32 Appreciation that comparisons can be made indirectly by use of an intermediary.
2.33 Development of concepts of conservation of weight, area and volume.
2.34 Appreciation of weight as a downward force.
2.35 Understanding of the speed, time, distance relation.

3.21 Appreciation that classification criteria are arbitrary.
3.22 Ability to distinguish observations which are relevant to the solution of a problem from those which are not.
3.23 Ability to estimate the order of magnitude of physical quantities.

3.31 Familiarity with relationships involving velocity, distance, time, acceleration.
3.32 Ability to separate, exclude or combine variables in approaching problems.
3.33 Ability to formulate hypotheses not dependent upon direct observation.
3.34 Ability to extend reasoning beyond the actual to the possible.
3.35 Ability to distinguish a logically sound proof from others less sound.

Posing questions and devising experiments or investigations to answer them

.40

1.41 Ability to find answers to simple problems by investigation.
1.42 Ability to make comparisons in terms of one property or variable.

1.43 Appreciation of the need for measurement.
1.44 Awareness that more than one variable may be involved in a particular change.

Acquiring knowledge and learning skills

.50/.60

1.51 Ability to discriminate between different materials.
1.52 Awareness of the characteristics of living things.
1.53 Awareness of properties which materials can have.
1.54 Ability to use displayed reference material for identifying living and non-living things.

1.55 Familiarity with sources of sound.
1.56 Awareness of sources of heat, light and electricity.
1.57 Knowledge that change can be produced in common substances.
1.58 Appreciation that ability to move or cause movement requires energy.
1.59 Knowledge of differences in properties between and within common groups of materials.
1.61 Appreciation of man's use of other living things and their products.
1.62 Awareness that man's way of life has changed through the ages.
1.63 Skill in manipulating tools and materials.
1.64 Development of techniques for handling living things correctly.
1.65 Ability to use books for supplementing ideas or information.

2.41 Ability to frame questions likely to be answered through investigations.
2.42 Ability to investigate variables and to discover effective ones.
2.43 Appreciation of the need to control variables and use controls in investigations.
2.44 Ability to choose and use either arbitrary or standard units of measurement as appropriate.
2.45 Ability to select a suitable degree of approximation and work to it.
2.46 Ability to use representational models for investigating problems or relationships.

2.51 Knowledge of conditions which promote changes in living things and non-living materials.
2.52 Familiarity with a wide range of forces and of ways in which they can be changed.
2.53 Knowledge of sources and simple properties of common forms of energy.
2.54 Knowledge of the origins of common materials.
2.55 Awareness of some discoveries and inventions by famous scientists.
2.56 Knowledge of ways to investigate and measure properties of living things and non-living materials.
2.57 Awareness of changes in the design of measuring instruments and tools during man's history.
2.58 Skill in devising and constructing simple apparatus.
2.59 Ability to select relevant information from books or other reference material.

3.41 Attempting to identify the essential steps in approaching a problem scientifically.
3.42 Ability to design experiments with effective controls for testing hypotheses.
3.43 Ability to visualise a hypothetical situation as a useful simplification of actual observations.
3.44 Ability to construct scale models for investigation and to appreciate implications of changing the scale.

3.51 Knowledge that chemical change results from interaction.
3.52 Knowledge that energy can be stored and converted in various ways.
3.53 Awareness of the universal nature of gravity.
3.54 Knowledge of the main constituents and variations in the composition of soil and of the earth.
3.55 Knowledge that properties of matter can be explained by reference to its particulate nature.
3.56 Knowledge of certain properties of heat, light, sound, electrical, mechanical and chemical energy.
3.57 Knowledge of a wide range of living organisms.
3.58 Development of the concept of an internal environment.
3.59 Knowledge of the nature and variations in basic life processes.
3.61 Appreciation of levels of organisation in living things.
3.62 Appreciation of the significance of the work and ideas of some famous scientists.
3.63 Ability to apply relevant knowledge without help of contextual cues.
3.64 Ability to use scientific equipment and instruments for extending the range of human senses.

Communicating

.70

1.71 Ability to use new words appropriately.
1.72 Ability to record events in their sequences.
1.73 Ability to discuss and record impressions of living and non-living things in the environment.
1.74 Ability to use representational symbols for recording information on charts or block graphs.

1.75 Ability to tabulate information and use tables.
1.76 Familiarity with names of living things and non-living materials.
1.77 Ability to record impressions by making models, painting or drawing.

2.71 Ability to use non-representational symbols in plans, charts, etc.
2.72 Ability to interpret observations in terms of trends and rates of change.
2.73 Ability to use histograms and other simple graphical forms for communicating data.
2.74 Ability to construct models as a means of recording observations.

Appreciating patterns and relationships

.80

1.81 Awareness of cause-effect relationships.

1.82 Development of a concept of environment.
1.83 Formation of a broad idea of variation in living things.
1.84 Awareness of seasonal changes in living things.
1.85 Awareness of differences in physical conditions between different parts of the Earth.

2.81 Awareness of sequences of change in natural phenomena.
2.82 Awareness of structure-function relationship in parts of living things.
2.83 Appreciation of interdependence among living things.
2.84 Awareness of the impact of man's activities on other living things.
2.85 Awareness of the changes in the physical environment brought about by man's activity.
2.86 Appreciation of the relationships of parts and wholes.

3.71 Ability to select the graphical form most appropriate to the information being recorded.
3.72 Ability to use three-dimensional models or graphs for recording results.
3.73 Ability to deduce information from graphs : from gradient, area, intercept.
3.74 Ability to use analogies to explain scientific ideas and theories.

3.81 Recognition that the ratio of volume to surface area is significant.
3.82 Appreciation of the scale of the universe.
3.83 Understanding of the nature and significance of changes in living and non-living things.
3.84 Recognition that energy has many forms and is conserved when it is changed from one form to another.
3.85 Recognition of man's impact on living things—conservation, change, control.
3.86 Appreciation of the social implications of man's changing use of materials, historical and contemporary.
3.87 Appreciation of the social implications of research in science.
3.88 Appreciation of the role of science in the changing pattern of provision for human needs.

327

Interpreting findings critically

.90

1.91 Awareness that the apparent size, shape and relationships of things depend on the position of the observer.
1.92 Appreciation that properties of materials influence their use.

2.91 Appreciation of adaptation to environment.
2.92 Appreciation of how the form and structure of materials relate to their function and properties.
2.93 Awareness that many factors need to be considered when choosing a material for a particular use.
2.94 Recognition of the role of chance in making measurements and experiments.

3.91 Ability to draw from observations conclusions that are unbiased by preconception.
3.92 Willingness to accept factual evidence despite preceptual contradictions.
3.93 Awareness that the degree of accuracy of measurements has to be taken into account when results are interpreted.
3.94 Awareness that unstated assumptions can affect conclusions drawn from argument or experimental results.
3.95 Appreciation of the need to integrate findings into a simplifying generalisation.
3.96 Willingness to check that conclusions are consistent with further evidence.

Appendix C

Aims of primary education

These aims, which are here listed in random order, were published by the Schools Council Aims of Primary Education Project (Ashton *et al.*, 1975a), and represent what a group of teachers believed that children in the middle range of ability should have achieved by the end of their primary education.

1 The child should be able to communicate his feelings through some art forms; for example, painting, music, drama, move-ment.
2 The child should have an understanding of how his body works.
3 The child should know how to acquire information other than by reading; for example, by asking questions, by experimenting, from watching television.
4 The child should know how to use mathematical techniques in his everyday life; for instance, estimating distances, classifying objects, using money.
5 The child should know the correct spelling of a basic general vocabulary.
6 The child should have some knowledge of the Bible and Chris-tian beliefs.
7 The child should be an individual, developing in his own way.
8 The child should be able to write legibly and know how to present his work attractively.
9 The child should be developing the ability to make reasoned judgments and choices, based on the interpretation and evalua-tion of relevant information.
10 The child should be developing awareness of the spiritual

aspects of prayer and worship.

11 The child should find enjoyment in some purposeful leisure-time interests and activities both on his own and with others.

12 The child should be able to read fluently and accurately at a minimum reading age of 11.

13 The child should find enjoyment in a variety of aspects of school work and gain satisfaction from his own achievements.

14 The child should have a wide general (not subject-based) knowledge of times and places beyond his immediate experience.

15 The child should know how to observe carefully, accurately and with sensitivity.

16 The child should have sufficient knowledge and skill to be able to engage in simple music-making; for example, singing, percussion, home-made instruments.

17 The child should be industrious, persistent and conscientious.

18 The child should be generally obedient to parents, teachers and all reasonable authority.

19 The child should try to behave in accordance with the ideals of his own religion whether or not this is Christian.

20 The child should know how to behave appropriately in a variety of situations; for example, talking to visitors, going on outings, answering the telephone.

21 The child should know how to convey his meaning clearly and accurately through speech for a variety of purposes; for example, description, explanation, narration.

22 The child should be developing the capacity to form a considered opinion and to act upon it even if this means rejecting conventional thought and behaviour.

23 The child should know how to apply the basic principles of health, hygiene and safety.

24 The child should be beginning to acquire a set of moral values on which to base his own behaviour; for example, honesty, sincerity, personal responsibility.

25 The child should be careful with and respectful of both his own and other people's property.

26 The child should be able to read with understanding material appropriate to his age-group and interests.

27 The child should be kind and considerate; he should, for example, be willing to give personal help to younger or new children, to consider the elderly, the disabled.

28 The child should know how to engage in discussion; for example, he should be able to talk about his own and others' opinions in a reasonable way.

29 The child should know how to compute in the four arithmetic rules using his knowledge of, for instance, number, multiplication tables and different units of measurement.

30 The child should be a good mixer; he should be able to make easy social contact with other children and adults in work and play situations.

31 The child should know those moral values, relating to people and property, which are shared by the majority of members of the society.

32 The child should know how to speak in a clear and fluent manner appropriate to different situations; for example, informal occasions with children and adults, formal occasions.

33 The child should have precise and economic body control for all ordinary physical activities including the handling of tools and equipment.

34 The child should know how to write clear and meaningful English appropriate to different formal purposes; for example, factual reports, letters, descriptive accounts.

35 The child should have ordered subject knowledge in, for example, history, geography.

36 The child should have some understanding of modern technological developments; for example, space travel, telecommunications, automation.

37 The child should be developing a critical and discriminating attitude towards his experiences; for example, of the mass media.

38 The child should be developing the ability to control his behaviour and his emotions.

39 The child should know how to write interestingly and with sensitivity.

40 The child should be self-confident; he should have a sense of personal adequacy and be able to cope with his environment at an appropriate level.

41 The child should know the basic facts of sex and reproduction.

42 The child should know the basic grammatical rules of written English.

43 The child should know how to behave with courtesy and good manners both in and out of school.

44 The child should be able to maintain lasting relationships with a few close friends.

45 The child should be adaptable to changing circumstances and flexible in outlook.

46 The child should be developing a personal appreciation of beauty in some of its forms, both natural and artistic.

47 The child should be enthusiastic and eager to put his best into all activities.

48 The child should be beginning to understand aesthetic experiences and should be able to talk about them; for example, looking at pictures and sculpture, listening to poetry and plays.

49 The child should be able to play a musical instrument such as a recorder, violin, guitar.

50 The child should be able to listen with concentration and understanding.

51 The child should have a general knowledge of his local environment in some of the following aspects: historical, geographical, natural, economic, social.

52 The child should be beginning to understand his own emotions.

53 The child should be able to swim.

54 The child should know the appropriate techniques of some arts and crafts; for example, how to use paint, clay.

55 The child should have a wide vocabulary.

56 The child should be developing the skills of acquiring knowledge and information from written material; for example, summarising, taking notes accurately, the use of libraries.

57 The child should be developing the ability to plan independent work and organise his own time.

58 The child should be happy, cheerful and well balanced.

59 The child should know what to do in emergencies; for example, fire, sickness, accident.

60 The child should be developing his inventiveness and creativity in some fields; for example, painting, music, mechanical things, poetry, movement.

61 The child should have some knowledge of the beliefs of the major world religions other than Christianity.

62 The child should know some simple scientific experimental procedures and some basic scientific concepts; for example, properties of materials, the nature and significance of changes in living things.

63 The child should know how to play a variety of games; for example, football, skittle-ball, rounders.

64 The child should be beginning to feel community responsibility; for example, he should be loyal to groups such as class and school of which he is a member and, where possible, the wider community, and willing to accept the responsibilities which membership implies.

65 The child should have a questioning attitude towards his environment.

66 The child should be developing tolerance: respecting and appreciating others, their feelings, views and capabilities.

67 The child should try to behave in accordance with the ideals of the Christian religion.

68 The child should be able to conduct a simple conversation in a foreign language.

69 The child should be beginning to realise that he can play an important part in his own development by, for example, recognising his strengths and limitations and setting his own goals accordingly.

70 The child should be able to listen to and enjoy a range of music; for example, pop, folk, classical.

71 The child should know how to think and solve problems mathematically using the appropriate basic concepts of, for example, the number system and place value, shape, spatial relationships, sets, symmetry and the appropriate language.

72 The child should have a range of movement and gymnastic skills.

Appendix D

The 97 bus

This is a proposal for organising part of the curriculum round a local bus route (Schools Council, 1967).

The purpose of the enquiry

(i)   To help the pupils to become familiar with the district where they live, and to appreciate some of the benefits and problems of their own locality.

(ii) To illustrate a local transport route through the people working it and using it.

(iii) To bring forward for discussion the differences between public and private transport.

(iv) To use a variety of techniques such as interviews with special people, social surveys, discussions and field studies into environment and local history through local records.

(v)   To bring out other social problems, e.g. of conveying people to work, shops and entertainment centres.

The methods of the enquiry

(i)   An opening point of departure.

(ii) Individual and group assignments. The nature of the enquiry lends itself to direct involvement and personal experience.

(iii) To make full use of people from outside the school to comment on their part in the undertaking.

(iv) To use a group composite display which will illustrate the results of the enquiry.

334

The point of departure

[A paragraph is omitted here which describes an imaginary film that is to serve as a point of departure.]

THE INDIVIDUAL AND GROUP ASSIGNMENTS

As the emphasis is through persons and personalities, most of the assignments will be of the interview type. Therefore it is important that the boys and girls have some training in inter-view techniques, and also that the people to be interviewed have agreed to help with the enquiry. These assignments are for two people together rather than individuals, and they are based on an actual bus journey which was investigated on these lines by a school in Kent. The bus passes the school on its way from the neighbouring town to another town 30 miles away. Many of the boys and girls use the bus to and from school. None had made the whole journey. It is a typical cross-country route which moves from orchard to hop-growing country to a pastoral sheep-raising area. Within a mile of the school is a large village where many of the children live.

Pair 1 will board the bus at its starting point at 9.00 a.m. making the complete journey (1½ hours), recording at each stop the number of people (men, women, children) boarding and leaving, and if possible recording the length of the journey each makes. They will try to assess the purpose of the journey, in simple terms: going to work, going to school, going to hospital, going to shop. This pair will return on the same bus repeating the observations.

Pair 2 will repeat this journey starting at 1.30 p.m.

Pair 3 will travel on the top of the bus and record the view — describing the nature of the country, the farming, the houses and the traffic en route. Simple categories will be suggested, e.g. large, medium, small, tiny, for the houses. This pair will need a large-scale map to which they can refer their observations.

Pair 4 will take the school camera and at points previously agreed with Pair 3 will take photographs to illustrate the observa-tions made by Pair 3. Colour transparency 35 mm film will be used.

Pair 5 will be left at village 'C' en route. They will talk to people waiting for the bus to find out why they are using it, how often they use it, what it means to the village. They will also visit the village general store and the village school to see how many children use the bus. They will also visit the local police constable. The purpose of this part of the enquiry is to try to assess what the bus means to the village.

Pair 6 will repeat the work of Pair 5 but at village 'B', which is nearer the other terminus of the route. This part of the investigation may lead to a comparison of shopping habits and preferences.

Pair 7 will visit the bus depot in the town where most of the boys and girls live. They will arrive in time to see the final stages of cleaning a 97 bus and watch the take-over procedure as the bus crew arrive for duty. They will talk to the cleaners and the manageress of the canteen and in general will build up that part of the picture represented by maintenance and behind the scenes preparation. They will go back to see the same bus going 'off duty'.

Pair 8 will have a similar task to Pair 7 but here the purpose is to uncover some of the administrative work. They will interview the traffic superintendent and an inspector. If possible they will tape record some of the inspector's problems – complaints both by and about the passengers. They will try to find out something of the personalities of the bus crews, including the problems of labour relations in this industry.

Pair 9 will visit one of the governors of the school who is chairman of the parish council of the large village nearby. He is an enthusiastic collector of local history and he has access to parish records which include correspondence between the parish and an earlier bus company which insisted on burying its dead horses in the village. This pair will visit this governor and endeavour to trace other references to parish correspondence over local bus traffic. Many of these will be recent but enough exists to provide a historical profile of the local bus. It is certain that other items in parish records will come to light which will suggest future enquiries and this pair should be briefed to be on the alert for these.

Pair 10 will carry out a similar survey of local transport history leading through the amalgamation of the private bus companies to the take-over by the railways of so many of them. They will find out the purpose of transport commissions and perhaps be able to attend one.

Pair 11 will visit the head office of the bus company so that the place of the local bus in the whole complexity of the bus company's operation can be realised.

Pair 12 will look at the local bus through the eyes of the Borough Surveyor and the town police. What are the problems of routing, of traffic congestion, of bus stations? Why is there no bus station in one town whereas there is in the other?

Pair 13 will talk to some of the bus drivers and learn as much as they can about good driving, road courtesy and dangerous actions by motorists, cyclists and pedestrians which lead to accidents.

Each of these assignments is timed to occupy each pair not less than half a day and possibly up to a whole day. It is a vital part of the operation that each pair reports back to the whole group so that the gradual building up of the profile is clear to all. There must be no sense of isolation.

THE PEOPLE FROM OUTSIDE THE SCHOOL

These visits will be more productive after the individual assignments have been started, possibly after the field work is finished. As many as possible of the following people can be brought in to contribute to the investigation.

1 Bus driver and conductor (often a local bus crew member may be a parent of one of the children in school). They will be asked to talk about their job in terms of hours of work, rates of pay, times of work. They may need careful selection and some briefing first as to the sort of questions that may arise. Do they like this route? Do they always do the same route? Do the same crews always work together? What about the customers? Any problems from the conductors' point of view, such as late-night drunks, teenagers, schoolboys and girls? What about productivity in this industry? One-man buses? Take-home pay? What is a PSV licence? How do you get one?
2 One or two regular users of the bus might come to talk about their problems.
3 The Borough Surveyor.
4 The police officers responsible for traffic.
5 The local education authority officers responsible for school bus arrangements. This school has no school bus — why not?

Many boys and girls use the 97 bus. When the weather is bad, it is often full of other people when it passes the school. How will bigger comprehensive schools affect the local education authority? How much does it cost to have a school bus?

EXTRA PROJECTS

A central team could provide the school with a work kit which might include.

(*a*) Technical data. Bus engines, chassis body assembly including emphasis on safety factors, braking distances, driver's field of vision, turning circle, centre of gravity when loaded and unloaded.
(*b*) Personnel data. Time sheets used by bus crews, log books, early and late working, overtime pay, wage rates in rural, town and metropolitan bus companies.
(*c*) Road data. Cost of upkeep of various types of roads, design and speed of special motorway buses.
(*d*) Foreign data. Buses in other countries.
(*e*) A summary of the procedure for increasing fares. Newspaper cuttings of protest meeting after recent increases in fares.

WORK TO FOLLOW

What alternatives have the people on the route for travel? What are their shopping needs today? Local history archives might show how shopping habits have changed. Analysis of users' needs would almost certainly throw up more lines of enquiry. How many people need the bus to visit relatives, friends, or people in hospitals? How many are going to work? How many to the nearest railhead?

It might be worthwhile drawing a local map showing the transport facilities in the neighbourhood. Should unprofitable railway lines be closed? What are the disadvantages of buses (luggage, children, etc.) compared with trains? A comparison of busy and slack times will illustrate the fundamental problem of all public transport. The misery of missing a full bus on a rainy night could be discussed in relation to the maximum number of hours a bus driver should work.

PRESENTATION

The exhibition at the end of this area of enquiry will be able to show some or all of these items:

(i) Public transport is a vital part of the urban and rural scene.

(ii) Many different kinds of travellers depend upon the 97 bus.

(iii) As well as travellers, the jobs of many people (drivers, conductors, maintenance men, cleaners, traffic superintendents, office staff) depend upon this bus.

(iv) The impact of the 97 bus on local traffic, police, industry, shopping and entertainment.

(v) The way local history and geography is reflected in the vast changes in public transport in the last 100 years.

(vi) Transport in other areas, not only in England, but all over the world.

(vii) Public transport depends on people (sometimes immigrants) and we depend on public transport for both work and leisure.

Appendix E

Curriculum documents from a middle school

These are intended for use by readers who do not have access to a school. However, it is both more interesting and more valuable to collect documents from a school that you know, though not all schools make their intentions as explicit as this one does. There are fifteen documents: you may decide whether or not they are all relevant to understanding what the intended curriculum is at G — School.

1 Mathematics information
2 Mathematics syllabuses
3 Individual record sheet of progress in mathematics
4 English syllabus
5 Geography syllabus
6 History syllabus
7 Science scheme of work
8 Religious education syllabus
9 Physical education syllabus
10 The Adjustment Unit
11 Guidelines for assessment
12 'Simple statistics'
13 'Welcome to G — Middle School' (This guide for parents is to be found not here but in Appendix L where it is Extract F on pp. 489-96.)

MATHEMATICS INFORMATION

Inside this information pack will be found all the policies, procedures,

340

methods, etc. that are needed to teach mathematics within the school. If there are any points not covered please contact the head of the department.

Aims of the mathematics department

Our aim is to educate each child to the highest level possible within the mathematics field. We would hope that all children leaving the school will have a good grounding in the basics of mathematics as well as having sampled a wide variety of other topics.

The setting system

When children have been in the school for one half-term they are assessed and on ability placed into a set. The sets are labelled A, X, Y, Z, R — A being the top set and R being the bottom or remedial set. Once put into a set the child usually stays in it for the rest of his time in the school. However, should a child improve his ability or the opposite then he will change sets. Any changes of children between sets is done with consultation between the two class teachers and the head of department. The numbers of children within each set varies; this is so that the bottom sets can have fewer pupils and allow the set more teacher/pupil time, as it is in this area of setting that major help has to be given to the children so that they may overcome their difficulties with the subject.

Departmental staff

Within the department there are two mathematics specialists, who will help anyone with any problems they have with mathematics. The rest of the staff are teachers with an interest in the subject and wish to teach it. The staff select to take mathematics before the start of the academic year and have a choice as to whether they take mathematics or not.

Examinations and testing

After two or three weeks in the school the new intake of children are all given the Nottingham Number Test. This test has no reading content so that they do not encounter language difficulties which would distort their mathematics result. Of course this does not mean that they will be able to follow oral instructions!

At the end of each academic year each child is given the NFER Mathematics Test appropriate to his or her age. Along with this it is proposed that there will be an internal school examination. In the fourth year the children are also given a local examination for children leaving middle school.

Departmental meetings

Departmental meetings take place every two to three weeks depending on demand. At these meetings any problems which have been encountered in the teaching or organisation are discussed, along with suggestions as to approaches to different topics. This is also an ideal opportunity for staff to consult each other about set changes.

Children's work

The children work in mathematics books provided by the school. The pages are folded in half and the work is completed down one side of the page and then down the other side. Margins are not used in mathematics. If the work dictates the use of more space then whole pages may be used or the book turned sideways. Children are expected to write in pen at all times and use rulers to draw all lines. Covers of exercise books are not to be written on except to write the name, class set and mathematics teacher. If a book is lost or misplaced then after a reasonable amount of time the child will be given a replacement. Any book that is carelessly lost or damaged has to be paid for by the child. When a book is full it is checked by the teacher who then gives a new book to the child; the teacher will obtain new books from the head of department.

Textbooks

All mathematics textbooks are stacked on shelves in U5. The answer books are with the set of books. If an answer book is not with the set then a reference copy is kept on the answer shelf in U6. Would staff please ensure that all books are returned to U5 and put on the correct shelf as they are most likely used by another set in a different year.

Mathematics syllabus

The syllabus attached is the ground which we expect to cover while a child is in the school. Please do not regard it as a rigid document; it is to be used to suit the children and staff and can be flexible. It will be seen that it is split into years, but this is only a guide, and children will continue through the syllabus regardless of their academic year. At present work is being completed to provide a syllabus with linked textbooks, and it is hoped that by September this will come into operation. The following topics are the top priority and must be practised and used as much as possible.

Tables

It cannot be stressed hard enough how important to our children these are. They should be tested at least once per week and all children should know at least as far as the 10 times and preferably to 12. Please try and ensure that the children can extract a product without having to go through the complete table.

The remedial children who find difficulty in learning tables may be taught the use of the number square and allowed to use this.

Basic four rules of number

All children should be able to use the four rules of number both numerically and mentally.

Subtraction

If a child has not been taught subtraction by decomposition and is confident in his working then he should be allowed to continue. However, the decomposition method is the policy method for our school and should be used where possible.

Operation signs

For addition, multiplication and subtraction the sign should be on the left-hand side of the calculation.

Television

Television is used in the school if the timetable will allow and we use such programmes as 'Mathshow', 'Maths Workshops', etc.

Equipment

The equipment list is attached; however, all the equipment on the list may not be available due to break-ins, vandals, etc. Please ask the head of department if you cannot find what you require. All equipment is housed either in U8 or in U6 cupboards. Graph paper is available in U6 in various sizes. The type you require can be seen by looking in the filing cabinet at the sample sheets.

Mathematics worksheets

It is requested of staff that any duplicated sheets which are produced are placed in the filing cabinet, so that they may be used by other sets and teachers. The sheets already in the file are numbered and filed, and a reference file will be found in the cabinet which has the sheets in order with a single copy of each sheet available. If any sheets are used would staff please ensure that they are replaced in the right order.

Mathematics filing cabinets

The filing cabinets are situated in U6. They contain: set list spares, mathematics glossaries, record sheets for all sets, any sets of work-cards which are in school, mathematics catalogues, any mathematics information, for example, *The Times Educational Supplement* reports on mathematics, any local authority notices, etc.

Final note

If any member of the staff has any suggestions would they please convey them at the meetings so that the department may give to the children the best that is possible in the teaching of mathematics.

Record system in mathematics

The record system is an individual-child record system and is designed so that all mathematical work undertaken by a child is recorded in one booklet. The content tries to cover all topics which a child will encounter and to cater for all levels of ability. The wording of the booklet is such that it matches the wording of the syllabus in order to try and standardise syllabus, records, sets and teachers.

The system within the record booklet is as follows:

A   the child has met this;
B   the child has grasped the idea;
C   the child fully understands and can handle most assignments
     set on this particular topic.

A tick is placed in the appropriate column when work has been marked. The comments section is designed so that the member of staff may note any weaknesses or comments of value.

The records are situated in the mathematics department filing cabinets with each set having its own folder and these may be removed at any time in order to complete, but would it be possible for records to be returned as soon as possible and placed in the correct order.

MATHEMATICS SYLLABUS

First year

It is not essential to teach topics in the order they appear. Tables up to 10 X 10 should be stressed at all times.

Units

Understanding of units is dealt with from a practical standpoint.

Money	£ p
Time	a.m., p.m., 24-hour clock system
Length	mm, cm, m, km
Capacity	l, ml, kl
Mass (weight)	g, kg

Number

Initial work on number bonds is essential.

Whole numbers
Emphasise place value
Simple estimation of answers as an aid to calculations
Addition
Subtraction: by *decomposition*
Multiplication: tables up to 10 X 10; simple long multiplication (e.g. 23 X 27)
Division: simple short division (e.g. 1233 ÷ 9)

Appendix E

Approximations
Discussion about the need for and uses of approximations
Approximations to the nearest whole number, 10; 100; 1,000

Signs
Understanding of signs in general use $+ - \times \div =$

Number patterns
Patterns in number squares
Patterns in multiplication tables
Special feature of the 9 times table
Square and triangular numbers
Prime, even, odd and square numbers

Fractions

Informal play
Recognition of: ½ ¼ ⅓ ⅕ ⅛ ¹⁄₁₀
Diagrammatic work e.g.   +   = 1¼
Terminology — numerator, denominator

Money

Recognition of all coins and notes
Shopping, giving change from £1 to £5
Recording amounts, e.g. £1.05, 35p, £0.35, etc.
Calculations and problems involving $+ - \times \div$

Time

Ancient time — candle, water clocks, etc.
Telling the time to nearest hour (12-hour clock), ½ hr, ¼ hr, 5 mins, 1 min

Calendar
Days of the week
Weeks of the year
Months of the year
Years

Date
Written month rhyme
Day date, e.g. 6 September 1976

Abbreviation — 6.9.76
Meaning of AD, BC
Conversion of: secs — mins; mins — hours; hours — days; days — weeks; weeks — months; months — years
24-hour clock system
Calculation of + —

Length

Practical measuring to the nearest metre, centimetre, millimetre
Understanding of abbreviations: mm, cm, m, km
Comparison with imperial measure (inch, foot, yard)

Weight

Practical weighing up to 1 kg, 500g, 200g, 100g, 50g
Understanding of abbreviations: kg, g
Comparison with imperial measure (oz, lb, st, cwt, ton)

Capacity

Practical measuring to the nearest litre, 500 ml, 250 ml, 100 ml, 50 ml
Understanding of abbreviations: 1, ml
Comparison with imperial measure (pint, gallon)

Coordinates

The use of coordinates in maps, etc.
Simple x, y coordinates

Second year

Number

Revision of first-year work
Long division (e.g. $672 \div 15$)
Mental arithmetic problems
Tables — (10×10)
Powers — ideas and notation (e.g. $3^2 = 3 \times 3$) up to 'cubes'; links with units of area (m^2, cm^2, etc.)

Fractions

Revision of first-year work
Comparison of $\frac{1}{4} \leftrightarrow \frac{1}{4}$, $\frac{1}{4} \leftrightarrow \frac{1}{2}$, $\frac{1}{2} \leftrightarrow 1$
Equivalent fractions $\frac{2}{8} = \frac{1}{4}$, $\frac{2}{4} = \frac{4}{4} = 1$, etc.

Mixed numbers, e.g. 1⅔ , etc.
Improper fractions and conversions, e.g. ⁵⁄₃ = 1⅔
Calculations   + and − using equivalent fractions; × by whole numbers, e.g. 4 × 3¼, etc.
Simple cancelling ⁴⁄₈ = ½

Decimals

Please emphasise place value and the significance of noughts:

tth	th	h	t	u	¹⁄₁₀	¹⁄₁₀₀	¹⁄₁₀₀₀
	1	2	3	4	1	2	3

= 1234.123

Equivalence of fractions and decimals:
0.1 = ¹⁄₁₀   0.5 = ½   0.2 = ²⁄₁₀ or ⅕   0.25 = ¼   0.333 = ⅓   0.666 = ⅔
0.75 = ¾

Calculations   + e.g. 12.4 + 6.78
− e.g. 12.4 − 6.78
× by whole numbers up to 10, e.g. 9 × 2.73
÷ by whole numbers up to 10, e.g. 7.35 ÷ 5
Multiplication by 10 and 100

Sets

Meaning of a set
Sets in everyday life
Sorting sets of objects
Intersection −
Union −
'Is a member of' −
'Is a subset of' −
Empty set −
Venn Diagrams −

Length

Practical measuring using body measure, e.g. spans, stride, etc.
Measuring using metric measurements
Understanding of comparisons with imperial system (yd, ft, ins)
Calculations and problems involving + − × ÷
Conversion of: km ↔ m
m ↔ cm
cm ↔ mm
Perimeter of regular and irregular shapes

Weight

Practical weighing of objects
Personal weight
Balancing
Calculations and problems involving + − × ÷
Conversion of metric to imperial (in general), e.g. lb to g, etc.

Area

Calculating area by means of squares and practical measuring
Simple calculations of squares and rectangles using $l \times b$ = Area
Understanding of cm^2, m^2

Third year

Number

Revision of the four rules
Tables (10×10)
Mental arithmetic problems
Everyday-life problems
Simple percentages (%)

Geometry

Introduce the idea of an angle as a rotation or a turn
Points of the compass (eight in all)
Introduce right angles
Degrees
Use of the right angle as an aid to angle estimation
Sets of angles — acute, obtuse
Three-figure bearings e.g. $120°$, $073°$, $270°$ etc.

Instruments
Ability to use a pencil, ruler compass, protractor and set square to produce accurate drawings

Lines
The naming of lines — vertical, horizontal, oblique, perpendicular, parallel

Appendix E

Circle
Recognition of and construction of a circle
Examples in everyday life
Terminology — radius, radii, circumference, diameter, semicircle, etc.

Triangle
Recognition of a triangle and construction using instruments
Types of triangle — right-angled, scalene, isosceles, equilateral
Angle properties (180°)

Solids
Recognition of cuboid, cube, sphere, cylinder, pyramid, cone
Nets of solids leading to construction of easy solids

Shape
Properties and recognition of square, circle, rectangle, quadrilateral
pentagon, hexagon, octagon, parallelogram

Symmetry
Mirror and rotational symmetry

Volume

Concept of volume as a measure of space taken up by the actual
material of the body and capacity as a measure of the space available
within it
Experiments on regular and irregular solids using displacement
Construction of cuboids from unit cubes
Understanding of the term 'cubed'
Practical measuring to the nearest cm^3, m^3
Formal calculations of the volume of a cuboid

Coordinate geometry

Introduce basic terms — axis, origin $(0, 0)$
Plotting sets of points (positive coordinates only)
Coordinates as a set of ordered pairs, e.g. $(3, 4)$
Patterns in ordered pairs, e.g. $(2, 3)$ $(2, 4)$ $(2, 5)$ $(2, 6)$ are all $x = 2$

Fourth year

Number

Revision of four rules
Tables (10×10)
Mental arithmetic problems
Everyday-life problems
Base work — bases other than 10

Algebra

Use of flow charts to develop logical thought
Mastermind
Solution of simple statements using as unknown, e.g. ($2\Box + 3 = 11$)
Basic ideas and the use of letters
Meaning of terms, e.g. $2x$ means 2 times x, etc.
Substitution of whole positive numbers for letters
Solution of simple equations in x, e.g. $3x - 2 = 10$

Directed numbers

Introduce concept through practical work with reference to bank accounts and to the measure of temperature, etc., indicating the need and uses for negative numbers
Number lines as visual aids

Statistics

Simple terminology — survey, data, population, etc.
Collection and tabulation of data
Block graphs
Pie graphs
Practical work, e.g. birthdays, pets, heights, weights, etc.
Mode — most popular value
Median — centrally placed value when arranged in order
Mean — 'usual' average

Surveying

Plans — simple drawing from measurements
Distance and height measuring, using clinometer, trundle wheel, etc.
Use and construction of scale drawings

Appendix E

INDIVIDUAL RECORD SHEET OF PROGRESS IN MATHEMATICS

Number

Number bonds	A	B	C	Comments
10				
15				
20				
25				

Place value

	A	B	C	Comments
Understanding of				
units				
tens and units				
hundreds, tens and units				
thousands, hundreds, tens and units				
function of zero				

Signs

	A	B	C	Comments
Understanding of signs used				
+ add or plus				
− 'take away', subtract, or minus				
× 'times', or multiply				
÷ 'share' or divide				
> greater than				
< less than				
= equal to or 'equals'				

Number

	A	B	C	Comments
Counting objects				
1-9				
10-29				
20-29				
30-39				
40-49				
50-59				
60-100				
100-1000				
In groups of (tables)				
2				

	A	B	C	Comments
3				
4				
5				
6				
7				
8				
9				
10				
11				
12				

Number

	Oral and practical experience	Units (to 9)	Tens and units (to 20)	Tens and units without carrying	Tens and units with carrying	Hundreds, tens and units or Long	Thousands, hundreds, tens and units or Long
+							
×							
÷							
−							

Subtraction

By decomposition

$$
\begin{array}{ccccc}
0 & 1 & 12 & 9 & 99 \\
\cancel{1}0 & \cancel{2}4 & \cancel{1}\cancel{3}7 & \cancel{1}\cancel{0}8 & \cancel{1}\cancel{0}\cancel{0}4 \\
-\ 7 & -\ 9 & -\ 89 & -\ 89 & -\ 768 \\
\hline
3 & 15 & 48 & 19 & 236 \\
\end{array}
$$

	A	B	C	Comments

Number patterns

Patterns in number squares
Patterns in multiplication tables

Special feature of 9 times table	A	B	C	*Comments*
Square numbers				
Triangular numbers				
Magic squares				
Number series: arithmetic				
Number series: geometric				
Prime numbers $- 1, 3, 5, 7, 11$, etc.				
Square numbers $- 2^2 = 4$				

Measure

Weight

Free play				
impromptu measures, e.g. a brick or stone as a standard measure				
Balancing				
Practical weighing up to kilogram				
500 grams				
200 grams				
100 grams				
50 grams				
Use of abbreviation				
kg				
g				
Understanding of other units				
Calculations +				
−				
×				
÷				
Conversion to units				
milligrams ↔ grams;				
grams ↔ kilograms				

Length

Free measurement				
Impromptu measures, e.g. body measure −				
spans				
feet				
arms				
fingers				

Practical measuring to nearest metre	A	B	C	*Comments*

Practical measuring to nearest   metre
                                 centimetre
                                 millimetre
Understanding of other units, e.g. yd, ft, in.
Calculations   +
               —
               ×
               ÷
Conversion of units, e.g.
   kilometres ↔ metres;
   metres   ↔ centimetres;
   centimetres ↔ millimetres.
Understanding of abbreviations
   mm
   cm
   m
   km

Area

Theory of area
Understanding of squares
Impromptu measures
Practical measuring to nearest
   cm²
   m²
Abbreviations for centimetre squared — cm²
                metre squared   — m²
Understanding of other units: ft², sq. in, sq. yd
Calculations   +
               —
               ×
               ÷
Conversion of m² ↔ cm²
             cm² ↔ m²

Volume

Theory of volume
Understanding of 'cubed'
Impromptu measures, e.g. use of sand, water,
blocks

Appendix E

Practical measuring to nearest cm³	A	B	C	Comments
m³				

Understanding of other units e.g. ft³, cubic in.
Abbreviations for centimetre cubed
metre cubed
Calculations   +

      −

      ×

      ÷

Conversion of km³ ↔ m³
          m³   ↔ cm³

Temperature

Theory of temperature
Understanding of units °C
Ability to use a thermometer
Body temperature
Maximum temperature
Minimum temperature
Freezing point

Capacity

Free play with
   (a) wet materials
   (b) dry materials e.g. sand, rice, peas, etc.
Comparison of capacities: tall jar can hold less than square box, etc.
Impromptu measure, e.g. box, tube, cup, etc.
Practical measure to nearest litre
               500 ml
               250 ml
               100 ml
                50 ml
Understanding of other units, e.g. pints, gallons, etc.
Calculations   +

      −

      ×

      ÷

Conversion of units
   millilitres ↔ litres

356

litres ↔ kilolitres	A	B	C	Comments

Understanding of abbreviations
  mg
  g
  kg

Time

Free play with clocks
Informal measuring of time
Ancient time, e.g. candle, water clock, etc.
Telling time to nearest hour (12-hour clock)
              ½ hour
              ¼ hour
              5 min
              1 min

Calendar
Days of the week
Weeks of the year
Months of the year
Years

Date
Written month rhyme
Day date, e.g. 6 September 1975
  abbreviation, e.g. 6.9.75
Meaning of AD and BC
Calculation   +
              —
              X
              ÷
Conversion of units
  seconds ↔ minutes
  minutes ↔ hours
  hours ↔ days
  days ↔ weeks
  weeks ↔ months
  months ↔ years
24-hour clock
Speeds

Money	A	B	C	*Comments*
Free play and oral expression of amounts				
Recognition of ½p				
1p				
2p				
5p				
10p				
50p				
£1				
£5				
Shopping giving change to £1				
£5				
Recording of amounts, e.g. £1.05, 35p, £0.35				
Calculations +				
–				
×				
÷				
Fractions				
Informal play				
Recognition of				
½				
¼				
⅓				
⅔				
¾				
⅕				
⅛				
⅒				
Comparison of				
⅛ → ¼				
¼ → ½				
½ → 1				
Equivalent fractions				
2/8 → ¼				
2/4 → ½				
4/4 → 1				
8/8 → 1				
2/10 → ⅕				

Fractions	A	B	C	Comments

Conversion of fractions, e.g.
$\frac{4}{6} = \frac{2}{3}$
$\frac{1}{2} + \frac{1}{4} = \frac{2}{4} + \frac{1}{4} = \frac{3}{4}$
Calculations: these need only concern eighths,
quarters, halves, thirds, sixths, fifths, tenths
+
−
×
÷

Decimals

Theory of decimals (metric fractions)
$0.1 \quad = \frac{1}{10}$
$0.01 \quad = \frac{1}{100}$
$0.001 = \frac{1}{1000}$
Conversion of fractions to decimals
Equivalence of fractions and decimals, e.g.
$0.01 \quad = \frac{1}{10}$
$0.5 \quad = \frac{1}{2}$
$0.2 \quad = \frac{2}{10}$
$0.25 \quad = \frac{1}{4}$
$0.333 = \frac{1}{3}$
$0.666 = \frac{2}{3}$
$0.125 = \frac{1}{8}$

Graphical work

General

Portraying mathematical situations with diagrams
   (*a*) simple
   (*b*) harder

Block graphs

Graph made by piling up real objects, e.g. deans
blocks, unifix, etc.
Real objects fixed to a chart, e.g. sweet wrappers
Representation of real objects on graph

One square represents one object on graph	A	B	C	*Comments*
One square represents several objects				

Practical work

Birthdays of class
Pets of class
Heights of children in class
Colours of jumpers in class
Brothers and sisters in class

Travel charts

Diagrams of distances and times
Simple journey plotting
Overtaking and crossing paths

Pictograms

Construction and use of pictograms
Advantages and disadvantages

Pie charts

Construction and use of pie charts
Advantages and disadvantages

Tabulation

Construction and use of tables
Advantages and disadvantages

Space and shape

Accurate use of a ruler to draw lines
Accurate use of compasses
Accurate use of protractor

Lines

naming and drawing of lines
   vertical
   horizontal
   perpendicular
   parallel

Circle	A	B	C	*Comments*
Recognition of a circle				
Example of everyday life				
Circumference				
Radius (and properties, e.g. same length all round)				
Diameter				
Relationship between radius and diameter				

Surveying

Plans

Simple drawing from measurements
Harder ground plans

Measuring weight and distance

Use of clinometer
Measuring by sun's shadow
Measurement by scale drawings
Use of trundle wheel

Number base work

Idea of base 10 — our own number system
Grouping at numbers, e.g. into 4, 5, 6, etc.
Decimals in different bases

Further topics

ENGLISH SYLLABUS

General aim

To create a language policy throughout the school, within which a pupil's language may develop productively and receptively.

Appendix E

Objectives

Language may be divided into four areas: reading, writing, speaking and listening. It is within these areas that our objectives and activities will lie.

I Reading

1 They will be able to build words using phonics.
2 They will be able to retain those words which cannot be phonetically built (look-say).
3 They will be able to attain a reading age similar to that of their chronological age.
4 They will be able to write and recite the alphabet.
5 They will be able to comprehend what they read.
6 They will be able to retain what is important in their material.
7 They will be able to read aloud with meaning.
8 They will be able to use alphabetical order in dictionaries and reference books in order to find information.
9 They will be able to classify subjects into categories.
10 They will be able to find a selected category of book in a library by using a number/letter classification system.
11 They will be able to return that book or information material to its place in the classification.
12 They will use reading as a source of pleasure and use both class and school libraries.
13 They will appreciate and become familiar with different forms of the written word in poetry, journalism, etc.

II Writing

1 They will be able to put capital letters to their correct use.
2 They will be able to put full stops to their correct use.
3 They will be able to write in sentences.
4 They will be able to put commas to their correct use.
5 They will be able to write with order using groups of sentences.
6 They will be able to write coherently, that is, with meaning.
7 They will be able to write a story with a beginning, a middle and an end.
8 They will be able to report speech using quotation marks.
9 They will be able to use and recognise a verb.
10 They will be able to use and recognise an adjective.

11 They will be able to use and recognise a noun.
12 They will be able to use and recognise an adverb.
13 They will be able to write a formal letter.
14 They will be able to pair selected opposites.
15 They will be able to pair male and female nouns.
16 Their spelling age will correspond with Schonell.
17 They will know that 'i' comes before 'e' except after 'c'.
18 They will be able to spell selected plurals and singulars; plural —
    add 'es', add 's'; change from 'f' to 'ves'; singular — no change.
19 They will be able to spell words which sound the same but are
    of different spelling.
20 They will be able to spell words which are connected with their
    own environment.
21 They will constantly extend their vocabulary.
22 They will become accurate in their choice of words.
23 They will write imaginatively and attempt to be original in thought
    and expression.
24 They will become aware of audience and their role as a writer.
25 They will be able to record and take notes.

III Speaking

1 They will develop a flow of speech.
2 They can express ideas formally.
3 They can explain and be cross-examined on their ideas.
4 They can function in a group discussion.
5 They respond in oral work.
6 They can convey directions.
7 They can formulate questions.

IV Listening

1 They can concentrate on what is being spoken.
2 They can listen at length.
3 They use it as a source of information.
4 They can retain the information they hear.
5 They use it as an aid in forming coherent speech and verbal expression.
6 They can recognise and become familiar with different language models.

363

Appendix E

GEOGRAPHY SYLLABUS

In drawing up this new syllabus I have tried to get the opinions and views of those who taught it last year – and to modify it, hopefully for the better. The overall skills and concepts which I feel essential to all middle-school geography, I have listed below and have tried to incorporate them in each year's work. The skills and concepts which I feel are essential are as follows.

Essential concepts

1 Values and beliefs
2 Conflicts/consensus
3 Similarity/difference
4 Continuity/change
5 Distribution
6 Region
7 Communication
8 Interdependence
9 Culture
10 Evidence

Essential skills

1 Mapwork/use of atlas/globe
2 Terminology (use of and understanding)
3 Primary and secondary evidence (e.g. photographs, etc.)
4 Empathy
5 Field skills and the collection of material and data

My aim has been to promote interest and curiosity in the subject and to foster in the children an awareness of the world around us and an understanding of the working of human society; to bring out in the children attitudes, concepts, values and skills which will help them in future life, and the enthusiasm to develop these in their later school life.

It is not suggested that we should do all of these concepts and skills in the first year, as one particular part of the topic may lend itself more readily to the development of a particular concept or skill. Therefore it is more likely each concept or skill will be met at some time, in fact, many times during that year.

Year 1   Family, home, school, neighbourhood

The concepts which should be studied in these topics are:

(*a*) similarity/difference;
(*b*) values/beliefs;
(*c*) region;
(*d*) distribution;
(*e*) interdependence.

The skills for year 1 are as follows.

1 The ability to understand plan views: (*a*) articles drawn from above, (*b*) the desk, (*c*) the classroom, (*d*) the school, (*e*) their home, (*f*) route to school.
2 Ability to appreciate direction – compass points.
3 Simple grid references – four-figure references.
4 Ability to recognise other information on maps; put their own key on maps.
5 Be able to draw and annotate a building.
6 Shade correctly, e.g. a map of the area.
7 Be able to record movement of people and vehicles.
8 Introduction to field work.
9 Be able to use (*a*) tape measure, (*b*) other methods of measurement, (*c*) home-made clinometer.
10 Be able to look at photographs and *see*.
11 Be able to write their complete address and know the significance of it.
12 Place their nearest town or city on a map of Great Britain.
13 Be able to record information obtained by various methods: (*a*) graphs, (*b*) pie-charts, (*c*) matrices.
14 Be able to write of what they have done and why they did it.
15 Be able to produce hardware models.
16 Be able to put themselves in others' shoes, e.g. role play.
17 Be able to situate services on a map, e.g. police, fire station, clinic, shops, etc.
18 Know the difference in the seasons.

Content of first-year work

Family
(*a*) Position in family.
(*b*) Size of family.

365

(*c*)   Different roles in family.

(*d*)   What the family do with their time.

(*e*)   Family rules.

(*f*)   Layout of house — who spends most time where.

(*g*)   Families in other lands.

Home

(*a*)   Plan of own room.

(*b*)   Plan of house.

(*c*)   Where it is in the neighbourhood.

(*d*)   Drawing of house.

(*e*)   Materials from which it is made.

(*f*)   Homes in different lands.

(*g*)   Reflection of environment.

(*h*)   Things in house/technical innovations.

School

(*a*)   Plan of classroom.

(*b*)   Whereabouts they sit (grid on class plan).

(*c*)   Position of classroom in school.

(*d*)   Drawing of school.

(*e*)   Materials used in school.

(*f*)   Age of school.

(*g*)   Different departments of school (zones of school).

(*h*)   Routes along corridors — flows of people.

(*i*)   Danger points.

(*j*)   School rules.

(*k*)   Authority/rules (position of staff).

(*l*)   Time in school — lesson, assembly play, lunch.

Neighbourhood

(*a*)   Map of area.

(*b*)   Pick out own house.

(*c*)   Route to school.

(*d*)   Types of houses.

(*e*)   Different materials.

(*f*)   Services in the area — police, shops, buses, etc.

(*g*)   Play areas.

(*h*)   Position of shops — why in such a position.

(*i*)   Why people live in the area.

(*j*) Movement of pedestrian/vehicles in the area.
(*k*) Go and do a local nature trail.

Year 2   Mapwork, public services, local city

The key concepts to be studied in these topics are:

(*a*) continuity/change;
(*b*) distribution;
(*c*) conflict/consensus;
(*d*) similarity/difference;
(*e*) communication;
(*f*) interdependence.

The skills for year 2 are listed below.

1   Go through the skills of year 1. Re-enforce them ready to build on them.
2   Ability to appreciate (*a*) scale/distance on a map, (*b*) true north and magnetic north.
3   Ability to interpret symbols on OS maps. Show all maps have symbols (key). Compare types of maps.
4   Introduce methods of showing height — contours. Opportunity to produce hardware models.
5   Introduction of globe, difference between globe and atlas.
6   Know how to use an atlas.
7   Be able to mark major oceans, mountains and continents on a blank world map.
8   Be able to put on a blank world map the equator, tropics and poles.
9   Be able to use and interpret photographs.
10 Place major cities of Britain on a map of Great Britain.
11 Be able to recognise different areas of a city — industrial area, commercial and residential.
12 Interpret things from old documents/newspapers, etc.
13 Know technical terms of geographical features — valley, bay, peninsula, etc.
14 Ability to relate photographs to land surface.
15 Ability to listen to outside speakers and formulate questions.
16 Ability to find information through observation.
17 Ability to participate in a group.
18 Be able to use a reference book correctly to find information.

Content of second-year work

Mapwork

(*a*) Look at 6″, 2½″ and 1″ maps and metric equivalents.

(*b*) Use of symbols.

(*c*) Scale.

(*d*) Points of the compass.

(*e*) Grid references (four and six figures).

(*f*) To be able to follow a route.

(*g*) Atlas.

(*h*) Globe.

Public services

(*a*) Local government:
    (i)   housing;
    (ii) education;
    (iii) welfare/social services;
    (iv) refuse, etc.

(*b*) Post Office — letters, telegrams, parcels, etc.

(*c*) Fire station.

(*d*) Police station.

(*e*) Health — doctors, nurses, hospitals, clinics, ambulance.

The city

(*a*) Position and size.

(*b*) Growth and development.

(*c*) Major routeways in city.

(*d*) Different areas, neighbourhoods in city.

(*e*) Industry.

(*f*) What sort of industry today.

(*g*) What is the city famous for?

(*h*) Go on the city trail.

(*i*) Compare the city with other major cities of Britain.

Year 3   Water, services, weather

The key concepts to be studied in these topics are:

(*a*) similarity/difference;

(*b*) continuity/change;

(*c*) distribution;

(*d*) region;
(*e*) interdependence;
(*f*) communication;
(*g*) evidence.

The skills for year 3 are listed below.

1 To re-enforce the skills of the previous two years.
2 Ability to recognise and relate features on the land from a map, e.g. valley, spur, etc.
3 Latitude and longitude.
4 Day and night. Effect of sun and moon on earth.
5 Draw cross-sections from maps and also produce hardware models.
6 On a blank map of the county draw the main rivers.
7 On a map be able to relate the following: rainfall, highland, geology of a certain area.
8 Be able to understand a weather map and its symbols.
9 Be able to measure temperature, rainfall and windspeed.
10 Be able to record these graphically.
11 Be able to recognise cloud type and amount.
12 Be able to measure the flow of a river.
13 Be able to 'survey' the beck, measuring depth, width, etc.
14 Be able to collect and label soil samples.
15 Ability to collect and label rock samples.
16 Collection of river bank plants.
17 Be able to use a microscope.
18 Needs for water on plants and seeds. Grow some.
19 Know major cities of the world.
20 Know geographical terms such as erode, deposit, valley, etc.
21 Be able to use official/newspapers about water services, etc.

Content of third-year work

Water
(*a*) Drought.
(*b*) Flood.
(*c*) Pollution.
(*d*) Soil and rock erosion.
(*e*) Deposition and erosion — effect of sea.
(*f*) Drainage, irrigation.
(*g*) Transport (canals and rivers).
(*h*) Water cycle.

(*i*) Water supply and power.
(*j*) Recreation – fishing, living on water.
(*k*) Effect on plant life.
(*l*) River valley.
(*m*) The Beck.

Services (local government)
(*a*) Gas and electricity.
(*b*) Water supply.
(*c*) Post.
(*d*) Police and fire services.
(*e*) Local government – refuse, education, housing, hospitals.

Weather
(*a*) Temperature – measure and graph.
(*b*) Windspeed, direction, Beaufort scale.
(*c*) Humidity and effects.
(*d*) Cloud types and amount.
(*e*) Rainfall – measure and record.
(*f*) Pressure – what makes wind?
(*g*) Differences over world.
(*h*) Anomalies in weather – drought, hurricane, flood.
(*i*) Climate.

Year 4   Agriculture, industry, rocks and maps

The key concepts to be studied in these topics are:

(*a*) values/beliefs;
(*b*) conflict/consensus;
(*c*) similarity/difference;
(*d*) continuity/change;
(*e*) distribution;
(*f*) region;
(*g*) communication;
(*h*) interdependence;
(*i*) culture;
(*j*) evidence.

The skills for year 4 are listed below.

1 Enforce the skills of the previous years.
2 Be able to understand and use maps and produce their own.
3 Be able to relate these maps with other maps, e.g. geology, natural vegetation, population.
4 Collect soil samples and be able to test them.
5 Know the types of soil and their structure.
6 Collect and recognise rock specimens.
7 State rock type (igneous, metamorphic; be able to comment on their permeability).
8 Be able to recognise certain crops, draw them, and know what types of climate they grow in.
9 Be able to understand the problems of other people and countries.
10 Be able to record and display information collected without the help of the teacher.
11 Be able to evaluate evidence and present the evidence orally.
12 Be able to formulate and test hypotheses and generalisations.
13 Be able to compare different types of agriculture and industry with other types.
14 Be able to produce input/output diagrams of their own.
15 Be able to produce their own questionnaire and use it by questioning adults and strangers.
16 Cover all the mapwork of previous three years on 1″, 2½″ and 6″ maps (or metric equivalent).
17 Know the difference between types of maps and what each is used for.
18 Know the structure of the earth and its beginnings.
19 Be able to recognise the best sites for certain industries, given different sets of conditions.
20 Be able to discuss the cost of situating certain types of industry and agriculture in different areas of the world.

Content of fourth-year work

Agriculture
(a) Look at one farm.
(b) Types of farm: mixed, dairy, sheep (hill), beef, arable, etc.
(c) Look at them individually then compare them.
(d) Types of world farming.
(e) Types of climate/vegetation/geology/soil type which effect farming in Britain and the world.
(f) Farming in underdeveloped countries.

(g) Cost of starting and 'keeping up' a modern farm — its equipment, animals, etc.

Industry
(a) Look at one factory.
(b) Inputs/outputs of a single factory.
(c) Industry in different parts of the world: USA, USSR, China.
(d) Industrial areas in Britain: coal, shipbuilding, chemical, steel, wool, oil, car industries.
(e) How these industries built up.
(f) How the industries have decayed.
(g) Industries help struggling countries.
(h) New industries in new towns.
(i) Strikes, unions, etc.
(j) Different ways of working, e.g. compare Russia, China and USA.
(k) Link of industry with geology/soil/natural resources/population.
(l) The cost of siting certain industries and the influence of items in (k).

Maps
(a) Study of symbols, grid reference and scale on the 1″, 2½″ and 6″ maps (or metric equivalent).
(b) Look at tourist maps, AA maps, etc. Find out the differences.
(c) Be able to follow a route.
(d) Give route directions orally.
(e) Look at old maps: (i) how different they are; (ii) how they were drawn.
(f) Make own maps using simple techniques.
(g) Be able to draw cross-sections.
(h) Be able to relate maps to photographs.

Rocks
(a) Know how the earth was formed.
(b) Know differences and how igneous, metamorphic and sedimentary rocks were formed.
(c) Be able to recognise these types of rock.
(d) Build up small rock collection.
(e) Know what the landscape of each rock type looks like — igneous, metamorphic and sedimentary.
(f) Use of these types of rocks.

(*g*) Look at permeability and general erosion forces of these rocks.

(*h*) Look at geological maps.

As I stated in last year's syllabus, the syllabus may need cutting down or building up depending on how it goes over the next year. Therefore I would be grateful for any suggestions or documents on how it could be improved. If anyone needs any help they can come to me for any advice I can give.

HISTORY SYLLABUS

To satisfy pupils' curiosity about people of the past
To provide vicarious experience for studying people of the past.
To develop the pupils' imagination.
To foster an awareness of our cultural heritage.
To develop an awareness of ways in which the past has influenced the present.
To develop analytical skills.
To encourage the development of hobbies and leisure pursuits based upon historical activities.

Objectives and acquisition of skills

First year

Reference skills
The ability to find information from a variety of sources.
The ability to find a reference book and use its index.
The ability to use primary and secondary sources (museum material, books, etc.).

Comprehension skills
The ability to understand simple historical terminology, e.g. king, reign, conquer, invasion, defeat, trade, government.
The ability to order sequences on a time-scale and to use the chronological conventions of historians, e.g. BC, AD, century, decade, the dating of centuries.

Communication skills
The ability to work from an assignment card.

373

The ability to present reports in the form of drawings with notes, of diagrams and charts, of tape-recordings, of role play and drama, of models of a composition and of maps.

Social skills
The ability to work independently.
The ability to work in groups and co-operate in a common venture.

Key concepts
Chronology.
Similarity and difference.

Second year

The objectives and skills of the first year are to be re-enforced and developed. Upon this foundation new skills can be built up.

Comprehension skills
The ability to frame questions to investigate aspects of the past e.g. What happened? Why did it happen? What were the consequences?

Evaluation skills
The ability to appreciate the variety of types of evidence available for historical study.

Social skills
The ability to exercise empathy — to understand and appreciate what it would be like to be someone else, e.g. through role play.

Key concepts
Chronology.
Similarity and difference.
Causes and consequences.

Third year

The skills of the first two years are to be re-enforced and developed. Upon this foundation the following new skills can be built.

Comprehension skills
The ability to *interpret* and to understand a variety of sources, e.g. documents, textbooks, pictures, maps, charts, statistics, visible remains

of the past.

Communicative skills
The ability to communicate findings clearly and accurately through an appropriate medium – oral, visual, written.
The ability to write a story disciplined by evidence.

Evaluation skills
The ability to compare two accounts of the same event and to notice similarities and differences.
The ability to *distinguish* between primary and secondary sources in history.

Key concepts
Continuity and change.
Evidence.

Fourth year

The skills of the other three years are to be re-enforced and developed. The new skills to be added are as follows.

Communication skills
The ability to draw up a plan for the investigation of a topic.
The ability to summarise and express in note form the main points of information collected.

Evaluation skills
The ability to weigh evidence, to detect bias, to distinguish fact from opinion, to appreciate that evidence can be conflicting and sometimes insufficient.
The ability to organise information through concepts or generalisations.

Key concepts
Continuity and change.
Causes and consequences.
Similarity and difference.
Evidence.
Chronology.
By the end of the fourth year the five major key concepts will have been introduced with the aim to show that they are an integral part

of historical study, investigation and explanation.

Personal qualities

Throughout the course of study it is hoped that certain personal qualities will be developed, including an interest in historical studies and an understanding of social attitudes and values.

It is hoped that the pupil will:

show a curiosity concerning the past;

show an inquiring attitude concerning the past;

show an interest in human affairs and people and their values and beliefs;

show an interest in the remains of the past (and their preservation);

practise caution concerning the simple and single explanation of human affairs.

Content

First year

Prehistoric man in Europe

Early hunting/collecting society: weapons; methods of hunting; cave dwelling; animals hunted for food; the use of fire; dress.

The Lake dwellers: fishing culture; early agriculture; hut dwellings; social organisation; beginnings of specialisation; tribal organisation.

Religious mystic beliefs: early art, wall paintings.

Communication: the growth of language; writing.

Homes and houses through the ages

Study of typical Roman villa, Norman castle and manor house, a Tudor mansion, the Victorian house, and the modern dwelling (house, flat, etc.): construction and building materials; furniture; social organisation of the family unit within the home.

The Golden Age of Rome AD

Government: Caesar; the Senate. The army: training; equipment; organisation of fighting units; military successes. The villa, houses and slums. Home and school: home life, dress, education. Clothes and fashion; the Roman bath. Shopping in Rome: the forum; markets; food and banquets. Sports and pastimes: the Colosseum, charioteers and gladiators; the games. Religious beliefs: gods and sacrifices. Trade and conquest: roads to travel; shipping; expansion outwards from

Italy as far as Great Britain.

Second year

First term
Roman Britain
Julius Caesar; Conquest; Claudius, Caractacus, Boadicea, Hadrian's wall.
Settlement: forts, signal stations, camps as nucleii of British towns and cities. Plan of Londinium.
Roads, buildings, baths, temples, aqueducts. Plan of a villa.
Life: food, furniture, dress, shops, pastimes.
Place names.

Saxon England
The English settle in Britain; kingdoms; King Alfred.
Saxon village: hall, farming, food, dress.
Language: place names.

Second term
Norman Britain
William: conquest; 'harrying the North'.
Feudal system: earls, lords, tenants, vassals.
Norman village and manor: villeins, serfs.
Norman castle: training a knight.
Law; monasteries.
Town life: shops, craftsmen, guilds, streets, clothes, plays, homes.

Third term
The City
History and geography of the city.
Planning; buildings.
Industries. Living in the city.
Leisure.

Third year

A scheme has been proposed for the first term only.

First term   Elizabethan England, 1558-1603
Topic: Elizabethan transport and sailors
Week 1   Comparison of settlement pattern 1558 and 1977 (map

377

interpretation). Movement: journey; markets; shops; trading (comprehension, different ways of life, time changes, farming, lack of education, communities). Presentation of reports, drawing, labelling signs.

Week 2   Transport in Elizabethan times: water transport (drawn and written descriptions, knowledge of names, different transport, identifying why water transport was more favoured).

Week 3   The Slave trade (assignment-card work, interpreting maps). Why was it accepted morally? Lack of education and mass media.

Week 4/5 Drake and the Spaniards: use of film strips.
          Food
          Jobs
          (assignment-card work; comprehension, illustration, research and reference skills; atlas work).

Week 10   Exhibition: pictures, artefacts, music, costume, models of the period (observation, recording, working from an assignment card, oral presentation of part of work done).

Week 11   Assignment involving reference skills, knowledge recall, etc.

Fourth year

Land transport through the ages
Early man: walking; use of animals, e.g. the horse. The age of coaching; development of the railway; the motor car. Modern changes in established transport system, e.g. steam and electric train, etc.

Industrial Britain, 1760-1815
Review of industry pre-1760: changes in power; factory system; social changes; moral abuses; increased population; new inventions. Linked changes in agriculture, new techniques in farming; social changes in land holding; profit farming.

Victorian Britain, 1815-1900
Linkage between growing industry and transport changes: the motor car; changes in towns; society; the development of the post; the reformers and child labour (linked to town life); houses and home life; dress, furniture, etc.; education; notable people, e.g. Prince Albert, etc.

Modern world studies
The development of the Commonwealth; colonies.

The defeat of the French and the 'capture' of India; North America; the loss of the USA and the development of Canada.
The discovery of Australia by Cook; settlement and growth; sheep-rearing.
South African interests.

The rise of USA, Russia and China

Independence of the USA from Great Britain; constitution; uniting the nation in the nineteenth century; economic growth of industry and world power.
Russia westernised by Peter the Great; slow growth in the 1880s; agricultural reform; war of ideology, 1900-21, uniting the many peoples; industrial and agricultural growth through planning; life in Russia today.
The development of China; British nineteenth-century interests and trade; the Second World War and the rise of Mao-Tse-Tung and Communist ideology; life in China today.

SCIENCE SCHEME OF WORK

The following is an outline of science work for the four years. It is offered as guidance only, and consists of recurring themes. The approach to a theme and the level of understanding expected varies according to the development of the pupils.

Aims

The subject-matter of science, even in the later years of middle school, is no more important than the attitudes and scientific ways of thinking and working.
1 The most important thing is that pupils should enjoy science and want to do more in the high school. They should appreciate the value of science in their everyday lives.
2 Science should give pupils an opportunity to explore their surroundings in the following ways:

(a) observing;
(b) measuring;
(c) sorting;
(d) looking for patterns;

    (*e*) drawing conclusions appropriate to their development;
    (*f*) attempting to explain what they see;
    (*g*) communicating and recording in words and numbers;
    (*h*) predicting;
    (*i*) planning and conducting experiments.

Even the youngest pupils will be able to use these skills in their own way. The development of these ways of thinking and working are of major importance and the following outline of work is presented, not as an end in itself, but as a vehicle for the pupils to practise and refine these ways of exploring their environment.

3   Pupils in middle schools should have extensive first-hand knowledge and experience of:
    (*a*) many different kinds of materials;
    (*b*) forms of energy;
    (*c*) living things;
    and the following outlines try and suggest a balance of activities in these areas.

It is envisaged that the following activities be explored practically, and therefore they are not directly related to any textbooks; instructions may be given verbally, on the blackboard, on workcards, assignment sheets, etc. The children may record their results verbally, in books, in graphical form, as a poster or any other way that is felt to be appropriate by the teacher. It is hoped that the children will always get a chance to discuss the results and their implications after each piece of practical work.

Testing can be by means of simple objective tests to check factual knowledge and short practical exercises to check skills learnt. Results will be recorded by the science teacher. The most appropriate time for testing would be after each main topic.

Science syllabus

Tables E.1, E.2, E.3 and E.4 show the main themes for each year split up into activities and there is an outline of the possible content of each activity and method of work. Although it is hoped that there will be as much practical work as possible, not every topic can be taught exclusively this way, and it will be up to the individual teacher to decide what the practical/theory balance will be.

Each theme is classed as either essential (E) or important (I). If

TABLE E.1 *Suggested science activities for first-year pupils*

Suggested number of lessons	Topic	Suggested outline of work	Importance	Completed
1	Sound			
	Making sounds	Make as many different sounds as possible	I	
1	Transmitting sounds	Through solids, liquids and gases	I	
1	Loudness and pitch	Different notes produced by different sizes	I	
1	Music	Hearing and making	I	
1	Sound insulation	How can we cut out sound?	I	
(5 weeks)				
	Light and colour			
1	Mirrors and lenses	Handling, using, etc.	I	
1	Coloured light and paint	Comparing, mixing	I	
(2 weeks)				
	Electricity			
1	Lighting bulbs	Simple circuits	I	
1	Conductors and insulators	What can and cannot conduct	I	
(2 weeks)				
	Magnets			
1	Testing materials	Pick up many different items	I	
1	Magnets and each other	Attraction/repulsion, etc.	I	
(2 weeks)				
	Air			
Ongoing	Weather	Record rain, temperature, wind, etc.	I	
1	Wind-driven models	Make and work models	I	
1	Wings/kites: balloons/ parachutes	Making and working	I	
1	What air feels like	Moving air, wind, draughts, etc.	I	
(3 weeks)				
	Water			
1	Straining	Simple filtering	E	
1	Needing water	Animals and plants need water	E	
1	Water play	Pouring, measuring, decanting	E	

381

Suggested number of lessons	Topic	Suggested outline of work	Importance	Completed
1	Drops and flow	Making drops, pouring	E	
1	Other liquids	Compare with water	E	
1	Water surfaces	Simple surface tension	E	
1 (7 weeks)	Seeing through water	Transparency/refraction	E	
	Animals and people			
1	Reproduction in mammals	Animals and young (school pets?)	E	
2 (3 weeks)	Ourselves	Height, weight, skin, hair, growth	E	
1	Senses and measuring	Estimate length, loud, etc.	I	
1 (2 weeks)	Variation	How are people different?	I	
	Plants			
1	Ecology	Simple counting, identification, etc.	I	
1	Seeds 'food' stores	For growth and eating	I	
Ongoing (2 weeks)	Collecting and growing seeds	Collect, plant and grow	I	
	Time			
1	Regular events	Vibration, seasons, clocks	E	
1	24-hour clock	Conversion and use	E	
1 (3 weeks)	Timing things	Using watch, clock, etc	E	
	Materials			
1	Sorting	Simple classification and groups	E	
1	Heaviness	Weight/floating/density	E	
1	Corrosion	Rusting and rotting	E	
1	Materials in water	Floating/sinking/wetting	E	
1 (5 weeks)	Heat conduct	Which material conducts?	E	

possible, every essential theme should be covered and the rest of the time used for important themes of the teacher's choice. A record should be kept of each theme and activity covered.

Year 1

Assuming an approximate number of double periods for the year as 35, each activity can be treated as one double period, although of course the teacher is free to develop each activity in more depth if he wishes. Themes can be taught in any order.

Year 2

Again, I have assumed a 35-period year; there are approximately 20 activities in year 2, so some of these can be developed over two weeks.

TABLE E.2 *Suggested science activities for second-year pupils*

Suggested number of lessons	Topic	Suggested outline of work	Importance	Completed
	Air			
3 (3 weeks)	Effects of air	Wind/pressure/vacuum/ flight	E	
	Water			
3 (3 weeks)	Dissolving	Solution/evaporation/ suspension	E	
	Heating and cooling			
1	Flames	Use of Bunsen burner	E	
1	Temperature	Estimating and measuring	E	
2	Heating	Cooking oil and water	E	
1	Cooling	Simple cooling curves	E	
2	Melting and boiling	Different liquids and solids	E	
2 (9 weeks)	Expansion and contraction	Metal/water; bar, beaker, etc.	E	
1	Thermometer	Making own thermometer	I	
1 (2 weeks)	Keeping warm and dry	Humans and animals	I	
	Plants			
1	Trees	Signs of growth/branches/ rings	E	
1	Leaves	Variation and structure	E	
1	Keys	Leaf and plant identification	E	
1	Vegetable reproduction	Compare seeds/potato/ bulbs	E	
Ongoing (4 weeks)	Observing and recording	Measure and observe first-year plants	E	

383

Suggested number of lessons	Topic	Suggested outline of work	Importance	Completed
	growth			
1	Plant structure	Internal/external	I	
1 (2 weeks)	Plant debris	Rotting/leaf/litter/peat	I	
	Animals			
2	Comparison of vertebrates	Classification on structure/appearance	I	
3 (5 weeks)	Human reproduction Parental care	From biological basis but possibly linked with health education	I	

Year 3

There are approximately 35 activities in year 3, so each will occupy one week (that is two double periods). This will give more time for greater depth of treatment, more recording and discussion and development.

TABLE E.3 *Suggested science activities for third-year pupils*

Suggested number of lessons	Topic	Suggested outline of work	Importance	Completed
	Purifying things			
2	Purifying rock salt	Filtering/evaporating	E	
2	Ink	How can we separate ink?	E	
2	Condensing	Distilled water, ink, etc.	E	
2	Distillation	Efficient condensing experiments	E	
2 (5 weeks)	Chlorophyll	Separate from plant/chromatography	E	
	Air			
2	Gases in air	$O_2/CO_2/N_2$	E	
2	Breathing	Human/animal, physiology, etc.	E	
2	Respiration	Respiration mechanics and rates	E	

Suggested number of lessons	Topic	Suggested outline of work	Importance	Completed
2 (4 weeks)	Plant respiration	Compare with humans, role of CO_2	E	
	Acids and Alkalis			
2	Extracts from plants	Plant juices, lemons, etc.	I	
2	Curing sourness	How can we neutralise acidity?	I	
2	Acids and alkalis	Properties of common acids/alkalis	I	
2 (4 weeks)	Indicators	Use of litmus, methyl red, etc.	I	
	Soil			
2	Soil samples	Home, school, field, wood	I	
2	Soil key	How classify soil? Feel, look, etc.	I	
2	Air in soil	How much, how measure, why?	I	
2	Drainage	How fast, how measure, different soils	I	
2	Particles and floatation	Soil grains, suspension, settling	I	
2 (6 weeks)	Humus and animals	Composition and extraction	I	
	Heating things			
2	Effect of heat	On metals, liquids, gases, etc	E	
2	Mass change	Effect of heat on mass	E	
2	Heating copper sulphate	Boiling, crystallisation	E	
2	Melting ice, boiling water	What temperature? How quick?	E	
2 (5 weeks)	Change of state	Ice, water, steam. Latent heat?	E	
	Electricity			
2	Circuits	Series/parallel	E	
2 (2 weeks)	Conductors and insulators	What does and does not conduct?	E	
	Forces			
2	Effect of forces	Pull/push/gravity/spinning	E	
2	Springs	Stretching/vibration/elasticity	E	

Suggested number of lessons	Topic	Suggested outline of work	Importance	Completed
2	Measuring	Newtonmeter, how to measure?	E	
2	Levers and balances	Levers law/balancing/ weighing	E	
2 (5 weeks)	Friction and lubrication	Effect of friction and how to stop it	E	
	Animals			
2	Soil and water invertebrates	Collect, examine, classify	I	
2	Insects	Structure and life history	I	
2 (3 weeks)	Animal move- ment	Structure in relation to function	I	

Year 4

This year has approximately 30 activities, each taking up about two double periods each week and leaving extra time for development and discussion and also the examinations at the end of the year.

TABLE E.4 *Suggested science activities for fourth-year pupils*

Suggested number of lessons	Topic	Suggested outline of work	Importance	Completed
	Electricity			
2	Measuring currents	Simple circuits and ammeters	E	
2	Batteries	Examining and making batteries	E	
2	Heating effect	Hot wires, bulbs, fires, resistance	E	
2	Magnetic effect	Plot fields round wire	E	
2	Static	Making and measuring, electroscopes	E	
2	Van der Graaf	Use and abuse!	E	
2	Like charges	Magnets and static repulsion	E	
2 (8 weeks)	Static, mag- netic and current links	How all three are related	E	

Suggested number of lessons	Topic	Suggested outline of work	Importance	Completed
	Kinetic theory			
2	Diffusion	Through air and water	E	
2	Conduction	How in relation to kinetic theory	E	
2	Convection		E	
2 (4 weeks)	Radiation		E	
	Air			
2	Pressure	Laboratory experiments on suction, vacuum, etc.	E	
2	Pressures	Effect on weather, wind, etc.	E	
2	Measuring pressure	Use of manometers, anemometers	E	
2 (4 weeks)	Barometers	Use and own construction	E	
	Metals			
2	Extraction	Iron, lead, aluminium, etc.	I	
2	Reactivity	Experiments with Fe, Al, Mg	I	
2	Oxides	Of metals and non-metals/rust	I	
2 (4 weeks)	Displace-ment	Simple experiments on prepared solutions	I	
	Small things			
2	Cells	As units of life, cf. different cells		
2	Microscopes	Structure, function and use	I	
2 (ongoing)	Embryos	Hens' eggs and incubation	I	
2 (4 weeks)	Microbes	Structure, sterile techniques, etc.	I	
	People			
2	Skeleton	Names, structure and function	I	
2	Muscles	Names, structure and function	I	
2 (3 weeks)	Support	Cf. humans with animals	I	
	Environment			
2	Ecology	Simple methods of sampling	I	
2	Urban ecology	Investigating at home and school	I	
2 (3 weeks)	Pollution	How to make and prevent it	I	

This outline of work has been based on a 'Draft outline of a Middle School Science curriculum', prepared by the Science Curriculum Study Group: Middle School Science Working Party. It does not represent the conclusions of the working party, and is presented as an interim document. At the end of the year, comments and constructive criticisms will be welcome as to its success or failure at this school.

RELIGIOUS EDUCATION SYLLABUS

Various definitions of the aim of religious education are subscribed to by different pressure groups and interested parties within and outside education. It is not our job to duplicate or even extend the role played by the church or Sunday School; indeed, which 'church' should we consider working with? If religious education is to be taken seriously by our colleagues in the teaching profession, we ought to have definite educational aims and specific objectives for the teaching of it, otherwise we cannot expect the retention of the subject in the curriculum.

The overall aim of religious education is to enable pupils to reflect upon their experience and upon mankind's quest for and expression of meaning. Part of this is to acquire an understanding of religions and religious ways of living.

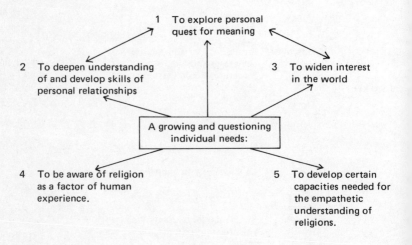

1   To explore personal quest for meaning

2   To deepen understanding of and develop skills of personal relationships

3   To widen interest in the world

A growing and questioning individual needs:

4   To be aware of religion as a factor of human experience.

5   To develop certain capacities needed for the empathetic understanding of religions.

Figure E.1   *Recognition of pupils' needs*

Specific objectives for the teaching of religious education

1 The children will have knowledge of the subject-matter and the facts associated with schemes outlined in the syllabus. (They will certainly be able to recognise the terms and vocabulary employed.)

2 They will identify and understand the reasons for various ideas and beliefs held by people in their quest for meaning.

3 They will be able to recognise and describe the similarities and the differences between various conflicting or agreeing ideas.

4 They will be able to apply knowledge to new situations in their continuing development of self-knowledge and understanding.

5 They will discover that religion is partly concerned with man's questions and they will be able to identify those questions which religion attempts to answer.

6 They will be able to discuss the possibilities of a relationship between man and the Absolute.

7 They will have knowledge of the various ways we can relate to others.

8 They will be able to identify ways of thinking of others, treating others.

9 They will be able to recognise and describe examples of the principles of tolerance, respect of others' beliefs, fair play, and their opposites.

10 They will widen their interest in the world, as the *place* we are given or which we hold.

11 They will accept the idea and existence of the varied and wider society to which we belong.

12 They will develop certain capacities which are needed for the empathetic understanding of religions through the study of symbolic communications, including the development of an interest in symbol and language. (Nos 13-18 are included in these 'certain capacities'.)

13 They will be able to recognise symbolic language.

14 They will be able to recognise the tone of poetic language.

15 They will understand the use of metaphor and analogy.

16 They will be able to identify the true meaning of an allegorical story.

17 They will be able to recognise and describe examples of situations where this method of teaching would be successful.

18 They will be able to think at depth about a subject — exploring connotations, connections, implications and symbolic references

(that is, reading 'between the lines').

19 They will recognise and describe examples of the principle of commitment.
20 They will accept the idea that religious beliefs are worthy of respect and serious consideration.
21 They will be able to recognise and describe the place of religion in people's lives in the neighbourhood and in the larger world.
22 They will have been introduced to the Bible and they will know what it is, and what it consists of.
23 They will experience the awe of a religious mode of thought by participation in worship/celebration of a religious kind.
24 They will want to know more about God and religion.
25 They will want to act in a moral way.

Religious education syllabus

Time allocation

Time will be taken from the Humanities? rather than one period a week I suggest one session a fortnight, for example, from break to lunch.

Books

Exercise books will be provided for the whole school.

Year 1

It is suggested that each theme is studied for a full term.

Courage

Consider examples of the following types of courage.

(*a*) Physical courage: soldiers, sailors, airmen, policemen, firemen, miners (use newspapers, etc).
(*b*) Moral courage: people who speak out against wrong, differ from the majority.
(*c*) Examples in the Bible: Abraham leaving Haran (Gen. 12: 1-9); Gideon and the 300 men (Judg. 7: 108, 16-23); David (1 Sam. 17: 34-50); Nathan (2 Sam. 12: 1-12); Nehemiah (Neh. 2: 11-20); Jesus (Matt. 26: 47-50), (Luke 4: 28-30), (John 2: 13-16); Stephen (Acts 7: 54-60); Paul (Acts 14: 1-7, 19-22; 16: 16-24).
(*d*) Courage through the ages: Patrick in Ireland, Bede of Barrow, Joan of Arc, William Carey in Bengal, William Wilberforce (Slavery), Wilfred Grenfell, Albert Schweitzer.

Life in biblical times
Dwellings: tents in nomadic period; one-room mud huts with earth floors for poor people, lower level for animals, upper level for family. Brick, store houses for rich, with ivory decorations, flat roof, an outside staircase and a parapet; upper room for guests.
Furniture: a low table, meals taken reclining; rush mats on floor for beds; oil lamps for lighting; primitive oven built in wall, using dried grass as fuel; pots or cisterns for storing water.
(Children could make models of above.)
Throughout the first year it is suggested the celebrations associated with the Christian calendar should be studied and the child's knowledge deepened.

Harvest
Different kinds of harvest: land, sea; harvests in other parts of the world, e.g. citrus fruit, cocoa, rubber.
Different ways of celebrating harvest.

Christmas
The story of the birth, the Shepherds, the Magi and Epiphany (Matt. 2: 1-12).

Easter
Different ways of celebrating Easter: the Origin of the Easter egg, egg rolling, hot cross bun. Events between Palm Sunday and Easter.

Whitsun
Birthday of the Church, festival of the Holy Spirit, growth of the Church.

Year 2

Forgiveness
Children are beginning to experience personal relationships; many face problems of argument and broken friendships.

(*a*) People who do not/have not borne a grudge. Discussion of reactions when hurt, insulted or offended; retaliation, revenge, forgetting the incident, forgiving the offender. Discussion of reactions when we have hurt, insulted or offended others: indifference, feeling sorry, showing we are sorry.

(b) Examples from the Bible: Joseph forgives his brothers (Gen. 50: 15-21); David forgives Saul (1 Sam 24: 1-12); Jesus and Zacchaeus (Luke 19: 1-8); Jesus forgives his enemies (Luke 23: 34), Stephen forgives his enemies (Acts 7: 54-60); the teaching of Jesus (Matt. 6: 15, 18, 23-5), (Mark 11: 25), (Luke 15: 11-24).

(c) Other examples: Columba becomes a missionary, Alfred and the treaty with the Danes, John Wesley and crowds which attacked him.

The Bible lands

Palestine occupied a central position in the ancient world. A small country, the size of Yorkshire; use maps: 140 miles north to south, 75 miles east to west, and divide the land into four strips of land running north to south.

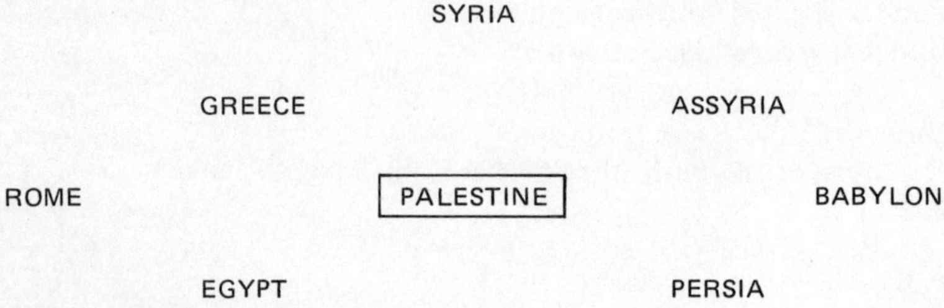

SYRIA

GREECE   ASSYRIA

ROME   PALESTINE   BABYLON

EGYPT   PERSIA

Figure E.2   *Position of Palestine in the ancient world*

1   Mediterranean coastal strip: a straight coastline except for Carmel (Flamborough, the Great Orme or Beachy Head).
2   A high ridge, barren west of Jordan (wilderness, Matt. 4: 1). Jerusalem was on this ridge; Jerusalem-Jericho descent 3,000 ft (height of Snowdon) 20 miles of winding road.
3   Jordan valley: the deepest rift on earth's surface. River Jordan rises near Caesarea Philipp (from underground like River Aire at Malham Cove); Sea of Galilee (harp-shaped, 12 miles long, 8 miles wide); Dead Sea, ¼ mile below sea level.
4   High ridge: barren, east of Jordan. Difference in height: Mt Hermon 9,000 ft above sea level and Sodom 1,200 ft below sea level. Considerable variation in temperature, rainfall and scenery. (Hermon snow-covered, Negev desert, barren slopes above Jericho, dense jungle Jordan valley, wild flowers in Galilee).

Boyhood of Jesus against this background.

The Bible
A closer look at the Bible to discover the different kinds of material it contains.

Myth, e.g. Gen. 1: 1-23; other Creation stories.

Saga, e.g. Judg. 16: 4-21.

Allegory, e.g. 1 Sam 5: 1-7 (every detail has a hidden meaning).

Parable, e.g. Luke 10: 30-7.

History, e.g. Acts 27: 1-44.

Poetry, Proverbs 31: 10-31.

Letters, e.g., Philemon.

Year 3

The spread of Christianity
Christian martyrs: Stephen (Act 6: 8-15; 7: 54-83); Saul the persecutor (Acts 9); opposition and persecution Paul faced after conversion from Jews (Acts 9: 23-5; 17, 1-9); from Gentiles (Acts 16: 19-40).

Paul's journeys: Rome, imprisonment (Acts 27: 1, 28-31).

Missionaries	Paul and Barnabas (Acts 13: 1, 14, 28);
	Paul and Silas (Acts 15: 36-41);
	Paul in Asia Minor (Acts 14: 1-28);
	Paul in Europe (Acts 16: 5-40; 17: 1-34);
	Paul in Rome (Acts 28: 16-31).

Growth of the Church — in Roman Empire, Constantine.

Church grows in England
Pope Gregory, Aidan of Lindisfarne, monks and friars, monastic life, Wesley and Methodists; British missionaries: Carey (India); Livingstone (Africa); Fleming (Arctic); Grenfell (Labrador); Gladys Aylward (China).

Social reformers — people with a purpose:
Elizabeth Fry (prisons); Lord Shaftesbury (child labour); Florence Nightingale and Edith Cavell (nurses); Father Damien (lepers); Dr Barnardo (poverty); Wilberforce, Granville, Sharp, Abraham Lincoln (slavery).

393

Year 4

Worship: What do we mean?
Early religion — tops of hills (high places); idolatry (e.g. 1 Kings 11: 7f; 21:3) condemned in Israel (e.g. Num. 33: 52; Deut. 12.2).
Stone pillars and wooden poles — destroyed because idolatrous worship.
Altar (mounds of earth Ex. 20:24) piles of stones (Deut. 27:5).
Natural rocks (Judg. 6:20) places of sacrifice.
The burnt offering (Lev. 22: 17-20) (homage).
The peace offering (Lev. 3: 1-17) (surrender).
The sin offering (Lev. 4: 1-5, 13) (gratitude).
The guilt offering (Lev. 5: 14, 6: 7) (sorrow).

Biblical Judaism
Jewish festivals: Passover unleavened bread, ass with Exodus; Feast of Weeks; Feast of Ingathering, Booths or Tabernacles; The Day of Atonement.

Sacred buildings
Types of worship past and present
Temples: plan of a temple
Synagogues: after Exile (plan)

The Law — first five books of the Old Testament.
Other religions: basic beliefs, worship, rituals, holy books.
Judaism
Muslim way of Life, Islam
Immigrants to Britain, and their religions

Christian worship and Christianity today
Baptism, Communion, Sunday, Churches — types.

World development and the Third World
Hunger a problem in the Third World: Important to distinguish between emergency steps to realise hunger and the campaign to conquer hunger by economic development and international understanding.
Discuss example and teaching of Jesus (Matt. 25: 31-46).
Work of Church here/overseas in practical caring through education, agriculture and hospitals.
Investigate work of Christian Aid.

Projects on topics: Responsibility for others; caring for hungry and homeless.
Information from: Freedom from Hunger Campaign,
69 Victoria Street, London SW1.

Christian Aid,
10 Eaton Gate, London SW1.

This syllabus is a basic outline for religious education throughout the school. If there are any problems, please ask.

Book lists

There are sets of books in the cupboard outside the smallest classroom in the lower school (Room L 14). These books were not ordered by me, but can be used for parts of the syllabus. It may be a better idea to use these for inspiration, for ideas from which to make duplicates worksheets.
The School Study Bible Books 1-4: sets of each
Religions of the World (in the *SSB* series)
Patchett: *New Testament History* (Life of Christ) (Spread of Christianity)
             Old Testament History: sets of each
The Westminster Smaller Bible Atlas can be used in conjunction with ordinary atlases.
Goldman   *Symbols* 1-4
           What is the Bible? 2 and 3, plus notes for teachers
           About Myself 2, 3, 4 and 5
The Christian Adventure Series: *King for Ever*
                                Heralds of Jesus
                                Knights of Jesus: Sets of each
Bull: *A Book of Bible Activities* (some of them useful)

New books, highly recommended:

Sets of the *Good News Bible*, *Mark's Gospel*
The Lion Handbook to the Bible
The Children's Bible (my own copy but it may be borrowed)

The Adviser for this subject has made it known to me that he considers the use of duplicated worksheets to be superior to that of old textbooks. I can supply anyone with details of what I have done with classes in any year. (I am teaching religious education to at least one class in each year, so doubtless there will be some duplicated sheets there.) Please let me have one copy of any worksheet you make, for my next year's plans.

PHYSICAL EDUCATION SYLLABUS

Aims

1   To provide a meaningful progression to all games skills.
2   To provide situations in which each child will discover the satisfaction of success in movement through practical challenges and problems.
3   For each child to develop his/her full potential and to success.
4   To develop gamesmanship and social awareness, e.g. sharing, helping and co-operating with others.
5   To provide a variety of apparatus, e.g. different sized bats, balls and types of equipment for the child to explore and experience.
6   To provide maximum activity and participation.

Time allocation

One double lesson per class for four years.
First years have swimming as an addition.

Notes:

Whenever possible children are expected to shower at the end of the lesson.
Children should be encouraged to bring full kit for the lesson.
Staff will only accept responsibility for watches and money, which should be locked away at the beginning of the lesson.
Games and physical education is part of the school curriculum and unless covered by a note from home every child is expected to participate.
A foot check for verrucas and athlete's foot should be carried out at the beginning of every term.
No child must use gymnastics apparatus unless a member of staff is present.

Year 1

Within the first year each child must be given the opportunity to experience a variety of implements and apparatus within 'small games' situations.

First term

Large-ball skills — throwing, catching, striking with implements and different parts of the body.

Teaching points
1 Watch the ball; be alert at all times.
2 Opposite hand/foot when throwing. Encourage children to try with both hands and feet.
3 Sideways stance when striking.
4 Mobility.
5 Use of space.
6 Possession.
7 Aiming for objects stationary and moving.
8 Contact and non-contact.

See below (p. 402) for ideas of small games. Do not be afraid to adapt to situations and adapt and improvise where necessary.

Second term

It is anticipated that the weather during this term will be more inclement. Therefore, it is suggested that physical education is done.

Themes concerned with travelling
Moving, stopping, starting.
Variety in speed.
Jumping, landing, recovery.
Travelling on different parts of the body using change of speed, direction and level.

Use of simple apparatus
1 How to get apparatus out.
2 Where it belongs.
3 How to put apparatus away quickly, quietly, neatly.

Each child should be able to produce a simple gymnastics sequence.

Third term

Small-ball skills and games (see first term).

Athletics

1 Running: competitive against self, others and clock.
2 Jumping: standing, long jumps, competitive, self-measurement, how to measure.
3 Relay running, team work, baton passing.
4 Throwing: rounders and cricket ball.

Year 2

It is hoped that during the second year the children will become more proficient in the basic skills and will feel at ease working alone and in group situations.

First term

Dance
Themes concerned with dance:

1 body awareness;
2 space;
3 resistance;
4 flow.

Children should experience work alone and with partners.
A variety of stimuli may be used, e.g. Literature, art, sculpture, music, percussion. (See 'Additional ideas for dance', pp. 407-9)
Throughout this term in fine weather games skills should be continued outside, e.g. types of throwing – shoulder, chest, overarm passes, etc.

Second term

Gymnastics
Themes concerned with gymnastics:

1 weight transference;
2 control of body weight;
3 flight, recovery;
4 bending, stretching, twisting, turning.

Begin with floor work and move on to small, then large apparatus. Simple sequence work.

Third term

Athletics

Long jump, high jump, running, throwing.

NB Could make use of 'five-star award scheme'.

Also small-ball skills in different small-game situations (see p. 402).

Making use of throwing, catching, striking.

Emphasise team work and fielding techniques.

Year 3

Games at this stage will be single sex. Through a gradual progression it is hoped to introduce children to larger games situations and teach rules of set games. In third year children should have the chance to improve their own personal standard in dance and gymnastics. It is hoped that some set movements will be taught in gymnastics.

First term

'Netball' and 'basketball' type games. Emphasise

1 space;
2 non-contact;
3 differences between games;
4 rules of game.

Second term

Dance

More adventurous dance should be undertaken, e.g. small to large groups. Stories re-enacted in dance to include:

1 movement shapes;
2 use of space;
3 use of different parts of body.

Gymnastics

1 Flight.
2 Balance.
3 Partner work.
4 Group work.

Development of the above together with bending, stretching and twisting, that is composite movement.

399

Appendix E

Development of sequence work.
Development of group work.
Development of large-apparatus work.
Children should be given directions on set movements, e.g. rolls
(forward/backward); handstands; cartwheels, vaulting, etc.

Third term

Continue with small-ball skills leading to introduction of larger game.
Danish rounders, circular rounders, leading up to rounders: rules of the
game.

Year 4

Within the year children should be given the opportunity to experience
a variety of larger game situations, e.g. netball, basketball, volleyball,
badminton. Continue to teach basic skills at the beginning of each
lesson, but move towards the major game.

First term

Netball and basketball.

Second term

Gymnastics
Development of sequence work on and off apparatus. Themes:

1 meeting and parting;
2 symmetry;
3 asymmetry;
4 simultaneous and successive movement.

Indoor games
Volleyball and badminton. The different basic skills of these games
should be taught, together with simple rules, leading on to the more
complex rules of the full game.

Third term

The continuation of rounders and athletics.

This syllabus is a guide to all those teaching games or physical education
in the first two years of the school and for the girls games or physical

education in third and fourth years. If there are any problems or questions arising from the syllabus I will be pleased to discuss them with other members of staff.

Tag games

Free-tag: one chaser/players touched sit down.
All-in tag: one chaser/players touched collect braid and chase.
Release tag: two chasers/one releaser.
Couple tag: one couple/players caught join on four and split into two couples.
Tail tag: one chaser catching tails.
Team tag: one team/one minute sit down when touched.
Chain tag: one chaser/players touched join chain.

Races

'All-in'

Running, crawling; hopping; kangaroo jumps; skipping; crow-hops.

In pairs

No. 1 runs then no. 2; wheelbarrows; piggy back; horse and jockey.

'All-in' with apparatus

Bouncing; dribbling; run, bounce, throw.

Circle 2's (horse and jockeys)

Scoring runs; running tunnel ball; captain passing; clock relay; baton relay; shuttle or exchange; (+ non-stop).

Relays

In file

Over the backs; through the legs; in and out of the files; over the legs; fetch and carry; tunnel ball; passing over the head; passing over and under; shuttle relay.

401

Ball games

Team passing

One large ball. Count number of consecutive passes.
Start with 'jump ball', no tackling, no running with ball, no rough play.
Possession gained by intercepting.

Post ball

A target (skittle, jumping stand, post, etc.) is set up in a small circle
approximately 5' radius at each end of the court. One player guards
the target from outside the circle. The remaining players mark each
other and the object of the game is to hit the opponent's target. Ball
thrown out by guard after score.

Bucket ball

One player, holding a waste-paper basket, stands in circle at each end of
the court. Start with 'jump ball'. No tackling, no running with ball, no
rough play. Possession gained by intercepting. Score by throwing ball
into basket.

Ring the stick

One player holding a stick or relay baton, *vertically*, stands in a circle
or on a chair at each end of the court. Method of play as for team
passing. Players throw quoit over stick to score.

Corner ball

Two 'scouts' of each team standing in corners at opposite ends of court.
Players closely mark each other and try to get ball to their own 'scouts'
for a point.

Free dodgeball

One large soft ball. Anyone may throw the ball to hit another player
below the knees. Players who have been hit put on a braid and become
chasers. When a catch is made the thrower is out.

Circle dodgeball

Five or six players form a large circle with one player in the centre.
Players aim to hit the player in the centre below the knees. Player
who scores a hit then takes the place of the centre player.

Four-court dodgeball

Court divided into four equal parts. Teams occupy two central courts and throw ball(s) to hit opponents below the knee. When hit, players retire to court behind 'enemy line' and continue to attack from the rear. Winning team is the one which completely eliminates opponents from central court.

Three-court dodgeball

Three equal teams. The object of the game is for the teams in the two end courts to hit players in the middle court with the ball. A point is scored for every hit below the knee, each team occupying the middle court for a specified time. More than one ball may be used.

Rugby dodgeball

Two equal teams. One rugby ball. Team A have possession and attempt to touch players of the team B with the ball. Count touches in a given period of time, then give possession to other team. No running with the ball.

Circle skittleball

As for circle dodgeball. Centre player guards skittle.

Skittleball

Skittle placed in circle at either end of court. No players allowed in circle. Object of game to knock down opponent's skittle. Variations:
 (a) Players may not move with ball.
 (b) Players may bounce the ball — Basketball skittleball.
 (c) Ball played with feet only — Soccer skittleball.

Rugby touch

The object of the game is to score a try by carrying the ball and placing it over the opponent's goal line without being touched by a defender. When in possession of the ball a player should run with it and try to make as much ground as possible but should be encouraged to pass the ball before being touched. A player *must* pass as soon as he is touched *or* must put the ball on the ground. Kicking is not allowed. Game started and restarted by a pass at the centre. Forward passes not allowed.

Newcombe

Rope or net stretched height. Large ball thrown back and forth over net, the object being to get the ball on the ground in opponent's court. Game started by underarm throw from baseline directly over net. No running with ball allowed. Up to three passes can be made between members of same team. Only serving side may score.

Deck tennis

Low net, court markings. Quoit thrown back and forth over net until one side fails to return it. Rules and scoring as for tennis.

Moving target

Teams take up position around a square, each player equipped with a tennis ball. A football is placed in the centre of the square as a target. At a signal each team attempts to drive the football over the opponent's line by hitting it with the tennis balls.

Longball

Rectangular pitch. Ball is hit by bat or hand. Batsman scores by reaching far end of pitch and returning without being hit by ball. Batsman may rest at far end of pitch. Fielders not allowed to run with ball.
Variation: Team longball – Whole team run and return without stopping.

Stoolball

1 foot square target on posts 12-14 yards apart. Two batsmen; bowler at midpoint between posts bowls underarm. Batsmen out caught, bowled, run out. Each player bowls in turn.

Circular rounders

Batsmen must run on good ball and must attempt to complete a rounder before fielding side have thrown ball around all the bases, i.e. running v. throwing and catching.

Danish rounders

Soft ball, hit with hand. Batsman/men out if between bases when ball is returned to bowler. Any number of batsmen may occupy any base. A non-stop rounder scores two points and may bring back an 'out' player.

Soccer rounders/Netball rounders

'Batting' side kick, head or throw ball (according to game) and then dribble or bounce another ball around the bases while fielders try to get the ball round the bases as in circular rounders.

French cricket

Soft ball, cricket bat. Players form large circle around batsman who has to prevent his legs being hit by ball. Batsman must not move his feet. Runs scored by passing bat around body.

Class activity lesson

1 *Introductory activity*: dodge and mark or tag game.
2 *Small ball each*: free practice, competition.
3 *In pairs* with two balls: throwing, catching, bounce pass.
4 One ball away, still in pairs: aiming and fielding. No. 1 throws no. 2 collects.
5 Into fours: small balls away, one large ball per four – 2 v. 2.
6 Four games 4 v. 4 team passing.
7 Four games post ball *or* 1 game post ball; 1 game netball posts; 1 game skittles; 1 game buckets/benches.
8 Run and bounce relay: 8 × 4.

Mixed activity lesson

1 Introductory activity: 'all in race' tag game.
2 Individual free practice: free choice of apparatus or specified apparatus.
3 Partners work: free choice of apparatus or specified apparatus.
4 Group activities:

A	B
(*a*) Low net, playbats, shuttles, tennis balls.	(*a*) 'Keep it up'. Padder tennis.
(*b*) Netball ring, three balls – shooting practice	(*b*) Netball 3 v. 3. defence v. attack.
(*c*) 6 hockey/shinty sticks, 6 balls, at wall. Pushing, hitting, stopping.	(*c*) Hockey 3 v. 3.
(*d*) 1 ball, circle.	(*d*) Circle dodgeball.

	Throw and catch.		Circle skittleball.
(*e*)	3 footballs, skittles: dribbling, bouncing. Aiming.	(*e*)	Skittle football 3 v. 3.
(*f*)	Jumping stands, ropes, quoits, or balls. Throw and catch.	(*f*)	Deck tennis. Newcombe. Throwing tennis. Volleyball.
(*g*)	2 rounders/cricket balls 2 rounders/cricket bats Bowl, bat, field.	(*g*)	Non-stop cricket. Circular cricket.

5 Relay race.

Note

Only modest amount of equipment required, group activities *A* are simple technique practices which may lead to *B* small sided games.

Additional ideas for gym lessons

Specimen lessons

Main theme: awareness of weight transference.
Sub-themes: space/direction, speed, levels.

Introduction
1 Run around hall.
2 Weave in and out. No touching. Pay attention to:
   (*a*) space;
   (*b*) speed;
   (*c*) levels.
3 As above, but make different body parts important:
   (*a*) elbows;
   (*b*) knees;
   (*c*) hands.

Main experience
1 Travel about on parts of body not legs.
2 What is body doing? Sliding? Rolling?
3 Travel in two very different ways.
4 Repeat but get off ground.

Apparatus
1 Different ways of travelling using all apparatus.
2 Choose words which apply to your apparatus — under, over, along, through, across, on to, off, etc.
3 Combine any two as you travel.
4 Produce short sequence using three ways of travelling.

Other themes and sub-themes

Twisting
Pathways, parts that can support weight, arts that can start movement.

Flight
Turning, pathways and direction, shape, acceleration/deceleration, tension.

Balance
Stillness, parts that can support weight, parts that start movement.

Transference of weight and balance
Shape and pathways.

Curling and stretching
Body shapes, parts of body, levels.

Twisting and turning
Fixed parts.

Additional ideas for dance

As well as all suggestions given any stimulus can be used; topical events — Bonfire night 'be fireworks', etc., winter, stories, poems.
Interpretations. Sounds used for movements, words, percussion, body sounds — clicking, snapping, music, simple rhythms. All can be used with action phrases — words suggest movement, e.g. stamp, patter, twine, then balance with feet on floor.

1 Whole sequence done same time as partner.
2 Whole sequence done by one and then the other.
3 Whole sequence started near to or far from partner, facing, etc.
4 Sequence started by one, carried on by the other.

Action phrases can lead to partner and group work

Method
Breakdown of phrase.

1 Practise each word or part in isolation, then put together bit by bit. Encourage clarity and quality of movement.
2 Try sequence out and practise it as a whole several times.
3 May want to do partner work . . . will they do it simultaneously part for part or each do whole, what pathway will they take, where do they start and finish?
4 When making up own action phrases ensure that they have 'movement logic', not too many similar words and a balance between stillness and vigorous movement. It may help to make up a story about the phrase.

Poems

Words, interpretation of words, extract action words. Select poems that contain action or have a story, e.g. 'Pied Piper' 'Dulce et decorum est' 'The Hypercrump'.

Stories

Select characters with typical movements, e.g. old woman/man, young person, policeman's walk, 'Farmer Giles', etc. Village market scene. Mime situations (more advanced).

Rhythm

Simple metric rhythm shifting accent:

①	2	3	4
1	②	3	4
1	2	③	4
1	2	3	④
①	2	3	4

When making up rhythms, passing rhythm round group (one more in group than parts in rhythm). Get rhythm on the move, stepping to certain rhythms: (*a*) step patterns; (*b*) body parts – clicking, clapping, slapping.

Improvisations

Small groups, four or five, e.g. point and move – can be done slowly, leisurely or sharp and defined.

Group work

Many themes can be used here, several already mentioned — poems, stories, etc.

Seasons

Winter — rolling snowballs, walking through the snow; summer — long movements; autumn — bonfire night, leaves falling, etc.

Ordinary movements

Walking — through snow, on ice, through water, sand, kicking leaves/tin can; show difference. Running doing same things.

Music

Vast possibilities: themes from films, westerns, e.g. *2001* — rising and falling movements.

Others

Jungle scene — walking through jungle, animals, trees, etc.

Additional ideas for games

Games

Try to engineer small games situations and practices, build up from these. Use as basis for skill-training rather than other way round. Use changed games, adapt rules to suit situation, number of children, space available, etc. e.g. benchball, useful introduction to basketball and netball. Build up rules to suit whichever game is being played.

Volleyball

Have unlimited touches on each side; it may also be necessary to allow one bounce on floor — break down into small situations.

Cricket/rounders

Smaller side situations; everybody bats and bowls. Limit overs in cricket. Always try to balance small situations against children's needs and demand for a 'proper game'. Extract skills from games situations, rather than use isolated skill practice to try build up game (applies to games lessons rather than team practices).

Appendix E

Suggested suitable main games

Netball, football, cricket, rounders, rugby, basketball, volleyball, hockey (small groups), badminton (small groups), table tennis (small groups).

Others

Murder ball, pirates, continuous cricket, chair cricket, various team and obstacle games, chasing games, dodging games, bench ball.

THE ADJUSTMENT UNIT

Aim

To improve the behaviour, manner, attitudes and self-confidence of maladjusted and deviant children so that they may be able to resume working in a normal classroom. To encourage truants and school refusals to attend school more readily.

Method

Children spend one or two sessions per week in the unit, in extreme cases individuals may stay full time for a period, or be sent in more frequently. Family grouping is used, that is children from all the years are in together to prevent comparisons amongst year-groups and to encourage the older members to help the younger ones. As every child needs individual attention I prefer to keep the numbers below six, but recently, due to major behavioural problems, it has reached ten on occasions and I have taken up to twelve out on a trip.

The children can choose any activity they wish, but the choice is directed by me and more structured than it appears. A reasonable standard is required, as I do not see the value of praising something that does not deserve it, and yet the children are in need of encouragement. This is why much of the work centres around my interests, baking, sewing and art. I aim to correct their misuse of materials and improve manual dexterity.

They are not taught academic subjects directly unless they request it, but mathematics occurs in a practical manner when measuring ingredients and working out the cost of articles made. Reading is encouraged by having 'wordy' notices on the walls and cards with instructions for baking and craft.

410

The second room has been named the quiet room and this can be used when a child wishes to read the books on display or work on his own at drawing.

To improve the child's self-confidence I like to have a sample of something every child has done on display.

Discussions are very important and they know that they can talk about any topic. I like them to pass opinions then we can discuss my ideas as well. A long-term hope from these miniature debates is that they may see the other person's point of view and not be so ready to steal or inflict pain on smaller children.

Activities

These are just some. Painting, sketching, modelling, baking, sewing, making soft toys, reading, construction sets, lego, mosaic patterns, draughts, mime (they usually choose beating old men or prison break-outs), gymnastics, football and trips to any place of interest, usually out of doors.

Entry to unit

By recommendation from any of the following:
1   educational psychologist;
2   medical officer;
3   headteacher;
4   any member of staff.
Before the child is brought in, I check with the year leader and class teacher and if necessary a Bristol Social Adjustment Guide is done by the class teacher.

Members of the unit

1   Since September 1976 thirty-three children have made use of the unit, at the present moment there are thirty. One has left the district, one is in an ESN school and the most recent departure was taken 'into care'.
2   Seven children are in the fourth year; fourteen children are in the third year; five children are in the second year; and four children are in the first year.
   Maladjusted and deviant behaviour seems to make itself more

apparent in the older year-bands, this may be because there is less movement between classes in the first year.

3   Of the eighteen who have had a Bristol Social Adjustment Guide, ten have been classed as maladjusted or severely maladjusted.

4   Twenty-two children have been seen by the educational psychologist, but some only because of academic problems.

5   Of the remainder, at least three present problems needing the psychologist's assessment, but no more can be taken on at the moment unless the child's case is extreme.

6   There are three genuine school refusals, children who would refuse to attend school without the refuge of the unit.

7   Fifteen children are either persistent truants or truant at widely spaced irregular intervals, possibly when home problems get too much.

8   One child who has just joined us is severely disturbed and refuses to co-operate at all in the normal class.

9   Twenty-two children are violent and easily provoked.

10 Two are withdrawn, one probably due to a neurotic mother.

11 It is impossible to state how many would thieve, but it is certainly over twenty.

12 At least four have appeared in court on charges of breaking and entering; the educational welfare officer can name fourteen who come from families who have had dealings with the law, he feels that this is a conservative estimate.

13 At least four have spent a long period in hospital.
    At least six have an eye defect.
    At least four have a hearing defect.
    At least four have nocturnal enuresis.
    At least three have a speech impediment.

14 The average family size for children in the unit is six and a half.
    The smallest family consists of three children, the largest fifteen.

15 As liaison teacher, I have visited thirty homes, and of those twenty-one have children in the unit. Of these about five were well cared for, the owners taking a pride in them, a further five could be classed as adequate, i.e. having sufficient furniture for the size of family and a reasonable standard of hygiene. Many of the others were hopelessly inadequate, windows and furniture broken, surroundings dirty and wallpaper torn, no carpets, small table, and no room for every member of the family to be present together in the same room; windows boarded up or stuffed with paper and in one

instance toadstool-like fungus hanging from the kitchen ceiling.
In most cases the lounge is turned into a fourth bedroom and
the family live in the dining-room.

GUIDELINES FOR ASSESSMENT

1   The course *must* dictate the assessment, not the converse.
2   All course objectives should be assessed. These include: skills,
    knowledge and attitudes.
3   As much assessment as possible should be entrusted to those who
    teach the course.
4   Assessments should be used as a means of motivating pupils, by
    encouraging them to exhibit their particular strengths.
5   Assessment must act as a feedback to both pupils and teachers.

Types of assessment

1   Assessment will be mainly continual internal assessment of day-to-
    day progress in written, oral and practical work by the class teacher.
2   Objective tests which are either nationally verified or school based
    may also be used.

| Internal (continuous) | Tests, Classwork, Homework, Projects, Experiments | Oral, Practical skills, Attitudes, Interests, Effort | Feedback to:— Teachers, Parents, High school |

Figure E.3   *Types of assessment*

Continuous internal assessment

1   Day-to-day progress   oral techniques (the teacher as listener);
                          written techniques (short-answer tests, long-
                          answer tests, quiz tests, written exercises —
                          descriptive, numerical, comprehension,
                          interpretation, open-ended tasks, creative
                          tasks);
                          skill mastery (checklists, e.g. use of apparatus);

		homework (written assignments, reading, revision).
2	Broader aspects — (teachers' notes)	effort (conscientiousness, concentration, tenacity); attitudes and interest; problem-solving skills.
3	Marking and grading	regular marking (good routine); impression marking (good presentation); always give oral and written comments (encouragement); pupil marked work.
4	Records	should be kept in the department and in the school.

```
                        Assessment in subject
                                 |
                            Subject tutor
                          /              \
        Departmental records              Pupil's form teacher
          /            \                          |
  Pupil's needs   Course evaluation          School records
```

Figure E.4

Note.
Use of the five-point scale when grading.

Attainment		*Effort*	
1	Very good	A	Outstanding effort
2	Above average	B	Good effort
3	Average	C	Satisfactory effort
4	Below average	D	Less than satisfactory
5	Weak	E	Not trying

Presentation and marking of children's work

All work should have a margin, except for mathematics (in pencil).
Previous work should be ruled off: right across the page.
Date at the top left-hand side (not in margin).
Headings and date underlined with a ruler and the next line left clear.
Rule off each piece of work on the next line — with ruler.

All writing should be done in ink (blue or black).
All drawings should be done in pencil — label in ink (underline) and put date and headings on every drawing.
Ensure children know correct place for starting paragraphs.
Mark and correct punctuation where necessary.
Spellings: correct (if necessary) by letter S through word and correct example at end of passage — underline any specific words to be copied at back of book.

General notes

Children may margin all of book when new.
Writing must be clear and legible (please discourage printing except in very poor cases).
Children correct own mistakes by crossing out words with one horizontal line.
Number of sums should be circled.

Reports on pupils

Besides the usual report to parents on the child's attainment in each subject, the class teacher grades each pupil on a five-point scale for each of the eighteen qualities listed below.

Motivation   How keen he/she is to do well

Concentrates: Able to work for a length of time without interruption.
Persistent: Able to meet and work at, new or unfamiliar or difficult work.
Enthusiastic: Shows keen interest in what he/she does.
Inquisitive: Wants to find out, know or understand.
Thinks ahead: Able to find out what is required before starting work.

Personality

Patient: Able to wait for materials or success without getting agitated.
Dependable: Able to carry out instructions well.
Independent: Able to work alone; not easily distracted by others.
Shows initiative: Able to overcome problems or tackle unfamiliar situations.

Social How well he/she gets on with adults/children.

Communicates: Able to talk and mix with other children and adults.

Participates: Willing to join in, in classroom and playground.

Co-operates: Shows willingness to be flexible in working or playing with others.

Shows tolerance: Able to endure discomfort, e.g. when disciplined or when he/she realises work is incorrect.

Shows unselfishness: Willing to share equipment, skill and understanding.

Shows respect: For children, adults and property.

SIMPLE STATISTICS

It would be wrong to draw oversimplified conclusions from any one or all of the following statistics, without examining the context in which they occur. Nevertheless taken together and viewed in the light of the local circumstances of the school, they provide useful factual information which may be borne in mind when answers are sought to later questions. They may also form a basis for comparison from year to year.

1   A curriculum analysis of the kind recommended in the ILEA Inspectorate pamphlet *Curriculum analysis and planning*. This displays the deployment of staff teaching and non-teaching time. It enables one to discuss the educational implications of the arrangements and to cost the consequences of proposed changes.

2   Numbers of parents choosing the school at first and second choice, and the actual recruitment.

3   Number of primary schools from which first-year pupils came, together with schools from which a substantial number of the pupils came, i.e. main intake schools.

4   Number of pupils joining the school during the year other than at secondary-transfer stage.

5   Number of pupils leaving the school during the year other than at the completion of secondary education.

6   Number of pupils receiving free lunches.

7   Number of pupils receiving uniform grants.

8   Attendance rates for pupils, by year-groups and by individual classes.

9   Results in public examinations, related to the intake at 11+, if possible.
10 Number of pupils continuing in full-time education beyond the statutory school-leaving age, whether this be at school or at a college of further or higher education.
11 Facts about school-leavers' first employment.
12 Cost of furniture replacement and repair during the year.
13 Cost of repairs to windows, etc. during the year.
14 Number of accidents to pupils recorded.
15 Number of staff leaving the school for (*a*) retirement, (*b*) promotion, (*c*) family reasons, (*d*) other reasons.
16 Number of teacher-days absences due to sickness during the year.

The school environment

Some aspects of this can be evaluated subjectively by staff.

1   What is the general appearance of the school like – playground, corridors, classrooms, lavatories, etc.? What arrangements are made for ensuring that the school is kept in a state of good working order?
2   What visual evidence is there of the quality of pupil's work and school activities? Are there displays of work to stimulate interest among pupils, parents and visitors? Who ensures that displays in halls, corridors and other communal spaces are well mounted and regularly changed?
3   How would one describe the manner in which pupils move around the school between lessons, during breaks and in the playground?
4   How would one describe the noise level, and the kind of noise, at various times and places?
5   Are the appearance and use of the hall, the various common rooms, the library, the resource centre(s) satisfactory? In what ways could they be improved?
6   Is the reception of visitors by staff and pupils friendly, courteous and helpful, especially for unscheduled visits? Is the way to the school office clearly indicated?
7   What comments have we on the appearance and care of pupils' workbooks, our class registers, school equipment?

417

Resources

1 In addition to teaching staff, what other staff are available: technicians, ancillary workers, media resources officers, librarians, and so on?
2 To whom are the various non-teaching staff responsible? Who is responsible for developing their skills and reviewing their relationships within the school?
3 Are there any staff vacancies, teaching or non-teaching? If so, for how long have they remained unfilled? Why? Is there any resulting distortion of the curriculum?
4 Do the numbers of teachers in various specialisms match the curriculum the school believes to be appropriate?
5 In what respects is the school poorly equipped? Can these deficiencies be made good?
6 Are there any minor works needed to improve the accommodation? What priority do they command?
7 What procedures are there for a regular review of the provision of materials and equipment?
8 Does the school have a resources committee? If so what is its membership? Are its terms of reference defined? Does it publish its recommendations?
9 How is waste of materials and other resources avoided?

Decision-making and communications

1 What is the consultative structure used to help arrive at policy decisions?
2 Are there adequate opportunities to all members of staff to express their views?
3 What steps do senior staff take outside the formal consultative structure to keep in touch with the views and hopes of their colleagues?
4 How are decisions recorded and communicated?
5 What methods are used for making clear who is responsible for seeing that decisions are carried out?
6 What steps are taken for reviewing the effects of decisions?
7 Is there a staff bulletin? Who compiles it? Who produces it? Is it effective?
8 Is there a staff guide? How often is it reviewed? How is this review

conducted? Is the guide worth the trouble taken to produce it? If not, should it be altered or abolished?

9   Is there a tannoy system? If so, is it used usefully and without irritation to staff and pupils?

10 Should pupils have a part to play in the consultative structure? If so, do our arrangements work well? How might they be improved.

Staff

1   What is the structure of responsibilities? How does a new member of staff learn about it? Does this structure reflect the importance attached to various aspects of the school's work?

2   What arrangements are made for applicants for posts to acquaint themselves with the school prior to interview?

3   What are the arrangements for integrating new members of staff, both teaching and non-teaching, and ensuring that not only are they involved but feel themselves to be involved in the school's life and decisions-making?

4   What is the policy for staff deployment among teaching groups?

5   How effectively are non-teaching staff consulted about decisions affecting them, e.g. librarian, media resources officer, school-keeping staff, technicians, secretary, clerical staff?

6   What are the school's arrangements for staff development? What procedures are followed for induction? How are decisions made about appropriate in-service courses or conferences for individuals, for groups of staff or for the whole staff? What 'reporting-back' arrangements are made on return from courses or conferences?

7   What are the arrangements for covering classes for short-term staff absence? Can they be improved?

8   How does the school help student teachers?

9   What links are there with colleges of education, university and polytechnic education departments?

10 What use can we, and do we, make of various support services — the inspectorate, advisory teachers, teachers' centres, the learning materials service?

Pupils

1   How are new pupils welcomed to the school, particularly those who do not join at the secondary-transfer age?

2 What is the system of personal and individual attention to pupils? How well is it working and are there any ways in which we can improve it?

3 What are the systems of careers education, careers guidance and educational guidance? Are any weaknesses apparent in these areas? How might they be rectified?

4 To what extent are pupils fully informed about further and higher education?

5 What are the links with the education welfare service, the medical service and the schools' psychological service?

6 Praise, rewards and sanctions — what do we use and why? Are any improvements feasible?

7 If the school has any form of special unit, what are the arrangements for allocation to it, what happens to pupils while they are there and what are the ways by which they return to the mainstream?

8 Are our registration arrangements satisfactory? What is the procedure for checking lateness and absence? What measures are taken to check attendance at lessons?

9 What opportunities are given for the development of initiative and responsibility?

Parental and community links

1 How is a parent first introduced to the school? Is this satisfactory? Is there a prospectus for new parents?

2 Do parents of new first-formers meet personally the members of staff most responsible for their child, e.g. form teacher/house master and year head/house head?

3 Is there any form of parents' association? What are its functions? Is it effective?

4 What opportunities are there for parents to see staff (*a*) as a matter of routine, (*b*) at their own or the school's request?

5 What are the various kinds of meetings held for parents? What proportion of parents come to each kind? How do we get in touch with non-attenders?

6 What is done to give parents an understanding of what the school is trying to do?

7 How are parents helped and encouraged to be interested in helping their children to learn?

8 Have we looked at the language in which we couch letters to parents?

9   Are arrangements made to help non-English-speaking parents to participate in the life of the school?
10   How are complaints and difficulties dealt with?
11   How are parents/pupils consulted about curriculum choice at various stages in the pupil's career? Does the school issue pamphlets about fourth-year and sixth-year courses? Are they comprehensible to parents?
12   What reports go home to parents? What form of assessment is used? Can parents comment on the reports?
13   Does the school have any contact with external voluntary or local government agencies?
14   How fruitful is our association with the Adult Education Institute, the Youth Service, the Careers Service and employers?
15   To what extent is the school concerned with the local neighbourhood?
16   How do we ensure good relationships with local residents and traders?
17   Are pupils involved in any way with local community service?
18   What are our relationships with other users of the building?

Arrangements for learning

1   (*a*) What initiatives does the school take about getting to know children to the school for the first time?
     (*b*) Who is responsible for assisting continuity from primary school; from class to class; from school to work, to further education, to higher education?
     (*c*) What records are passed from stage to stage?
     (*d*) Are there any serious obstacles to achieving continuity? How are they being tackled?
     (*e*) Do we, while using the benefits of continuity, allow for the possibility of change in the pupil's motivation and relationships?
2   How are curriculum and syllabuses determined? How do they relate to the ends we have in view?
3   How and when is the timetable constructed and presented to staff?
4   What provision is there for pupils of all abilities? What is done to diagnose and remedy learning deficiencies and to extend the most able? Have we considered any special needs of pupils of varying ethnic backgrounds?

5 How do we assess the quality and quantity of work produced?

6 What is the policy about homework? Is it being followed? Does it need changing?

7 What range of subjects and levels are we offering at 14+ and 16+. Are these appropriate?

8 Are we aware of information about courses in colleges of further and higher education in the area and in —— generally? Have we, or have we considered, links with further education for older pupils?

9 Do we need to make arrangements to co-operate with other institutions to broaden the range we offer, or to release staff for time to effect other improvements to the curriculum?

10 What is the school's language policy? How is it effected in practice? What arrangements are made to improve the language skills of pupils of all abilities?

11 Have we examined the question of mathematics across the curriculum?

12 Have we examined the success of curriculum changes made in the last five years?

13 On what basis are pupils arranged in classes? Are we satisfied with it?

14 If pupils are extracted from classes:
   (*a*) for what reasons are they extracted?
   (*b*) how are they enabled to fit in with the class when they return to it?

15 What does the school regard as a 'balanced' curriculum in the fourth and fifth years? Does it include a common core? Does the common core need a review?

16 Who is responsible for seeing that a given pupil receives a balanced curriculum as a result of any option system?

17 Are departments sufficiently aware of the educational standards demanded for employment? How could we ensure that all our pupils have reached an adequate level of attainment in basic skills to meet the needs of employment?

18 What part do educational visits and journeys play in the curriculum? How are decisions made about the frequency and timing? Who assesses their effectiveness? What checks are there on their conduct?

Department (or faculty) self-assessment

1   Is communication and consultation within the department sufficient? Do the staff feel effective members of a departmental team?
2   When are departmental meetings held? Are minutes kept?
3   How are responsibilities other than class teaching distributed within the department?
4   How is it decided which teacher takes which classes?
5   Who makes the syllabuses? When were they last revised? Do all members of the department have copies? Do new teachers receive copies in advance as a matter of course?
6   Do members of the department discuss together syllabuses, books, materials, equipment, pupils' work, examination entries?
7   Do staff keep regular records of their plans of work? At what intervals of time are these compiled?
8   What do we know about schemes of work and attainments in feeder primary schools? What steps do we take to assess and record progress? What do we do about (*a*) setting homework; (*b*) setting work for classes when teachers are absent; (*c*) marking work; (*d*) testing? Can we make improvements?
9   What is done to prevent loss of materials, books and equipment while ensuring they are used?
10 What use is made of the school's resource centre?
11 Are pupils' standards capable of improvement? What improvements are we aiming at in the next twelve months?
12 How do we ensure continuity in a pupil's work as he or she moves up the school?
13 Is everyone aware of relevant safety precautions and carrying them out?

Questions for the headteacher to ask himself or herself

The head will, of course, be intimately involved in the answers to all other sections concerning resources, the academic programme, the care of the individual and the general organisation, and with the strategies to adopt in order to maintain strengths and improve weaknesses. He or she will want to consider whether the school's policies are appropriate to the actual conditions obtaining. The following questions are more concerned with style and *modus operandi* and, because of this, most of them are equally applicable to deputy heads and other senior staff.

Time

1 Keep a detailed diary for a fortnight on two occasions separated by at least a month.
2 How often did I:
   (*a*) tour the school?
   (*b*) talk to people in the playground?
   (*c*) go to a school gate at the beginning or end of school?
   (*d*) go into classrooms to see pupils at work?
   (*e*) teach?
   (*f*) observe pupils during lesson changes?
3 What time did I give to meeting staff individually and in groups?
4 How much time did I spend out of school:
   (*a*) at County Hall?
   (*b*) at divisional meetings?
   (*c*) at other schools?
   (*d*) at conferences or in-service courses?
   (*e*) elsewhere?
   Was this time:
   (*a*) necessary?
   (*b*) useful to the school or service?
5 How much time did I spend on administration and meetings in school?
6 How much time did I give to visitors, including parents, inspectors and local education authority officers?
7 Do I need to try to change the time distribution revealed by the answers to questions 2-6.

Objectives and organisation

1 What do I see as the priorities for the school in the next term; year; five years?
2 To what extent is my view shared by others?
3 What constraints exist?
4 Are any organisational changes desirable or necessary?
5 Am I satisfied with the rolling programme of meetings? Are the necessary preparatory documents forthcoming? Are agendas well prepared? Are minutes well done?
6 Am I satisfied with the curriculum?
7 Which departments are flourishing, acceptable, needing attention?
8 Does every person in the school know to whom he or she is immediately responsible and for what?

9   Am I confident that there is a system for looking after the interests of every child?
10 How do I ensure that resources are distributed in a balanced way?

Staffing

1   How available am I — formally and informally?
2   Do staff feel I am interested in their professional development and advancement and their personal welfare?
3   When, for example, did I last speak to:
    (*a*) the part-time teacher in so-and-so department?
    (*b*) a cleaner?
    (*c*) the new teacher in such-and-such department?
    (*d*) the senior laboratory technician?
    (*e*) the second-in-charge of department X?
    (*f*) the head of department Y?
4   Who needs promotion?
5   How accurate is my awareness of the load carried by different individual teachers: (*a*) on the timetable, (*b*) in voluntary activities, (*c*) in unostentatious pupils and colleagues?
6   How accurate is my awareness of the load carried by non-teaching staff?

External relations

1   What is the first impact of the school on visitors?
2   Do I know what impression is given to telephone callers?
3   Have I satisfied myself that parents know to whom they can turn for help and that it will be forthcoming?
4   Are relationships with governors positive and fruitful?
5   Have I a sufficient knowledge of the local education authority administrative structure and inspectorate to ensure the school is properly supported?
6   Do I make good professional relationships and personal relationships with (*a*) local primary-school heads, (*b*) nearby secondary-school heads, (*c*) principals of local college of further and higher education?
7   Do I know, and am I known by:
    (*a*) local community leaders?
    (*b*) police and welfare agencies?
    (*c*) local shopkeepers?
    (*d*) neighbours of the school?

Appendix E

General

When did I last follow a class round the school for a day?

Questions for the individual teacher to ask himself or herself

My lessons

Do I prepare properly? What do I think of the presentation of my work? Am I using appropiiate materials and teaching aids? What improvements can I make in class organisation? Am I evaluating my lessons? How satisfied am I with my class control and relationships? Do I convince the pupils that I am interested in the work they produce? What kind of comments do I make on their work?

Knowledge of pupils

How much do I know about the work done in the top classes of feeder primary schools? To what extent am I aware of, and do I take account of, individual differences in the members of the class? Do I 'label' pupils prematurely? Why is it that some of my colleagues get good work from pupils with whom I fail and do I succeed with others that some of my colleagues find difficult? Am I aware of pupils with particular problems? How do I cope with them? How successful is my writing of reports?

General

Whose responsibility is it to help my professional development? What help do I need? Who am I going to ask for it? What contact have I with (*a*) the teachers' centre; (*b*) a specialist centre for my subjects?

What contribution do I make to my department/faculty and to my year-group? What part do I play in various levels of staff meetings? How do I contribute to the development of good relationships with pupils, colleagues and parents?

Administration

Am I punctual in arrival at school and at lessons?
Do I keep records of pupils' attendance and progress?
Do I keep lessons and evaluation notes?
Do I read the day's notices and act on them?

The acid test

Each member of staff asks the following questions.

1 Would I recommend a colleague to apply for a post at the school?
2 Would I recommend the school to friends for their children?

If *yes*:

What are the strengths of the school that led me to this decision?
What areas of the school's work and life need improvement?
How might this be achieved?

If *no*:

Why not?
Having identified what is amiss, make suggestions as to how to set about putting things right, including what you personally might contribute.

Action

1 Are we clear what we have been trying to do? How far are we meeting those intentions?
2 What are the priorities for action:
    (*a*) next term?
    (*b*) in the coming year?
3 Do these priorities imply any re-distribution of our resources?
4 Do we need any outside support and advice? If so, what?

The question is posed 'How and when is the timetable constructed and presented to staff?' The question immediately suggests a further set of questions.

1 What discussions with departments precede timetabling?
2 What consultation within departments precedes the allocation by the head of department of his or her staff to forms or sets for the ensuing year?
3 Is the present process of timetabling effective and satisfactory to those concerned?
4 In what ways could it be improved?
5 Is the timetable presented to staff at the right time and in the right form?
6 Are the arrangements for giving the pupils their timetables satisfactory?

Appendix F

An ethical classification

This classification is an extract from McPhail (1972). A boy or girl of your own age, with whom you are friendly, appears to be very upset for some reason unknown to you. What do you do?

Response	*Classification*
Do nothing.	Passive
Feel disturbed but do not know what to do.	Passive-emotional
Point the situation out to some adult.	Dependent-adult
Talk to your friends about the situation.	Dependent-peer
Tell the person concerned to pull himself/ herself together.	Aggressive
Jeer at that boy or girl.	Very aggressive
Avoid him/her.	Avoidance
Ask your friend what is the matter.	Experimental-crude
Try to talk to him/her as if you have not noticed that anything is wrong.	Experimental-sophisticated
Comfort your friend.	Mature-conventional
Set about interesting the person concerned in something which is going on, at the same time being available to help if asked.	Mature-imaginative

Appendix G

Seven worksheets for analysis

This worksheet is an extract from a book by Darke and Hughes (1974).

10.19   Starch contains energy locked within it. This is why we eat so many starchy foods, like bread, potatoes, rice and pastry. It is useful to be able to detect starch in foods.

Finding a starch detector

10.20   You need: flour; two beakers; glass rod; something on which to smear flour paste, such as a watch glass or sheet of polythene; solutions of iodine, alcohol, dilute (weak) hydrochloric acid, vinegar.

Make a table like Table G.1 in your notebook.

TABLE G.1   *Reactions of chemicals when mixed with flour paste*

Solution of chemical	Colour of solution alone	Colour of solution after mixing with flour paste
Alcohol		
Hydrochloric acid		
Vinegar		
Iodine		

Gradually add water to 5 g of starch powder. Stir with a glass rod to make a paste as thick as toothpaste. Make a smear of the paste on the polythene, about 15 cm long. Dip one end of the glass rod in the vinegar solution and add one drop to the paste smear. Immediately wash the rod in your other beaker. Continue with the alcohol, and other solutions, washing the rod each time after adding the solution to the paste. Fill in the table in your notebook as you get the results. Make sure that the test liquids are kept separate on the paste smear.

10.21 Which, if any, of the solutions changed colour with starch? Using this same solution, now try pure starch and then other foods mentioned above (10.19) to see that they really do contain starch.

How to detect starch in green plants

10.22 Ask the teacher for permission to do this experiment. It is dangerous. Read all the instructions before starting.

The green colouring matter in the leaf may stop you from seeing any colour change which might happen with your successful solution from the last experiment. This chlorophyll (the green matter) has to be removed. This is done by boiling it in alcohol. Alcohol catches fire easily and burns with an almost invisible flame. Take care not to spill any and keep it away from any naked flame.

You need: 250 cm beaker; test tube; tripod; gauze; burner; thermometer; 10 cm of alcohol; petri dish.

Half fill the beaker with water and set it on the gauze and tripod. Boil the water. Make sure the outside of the beaker is dry to start with or it may crack. Put the thermometer in the water to check that the water boils. While the water is heating, take a leaf and put it in the water. It will be killed as the water boils. This allows the alcohol to get into the leaf later on. When the water has boiled, turn out the flame for safety.

Pour the 10 cm of alcohol into the test tube, making sure that none is spilt. Keep it away from any bunsen flame. Put the dead leaf into the test tube so that the alcohol can get at it. Immediately afterwards, hold the test tube in the boiling water. On *no* account must the bunsen be alight when this is being done. The boiling water will boil the alcohol, which in turn will dissolve the chlorophyll out of the leaf. Leave the test leaf in the alcohol for 5 minutes to allow all the colouring to be extracted.

At the end of this time, the leaf should be either white or pale green. It will also be stiff because the alcohol also extracts all the water from the leaf. Dip the leaf into the hot water to soften it. Immediately spread out the leaf in the clean petri dish. Tilt the leaf so that the excess water drains off. Pour any excess water away and add enough iodine solution to cover the leaf on one half only. This will allow you to compare the tested portion with an untested portion. Finally, having allowed it to stay on the leaf for 5 minutes, wash the iodine solution off.

Draw the pattern of colours on the leaf. Iodine-stained leaf will be the same sort of reddish brown that nicotine makes on a smoker's fingers. The starch will show as black or bluish black, if it is there.

10.23 Not all plants store energy in starch for their own use later on. Some store the energy in sugars instead. By using the method described earlier, find out which of your aquarium plants contain starch.

FINDING OUT ABOUT OXYGEN AND NITROGEN

Experiment 1

In this experiment you will need corked test tubes containing the different gases. Make sure you know which is which. Can you tell the gases apart simply by looking at them — by smelling them?

To help you *burn* things *safely* use the following method (see Figure G.1). Fix the substance to be heated in the loop at the end of the nichrome wire. (If you are using a powder just wet the end of the loop in distilled water first.)

Holding the wire at an angle and using the asbestos paper as a heat shield, heat each substance in turn in a burner flame until it burns or glows red. How well does each substance burn?

When the substance is burning or glowing remove the cork from a test tube of gas and place the wire inside. How well does each substance burn?

Look at the burning substance through blue glass to begin with and then without if the flame is not too bright.

Appendix G

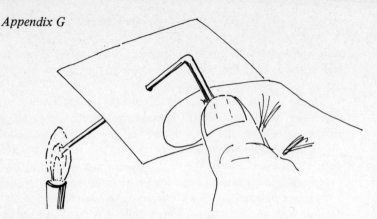

Figure G.1   *Safe method for heating substances*

Make a table of your results noting what happens to each of the substances in first one gas and then the other.

Task 1

Write this experiment up correctly making the differences between oxygen and nitrogen very clear.

Extra science project

'What is the difference between air and nothing?'

Task A

Draw quickly an empty box. Look at an empty box. We see nothing inside the box so we say it is empty.

If somebody asked us what outer space was like we might also say there is nothing there. Does this mean that the inside of the box is the same as outer space? What is there in the box which is not in outer space?

Task B

Write three sentences, each one giving a reason for thinking that there is something in the box.

Task C

You may have a vacuum cleaner at home — can you find out how it works? Does it really use a vacuum to do its job?

432

Task D

Have you seen tins or bottles with the words 'vacuum sealed' or 'vacuum packed' written on them? What do you hear when these tins are opened? Why?

But when you open a can of lemonade or a bottle of shandy you hear a similar noise. Is it for the same reason?

THE TEMPLE

1 Make a list of famous big cathedrals or abbeys in this country. (Remember to head your work.) Choose one of these and write a paragraph about it *in your own words*; if possible find a picture.
2 What is the capital of Great Britain? Name some of the important buildings in the capital. Why do you think we have more important buildings there than anywhere else?
3 Find out the capital of Palestine at the time of Jesus. (Look at the map on the wall.) What was the most important building in all the city? Draw a diagram or picture of the temple.
4 For the Jewish people, the *temple* was a very important place and no matter how far away you lived you would try to visit it at least once in your life. Very often people would travel together to Jerusalem for safety and they were called *pilgrims*. This was a very happy occasion. As the pilgrims were approaching Jerusalem they would begin to sing psalms (these are like our hymns and religious poems).
5 Look up Psalm 95. Write out verses 1 and 2. Leave a line and write out a sentence explaining how it was used.

LIFE IN A VILLAGE IN THE MIDDLE AGES

[In the original, references to four textbooks were supplied for each item.]

The village

(*a*) Draw and label an imaginary mediaeval village showing forest, commons, meadow, fields, church, houses, river mill.

433

(*b*) Study the village sketched in reference book **A** on page 130 and
then answer the following.
 (i) How big was a villein's holding?
 (ii) Make a guess at the population of the village and explain how
you reach your answer.
 (iii) What do you notice about the positions of the hall, the mill
and the villagers' houses?

The people of the village

Who were: villeins, cottars, freeholders, bailiff, reeve, steward, tithing-
men, constable?

People's homes

Either: describe and draw a cruck-framed house. List the differences
between it and your home;
or: make a model of a cruck house.

The work of the people

 (i) How was land split up between the people?
 (ii) Write to explain the three-field system of farming. (Describe
the crop rotation used, strips, fallow, commons.)
 (iii) *Either*: write a short scene describing the discussion of a villein
and a modern farmer about the merits and disadvantages
of the three-field system;
 or: list the advantages and disadvantages of the three-field
system.
 (iv) Draw sketches to show the various kinds of work done by a
villein during the year;
or
make up a calendar, picturing the work to be done each month.

Amusements

 (i) Briefly describe how you spend your Sunday.
 (ii) Describe how villagers spent a Sunday in medieval days, writing
and/or drawing about all the games they might have played.

Food

(i) List menus for a day's meals today.
(ii) List menus for a day's meals in 1300 for:
  (*a*) a villein;
  (*b*) a lord of the manor.

Law and order

Write or illustrate a scene in a medieval manor court, showing three typical offences, how the offenders were caught, how a decision about their guilt was reached and what punishments were ordered.

TRANSPORT

This booklet is designed to help you find out about transport. There are some maps to be drawn, graphs to be drawn, and so on. Try to write in good, clear English and draw your diagrams carefully.

First, list here the types of transport which you know of: the first letter may help you, for example:

R . . . . . . Railways   H . . . . . . ——
R . . . . . . ——   C . . . . . . ——
A . . . . . . ——   P . . . . . . ——
S . . . . . . ——   T . . . . . . ——

Answers: Roads, aircraft, sea transport, hovercraft, canals, pipelines and lastly, telecommunications. Yes, these last two are also types of transport.

Draw a map of —— (the town where the school is situated). Mark on it the main streets and all the areas connected with transport, e.g. bus stations, wharves, etc.

On the next two pages you will find two maps of Britain. Follow these instructions carefully and complete each map *carefully*.

Map 1 The main roads of England, Scotland and Wales.

Draw in the cities of Liverpool, Bristol, Southampton, Wakefield, Hull, Newcastle and Edinburgh.
Draw, in *red* lines, the *motorways*.
Draw, in *orange* lines, the trunk roads, e.g. A1 (T).

435

Write down the answer to this question on one of the writing sheets which you will find after the second map of Britain:

Why do the main roads of Britain appear where they do and why are they so important to the commercial activity of Britain?

Map 2   Railways in Britain

Draw in the cities of Liverpool, Bristol, Southampton, Wakefield, Hull, Newcastle and Edinburgh.

Draw, in *black* lines, the main railway lines.

Many railway lines run towards the coast, often to ports. Mark on the map some of the main ports and ferry-ports used by British Rail.

Write the answer to this question on the writing sheet which appears immediately after this map:

What service does British Rail offer (1) the general public and (2) the industrial and commercial user in Britain?

Draw the signs for the following:

traffic signals ahead;

level crossing with automatic half-barriers ahead

You will find these in the *Highway Code*.

Pipelines and communication by television and radio

Name *three* things which are 'transported' by pipeline

1   ————

2   ————

3   ————

What is transported by wire and cable?

What do you understand by the term *telex*?

What does the IBA stand for?

What does the BBC stand for?

Name *three* local radio stations.

Answer this question in the form of a short essay:

Taking *either* pipelines *or* communication by radio, TV, telex, cable, etc. state how each is an aid to the commercial life of Britain.

Comments:

Marks:

Air and sea routes

On the map of the world opposite write the title:
The main air and sea routes of the world.
Mark on the map the following ports and airports:

London   Air and Seaport.

New York   A/S

San Francisco   A/S

Rio de Janeiro   A/S

Cape Town   A/S

Sydney   A/S

Bombay   A/S

Paris   A

Moscow   A

Shanghai   A/S

Madrid   A

Tokyo   A

Marseilles   A/S

Liverpool   A/S

A = Airport
S = Seaport

Draw in the routes which you would think an aeroplane and/or a ship would take, from each of the places mentioned above, to London. Mark your map as follows:

Sea routes in *blue* thus -------------

Air routes in *red* thus   ———

Then answer this question below:

How important are Britain's links with the world? What would happen should one of our trade links with the world suddenly be terminated?

The waterways of Yorkshire

Study the map opposite and then answer the questions which follow.

1 To which North Sea port do you think the canals are heading?
2 Name the main rivers which are linked in the area.
3 Name six things which are made, quarried, etc. in the area.
4 On the map draw in the main rail links.
5 Answer this question in the form of a short essay. 'What sorts of goods are carried on the canals and why?'

437

Comments:
Marks:

Revision questions
Draw the symbol used by British Rail.
What is the name now adopted by BOAC and BEA?
Of what nationalised corporation is the NEGB a part?
What does YEB stand for?
Name *three* independent television companies.
Make a list of things which would be best suited to being carried by a specific form of transport: e.g. diamonds by air because they are small and very costly.

TABLE G.2   *Forms of transport best suited for specific items*

Item	Form of transport	Reasons
Diamonds	Air	They are small and very costly

MICROPOLIS

Equipment

1   A board $2' \times 2'$ covered with green paper. This gives a scale of $6''$ to one mile.
2   Felt-tipped pens. Each group to have three pens. Black: houses built before 1914, blue: houses built after 1914, red: shops.
3   Yellow adhesive plastic used to show factories.
4   Coloured pencils: brown to show contour lines, green to show marshes.

5 Black chinagraph pencils to number the factories.
6 A clear plastic template so that houses and factories can easily be drawn to scale.
7 White gummed paper to cover buildings which have been demolished.

Types of houses

Micropolis has four different kinds of houses.

Type 1

Rows of workpeople's houses built before 1914. These are shown as black lines drawn with a felt-tipped pen, and should be about ⅛″ wide. A one-inch row represents 50 houses.

Type 2

Larger, more expensive houses. These are shown as black squares ¼″ × ¼″. Each of these squares represents 5 houses.

Type 3

Modern semi-detached. These are shown as blue lines, drawn with the felt-tipped pen about ⅛″ wide. A one-inch row represents 25 houses.

Type 4

Flats built after the war. These are shown as blue squares ¼″ × ¼″.

Types of shops

Micropolis has three different kinds of shops.

Type 1

Local shops. These are shown as red lines, drawn with the felt-tipped pen about ⅛″ wide. A one-inch row represents 50 shops. A dot drawn with the pen, ⅛″ × ⅛″ represents about 6 shops.

Type 2

Larger central shops. These are shown as red squares about ¼″ × ¼″; one of these squares represents 5 shops. A row of 20 shops could be shown by drawing an area of red ¼″ × 1″.

Type 3

Major commercial establishments. These are shown as red squares ¼″ × ¼″. A square like this shows only one warehouse or department store.

Cycle I   How the town develops between 1500 and 1800

1 Discuss the site of the town.
2 Locate market square (roughly 1″ × 1″) and parish church (roughly 1″ × 1″).
3 Discuss relationship of town and countryside.
4 Locate first group of industry:
    corn mill ¼″ × ¼″;
    brewery ¼″ × ¼″;
    pottery and brickworks 1″ × 1″;
    agricultural machinery ¼″ × ¼″.
5 Locate associated houses, shops, churches and schools:
    houses   450 of type 1 (9″ × ⅛″);
                25 of type 2 (5 squares ¼″ × ¼″);
    shops   25 of type 1;
              10 of type 2;
    churches 2 (shown by a red cross about ¼″ × ¼″);
    schools   3 (shown by a square ¼″ × ¼″ with S in the middle).
6 Locate the second group of industries:
    woollen mills 1″ × ½″   (5);
    iron and brass foundries ¼″ × ¼″   (6);
    blanket and mattress factory ¼″ × ¼″   (7);
    tannery and glove works ½″ × ¼″   (8).
7 Locate associated services:
    houses   750 of type 1 (15″ × ⅛″);
                50 of type 2 (10 squares ¼″ × ¼″);
    shops   50 of type 1;
              5 of type 2;
    churches 3;
    schools   5.
8 Locate third group of industries:
    engineering works ¼″ × ¼″   (9);
    buttons ¼″ × ¼″   (10);
    soap ¼″ × ¼″   (11);

sawmills ¼″ × ¼″ (12);
printers ¼″ × ¼″ (13).

9 Locate associated services:
   houses   250 of type 1 (5″ × ⅛″);
            25 of type 2 (5 squares ¼″ × ¼″);
   shops   10 of type 1;
   churches 1;
   schools   1.

Cycle II   How the town develops between 1800 and 1830

1 Discuss the historical setting: growth in population and movement from country to town; great increase in numbers of industries and factories; river is straightened and made navigable.
2 Remove:
   tannery and gloves;
   soap.
3 Engineering works extends to 1″ × ½″.
4 Factories numbers 9, 10, 11, 12 and 13 need more workers, but the others need fewer.
   Add 50 houses of type 1 (1″ × ⅛″) and 12 shops of type 1.
5 Locate new industries:
   brewery ¼″ × ¼″ (14); (NB the town already has a brewery);
   metal works ¼″ × ¼″ (15);
   sand and gravel (½″ × ¼″) (16).
6 Add associated services:
   houses   350 of type 1 (7″ × ⅛″);
            25 of type 2 (5 squares ¼″ × ¼″);
   shops   10 of type 1;
            5 of type 2;
   churches 1;
   schools none.
7 Locate gas works ½″ × ½″
8 Locate new industries:
   clothing ½″ × ¼″ (17);
   leather goods ½″ × ¼″ (18);
   bakery ½″ × ¼″ (19).
9 Add associated services:
   houses   300 of type 1 (6″ × ⅛″);
   shops   10 of type 1;

      5 of type 2;
   churches none;
   schools none.

10 Locate railway and railway station (1″ × ½″).
   Notes: (*a*) marshland may be used;
       (*b*) shops and houses may have to be demolished;
       (*c*) any factories demolished must be relocated.

11 Locate new industries:
   barge-building 1″ × ½″ (20);
   timber industries 1″ × ½″ (21);
   engineering ¼″ × ¼″ (22).

12 Add associated services:
   houses 800 of type 1 (16″ × ⅛″);
        100 of type 2 (20 squares ¼″ × ¼″);
   shops   50 of type 1;
        30 of type 2;
         4 of type 3;
   churches 4;
   schools 3.

13 Locate new industries:
   furniture 1″ × ½″ (23);
   precision engineering ½″ × ½″ (24);
   chemicals ¼″ × ¼″ (25).

14 Add associated services:
   houses 800 of type 1 (16″ × ⅛″);
        100 of type 2 (20 squares ¼″ × ¼″);
   shops   50 of type 1;
        30 of type 2;
   churches 4;
   schools 2.

Cycle III How the town develops between 1830 and 1914

1 Discuss the historical setting.
2 Remove:
   agricultural machinery;
   buttons;
   chemicals;
   precision engineering.
3 Add extra services because of changing standards:

      houses   900 of type 1(18″ × ⅛″);
                    300 of type 2 (60 squares ¼″ × ¼″);
      shops   90 of type 1;
                  5 of type 2.

4 Locate fresh industry:
      brewery ½″ × ¼″   (26);
      pottery and brickworks 1″ × 1″   (27);
      second pottery and brickworks 1″ × 1″   (28).

5 Add associated services:
      houses   900 of type 1 (18″ × ⅛″);
                    300 of type 2 (60 squares ¼″ × ¼″);
      shops   90 of type 1;
                  5 of type 2;
      churches 2;
      schools   1.

6 Mark in hospital (½″ × ½″).

7 Locate new industries:
      wool 1″ × ½″   (29);
      clothing ¼″ × ¼″   (30);
      footwear ¼″ × ½″   (31);
      metalwork 1″ × ½″   (32);
      gas appliances ¼″ × ¼″   (33).

8 Add associated services:
      houses   1800 of type 1 (26″ × ⅛″);
                    500 of type 2 (100 squares ¼″ × ¼″);
      shops   200 of type 1;
                 10 of type 2;
                 10 of type 2;
      churches 4;
      schools   2.

9 Mark town hall (½″ × ½″), library (½″ × ½″) and museum (½″ × ½″).

10 Locate new industries:
      expanding engineering (½″ × ½″)   (34);
      machinery ¾″ × ¾″   (35);
      expanding timber 1″ × ½″   (36);
      wood 1″ × 1½″   (37);
      printers ¼″ × ¼″   (38);
      tents and ropes ½″ × ½″   (39).

11 Add associated services:

          houses   2700 of type 1 (54″ × ⅛″);
                    800 of type 2 (160 squares ¼″ × ¼″);
          shops   250 of type 1;
                     15 of type 2;
                     15 of type 3;
          churches   6;
          schools   3.
12 Mark power station (1″ × ½″).
13 Locate new industries:
          furniture ½″ × ¾″   (40);
          toolmakers ½″ × ¼″   (41);
          food and tobacco 1″ × 1″   (42);
          chemicals 1″ × ¾″   (43);
          electrical appliances ¼″ × ¼″   (44).
14 Add associated services:
          houses   2700 of type 1 (54″ × ⅛″);
                    800 of type 2 (160 squares ¼″ × ¼″);
          shops   250 of type 1;
                     15 of type 2;
                     15 of type 3;
          churches   8;
          schools   4.
15 Mark football stadium (1″ × 1½″) and cinema (½″ × ½″).

Cycle IV   How the town develops between 1914 and the present day

1 Discuss historical setting (two World Wars and a trade depression).
2 Insert industry growing after the First World War:
          jute ½″ × ¼″   (45);
          small metal goods ½″ × ¼″   (46).
3 Add expanding social services:
          park (large and irregularly shaped);
          hospital (1″ × 1″);
          higher education (1″ × 1″);
          further education (1½″ × 1″).
4 Add new housing:
          type 1   0;
          type 2   300 (60 squares ¼″ × ¼″);
          type 3   6,000 (240″ × ¼″).
          (Remember to use blue for types 3 and 4.)

Remove 1,000 of the oldest houses (20″ × ⅛″).
5 New shops:
    0 of type 1;
    50 of type 2;
    25 of type 3.
6 Schools: two new schools and one rebuilt to house more pupils.
7 Great depression causes many firms to go bankrupt. Remove:
    engineering;
    barge-building;
    pottery and brickworks;
    gas appliances;
    tents and ropes.
8 War damage and post-war clearance. Remove 1,500 of oldest houses (20″ × ⅛″ and 100 squares ¼″ × ¼″).
9 Locate post-war industries:
    precision engineering ¼″ × ¼″   (47);
    bread, cakes and biscuits 1″ × ¾″   (48);
    food processing ½″ × ½″   (49).
10 Add associated and expanding services:
    houses   0 of type 1;
              200 of type 2 (40 squares ¼″ × ¼″);
           6,000 of type 3 (240″ × ⅛″);
              10 of type 4 (10 squares ¼″ × ¼″);
    shops   0 of type 1;
              50 of type 2;
              25 of type 3;
    schools   3 and one rebuilt to house more pupils.
11 Mark expanding further education (1½″ × 1″).

LISTENING AND TALKING – THE MOB

[This worksheet was prepared by Elizabeth Hardman for the Nuffield Resources for Learning Project, but has not been published.]

Listen to the first extract on the tape called *The Mob*. The story is called 'A Lynching'. If you want to, you can follow the script of the tape while you are listening.

Here are a few points to talk about in your group after listening to 'A Lynching'.

1 This is no ordinary fire. Who has started it? What do you think the 'ends of a few posts and planks in the middle of the fire' have been? What is the mob doing when Horace arrives on the scene? How do they seem to feel?

2 'Here's the man that defended him. That tried to get him clear.' 'Put him in too. There's enough left to burn the lawyer.' What do you think of this suggestion? The lawyer is an innocent man and the crook has not committed the murder, although he is a criminal. Have you ever known of people behaving in this way, 'taking justice into their own hands'? What happened? Were they right?

3 Try to imagine how the night of 'A Lynching' began. Who collected the mob together? What was said to them? Who had been murdered? Each of you will probably have a different idea. Tell each other or write the ideas down.

4 How do you think the mob will feel in the morning? What will they say to each other about the night before?

If you want to hear about another mass killing and what did happen the next day, listen to Extract Two on the tape, *The Mob*. It comes from the book, *Lord of the Flies*. Follow the script if you want.

Things to do

Here are a number of suggestions. You can choose to work on any one of them or, if you prefer, you can work on an idea of your own. You can go on working as a group if you want, or you can work on your own or split up into pairs. When you have finished one activity, choose another.

1 Collect newspaper pictures and stories about mob violence. Ask the whole group to bring some in for you. Ask yourself three questions.
   (i) What was the mob wanting?
   (ii) How did they try to get it?
   (iii) Did they succeed?
   Make a scrapbook of your pictures and the answers to these questions. Try to find as many *different* types of crowds with different aims as you can.

2 Listen to the poem 'Street Gang', which is Extract Three on

the tape *The Mob*. You can follow it in the tape script.

It says 'None of them know why' they attack the victim, but what is their mood at the beginning of the poem? Does this suggest to you a reason why?

Have you ever been so bored you 'didn't know what to do with yourself'? What *did* you do?

Can you remember attacking or hitting anyone or anything without a real reason? What did you feel at the time?

Have you ever been part of a mob that has turned violent?

Write about one of these memories. Try to remember your feelings at the time and to make it very dramatic.

3 Act the scene from 'A Lynching' where the people meet each other next morning. The fire is burnt out and the lawyer gone. What do they do next? (Remember the real murderer is still free but they think they have killed the right man.)

4 Make a tape of any historical event or recent event in which a mob was involved. It could be the assassination of Julius Caesar, the trial of Christ, the Paris student riots. Try to make sure that each person has a speaking part as well as using all of them for crowd scenes.

5 Have you personally ever been in a crowd which became violent or found its feelings so strong that it acted as a body? When did you first realise what was happening? Did you join in? What did you feel at the time? Think about this and then write about it.

6 Have you yourself ever been on a march or demonstration? What was its purpose? Who else was with you? Did you come to know the other people well by the end of the march? What did you feel like by the end?

When you have remembered all about this, write about what you remember. Perhaps you have kept newspaper cuttings or photographs of the demonstration. Make a scrapbook of them.

7 Do you think you live in a violent world? How often have you yourself seen and heard fights? How often does violence take up part of the newspaper or TV news? You could watch out for this and make a list of the number of violent things going on in London and the world in the week you're working on this.

Look at the pictures called Violence in Art. All the painters lived in this century. Ask yourself what they thought it was like to live in this twentieth-century world. Then write a poem or very short piece of work using one of the pictures as a starting-point.

447

Appendix H

Evaluation of an experimental course

The following four extracts come from a series of documents written by a senior teacher in a large secondary school while leading a team of colleagues in bringing into existence a highly innovative integrated course for first-year (11-year-old) pupils. Your task is to design an appropriate evaluation based on these extracts.

AIMS

It should be borne in mind that we are concerned only with the first year and only with science, English, history, geography, art and religious education. Mathematics and French are specifically excluded.

Fundamental aims

Our fundamental aims have emerged in terms of qualities of character. They may be roughly summarised:

1 autonomy;
2 self-confidence;
3 respect for others;
4 open-mindedness;
5 freedom from fear;
6 realisation that things can be changed;
7 co-operativeness in groups;
8 willingness to ask for help;
9 responsiveness to environment and to other people;

10   realism in self-assessment;
11   perseverance;
12   responsibility.

All these qualities are difficult to assess, but it seems to us that they are a great deal more important than many conventional objectives in education. The difficulty does not therefore excuse us from trying to set up an environment which actively nurtures them. Some amplification may clarify what we mean.

Autonomy

The ability to 'stand on one's feet', to act on one's own initiative obviously involves the whole person — intellectually, emotionally and in terms of practical ability in various skills, but the intellectual element is essential to successful autonomy and can be broken down into several operations. The autonomous person must be able to:

1   set his own goals;
2   plan how to achieve them;
3   act according to the plan;
4   evaluate his success.

It is this intellectual element which we intend by the first of our aims.

There is nothing novel in these four operations, of course — they are what we do all the time, more or less, but by making children more conscious of them, by deliberately planning for opportunities to exercise these abilities as a primary aim of our work, we hope to enable children to develop a much greater proficiency in their use and to be able ourselves to diagnose difficulties, obstacles and failures more effectively.

It should be relatively easy to evaluate our success in this area at least. Lastly, success in these four operations, while desirable for itself, is fundamental to any problem-solving situation and can be applied to any problems, intellectual, social, communication, etc. which children meet.

Self-confidence and a respect for others

Despite difficulties of definition, these are worth including because they are the qualities which underpin all the others; the first with respect to the individual and the second, his relations with others. They are linked together because we see them as acting as a check on each

449

other – preserving a balance in the personality. The highly self-confident person might well ignore or despise others. Too strong a respect for others might inhibit the growth of a healthy self-confidence. These two qualities will be difficult to evaluate, but it will be possible to provide a subjective judgment and to base this on close observation of many specific incidents.

Open-mindedness

The opposite of bigotry.

Freedom from fear

We are not so much concerned here with obvious gross causes of fear, we assume these will be eliminated, but particularly with freedom from fear of failure, of injustice and lack of understanding from others. What we want to get rid of are, for instance, (*a*) the feeling of some children that they can never succeed at anything – we want to try to provide every child with *some* successes as a basis for increased self-confidence; (*b*) the hesitancy of even able children to risk being wrong – in short, any form of fear of failure which may inhibit a child from making the progress or taking as large a part in events as he is capable of.

Realisation that things can be changed

'The way things are' always seems to be immutable, but in fact society does change. If children are to cope with these changes and understand and participate in them effectively in later life, they must be involved in active ways from an early age. They must be able to see faults and inadequacies; to realise changes can be made; to explore ways of making improvements and to advocate sensible changes rationally. In short, they must be helped towards an intelligent participation in change, rather than be left to become uncomprehending and helpless victims.

Co-operativeness in groups

In almost any career a child eventually chooses, he or she will be working more or less closely with other people. Learning how to co-operate with them effectively in the *working* situation seems to us of major importance. It involves learning strategies for dividing work, for avoiding unnecessary work, for getting reluctant members to help, etc. It requires the recognition of which jobs are best done in groups and which individually and of the strengths and weaknesses of others –

not to mention oneself. It calls upon traditional virtues of courtesy, tidiness, honesty, truthfulness, toleration and responsibility.

Wilingness to ask for help

Whether from teachers or peers, this involves realistic self-assessment and ability to recognise when help is needed.

Responsiveness to the environment and to other people

This is intended to mean a certain eagerness, an active interest and involvement; but also a sensitivity and trained awareness, of colour, of shape, of sound, of others' feelings, etc.

Responsibility

Responsibility is intended to mean an internal sense of duty; a recognition of belonging to a community in which one is valued and which one values with a concomitant sense of what it is right to do or not to do. These qualities of character provide the basic framework within which we wish to work and to which we will constantly refer if in doubt.

All contents, all methods *must be consonant with these*, but these qualities of character clearly do not provide the bread and butter of the classroom. They do, however, have implications for teacher-child relationships, for the overall organisation of work, for content in the sense of bodies of knowledge, for the minute details of how we and the children conduct ourselves both in and out of the classroom.

Subsidiary aims/objectives

The fundamental aims can be broken down into various types of subsidiary aims seen in terms of skills:
1 general 'practical' skills;
2 sensory 'observational' skills;
3 communication skills;
4 intellectual skills;
5 social skills;
but before dealing with these we wish to emphasise the importance of *basic* skills.

Basic skills

Reading to a reading age of 10.00, and writing. These we consider on a par with the fundamental aims in the priority we give them in our thinking. So much of any work we may choose to do must depend on prior acquisition of a reasonable standard in these two skills, that remedial attention will have the highest possible priority.

General 'practical' skills

These are skills which should be useful in almost any learning context — not related to a particular 'subject'. Examples include using a library/resource centre; using a book — contents, index, skimming; note-making; using rulers, pencils, rubbers, scissors, etc.; effective display and presentation techniques.

Sensory 'observational' skills

These are skills related to looking, hearing, touching, smelling, etc. more sensitively and accurately. They may apply to the scientific observation of a leaf, the aesthetic observation of the same leaf in terms of colour, shape, composition, etc. or the observation of the child's own feelings or behaviour in a group.

Communication skills

These comprise a wider range of skills in the use of language — in writing and orally.

(a) Children need to be able to recognise the appropriateness, and to be competent in, a range of different 'registers' — to understand the language and syntax used in, for example, informal discussion; a formal talk to the rest of the class; chatting amongst themselves; a science report; a poem; etc.

(b) Many children find discipline-based work difficult in later years because they have never been able to internalise the specialist language required — they may have copied it, even quite proficiently — but they have never made it their own by translating it into the terms of their own personal language. This process of internalisation will be a major concern.

(c) The ability to verbalise one's own ideas is an enormous help to thinking. This verbalisation may take place within one's head, it may be spoken or written, but we think that the process of finding words to express what one means is an essential part of the process of clarifying one's meaning to oneself.

Intellectual skills

These comprise the four skills listed under autonomy. In addition — and implied by those four — we would add:

(*a*) the ability to ask relevant questions;
(*b*) the ability to think logically.

Social skills

These are partly dealt with in the fundamental aims and in the section on co-operativeness in groups, but further breakdown of some additional areas is necessary.

Creativity

The group does not see creativity as a separate category, but rather a quality which can emerge in almost any context and at any level. Essentially we see it as 'making' something which is new to oneself, it may be an idea, the working out of a combination of ideas, an ingenious practical contrivance, a pot or a picture or a dance in which the finished object is arrived at by an almost unverbalised process or the skilled motivation of a group.

All the skills mentioned so far could be practical without any *necessary* reference to specialist disciplines. We do anticipate, however, that children will be going on to learn within specialist disciplines, and that the existence of disciplines does reflect *different ways of knowing about the world*. It is therefore desirable that children begin to acquire aesthetic, historical, scientific, etc. ways of thinking and practical skills appropriate to those areas. Their acquisition is part of the overall process of enabling them to become more sensitive and responsive and better able to think and talk about the world. The group has been repeatedly struck by the amount which apparently unrelated disciplines have in common. All disciplines want to foster practical, observational, communication, intellectual and social aims of the sort we have outlined above. Even where these do not appear in the respective syllabuses, they are implicit in the behaviour of the teacher in the classroom. Nevertheless, there is a broad difference between what we envisage and some of the subject disciplines. The aspects of subject disciplines which remain important distinguishing features are, for example:

1 the approach to one's subject-matter — aesthetic, scientific, etc.;

453

2 the habits of thinking and attitudes which this approach engenders;
3 practical skills peculiar to the particular study;
4 specialised intellectual skills;
5 sets of concepts central to the disciplines.

The concepts (in no. 5) must form a sort of template against which sets of subject-matter we choose must be matched so that we can say, for instance, that whenever a child has chosen scientific work to do it is desirable that the work should contribute towards building up an understanding of one or more of these basic concepts. A few examples will illustrate what we mean.

In science the difference between living and non-living.
In history the fact that society has changed.
In art ideas of lines, colour, etc.
In movement ideas of rhythm, effort, etc.

One of our next jobs will be to explore this area of concepts essential to subject disciplines.

This outline lists the things which we feel it is most important for children to learn. The absence of content — in the sense of 'bodies of knowledge' — is deliberate. This does not mean there will be no content in our teaching or the children's learning. Of course there must be; one could not teach all the skills listed in the abstract — they will be learnt by doing things which require their exercise.

BASIC SKILLS

The following basic skills will be our concern:

I Reading skills, writing skills, speaking skills

These are more fundamental than any others we will have to deal with. They are complicated by the need of some children for remedial attention.

II Inquiry skills

The most basic of these, 'using a book' and 'using the library' must be done before we start thematic work. Since all will need it, we might as well do it as a class exercise. When it is done depends to a large extent on when the resource centre is actually ready. The best time is probably at the end of our introductory phase.

III   Laboratory skills

These must be learnt right at the beginning. Again as all need to learn them they can be done on a class basis using the Alt II worksheets.

IV   Map-reading

These are the only modern studies skills which we consider vital and, again, they can be taught on a class basis. The emphasis will be on the catchment area of the school rather than on the individual villages.

V   Art techniques

There are no basic techniques other than those which the children will learn as they go through the course, but there is no reason why they cannot start on these right away in class groups. They will need to find their way about their room and where equipment is kept, etc.

The Introductory phase in the case of English will be taken up with diagnosing the children's needs as under I above and then possibly by some work linking mime and dance with English, or a story pack.

VI   Display skills

These will be developed as the children go along.

TRANSITION TO MATURE WAY OF WORKING

Introduction

We cannot expect to start our mature mode of working immediately.

1 There is a new block and all its habits of routine to be established.
2 We have a number of new ways of working to adjust ourselves to — we do not intend to try them all out at once.
3 We need time to get to know the children, so that we can assess their probable response to the new ways of working.
4 The children need time to settle in.

Phase I   Settling-in period

Provisionally set at about half-term (6-7 weeks).

Work children should cover

Science
Laboratory techniques — by the end of the introductory period they should all be able to find their way about the laboratory, behave sensibly and safely, carry out various scientific processes correctly.

Modern studies
Map-reading:

(i)   Making and using large-scale maps based on school catchment area, *not* individual villages.
(ii)   Simple atlas work.

If time to spare some work on simple graphical techniques.

Art
Basic techniques as would normally do, avoiding themes likely to be relevant to major themes later. By half-term they should know their way about the room well.

English
Three aspects important in this period.

(i)   Diagnostic work to establish strengths and weaknesses of each child. In doing this transactional writing done in other subject contexts should be used from the start. Also reports and observations on oral work.
(ii)   Creative work — preferably closely associated with what is being done elsewhere, for example, in movement, in art, etc.
(iii) Introduction of movements — made possible by having four staff — adds extra dimension.

Also during this period we should establish:

(*a*) elementary inquiry skills: familiarity with equipment and facilities, especially the library; how to use a book; how to use a library (during the weekly library period);
(*b*) good standards of display;
(*c*) possibly some early work on planning.

Phase II Starting on theme-based work

1 Joint team introduction to 'Family', that is, a lead lesson(s).
2 Division into subject groups: discussion of possibilities.
3 Planning of individual and small-group work; worksheets ready for allocation to those who need them.
4 Looking at sources — if relevant.
5 Starting work.

This sounds like the mature method of working; in practice it will not be. We must restrict the range of choice at this stage. This can be done in a variety of ways within our general framework. The choice of method will depend on the judgment of the staff at the time. Some alternatives are:

(*a*) within a 'subject' section, start with some work they all do leading to a staggered start on own choice assignments;
(*b*) give an initial choice within a narrow range of alternatives;
(*c*) give a choice in one aspect, for example, how work is to be presented.

This phase will extend over the introductory half of the autumn term and the whole spring term, the object being to gradually increase children's skill in planning and thinking about and carrying out their own work. By the end of this time it should be possible to trace distinct improvements in the abilities of children to work in the way we wish. Probably the best and most convincing way to do this would be to follow through a number of 'life histories'.

A METHOD FOR HELPING CHILDREN TO CHOOSE THEIR GOALS

The steps might be as outlined below.

1 Introduction or lead sequence designed to fire imagination.
2 Brainstorming session — as many suggestions as possible, all jotted down as they come on board.
3 As a result of discussion, these are grouped into sensible related areas, for example:
    some will involve a time factor and might be roughly classed as historical;
    others would be mainly geographical;

others involve creative work in art or writing;
others might involve experiential work.

4 The team then organises these rough groupings into a large chart
which might well be put up for the duration of the theme, and
which shows a number of 'routes' through the theme.

5 The children have then to commit themselves initially to one of the
main *'routes'* and make a statement about what they want to do,
for example, 'I want to find out about . . .'

All these goals will probably involve divergence from the main route
chosen, but they must all be related to it and must relate back to it
as they proceed.

In following this 'path' children may choose to use any of a variety
of media — models, painting, writing, different types of writing, etc.
and will be encouraged to learn to choose what is most appropriate to
their purpose — to begin with they may need a good deal of guidance;
hopefully, as they gain experience and confidence, discussion with
individuals may be enough. The following of a particular path may
well lead into other 'subject' areas, for example, work on living conditions in the late nineteenth century, started as a path off the main
historical trunk-route, might lead to looking at methods of sanitation
and control of disease which would be best conducted under the
supervision of the science specialist. The child might diverge in this
way and then return to his main route or he might come on to the
science-biased path as a sequel to earlier historical work. The sequence
might work the other way round; equally, either of these two
approaches might lead, say, to writing based on experience of illness as
a result of infection, or of the effects of illness on the family; yet
another path might lead from study of the shapes of infective bac-
teria to art work in various media.

6 At the point of starting out on a particular path of investigation,
each individual or group would have to put down some sort of plan.
This should not be complete or considered as restrictive — rather a
preliminary attempt to chart a course.
Such a plan might include:
general but accurate statement of goal;
list of questions to find answers to;
ideas about the sort of information needed;
list of possible sources of information;
an idea of what sort of final product would be appropriate.

We would probably need to help them considerably at this stage — possible methods of doing so might include a standard format sheet which they can fill in (see Figure H.1).

Name:	Title of work:				Form: Date:
Questions Sources of information/ activities					

Figure H.1. *Standard format sheet for pupils following their own goals*

Appendix I

Primary school evaluation: a schedule for self appraisal

This appendix was issued by Lancashire Education Committee (1980) under the above title.

CURRICULUM

Aims

1 Are the aims of the school clear and evident to all members of staff — teaching and non-teaching?
2 Are they founded on a firm basis of realism?
3 In what form are they available to:
   (*a*) members of staff?
   (*b*) managers?
   (*c*) parents?
4 How is provision made for re-thinking and developing the aims of the school?
5 How does the daily life of the school and its learning programme reflect the school's aims?
6 In seeking to achieve these aims what are the school's priorities for the next term; next year; and next five years?
7 How might these priorities be affected by outside influences (falling rolls, etc.)?

Programmes of work or guidelines

1 Does the school possess written guidelines in the following areas of the curriculum:
   (*a*) language and literacy, including reading as a skill?
   (*b*) mathematics?
   (*c*) social and environmental studies (history and geography)?
   (*d*) science?

(*e*) physical education?

(*f*) aesthetic development (music, art, craft, drama)?

(*g*) religious, moral, social, health education?

2 When were these programmes written?

3 By whom were they written?

4 When were they last revised?

5 What guidance was sought from:

(*a*) inspectorate and advisory services?

(*b*) educational literature?

(*c*) other schools — in particular, feeder and receiving schools?

(*d*) colleges, universities, curriculum development centres?

(*e*) diocesan education departments?

6 Do all members of staff have a copy of the written guidelines?

7 What assistance is given to teachers to understand and follow the guidelines?

Is this by:

(*a*) staff discussion on the content, consistency and continuity of their work?

(*b*) guidance from the headteacher and members of staff with curriculum responsibilities?

8 How does the head ensure that each area of the curriculum receives an adequate allocation of school time?

9 How does the head ensure maximum use of learning time?

10 How does the head ensure continuity and development of skills in topic and thematic work?

11 Do the school's resources (teaching materials, library, audio-visual, reprographic) support adequately the work of the school and reflect its aims?

12 (*a*) Are school journeys and visits encouraged and considered part of the school curriculum?

(*b*) Is there a particular review of the number, type, purpose and participants of visits undertaken?

13 Are inter-school visits encouraged for the mutual benefit of children and staff?

14 What opportunities and facilities are there for children to develop interests and talents outside the framework of the normal curriculum?

Attainment and assessment

1 (*a*) How does the head assess the quality of the learning experiences provided for the children?
  (*b*) How do these experiences cater for different ages, abilities and aptitudes?
2 In what form do teachers keep a continuing record of the children's progress in physical, intellectual, social, emotional and aesthetic areas of development and how is it used?
3 Does the school have a common and continuous procedure for this recording?
4 How often is this information evaluated by the headteacher and members of staff with curricular responsibilities?
5 As a result of this evaluation what steps are taken to review and remedy any gaps and duplication in the learning process?
6 Are the school's current methods of assembling and recording information relevant to the needs of the staff, other schools and parents?
7 Is the headteacher clear in what circumstances he would regard pupil information and records as confidential to the school?

Internal screening

1 In assessing progress what use is made of:
  (*a*) standardised attainment tests?
  (*b*) criterion-based tests?
  (*c*) observational profiles?
2 What steps are taken to ensure consistency in the administration of tests?
3 (*a*) When was the testing structure, content and frequency last revised?
  (*b*) Who makes this review?
4 How are the results of these tests recorded and used?

SOCIAL CONSIDERATIONS

Children

Pre-school children

(*a*) What initiatives are taken to introduce the school to parents of pre-school children? For example, talks, meetings, written guidelines, invitations to school functions, home visits.

(*b*) How is the smooth introduction of the child to school ensured? For example, part-time attendance before full-time education, staggered admission.

(*c*) What contact is made with nursery schools, day nurseries and play-groups?

(*d*) Is there liaison with medical services before the child comes to school?

(*e*) Are the managers and staff consulted regarding the school's admission policy?

(*f*) What steps are taken to inform parents of this policy?

Children in school

In considering the needs and interests of individual children what provision is there for:

(*a*) compensating for social deprivation?

(*b*) children with behaviour problems?

(*c*) children from different ethnic groups?

(*d*) gifted children?

(*e*) children with specific talents?

(*f*) slow learners?

(*g*) integration with other age-groups within the school?

(*h*) providing opportunities to develop initiative and responsibility?

(*i*) developing relationships between children and other adults in the school?

(*j*) interesting children in outside organisations?

(*k*) encouraging children to participate in self-help school activities?

(*l*) involving children and staff in school assembly?

Children changing schools

What initiatives are taken to liaise with other schools on the transfer of children? For example:

passing and receiving information;
visits by parents, teachers, children;
involvement in activities between schools.

463

Parental and community involvement

1 What initiatives are taken to introduce the school to the community and how are links developed?
2 How are pupils helped to understand the local community and encouraged to contribute to it?
3 How is the community helped to understand the aims of the school?
4 What opportunities are there to give parents an understanding of what the school is trying to do, and their child's part in it?
5 How are parents helped and encouraged to be interested in helping their children to learn? For example:
   talks to parents on curriculum-areas;
   participation in the daily life of the school.
6 (*a*) What opportunities are there for parents to discuss their children's development and progress with the teacher and the headteacher?
   (*b*) How does the head establish contact with those parents who do not take advantage of these opportunities?
7 Are there any prepared leaflets of explanation and information for the parent to consider?
8 Is there a formal/informal parent/community association? How effective is it?
9 How and for what purposes does the school liaise with:
   (*a*) other primary schools?
   (*b*) secondary schools?
   (*c*) Adult Education Service?
   (*d*) colleges of further and higher education?
10 What contact is there between the staff and other users of the building?

The school managers

1 Are staff and parents aware of the identities and functions of the school managers?
2 What are the managers' contacts with the school:
   (*a*) in school time?
   (*b*) out of school time?
3 How are they informed of what the school is trying to do?
4 In the preparation for appointments of staff is there effective

consultation between the headteacher and the school managers?
5 Headteacher's report to the school managers: are the following points covered:
   (*a*) staffing – changes, attendance, deployment, involvement in in-service courses?
   (*b*) children – numbers on roll and forecasts?
   (*c*) the curriculum, its organisation, development and resources?
   (*d*) the school premises – state of repair, caretaking standards, adequacy of accommodation?
   (*e*) school's calendar?
   (*f*) unofficial school fund?
   (*g*) educational visits?
   (*h*) health and safety?
   (*i*) home/school/inter-school liaison?
   (*j*) community involvement?

ADMINISTRATION AND ORGANISATION

Admission and transition

1 What steps are taken and what contact is made to ensure smooth transition between home and school?
2 What arrangements are made for children transferring from another school?
3 What procedures are taken to ensure the smooth transfer of children from school to:
   (*a*) another primary school?
   (*b*) the receiving secondary school?
   (*c*) a special school?
   (*d*) an independent school?
4 How often are these procedures reviewed?

Grouping of pupils

1 By what criterion are children grouped:
   (*a*) age?
   (*b*) vertical grouping?
   (*c*) streaming?
   (*d*) mixed ability?
   (*e*) setting?

465

(*f*) withdrawal groups of children with special needs?
(*g*) remedial classes?
2 How often are these arrangements reviewed?
  How flexible are they?

Records

1 Does the head keep adequate records:
  (*a*) log book?
  (*b*) punishment book?
  (*c*) stock book?
  (*d*) sales book?
  (*e*) county record cards?
  (*f*) unofficial school funds?
2 (*a*) What provision is made for recording the individual progress of children?
  (*b*) How frequently are these records seen by the headteacher?
3 Where are these records kept and to whom are they available?
4 Do records of children's progress include samples of work?
5 Does the head have access to medical records?
6 (*a*) In what form do teachers record their work?
  (*b*) How frequently are these records seen?
7 Are records kept on staff service and development?

Discipline

1 What steps are taken by the staff, collectively, to reinforce good behaviour?
2 What strategies are there for dealing with:
  (*a*) truancy?
  (*b*) dishonesty?
  (*c*) bullying?
  (*d*) theft?
  (*e*) vandalism?
  (*f*) insolence?
  (*g*) deliberate disobedience?
3 Are these strategies clearly understood by children, staff and parents?
4 At what point are external agencies involved?

Communications – internal

1 What steps are taken to ensure effective two-way communication between staff and headteacher?
2 (*a*) Has the value of a staff handbook been considered?
   (*b*) What might such a handbook contain?
   (*c*) Who will be involved in compiling its contents?
3 How is the dissemination of information to all staff organised?
4 Staff meetings:
   (*a*) Are staff meetings held regularly?
   (*b*) For what purposes are they held?
   (*c*) Who initiates them?
   (*d*) Do they include full-time and part-time teaching staff?
   (*e*) Are there also meetings for non-teaching staff?
   (*f*) Is an agenda produced in advance?
   (*g*) Are staff encouraged to contribute to the agenda?
   (*h*) How is the implementation of decisions ensured?
   (*i*) Are discussion papers ever produced for staff meetings?
   (*j*) Are temporarily constituted working parties set up to consider aspects of a particular issue?
   (*k*) Is there a record of staff meetings? If so, who keeps it?

Communications – external

1 What means are there for contacting:
   (*a*) parents and relatives?
   (*b*) clinics and social services?
   (*c*) schools psychological service?
   (*d*) police – junior school liaison officers?
   (*e*) educational welfare officer?
   (*f*) chairman of the managers?
2 In what situations are written communications from home required, for example, in the case of absence/withdrawal/administration of medicines?
3 Are the contents of the school's handbook to parents as informative and up to date as they can be?
4 Is there a periodic newsletter to parents?
5 Are meetings held to present curriculum matters to parents?
6 What opportunities are there for parents to discuss their children's progress and problems?

7 Is there a link between a written report to parents on child's progress and these discussions?
8 Is the communication between the school and parents two-way? How is parental initiative and response encouraged?

Use of resources

Staff deployment

1 Are teachers' skills and interests catalogued?
2 Does the organisation facilitate maximum use of these talents?
3 In the allocation of responsibilities how are the major curriculum-areas covered?
4 Are individual organisation and curriculum responsibilities, including those of the head, clearly defined to all members of staff?
5 What considerations are given to inter-personal relationships in the deployment of staff?
6 (*a*) Do the responsibilities of teachers without classes meet the stated needs of the school?
   (*b*) When was their deployment last reviewed?
7 Are job descriptions of all non-teaching staff clearly defined to all members of staff?
8 (*a*) In what way does the head's personal teaching commitment contribute to staff and curriculum development?
   (*b*) How frequently does the head visit each class?
9 Is there systematic preparation for staff selection interviews and is all necessary information available?
10 (*a*) Does this process include the preparation of a job description?
   (*b*) Are short-listed candidates invited to visit the school?
11 What arrangements exist for the recruitment and deployment of relief teachers?
12 Is full use made of support services (for example, reading and language service)?

Staff development – internal

Headteacher
1 What steps does the head take to develop his/her professionalism?
2 How available is the head formally and informally?
3 Do the teachers feel that the head is interested in:
   (*a*) their professional development?
   (*b*) their personal welfare?

4 How aware is the head of the load of individual teachers:
   (*a*) in the classroom?
   (*b*) in voluntary activities?
   (*c*) in pastoral roles with children and colleagues?
5 (*a*) How aware is the head of the work of various members of the non-teaching staff?
   (*b*) Could their contribution to the school be increased?
6 What steps does the head regularly take to sustain and develop staff morale?

Probationary teachers

1 What considerations are given to a probationer's placement and teaching load?
2 Is there a member of staff responsible for the oversight of the probationers?
3 Is there a clearly-defined structured induction policy within the school?
4 How is the probationer's progress monitored and recorded?

Individual teachers

1 (*a*) Is there an induction policy for all teachers new to the staff?
   (*b*) Is there a policy for informing supply staff of aspects of school life?
2 What opportunities are there for individual teachers to extend their experience by teaching different age-groups within the school?
3 Is there a staff programme of assessment?
4 By what means does the head help individuals to become better teachers:
   (*a*) within their classrooms?
   (*b*) within the school?
   (*c*) within the profession?

Staff as a team

1 What use is made of staff/group meetings for staff development?
2 How frequent are such staff or group meetings?
3 What use is made of external expertise?

Students

1 On what criteria are students allocated within the school?
2 Who is responsible for their supervision and assessment?

Non-teaching staff

1 Is there an induction and development policy for non-teaching staff?

Staff development – external

In-service training

1 How is in-service provision used to match the needs of individual members and the needs of the school?
2 What provision is made for all teachers to gain experience from visits to other educational and allied agencies?
3 Is sufficient opportunity provided for teachers to report back after visits/courses?

School finance

1 (*a*) On what basis are decisions made with regard to the allocation of the annual capitation allowance?
   (*b*) To what degree are staff involved in these decisions?
2 Are the county guidelines on the management of official and unofficial school funds followed?
3 Who decides how unofficial school funds are allocated?

Building/accommodation fabric

1 What steps are taken to ensure that the school is maintained in a state of workmanlike tidiness?
2 What procedures are there to ensure that the fabric and installations are sound and in good repair?
3 (*a*) Are the grounds, pitches and play areas maintained satisfactorily?
   (*b*) Are there adequate and safe parking facilities?
4 Are storage facilities adequate and effectively used?
5 Is provision for display adequate throughout the school and is best use made of it?
6 What constraints does the use of the building outside school hours place upon the school?
7 Is the classroom furniture adequate, suitable and in good repair?

Design

1 To what extent does the design of the building constrain or facilitate the work of the school?
2 Is optimum use made of:

(*a*) hall?
(*b*) resource and library areas?
(*c*) foyer?
(*d*) dining areas?
(*e*) corridors?
(*f*) all classroom accommodation?

Day-to-day routines

1 How is the planning for assemblies conducted? Who is involved?
2 How are class timetables determined?
3 Who has responsibility for compiling and implementing duty rotas?
4 What arrangements are there in bad weather for break supervision by teaching and welfare staff?
5 Who is responsible for the supervision of children on entering and leaving school?
6 What arrangements are there for fire drill?
7 In the event of accidents to children are procedures clear to members of staff?
8 Are lunch-time arrangements clear to teaching and non-teaching members of staff?
9 Is there a policy for the moving of large or centrally shared equipment in preparation for lessons?
10 Is the system for the collecting and safe-keeping of monies and valuables brought into the school made clear to staff, pupils and parents?
11 What is the procedure for dealing with lost property?
12 (*a*) Are the daily duties of the caretaker and cleaning staff clear?
    (*b*) What degree of supervision do you undertake of the caretaker and cleaning staff?
13 How often do you review, by staff discussion, your day-to-day routines?

Appendix J

Classroom observation

Here is a transcription of parts of two lessons taught to younger pupils in two secondary schools. I have chosen them so that you may try out some of the category systems that you may have developed in response to Tasks 3.9 or 3.10 (if they happen to fit) or to one of the ready-made systems presented on pp. 219-33.

HISTORY LESSON TO 11-YEAR-OLDS

T. Now you have come along to this room this particular period because on your timetable it says the magic word history. I suppose that when you have gone along to other rooms, when on your timetable there has been, say, maths written on it, you have known very well that you are going along to a room and that because it says maths on your timetable you are going to work with figures. And I suppose that if you go along to a room and it says art on your timetable you know very well that you are going to draw or paint or model. But what do you expect to do when you come along to this room because it says on your timetable, history? Yes.

P. About the old things from the past.

T. We expect perhaps to talk about things of the past. Make a note of that. [*Writes on board*.] Anything else, any other suggestions? Yes.

P. Sir, about famous battles and the men who fought them, something like that.

T. Yes, famous battles. Anything else?

P. About heroes.

T. Heroes. Yes.

P. Inventors.

T. Heroes, inventors. Anything else?

P. Famous people.

T. Famous people. I suppose really we could class our heroes, our inventors in as famous people. So you expect to come along and you expect to talk, to read and write about things of the past, famous battles, heroes, inventors, famous people; but let's have a look more closely at this. What do we mean by things of the past? What do we mean by the past first of all, as far as history is concerned anyway? Yes.

P. Back in history.

T. Well, back in history. What do we mean by back in history then? Yes.

P. Things like the Vikings and the Saxons.

T. The Vikings, the Saxons.

P. Going back into time.

T. Going back into time. How far back into time?

P. As far as we . . . er . . . can remember or . . . have been told.

T. As far as we can remember, as far as we have been told. Perhaps it would be better to say as far as we can find out. I think that is probably what you meant. But, when does the past stop?

P. It doesn't stop, sir.

T. In a way it doesn't stop, no. Perhaps you'll explain that one. You know the answer. Yes.

P. Erm, the past is, erm, right up to the time you are in now.

T. Yes. The past is right up to the time you are in now. What you had for breakfast is history. What you did last night is history. So certainly history is things of the past, but remember, when we talk about the past we are not thinking of a thousand years ago all the time, we are thinking of five minutes ago, ten minutes ago, yesterday, fifty years ago, a hundred years ago and so on as far back as we can. So things of the past. Remember the past is yesterday. So when we talk about history we expect to know about yesterday as well as a thousand years ago. The second thing we mentioned we can put together, famous people, famous events. Is history only about famous people and famous events?

P. No sir. It's about the land as well isn't it sir?

T. About the?

P. About the land and animals and what lived on earth before man.

T. Well, not as far as we are concerned. We are not going back before man. I suppose we would call that prehistory really. Is it just about famous men? Are we only concerned with what the famous men did? How the famous men lived?

P. About the peasants.

T. We're concerned about those people who weren't famous at all. In other words we're concerned with . . . ?

P. Everyone.

T. Everybody. So history is not just about famous people but of everybody. We try and see how everybody lived in the past, and remember the past isn't necessarily a thousand years ago, it might be yesterday. So if we think about history this way, history is really a story, a true story of course, but nevertheless a story of . . . ?

P. Time.

T. Partly of time, yes.

P. The past.

T. Of the past.

P. Of man.

T. Of man, yes I think that's the one we want. It's the story of man. Not just famous men, and of course we include women in this but every man. So remember, history is the story of man. Now if we are going to tell the story of man, where do we begin?

P. Cavemen.

T. We do in fact begin with cavemen but, to be a little more general than that?

P. Prehistoric man.

T. Well that would be the same as caveman. If we are going to tell . . . erm . . . your story, the story of your life where do we begin?

P. Where . . . the place you were born.

T. Yes, the place you were born. In other words we begin at the . . . ?

P. Beginning.

T. We begin at the beginning. And, as you have already said, the beginning was with caveman when man first appeared on earth. And when do we end that story? Again let us assume that we are telling the story of your life. When do we end with that story? And remember it's your life now.

P. When you die.

T. Well you're not dead yet, we're telling your story so when are we going to end with your particular story?

P. When we get right up to date.

T.　When we get up to date. So what we shall be trying to do when you come along to the periods which we describe on the timetable as history, we shall be trying to tell the story of man.

BIOLOGY LESSON TO 12-YEAR-OLDS

The pupils are working in groups, trying to carry out their own experiments which will find answers to questions which they themselves have raised. The teacher moves from group to group: for example, the second group are weighing slugs to find out how fast they grow.

P.　There's a frost this morning sir.

T.　Is there a frost?

P.　Yes.

T.　Anybody seen frost this morning?

PP.　Yes.

T.　There's condensation but . . . was there frost?

P.　Well sir there's . . . [*Omission*] [*Other voices too*]

T.　Might have been dew mightn't it? . . . Did you feel it?

P.　It were cold.

PP.　Cold . . . cold . . .

T.　Of course what we need to do now is measure it . . . to see how cold it was.

[*One group*]

P.　[Inaudible]

T.　Look. Are you sure you haven't got them all mixed up? [*Looking at table of weights of slugs.*] You see point three four and point three five . . . are similar. Point two two and point two three are similar. You get . . . in your rough [work] . . . make two columns . . . like that . . . Write the . . . three weights down the first weighings down there . . . write the three weights second time down there . . . and see if they fit and if you've got them in the wrong order . . . because . . . if you (haven't) that's a very interesting figure . . . something that changes its weight.

P.　[*Sentence inaudible* . . .] (had three watch glasses) and he put one slug on each and then he . . .

T.　And had you numbered the watch glasses?

P.　No. We thought . . . [*Omission*] . . . (bit of paper)

T.　Well how do you know that you picked up the right watch glasses the same time . . . if you didn't have a number on the watch glass . . . Couldn't you have got them mixed up?

P. [*Mumbles*]

T. Now surely that needs doing again . . . and see if you can get one another (stack) of er slugs to change their minds . . . eh? . . . See what happens this time . . . because you've got a a a a much . . . different problem from the one you started out with. . . . You started out with a problem about slugs. . . . Now you've got to see if things change their weight . . . for no reason . . . apparently. That make sense?

P. (Yes)

T. Sure? It'll be interesting to see what happens.

[*Another group*]

T. You're with the wasp lot are you?

P. Yes sir.

T. (Haven't you got anything to do?)

P.1 There's no . . . there's no sign of life out there.

T. (Not that side out there?)

P.2 It's right frosty ground.

T. Is it frosty?

P.2 Yes sir it's frosted everywhere. . . . Well . . . it looks like it. It's a lot white . . .

T. How would you find out?

P.3 [*Inaudible*]

T. Temperature? How would *you* do it?

P. I dunno.

P. (I would find out with a temperature glass)

P.3? You couldn't do the temperature because it . . . mucks . . .

T. What's a 'temperature glass'?

P.? A thermometer.

T. Yes. Ah . . .

P.2? (It might not work) It might not get a temp . . . How do you know it's frost . . . unless you know . . . [*Interrupted*]

T. How *would* you know it was frost?

P.2 You'd have to know what frost . . .
[*Another pupil tries to interpose*]

P.2 You'd have to know that frost was . . . You know . . . you'd have to know what temp . . . um . . . what temperature frost was before you knew how you could do it.

T. I understand what you mean . . . Do you know that? [*Omission*]
    In which case what you need is a thermometer.
P.2 How do you measure it though sir . . . because it's all thawing
    out?
T. That's your problem . . . I'll ask you what you did.
T. Now what are you going to do about it . . . this is what I'm
    interested in.
P. Don't know.
T. You're waiting for me to tell you what to do aren't you? Well
    I'm not going to tell you what to do . . . I shall be interested to
    see what you *do* . . . OK? Your decision.

[*A third group has been attempting to measure the effect of fertiliser
on the growth of plants.*]
P. It's gone mouldy
P. Well (it's that one there)
P. [*Omission*]
P. We think it's with the fertiliser
T. Now you say 'It's gone mouldy' . . . What's 'it'?
P. Fertiliser
P. Fertiliser
T. It's the fertiliser that's gone mouldy. You're sure it's the ferti-
    liser that's gone mouldy?
P. Well . . .
T. You'll have evidence for that . . .
P. Because . . . last week [*Omission*] . . . the week before when we
    (planted the seed) it hadn't gone mouldy
T. Yes but . . . [*Interrupted*]
P.2 It hadn't gone mouldy last week
P.1 When did you come and last water it?
T. What's your object?
P.2 Two days ago.
PP. See . . . see . . . um . . . see
P.3 (Seeing) grass make . . .
P. Fertiliser makes grass grow
P.3 Yes, well . . . and seeing which grows faster . . . seeds in soil or
    seeds in sand
T. And where does the fertiliser come in?
P. Seeing whether fertiliser makes grass grow faster
T. Oh Yes . . . so you've got you've got the three things haven't you?

P.   sand, soil and fertiliser and you're mixing them up in different ways . . . That right? OK, Now you've come across this problem of . . . mould . . . and you say it's the . . . er . . .

P.   Ferti . . .

T.   The fertiliser that's going mouldy

P.   Well we left it a week without any top on

T.   Yes . . . well if you're right . . . presumably you'll be able to find *some* fertiliser . . . with mould on . . . where there's no grass next to it . . . because there you see it's rather difficult isn't it to say which is which is going mouldy either the grass or the fertiliser . . . Now then . . . can you on your dish anywhere see . . . a place . . . where the fertiliser only is going mouldy . . .

P.   Yes, there

T.   But that's against grass . . . What about these places out here look where it's where the fertiliser is away from the grass?
[*Pause*]

T.   How about you at that end Tich? You can't see anything can you?
[*Pause*]

T.   Why I asked you when I said 'You'll have evidence?' to to to . . . say that it's the fertiliser that's going mouldy what evidence have you got?
[*Pause*]

T.   Now look . . . er . . . I'm going to come back in a minute. You have a chat about it, right? You can leave it here. I I I'll . . . I'll [*Omission*] for a minute . . . I'm going to ask you about this again. OK?

[*Same group*]

T.   Now then . . .

P.   Sir it's the roots

T.   Pardon?

P.   Sir it's the roots

T.   It's the roots. Well you'll have evidence for that, won't you?

P.   We pulled some up

T.   You pulled some up? Yes. Did you pull all that up? Good heavens! . . . How did you come to the idea that it was roots?

P.   Oh I'd got a sort of feeling

P.   Yes

T.   But you said originally it was fertiliser didn't you? What made you change your mind?

P.1   Put some . . .

P.2   Well we don't know do we really? [*Omission*]

T.   Woah. One at a time . . . (Anita) first

PP.   [*Answers omitted*]

T.   Yes so you think it's the roots. Well the next question is . . .
you've said . . . or we've said it might be either the fertiliser . . .
or . . . the roots . . . It could be . . . something else.

P.   I didn't water it (till Monday) . . . I watered it again . . .

T.   Yes, but even then you've still got the problem of what is going
mouldy haven't you? Maybe the water helps to sort of speed it
up but then you've still got the problem what . . . is going
mouldy . . . Now you've said it might be the fertiliser it might
be the grass. It might be . . .

P.   (It might be the grass seeds we watered)

T.   But that would be the grass then wouldn't it? Still be the grass . . .
In which case it would be the fertiliser.

[*Same group*]

T.   What're you going to do with it next?

P.   We really ought to put it . . . [*Omission*]

T.   The other thing that I was thinking of . . . We've said that it
could be either grass or fertiliser . . . It may be . . . only . . . that
it happens when the grass is against fertiliser. It may be both of
the things together. It could be either . . . *or* . . . or both. [*Pause*]
Well now you go . . . you take it away now . . . and er . . . examine it as carefully as you possibly can . . . and try and sort out
what you really think is the case here. Is it the grass? Is it the
fertiliser? Or is it something else? Or alternatively if you think
that is what I call a red herring . . . it may be that you'd like to
go on with your original job anyway . . . What are you going to
do?

P.   We're going to examine it.

T.   All right then. Good-bye.

479

Appendix K

Freinet's study

Earlier in this century a famous French educationist, Célestin Freinet, carried out an informal study of what people from different walks of life thought their children ought to be able to do at the end of their schooling.

I do not have information about how the survey was conducted: the figures in the right-hand column represent the relative support given to the ability in question. This extract was quoted in Dottrens (1962).

Reading

Ability to read books or letters easily	10
Ability to read and understand newspapers and magazines	9
Ability to enjoy good and fine books	9
Ability to use a dictionary	9
Ability to grasp the contents of a newspaper at a glance	7
Ability to enjoy adventure books	6
Ability to enjoy poetry	6

Writing

Ability to write a letter without mistakes	10
Ability to write a report	8
Ability to draft a telegram	8
Ability to reply to a questionnaire	8
Ability to write an article	7
Ability to draft a resolution or appeal	7
Ability to write the minutes of a meeting	7
Ability to take notes during a lecture	7

Ability to write a poem or a story	6
Ability to write local dialect or patois	5

Speech

Ability to speak correct French	10
Ability to telephone	9
Ability to carry on a discussion	8
Ability to speak readily in public	8
Ability to put questions in public	7
Knowledge of a dialect or language	7
Ability to make a speech	6
Ability to take part in a play	6
Ability to tell a story	6

Numbers

Ability to add, subtract, divide and multiply	10
Ability to understand a pay-slip	10
Ability to calculate area, volume, profits, board	10
Ability to do rapid mental calculations	9
Ability to measure, weigh and count notes	9
Ability to read a plan or a map	9
Ability to calculate the cost price of a product	9
Ability to understand a tax assessment	9
Ability to make out a postal order	9
Ability to use a table, a scale, a price list	9
Ability to assess and estimate without measuring	8
Ability to read an insurance policy	8
Ability to calculate a health scheme reimbursement	8
Ability to understand a graph	8
Ability to read a map in order to find the distance between towns	8
Knowledge of geometry	7
Ability to make a dimensioned sketch	7
Knowledge of algebra	6

General skills and knowledge

Ability to look after an invalid	9
Ability to treat a wound	9
Ability to bandage	9
Ability to apply splints to a broken limb	9
Ability to apply artificial respiration	9

481

Ability to stop a haemorrhage	9
Ability to stop nose-bleeding	9
Ability to treat an injured person	9
Ability to read a prescription	9
Ability to handle dangerous or inflammable liquids	9
Ability to light or put out a fire	9
Ability to read a thermometer, a barometer and a chronometer	9
Knowledge of human physiology	8
Ability to remove a foreign body	8
Ability to carry out simple electrical work	8
Ability to grease and repair a bicycle	8
Ability to mend a tyre, to repair a puncture	8
Ability to read a meter	8
Knowledge of animals and their classification	7
Knowledge of vegetables	7
Knowledge of minerals	7
Knowledge of breeding of domestic animals	7
Knowledge of soldering and splicing	7
Ability to operate a radio set	7
Ability to assemble a torch	7
Ability to hunt and fish	6
Ability to mix concrete	6

History

Knowledge of the history of labour	8
Knowledge of the history of economic progress	8
Knowledge of the history of the workers' struggle and of revolutions	8
Knowledge of the history of the last two wars	8
Knowledge of the dates of major historical events	7
Knowledge of the history of religions	7
Local history	7
History of material progress	7
Ability to situate a given event in the right century	7
Knowledge of the dates of kings and emperors	6
Knowledge of wars and treaties	6
Knowledge of the history of other countries	6
Knowledge of folklore	6
Knowledge of local or national customs	6
Knowledge of ancient history	6

Knowledge of prehistory	6
Knowledge of styles	6
Knowledge of a period through the relics of that period	6

Geography

Highway code	10
Knowledge of the rivers, mountains and towns of France	9
Knowledge of communication routes	9
Ability to plan a long trip	9
Ability to use a timetable	9
Knowledge of agricultural and industrial production	8
Knowledge of the French colonies	8
Ability to read an ordnance map	8
Ability to read the Michelin map	8
Ability to use a compass and find one's bearings	8
Ability to use a town map	8
Knowledge of other countries	7
Astronomy	5
Ability to establish close relationship between human life and geographical relief and communication factors	4

Manual work and practical life

Ability to mend clothes and shoes	10
Washing clothes	9
Cleaning the house	9
Sewing on buttons	9
Riding a bicycle	8
Changing fuses	8
Finding names in a directory	8
Sewing and darning	8
Ironing	8
Preparing an ordinary meal	8
Doing the household washing	8
Looking after a baby	8
Asking for information without feeling shy	8
Not being a slave to tradition	8
Giving clear indications of the way to go	8
Using a sewing machine	7
Looking after a child	7
Painting	7

Driving a car 7
Fitting an electric lamp 7
Bringing up a child 7
Repairing a tyre 7
Putting up a tent 7
Sawing wood 6
Sharpening a saw 6
Driving nails 6
Planing timber 6
Putting in a window-pane 6
Wrapping a parcel 6
Sharpening a knife 6
Papering a wall 6
Knitting 6
Cleaning round, and outside the house 6
Making clothes 4
Tying knots 4
Climbing a wall 4
Making a model 2

Gymnastics, sports

Ability to swim 10
Mountain climbing 8
Rescue work 8
Knowing how to breath properly 7
Practising one or more sports 7
Camping 6
Becoming an athlete 5
Flying 5
Parachuting 5
Enjoying competitions 4

Music

Ability to enjoy good music 9
Ability to play an instrument 8
Ability to understand music 6
Ability to sing 5
Knowledge of famous composers 5
Ability to sing in public 4

Cinema, radio

Ability to understand radio	9
Ability to understand the cinema	8
Ability to criticise a film	7
Ability to criticise a broadcast	7

Art, social accomplishments, aesthetic sense, etc.

Ability to appreciate a fine edition	9
Dress sense	8
Appreciation of museums	8
Ability to appreciate works of art (sculpture, etc.)	8
A taste for interior decoration	7
Enjoyment of flowers	7
Ability to criticise a work of art	7
Ability to draw and paint pictures	6
Ability to make a dimensional sketch	6
Ability to classify	6
Ability to make a quick scale plan	5
Ability to appreciate a picture	5
Knowledge of outstanding artists	3
Knowledge of parlour games	2
Knowledge of the history of art	2
Ability to make a model of a given object	1

Moral characteristics

Knowledge of moral laws	10
Avoidance of sectarianism and class prejudice	10
Knowledge of oneself	10
Fairness	9
Community sense, willingness to help	9
Loyalty	9
Ability to be oneself	9
Co-operative living and mutual aid	8
Charity	8
Acceptance of responsibility	8
Knowledge of others	7

Citizenship

Knowledge of civic laws	10
Defence of life and property	10

485

Appendix K

Respect for human life and liberty	10
Knowledge of the Declaration of Human Rights	9
Readiness to fight for peace	9
Possession of a social ideal	9
Readiness to obey chosen authorities	8
Possession of a political ideal	7
Internationalism	6
Active participation in political life	5
Readiness to obey leaders placed in authority over one	5
Being a good soldier	5

Appendix L

Letters to parents

The passages in this appendix were all addressed to parents. Passages A-E are extracts from longer documents; Passages F and G are the whole of two guides to parents prepared in two middle schools.

EXTRACT A

This extract is from a duplicated brochure sent to parents by the head-teacher of a junior school.

Dear Parents,

       I hope that you find the information contained in this booklet to be of interest to you. As you may be aware, some parents have no real concept of 'what goes on in our school'. Therefore I have decided to write this small booklet to give you an idea of how your child is being educated, how best you can help him to take advantage of his education, what active part you can play in the life of the school, a few school rules which help in organisation and various items of information which you may find of value.

       Remember if at any time you are concerned about, or for, your child, do come and see me or the teachers, at a mutually convenient time.

EXTRACT B

The greatest single problem faced by every school in the country is
that of communication between parents and school. Parents have
always been welcome here and we have always invited you to make
an appointment, should you wish to have a private talk with me or
any member of staff. Far too often, however, the very children who
need most help are those whose parents we have not met. If it is
impossible for you to come to the school we will willingly visit you,
but I cannot overstress the importance of personal contact. Partly
the problem is that parents are too modest and feel that this is a
matter to be left to the teachers. In fact, your children's lives are
too important to be handed over to any professional, however
skilled or highly devoted he or she may be.

EXTRACT C

This extract presents the school's views about school rules, formulating
and enforcing them − here, the problem of smoking.

While we have one obvious duty to provide some protection against
these pressures [to conform to different moral standards] we have
another, to me equally obvious, which is to help boys to learn to
make the right choices when confronted with them. You cannot
learn to choose if you are not allowed to choose. Those who talk
of 'relaxing' discipline or 'being permissive' simply have not observed
the complexity of the problem.

EXTRACT D

The way the uniform is being worn is causing concern; tunics are
dirty, shoes are very rarely polished and are very often in need of
repair (some girls are even changing into uniform shoes on the train,
or out of them at the school gate!); coats are undone, hair is all
over the place and berets are not worn. Shoulder length hair should
be tied back and short hair that flops should have a band or a grip,
for the journey home as well as in school. Gloves are not being worn.
    The language of some girls is disgusting and I fear that it is being

brought into the school by those girls who frequent the stables . . .
We cannot send 'spies' on to every bus and train . . . so we do ask
you to let us know of girls who are letting the school down — with
names if possible — so that we can expel them.

EXTRACT E

This extract forms the preface to a course-planning handbook presented
to all students at an American High School.

This Course Planning Handbook was prepared for you and your
parents. It contains information important to planning for your
success at E — School and in later life.

Your growth at school, the knowledge that you gain in the
classroom and your ability to work cooperatively with other people
will largely determine your future. This handbook will help you to
think, to plan, to act, and re-plan to your best advantage as you
move from Freshman to Senior.

Your parents, your counselor, your teachers all stand ready to
assist. The initiative, however, is yours. You, alone, can determine
the direction of your life. You, alone, can decide where to apply
your talent and energies.

As you plan ahead, use the handbook to answer such important
questions as:

1 Am I meeting the requirements of each year and for graduation?
2 Am I preparing adequately for college entrance or for a good job?
3 Am I choosing courses most appropriate to my interests and
   abilities?

Best wishes for a successful life at E — School.

EXTRACT F

Welcome to G — Middle School

Dear Parents,

I would like to take this opportunity of welcoming your
child to — Middle School. The school offers a wide range of activities and we hope your child will take advantage of the opportunities
which are offered — we expect a high standard of work and behaviour.

I feel sure we can rely upon parents to give us their full support.

This booklet is designed to give you information about the school. However, parents are always welcome at school, if you have any further queries. Please would you sign and return the enclosed School Rules slip.

Yours sincerely,

Headteacher

The school-building

The school opened in 1940 as a Secondary Girls' School and remained as such until 1972 when it became a co-educational comprehensive Middle School for 9 to 13-year-olds. The school has approximately 500 pupils. As it was built as a secondary school we are fortunate to have specialist rooms, such as a full-sized gymnasium, science laboratory, library, home economics and needlework rooms and a hall in which the whole school can assemble. On re-organisation in 1972 we also had a woodwork/metalwork block added, with a photographic dark room and a small self-contained flat.

Aims

[A brief statement of aims has been omitted.]

The Staff

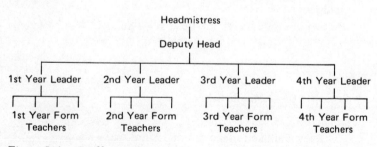

Figure L.1   *Staff structure*

The headmistress

Has final responsibility for all school matters.

The deputy head

Deputises for the Head and has some responsibilities in all aspects of school life.

The four year leaders

Each one is responsible for approximately a quarter of the school, and is concerned particularly with discipline within their respective year, and also for the pastoral care (interests, worries, problems) of the pupils in their year-group.

Organisation

Years 1 and 2 are taught in mixed-ability classes (i.e. children of all abilities in the same class) except in mathematics where children are grouped according to their ability in mathematics. In years 1 and 2 all pupils will have the following lessons:

English, mathematics, environmental studies (containing history, geography, religious education, science), music, games, physical education, needlework, art, woodwork, swimming, a library lesson and some health education.

Years 3 and 4 are taught mainly in streamed classes (i.e. children are grouped for most subjects according to their ability). In years 3 and 4 pupils will study:

English, mathematics, history, geography, science, music, games, physical education, health education, needlework, home economics, art, woodwork and some pupils will take French.

There are six lessons per day, each 45 minutes long.

Homework

In years 1 and 2 most homework is concerned with basic learning such as spelling, learning tables and practice in reading. In years 3 and 4 homework is an important part of the school work — it is essential that it is done at the correct time. Pupils in the third and fourth years will be given a homework notebook, which should be signed by a parent or guardian each week. We seek your help in

491

ensuring that the work is done conscientiously.

All pupils need a strong bag to carry their belongings to and from school.

Parents meetings

All parents are invited to a Parents' Evening during the year. This is usually after the February examinations and reports, and it gives staff and parents a chance to meet and discuss any problems which may have arisen. This does not preclude parents from visiting the school at any time if there are any worries.

Parents' Association

The support of parents is invaluable and there is a small, but lively, Parents' Association. They would be very happy to welcome new members at any time. Please return the enclosed Parents' Association slip to school if you are interested.

School meals

These are eaten in the School Hall — we have no kitchen and meals have to be transported to school after preparation elsewhere.

Dinner money *must* be paid on Monday for the week — even if a child only stays one day.

Attendance

Morning school	9.00 a.m. — 11.55 a.m.
Afternoon school	1.10 p.m. — 3.45 p.m.

If the afternoon is wet we have no break and pupils are then dismissed at 3.30 p.m.

An absence note must be sent by parents to cover every absence. If a dental card or medical appointment card is shown before a child is absent, then a medical mark is given. However, parents are asked *not* to make routine dental appointments during school time and absences are not allowed for such things as visiting the hairdresser or buying new clothes. Children do not learn the value of school if parents encourage absenteeism. There are prizes awarded each year for full attendance.

Pupils must arrive on time and, if a child is late three times in a term then their name is entered in the Detention Book on the fourth occasion.

Discipline

We expect our pupils to be well behaved. For cases of misconduct a pupil's name may be entered in the Detention Book. If this happens twice in a term, a letter is sent to the parents and on the *third* occasion the child is detained for half an hour after school. Parents are always given at least 24 hours notice if a child is to be kept in for detention.

In very *serious* cases of misconduct corporal punishment may be used.

School wear and appearance

The appearance of pupils plays a large part in creating a good impression, both within the school and to the community at large. Parents are asked to co-operate in ensuring that the children look clean, tidy and business-like.

Pupils attending G —— will require the following:

Essential PE equipment

Girls must have:
 Blue or *white* PE shirt (with a sleeve).
 Navy blue shorts or PE skirt.
 Pumps – to be kept in a pump bag
Boys must have:
 Blue or *white* PE or football shirt.
 Football shorts (black or navy).
 Pumps – to be kept in a pump bag.
 Football boots if possible, but not essential.

All to be
clearly
marked.

Classroom wear

Girls

Long or short-sleeved blouse, with collar	blue or white.
Plain skirt or pinafore dress	in grey, navy, green or maroon.
Plain cardigan or sweater	in grey, navy, green

493

	or maroon to match skirt.
Tie (optional)	maroon (these can be bought in school 90p).

Boys

Long or short-sleeved shirt with collar	blue, white or grey.
Long-sleeved sweater	grey, navy, dark green, or maroon to match trousers.
Plain trousers (Jeans are only allowed if they are navy blue with no designs.)	grey, navy, dark green or maroon.
Tie (optional)	maroon (on sale at school 90p).

Shoes should be safe and sensible.

School T shirts

These are also regarded as part of the accepted school wear during the summer.

All pupils are expected to wear the required school wear at all times, for it saves parents money and also eliminates the problem of keeping up with fashion. We may be able to give help in cases of real financial need.

Educational visits

All year-groups have at least one trip per year and we visit a variety of places. We hope most children will be able to take part. We always give parents plenty of notice and money can be paid in small quantities over a period of time. At the moment we run Bank books for children and they can be used for saving for visits and trips.

Club

We have a school Youth Club which meets one evening per week, usually from 6.00-8.00 p.m. At the moment it is only open to the third and fourth years.

Sports teams

We have four houses, and inter-house matches in football, netball, rounders and cricket are organised. We also have teams which compete against other schools. We expect a high standard of behaviour both from team members and supporters.

School library

We are fortunate to have a well-stocked school library. Pupils may borrow books as they would from a public library. However, it must be stressed that books must be looked after carefully, and must be replaced by the pupil if lost or damaged.

School rules

1 Valuables such as transistor radios, calculators, etc., may not be brought to school and only very essential money, such as bus fare is allowed. Any essential money should be handed to a teacher for safe keeping.
2 Jewellery is not allowed except for wrist watches, a plain signet ring and plain, circular, gold or silver-looking ear-studs for girls (boys may not wear ear-rings).
3 Girls may not wear trousers in school. In cold weather they may come to school in dark, plain trousers, but they must change in the cloakroom. Shoes with high heels and the single-strap Scholl-type sandals are not allowed.
4 No food or drink of any sort is allowed to be brought to school — except for fresh fruit.
5 Children must obtain a pass from a member of staff if they wish to leave the school early, or during break or dinner hour (if they stay to dinner).
6 Children must not run in the school building, they must move about in single file, keeping to the left.
7 The back of the school (behind the covered ways) is out of bounds at all play times.

We considered these rules very carefully and we ask for your help in encouraging your children to abide by them. They are based on principles of safety and good health.

Please sign and return the enclosed School Rules slip.

Parents' Association

I am interested in joining the Parents' Association. Please let me
know when the next Committee Meeting is taking place.

Name of Child ——————— Form ———————

                              Signed ———————————————

                                   Parent/Guardian

School Rules

Please return this slip.

I received your letter including the School Rules.

                              Signed ———————————————

                                   Parent/Guardian

Child's Name ——————— Form ———————

EXTRACT G

Information for parents

Dear Parent,

May I welcome you and your child to H —— Middle School.
If you do not know the school I hope it is only a short time before
you come to meet us. Perhaps this booklet will help you understand
our concern for your children's development, academically and
socially. However, if there is anything either now or in the future
that you do not understand or are unhappy about, do not hesitate
to call in and see me and I will do all I can to help.

School facilities

We have facilities for home studies, woodwork, science, needlework,
drama and library. All children, regardless of sex, follow the same
course in these subjects.

Although we are a divided school covering two buildings we have
the benefit of a gymnasium in each with showers and toilets.

School organisation

First year

Your child will be taught in sets in English, mathematics, French and science, so that each may work at his or her own rate. Humanities — our name for geography, history and religious education — is taught by the class teacher. The aim of the first year is to ensure that each child achieves a good standard in number work, reading and writing. Those who learn at a quicker rate will be given 'tangent' studies which they will choose themselves with the teacher's guidance.

Second year

In the second year your child will meet more specialist teachers, but generally they will be from the second-year team.

Third and fourth year

Because of the 'explosion' of interest, enthusiasm and desire for learning at this age your child will be taught by a range of teachers, each with a specialist skill. Although technical studies, woodwork, metalwork, home studies, art, physical education, etc. are taught in mixed-ability classes, for the more academic subjects — mathematics, English, French, science — the children will be 'setted'. This enables the brighter child to stride ahead while the slower child is able to receive the individual attention he also needs.

By the time your child leaves H — we hope he/she has developed sufficiently as a person to benefit his/her High School course and will be aiming for a worthwhile career and hoping to become a responsible citizen.

School rules	Explanation
1 Walk in the building and keep to the right.	1 To prevent accidents.
2 Stay in the yard at break time and if a dinner pupil do not leave the playground without permission.	2 We are responsible for pupils at this time and cannot have them wandering off into possible danger.
3 Always have correct equipment for your lessons. All pupils should own and bring	3 Valuable lesson time is wasted if kit has to be issued and collected.

pens and pencils, PE kit.

4 Do not risk damage to your-
selves or property by climbing
on gates, railings, trees, doors
or roofs.

4 All damage to buildings,
books or equipment is
expensive to restore. Any
damage must be *paid for in
full*.

5 Do not ask to go to the toilet
during lessons.

5 Breaks are frequent. Lesson
time is too valuable to lose.
Bring medical notes if you
have reasons to be excused.

6 No smoking is allowed.

6 This is a criminal offence
under sixteen. The safety of
all is at stake, and the health
of the individual.

7 No chewing in school.

7 This can be distracting to
both pupils and teacher.

8 No valuables should be brought
to school, e.g. transistors.

8 These can be stolen or
damaged.

9 Do not form gangs or bully
other pupils.

9 The health and happiness of
all pupils is important.

NB Children found:
1 being insolent to staff;
2 bullying;
3 forming gangs;
4 fighting;
5 damaging school property;
6 smoking;
will be caned.

A close watch is maintained on truants and culprits will be sent
to court if the need arises.

School uniform

Our children come from several first schools and it is important
that they develop a loyalty and pride in their new school. Uniform
is the outward symbol of school unity and helps pupils feel immediately a member of the community. In addition, a well-kept uniform
gives the pupil a smart appearance — we like our pupils to take pride
in themselves. We shall be grateful for your co-operation in this
matter.

Uniform – Boys	*Uniform – Girls*
Grey or navy trousers	Grey tunic
Blue or grey shirt	Blue/pink + white checked blouse
Grey pullover	Grey cardigan
Grey blazer	Grey blazer (optional)
Grey duffle coat	Grey duffle coat

This equipment is essential for PE:

Boys	*Girls*
White PE shorts	Black gym shoes
Black gym shoes	White socks
Football boots	Navy knickers
Towel for showers	Towel for showers

Satchel or drawstring bag
Pens, pencils, rubbers, rulers, etc. are also essential.

Friends of H ——

All parents are automatically enrolled in the Friends of H ——
Association and are able to take part in all the events which are run
during the year. On other occasions we also ask you to join in our
concern for the welfare of our pupils.

Everyone is welcome to the meetings.

A donation of not more than 25p a year would be appreciated
to help with school funds, out of which trips, equipment, entertainment and prizes are provided.

Other information

School phone no.
School day 9.00 a.m. – 12.00 noon
           1.00 p.m. – 3.30 p.m.
Clubs are held on most days at 3.30 p.m. for interested pupils.

Homework

This will be set for all 'A' and 'Y' group children.
Please see that all homework is done.
Always insist on reading practice.

Dinners

If you wish your child to stay to dinners please send the money each Tuesday.

Should you feel you are entitled to free dinners a visit to the Welfare Centre at G — C — or the Education Offices, would help you.

Absences

By law every absence must be explained by a parent. Please make sure that any absence is for a good reason and that it is explained by a note or telephone call. If the absence is longer than three days and we do not hear from you, then an Education Welfare Officer may call on you.

Any absence which is not covered by a parent's note will be treated as truancy.

In conclusion

I hope you have found this booklet interesting. Please contact me if there is anything that is not clear to you. I am available at any time during school hours, should you wish to consult me. Individual teachers should always be contacted through me so that I am aware of any difficulties and may help.

References

Ashton, P. *et al.* (1975a), *The Aims of Primary Education: A Study of Teachers' Opinions*, London, Macmillan.

Ashton, P., Kneen, P. and Davies, F. (1975b), *Aims into Practice in the Primary School*, London, Hodder & Stoughton.

Auld, R. (1976), *William Tyndale Junior and Infants Schools Public Inquiry*, London, Inner London Education Authority.

Ausubel, D.P. (1966), 'Meaningful reception learning and the acquisition of concepts', in H.J. Klausmeier and C.W. Harris (eds), *Analyses of Concept Learning*, London, Academic Press.

Barnes, D. (1971), 'Language in the secondary classroom', in D. Barnes, J.N. Britton and H. Rosen, *Language, the Learner and the School*, Harmondsworth, Middx, Penguin.

Barton, J. *et al.* (1980), 'Accountability in Education', in T. Bush *et al.* (eds), *Approaches to School Management*, New York, Harper & Row.

Becher, T. and Maclure, S. (1978), *The Politics of Curriculum Change*, London, Hutchinson.

Bernstein, B. (1971), 'On the classification and framing of educational knowledge', in M.F.D. Young (ed.), *Knowledge and Control*, London, Collier-Macmillan.

Bloom, B.S. (1956), *Taxonomy of Educational Objectives: I Cognitive Domain*, London, Longman, Green.

Blyth, A. *et al.* (1976), *Place, Time and Society 8-13: Curriculum Planning in History, Geography and Social Science*, London, Collins.

Brennan, W.K. (1978), *Reading for Slow Learners: A Curriculum Guide*, Schools Council Curriculum Bulletin 7, London, Evans/Methuen Educational.

Brent, A. (1978), *The Philosophical Foundations of the Curriculum*, London, Allen & Unwin.

Britton, J.N. (1970), *Language and Learning*, London, Allen Lane.

Bruner, J.S. (1966), *Toward a Theory of Instruction*, Cambridge, Mass., Harvard University Press.

501

Centre for Educational Research and Innovation (CERI) (1975), *Handbook on Curriculum Development*, Paris, OECD.

Centre for Educational Research and Innovation (CERI) (1979), *School-Based Curriculum Development*, Paris, OECD.

Coltham, J.B. and Fines, J. (1971), *Educational Objectives for the Study of History*, London, Historical Association.

Darke, J. and Hughes, G. (1974), *Explore and Discover: Science for the Middle Years*, New York, McGraw-Hill.

Davies, I.K. (1976), *Objectives in Curriculum Design*, New York, McGraw-Hill.

Department of Education and Science (undated), 'Assessment of Performance Unit: an introduction' (undated pamphlet).

Department of Education and Science/Assessment of Performance Unit (1978), *Language Performance*, London, HMSO.

Department of Education and Science/Assessment of Performance Unit (1980), *Mathematical Development: Primary Survey Report No. 1*, London, HMSO.

Department of Education and Science/Assessment of Performance Unit (undated), *Science Progress Report* (Appendix: 'List of science concepts and knowledge'), London, HMSO.

Department of Education and Science/Welsh Office (1977), *A New Partnership for Our Schools*, London, HMSO.

Department of Education and Science/Welsh Office (1977), *Education in Schools: A Consultative Document*, London, HMSO.

Department of Education and Science/Welsh Office (1979), *Local Authority Arrangements for the School Curriculum*, London, HMSO.

Department of Education and Science/Welsh Office (1980), *A Framework for the School Curriculum*, London, HMSO.

Dewsbury and Batley Technical and Art College (undated), 'General and Communication Studies, Units of a Diploma in Engineering for the Technician', Education Council (cyclostyled).

Donaldson, M. (1978), *Children's Minds*, London, Fontana.

Dottrens, R. (1962), *The Primary School Curriculum*, Paris, UNESCO.

Edwards, C.H. (1977), *A Systematic Approach to Instructional Design*, Champaign, Ill., Stripes Publishing Co.

Eggleston, J. (1980), *School-based Curriculum Development in Britain*, London, Routledge & Kegan Paul.

Eisner, E.W. (1969), 'Instructional and expressive educational objectives: their formulation and use in curriculum', in W. J. Popham *et al.*, *Instructional Objectives*, Chicago, Ill., Rand McNally.

Elliott, J. (1979), 'The case for school self-evaluation', *Forum*, vol. 22, no. 1, Autumn.

Ennever, L. and Harlen, W. (1972), *With Objectives in Mind*, London, Macdonald Educational.

Erant, M., Goad, L. and Smith, G. (1974), *Handbook for the Analysis of Curriculum Materials*, Falmer, Sussex, Centre for Educational Technology, University of Sussex.

Froome, S. (1975), 'Reading and the school handicap score', in C.B. Cox and R. Boyson, *The Fight for Education: Black Paper 1975*, London, Dent.

Gagné, R.M. (1975), *Essentials of Learning for Instruction*, Hinsdale, Ill., The Dryden Press.

Gagné, R.M. and Briggs, L.J. (1979), *Principles of Instructional Design*, New York, Holt, Rinehart & Winston.

Goldstein, H. and Seigle, D.M. (1971) (rev. edn), *A Curriculum Guide for Teachers of the Educable Mentally Handicapped*, ('The Illinois Plan'), Danville, Ill., The Interstate Printers and Publishers.

Gretton, J. and Jackson, M. (1976), *William Tyndale: Collapse of a School or a System?*, London, Allen & Unwin.

Gronlund, N.E. (1978), *Stating Objectives for Classroom Instruction*, London, Macmillan.

Gross, N., Giacquinta, J.B. and Bernstein, M. (1971), *Implementing Organizational Innovations*, New York, Harper & Row.

Harlen, W. (1973), 'Schools Council Science 5-13 Project', in *Evaluation in Curriculum Development: Twelve Case Studies*, London, Macmillan.

Henry, J. (1972), *Culture Against Man*, Harmondsworth, Middx, Penguin.

Herrick, V.E. (undated), *Strategies of Curriculum Development*, Merrill.

Hirst, P.H. (1974), *Knowledge and the Curriculum*, London, Routledge & Kegan Paul.

HM Inspectors of Schools (1978), *Primary Education in England*, London, HMSO.

HM Inspectors of Schools (1979), *Aspects of Secondary Education in England*, London, HMSO.

HM Inspectors of Schools (1980), *A View of the Curriculum*, London, HMSO.

Holroyde, G. (undated), 'The school and community college: community education' (cyclostyled), Sidney Stringer School and Community College, Coventry.

Holt, J.C. (1964), *How Children Fail*, London, Pitman.

Holt, J.C. (1967), *How Children Learn*, London, Pitman.

House, E.R. (1973), 'The conscience of educational evaluation', in E.R. House, *School Evaluation: The Politics and Process*, Berkeley, Ca., McCutchan.

House, E.R. (1974), *The Politics of Educational Innovation*, Berkeley, Ca., McCutchan.

Illich, I.D. (1971), *Deschooling Society*, London, Calder & Boyars.

Jackson, P.W. (1968), *Life in Classrooms*, New York, Holt, Rinehart & Winston.

Johnson, D.A. and Rising, G.R. (1967), *Guidelines for Teaching Mathematics*, Belmont, Ca., Wadsworth.

Kearney, C.P. and Huyser, R.J. (1973), 'The politics of reporting results', in E.R. House, *School Evaluation: The Politics and Process*, Berkeley, Ca., McCutchan.

Kogan, M. (1978), *The Politics of Educational Change*, Manchester University Press.

Lancashire Education Committee (1980), 'Primary school evaluation: a schedule for self appraisal' (cyclostyled).

Lawton, D. (1975), *Class, Culture and the Curriculum*, London, Routledge & Kegan Paul.

Lawton, D. (1980), *The Politics of the School Curriculum*, London, Routledge & Kegan Paul.

Lister, I. (1974), 'The whole curriculum and the hidden curriculum', In I. Lister (ed.), *De-Schooling: A Reader*, Cambridge University Press.

MacDonald, B. (1973), 'Innovation and incompetence', in D. Hamingson (ed.), *Towards Judgment*, Norwich, CARE, University of East Anglia.

MacDonald, B. and Walker, R. (1976), *Changing the Curriculum*, Shepton Mallet, Somerset, Open Books.

Maclure, J.S. (1970), 'The control of education', in J.S. Maclure, *Studies in the Government and Control of Education since 1860*, London, Methuen/History of Education Society.

McPhail, P. (1972), *In Other People's Shoes: Teacher's Guide*, London, Longman.

Mager, R.R. (1962), *Preparing Instructional Objectives*, Belmont, Ca., Fearon.

Manpower Services Commission (1975), Training Services Agency, *Pamphlet No. 13*.

Marjoram, T. (1977), 'Patience rewarded', *Times Educational Supplement*, 14 October.

Musgrove, F. (1968), 'The contribution of sociology to the study of the curriculum', in J.F. Kerr (ed.), *Changing the Curriculum*, University of London Press.

National Society for the Study of Education (1927), *The Foundations and Techniques of Curriculum Making*, Bloomington, Ill., Public School Publishing Association.

National Union of Teachers (1977), *Education in Schools: The NUT's Response to the Recommendations in the 1977 Green Paper*, London, National Union of Teachers.

Norris, E.E. (1973), 'The biological revolution and its impact on the curriculum', unpublished dissertation, University of Leeds.

Nuffield Combined Science Project (1970), *Teachers' Guide I*, London, Longman/Penguin.

Nuffield Combined Science Project (1970), *Teachers' Guide II*, Harmondsworth, Middx, Penguin.

Parsons, C. (1980), 'Geography for the Young School Leaver', in L. Stenhouse (ed.), *Curriculum Research and Development in Action*, London, Heinemann Educational Books.

Postman, N. and Weingartner, C. (1969), *Teaching as a Subversive Activity*, New York, Delacorte Press.

Pring, R. (1976a), *Knowledge and Schooling*, Shepton Mallet, Somerset,

Open Books.
Pring, R. (1976b), 'The integrated curriculum', Unit 12 of *Curriculum Design and Development*, Milton Keynes, Open University Press.
Rappaport, D. and Brown, O. (1971), 'Implementing a results-oriented budgeting system', in D.S. Bushnell and D. Rappaport (eds), *Planned Change in Education: A Systems Approach*, New York, Harcourt Brace.
Read, L.F. (1973), 'An assessment of the Michigan assessment', in E.R. House, *School Evaluation: The Politics and Process*, Berkeley, Ca., McCutchan.
Roethke, T. (1957), *Words for the Wind*, London, Secker & Warburg.
Rudduck, J. (1976), *Dissemination of Innovation: the Humanities Curriculum Project*, Schools Council Working Paper 56, London, Evans/Methuen.
Sharp, R. and Green, A. (1975), *Education and Social Control*, London, Routledge & Kegan Paul.
Shaw, D.M. and Reeve, J.M. (1978), *Design Education in the Middle Years*, London, Hodder & Stoughton.
Schools Council (1967), *Society and the Young School Leaver*, working paper no. 11, London, HMSO.
Schools Council (1968), *Enquiry 1: Young School Leavers*, London, HMSO.
Schools Council (1973), *Pattern and Variation in Curriculum Development Projects*, London, Macmillan.
Schools Council (1979), *Guiding Principles and Programmes of Work*, London, Schools Council.
Schools Council (undated: *c.* 1976), 'Local curriculum development preliminary information sheet' (cyclostyled), London, Schools Council.
Schools Council Geography for the Young School Leaver Project (1974), *Cities and People*, London, Nelson.
Schools Council History 13-16 Project (1976), *The Mystery of Mark Pullen*, in *What is History?*, Edinburgh, Holmes McDougall.
Schools Council Impact and Take-Up Project (1980), *Second Interim Report*, Falmer, Sussex, University of Sussex (cyclostyled).
Schools Council Integrated Science Project (1973), *Patterns I*, London, Longman/Penguin.
Schools Council Integrated Studies (1972), *Exploration Man: An Introduction to Integrated Studies*, Oxford University Press.
Schools Council/Avon Education Authority (1979), *Learning through Talking 11-16*, London, Evans/Methuen.
Schools Enquiry Commission (1867-8) (The Taunton Report), quoted by Lawton, D. (1973), *Social Change, Educational Theory and Curriculum Planning*, University of London Press, p. 87.
Science Teachers' Association of Nigeria (1972), *Nigerian Integrated Science Project: Teachers' Guide 1*, London, Heinemann Educational Books.
Scottish Central Council on Science (1977), *Scottish Integrated Science:*

Teachers' Guide to Sections 1-8, London, Heinemann Educational Books.

Scriven, M. (1973), 'Goal-free evaluation', in E.R. House (ed.), *School Evaluation: The Politics and Process*, Berkeley, Ca., McCutchan.

Shipman, M.D. (1973), 'The impact of a curriculum project', *Journal of Curriculum Studies*, vol. 5, no. 1, May.

Shipman, M. (1974), *Inside a Curriculum Project*, London, Methuen.

Skilbeck, M. (1972), 'School-based curriculum development: a functionalist-environmentalist approach to curriculum change' (cyclostyled), Coleraine, The New University of Ulster.

Stake, R.E. (1969), 'Language, rationality and assessment', in W.H. Beatty (ed.), *Improving Educational Assessment*, Alexandria, Va., Association for Supervision and Curriculum Development.

Stenhouse, L. (1968), 'The Humanities Curriculum Project', *Journal of Curriculum Studies*, vol. 1, no. 1, November.

Stenhouse, L. (1975), *An Introduction to Curriculum Research and Development*, London, Heinemann Educational Books.

Stenhouse, L. (1980), *Curriculum Research and Development in Action*, London, Heinemann Educational Books.

Taba, H. (1962), *Curriculum Development: Theory and Practice*, New York, Harcourt Brace & World.

Taba, H., Durkin, M.C., Fraenkel, J.R. and McNaughton, A.H. (1967), *Teachers' Handbook for Elementary Social Studies*, Reading, Mass., Addison-Wesley.

Taylor, P.H. (1970), *How Teachers Plan their Courses*, Windsor, Berks, NFER.

Tomlinson, P.D. (1980), 'Moral judgment and moral psychology: Piaget, Kohlberg and beyond', in S. Modgil and C. Modgil (eds), *Towards a Theory of Psychological Development*, Windsor, Berks, NFER.

Tomlinson, P.D. (1981), *Understanding Teaching: Interactive Educational Psychology*, New York, McGraw-Hill.

Tyler, R.W. (1949), *Basic Principles of Curriculum and Instruction*, Chicago University Press.

Walker, R. and Adelman, C. (1975), *A Guide to Classroom Observation*, London, Methuen.

Walton, J. and Welton, J. (1976), *Rational Curriculum Planning: Four Case Studies*, London, Ward Lock.

Warwick, D. (1974), 'Some aspects of the sociology of the curriculum', in M. Flude and J. Ahier (eds), *Educability, Schools and Ideology*, London, Croom Helm.

Watts, J. (1973), 'Countesthorpe: a case study', in P.H. Taylor and J. Walton (eds), *The Curriculum: Research, Innovation and Change*, London, Ward Lock.

Wheeler, D.K. (1967), *Curriculum Process*, University of London Press.

Whitehead, J. (1976), *Improving Learning for 11 to 14 year olds in Mixed Ability Science Groups*, Swindon, Wiltshire Curriculum Development Centre.

Whitehead, D.J. (1980), *The Dissemination of Educational Innovations in Britain*, London, Hodder & Stoughton.

Whitla, D.K. *et al.* (undated), 'Evaluation strategies' (cyclostyled; from MACOS evaluation team).

Wilson, J. *et al.* (1967), *Introduction to Moral Education*, Harmondsworth, Middx., Penguin.

Yeadon, A. (1974), *Toward Independence: The Use of Instructional Objectives in Teaching Daily Living Skills to the Blind*, New York, American Foundation for the Blind.

Yoloye, E.A. (1977), 'Observational techniques', in A. Lewy (ed.), *Handbook of Curriculum Evaluation*, Paris and New York, International Institute for Educational Planning, UNESCO.

Young, M.F.D. (1971), 'An approach to the study of curricula as socially organised knowledge', in M.F.D. Young (ed.), *Knowledge and Control*, London, Collier-Macmillan.

Young, M. (1977), 'Curriculum change: limits and possibilities', in M. Young and G. Whitty (eds), *Society, Stage and Schooling*, Lewes, Sussex, The Falmer Press.

Index

509